HABAKKUK

CHRISTIAN STANDARD
COMMENTARY

HABAKKUK

—

Susan Maxwell Booth

HOLMAN®
REFERENCE

Christian Standard Commentary: Habakkuk

Copyright © 2023

All rights reserved.

ISBN: 005811484

Dewey Decimal Classification: 224.90

Subject Heading: BIBLE. OT. HABAKKUK

1 2 3 4 5 6 • 26 25 24 23

Printed in China

RRD

DEDICATION

To Steve with gratitude—
"A strand of three cords . . ."
Ecclesiastes 4:12

TABLE OF CONTENTS

SERIES INTRODUCTION

The Christian Standard Commentary (CSC) aims to embody an "ancient-modern" approach to each volume in the series. The following explanation will help us unpack this seemingly paradoxical practice that brings together old and new.

The *modern commentary* tradition arose and proliferated during and after the Protestant Reformation. The growth of the biblical commentary tradition largely is a result of three factors: (1) *The recovery of classical learning* in the fifteenth–sixteenth centuries. This retrieval led to a revival of interest in biblical languages (Greek, Hebrew, and Aramaic). Biblical interpreters, preachers, and teachers interpreted Scripture based on the original languages rather than the Latin Vulgate. The commentaries of Martin Luther and John Calvin are exemplary in this regard because they return to the sources themselves (*ad fontes*). (2) *The rise of reformation movements* and the splintering of the Catholic Church. The German Reformation (Martin Luther), Swiss Reformation (John Calvin), and English Reformation (Anglican), among others (e.g., Anabaptist), generated commentaries that helped these new churches and their leaders interpret and preach Scripture with clarity and relevance, often with the theological tenets of the movements present in the commentaries. (3) *The historical turn in biblical interpretation* in the seventeenth and eighteenth centuries. This turning point emphasized the historical situation from which biblical books arise and in which they are contextualized.

In light of these factors, the CSC affirms traditional features of a *modern commentary*, evident even in recent commentaries:

- Authors analyze Old and New Testament books in their original languages.
- Authors present and explain significant text-critical problems as appropriate.
- Authors address and define the historical situations that gave rise to the biblical text (including date of composition, authorship, audience, social location, geographical and historical context, etc.) as appropriate to each biblical book.
- Authors identify possible growth and development of a biblical text so as to understand the book as it stands (e.g., how the book of Psalms came into its final form or how the Minor Prophets might be understood as a "book").

The CSC also exhibits recent shifts in biblical interpretation in the past fifty years. The first is the literary turn in biblical interpretation. Literary analysis arose in biblical interpretation during the 1970s and 1980s, and this movement significantly influenced modern biblical commentaries. Literary analysis attends to the structure and style of each section in a biblical book as well as the shape of the book as a whole. Because of this influence, modern commentaries assess a biblical book's style and structure, major themes and motifs, and how style impacts meaning. Literary interpretation recognizes that biblical books are works of art, arranged and crafted with rhetorical structure and purpose. Literary interpretation discovers the unique stylistic and rhetorical strategies of each book. Similarly, the CSC explores the literary dimensions of Scripture:

- Authors explore each book as a work of art that is a combination of style and structure, form and meaning.
- Authors assess the structure of the whole book and its communicative intent.
- Authors identify and explain the literary styles, poetics, and rhetorical devices of the biblical books as appropriate.
- Authors expound the literary themes and motifs that advance the communicative strategies in the book.

As an *ancient commentary,* the CSC is marked by a theological bent with respect to biblical interpretation. This bent is a tacit recognition that the Bible is not only a historical or literary document but is fundamentally the Word of God. That is, it recognizes Scripture as fundamentally both historical *and* theological. God is the primary speaker in Scripture, and readers must deal with him. Theological interpretation affirms that although God enabled many authors to write the books of the Bible (Heb 1:1), he is the divine author, the subject matter of Scripture, and the One who gives the Old and New Testaments to the people of God to facilitate their growth for their good (2 Tim 3:16–17). Theological interpretation reads Scripture as God's address to his church because he gives it to his people to be heard and lived. Any other approach (whether historical, literary, or otherwise) that diminishes emphasis on the theological stands deficient before the demands of the text.

Common to Christian (patristic, medieval, reformation, or modern) biblical interpretation in the past two millennia is a sanctified vision of Scripture in which it is read with attention to divine agency, truth, and relevance to the people of God. The *ancient commentary* tradition interprets Scripture as a product of complex and rich divine action. God has given his Word to his people so that they may know and love him, glorify him, and proclaim his praises to all creation. Scripture provides the information and power of God that leads to spiritual and practical transformation.

The transformative potential of Scripture emerges in the *ancient commentary* tradition as it attends to the centrality of Jesus Christ. Jesus is the One whom God sent to the world in the fullness of time and whom the OT anticipates, testifies to, and witnesses to. Further, he is the One whom the NT presents as the fulfillment of the OT promise, in whom the church lives and moves and has her being, who the OT and NT testify will return to judge the living and the dead, and who will make all things new.

With Christ as the center of Scripture, the *ancient commentary* tradition reveals an implicit biblical theology. Old and New Testaments work together as they reveal Christ; thus, the tradition works within a whole-Bible theology in which each Testament is read in dialectic relationship, one with the other.

Finally, the *ancient commentary* tradition is committed to spiritual transformation. The Spirit of God illumines the hearts of readers so they might hear God's voice, see Christ in his glory, and live in and through the power of the Spirit. The transformational dimensions of Scripture emerge in *ancient commentary* so that God's voice might be heard anew in every generation and God's Word might be embodied among his people for the sake of the world.

The CSC embodies the *ancient commentary* tradition in the following ways:

- Authors expound the proper subject of Scripture in each biblical book, who is God; further, they explore how he relates to his world in the biblical books.
- Authors explain the centrality of Jesus appropriate to each biblical book and in the light of a whole-Bible theology.
- Authors interpret the biblical text spiritually so that the transformative potential of God's Word might be released for the church.

In this endeavor, the CSC is ruled by a Trinitarian reading of Scripture. God the Father has given his Word to his people at various times and in various ways (Heb 1:1), which necessitates a sustained attention to historical, philological, social, geographical, linguistic, and grammatical aspects of the biblical books that derive from different authors in the history of Israel and of the early church. Despite its diversity, the totality of Scripture reveals Christ, who has been revealed in the Old and New Testaments as the Word of God (Heb 1:2; John 1:1) and the One in whom "all things hold together" (Col 1:15–20) and through whom all things will be made new (1 Cor 15; Rev 21:5). God has deposited his Spirit in his church so that they might read spiritually, being addressed by the voice of God and receiving the life-giving Word that comes by Scripture (2 Tim 3:15–17; Heb 4:12). In this way, the CSC contributes to the building up of Christ's church and the Great Commission to which all believers are called.

HABAKKUK: AUTHOR'S PREFACE

While writing this commentary, I've discovered many people love Habakkuk for many different reasons. Several people have mentioned the book contains a favorite verse or passage. Others appreciate Habakkuk's lament over the social injustices of his day. Still others admire the prophet's intimacy with God that allowed for honest questions.

My own love for this prophetic book goes back many years. I've always enjoyed introducing students to the Minor Prophets since they are often unfamiliar with the profound messages tucked away in these brief books. In writing my dissertation, I chose Hab 2:14 as the best succinct summary statement of the mission of God: "For the earth will be filled with the knowledge of the Lord's glory as the water covers the sea." Several years ago, when a student returned a borrowed book, she had inexplicably handwritten the closing verses of Hab 3:16–19 in a notecard to me. As soon as I read the verses, I felt a strong impression from the Lord that I needed to memorize them. I did, and the passage became precious to me, but I still didn't understand the directive. A few years passed before I was invited to write this commentary on Habakkuk. Although I knew the project would be challenging, there was no hesitation. The Lord had been preparing me for this assignment for some time, and he would walk me through it.

My background in literature has undoubtedly shaped my approach to this commentary. The structure of this brief prophetic book with its collection of diverse genres has intrigued me. After an in-depth study of the text, I became convinced the author had framed his message in three parts, which I have labeled a "literary triptych." The prophet's rich visual imagery also led me to describe his theology in terms of a painted triptych—much like church altarpieces that captivated the imaginations of congregants long ago. The three-part structure highlights clear contrasts between the outer panels, which compare, for example, the Babylonian soldiers and the Divine Warrior, as well as the voracity of the wicked and the contentment of the faithful.

The book's structure also emphasizes the contrast in the prophet himself from beginning to end. I identified the reason for the shift in the prophet's worldview at the center of the book: Hab 2:12–14. This location raised the possibility of concentric parallelism or even chiasm in the central panel, but there were still a few lingering questions. When I finally compared my findings to others, I discovered a variety of proposed structures for Habakkuk, but none seem to have carried the day convincingly. It wasn't until I stumbled across John Breck's explanation of a "rhetorical helix"—spiral parallelism—that the final puzzle pieces fell into place for me. I hope this humble volume adds to the ongoing discussion of Habakkuk's structure.

But why does the structure of the book even matter? Doesn't each proposal produce yet another outline, one of which is just as good as another? I would argue the prophet intentionally arranged his material to underscore the theological center of his message and to convey that message to his original audience. Understanding Habakkuk's structure can help today's readers comprehend his message more readily as well. The careful parallelism also stands as evidence that the book is not a haphazard patchwork of diverse sources as some argue, but rather the text displays an exquisite unity.

My background as a missiologist has prompted me to view Habakkuk through a missiological lens as well. The book plays a significant role in the unfolding metanarrative of God's mission, which points to the centrality of Christ. Habakkuk 2:13–14 stands as a beautiful description of the fulfillment of the Great Commission. Habakkuk's emphasis on the eschatological goal of that mission—a purified world overflowing with the knowledge of God's glory—is the answer to the prophet's heartfelt plea to understand life from the middle of the story. Some twenty-six hundred years later, the prophet's theological centerpiece gives us hope for redemption as well. Habakkuk's vision still conveys a sense of urgency: the whole earth needs to hear of the coming judgment and God's promised restoration.

As the prophet's own transformation attests, encountering God's word is not a mere academic exercise but rather a deeply transformative work of the Spirit. To that end, I've tried to keep in mind busy pastors and Bible study leaders who sometimes struggle to carve out time for deeper study. Along the way I've intentionally provided help toward illustration and application. I've also tried to write in a style that makes scholarship more engaging.

From beginning to end, this project has been a labor of love and a source of great joy. I am grateful for the opportunity to work in a commentary series whose convictions closely align with my own. (See Series Introduction.) I offer my sincere thanks to all the people at B&H who have worked hard on the CSC series. Special mention goes to my editor, Sheri Klouda-Sharp, whose helpful suggestions on rearranging and expanding sections have made this a much stronger volume.

I would like to express gratitude to Southern Baptists who have supported my life's work as a missionary. I am grateful for the International Mission Board's support and encouragement in my mid-career pursuit of a PhD in missional studies.

When I first began working on Habakkuk, Southeastern Baptist Theological Seminary kindly offered housing through their Scholar-in-Residence program. They also generously provided a research assistant, who just happened to be my son, Robbie Booth. My husband and I cherish the friendships we made during the semester we spent on the SEBTS campus.

I am especially grateful for the encouragement I've received from my own institution—the Canadian Baptist Theological Seminary and College. Our faculty, staff, and students all share a rare collegiality and sweet fellowship that is a gift from the Lord.

I also want to thank my family and friends for their faithful prayer support of this project. Your encouragement and prayers have sustained me through these years of research and writing. I am forever grateful to my parents, Bob and Barbara Maxwell, for teaching me to love the Lord and his Word from my earliest years.

My husband Steve deserves my deepest gratitude. Thank you for being my sounding board and first reader. Your suggestions have proven invaluable time and again. Never once have you complained about the many sacrifices this project required. You'll never know how much your encouragement and steadfast love have meant to me. I'll always be grateful to the Lord for giving me you.

Finally, all praise and honor go to the "God of my salvation." I have experienced your abiding faithfulness across these many years. I pray that you will keep me faithful—like Habakkuk—whatever the future may hold. What a joy it has been to walk alongside the One who "enables me to walk on the heights." Lord, please use each of us to spread the knowledge of your glory until it fills the earth "as the waters cover the sea."

ABBREVIATIONS

BIBLE BOOKS

Gen
Exod
Lev
Num
Deut
Josh
Judg
Ruth
1, 2 Sam
1, 2 Kgs
1, 2 Chr
Ezra
Neh
Esth
Job
Ps (pl. Pss)
Prov
Eccl
Song

Isa
Jer
Lam
Ezek
Dan
Hos
Joel
Amos
Obad
Jonah
Mic
Nah
Hab
Zeph
Hag
Zech
Mal
Matt
Mark

Luke
John
Acts
Rom
1, 2 Cor
Gal
Eph
Phil
Col
1, 2 Thess
1, 2 Tim
Titus
Phlm
Heb
Jas
1, 2 Pet
1, 2, 3 John
Jude
Rev

GENERAL ABBREVIATIONS

AB	Anchor Bible Commentary
ABD	*Anchor Bible Dictionary*. Edited by David Noel Freedman. 6 vols. New York: Doubleday, 1992.
ABRL	Anchor Bible Reference Library
ANEM	Ancient Near East Monographs
AT	Author's Translation
BAGD	W. Bauer, F. W. Danker, W. F. Arndt, and F. W. Gingrich. *A Greek-English Lexicon of the NT and Other Early Christian Literature*. Revised and edited by F. W. Danker. 3rd ed. Chicago: University of Chicago Press, 1979.
BBR	*Bulletin for Biblical Research*
BDB	Francis Brown, S. R. Driver, and Charles A. Briggs. *The Brown-Driver-Briggs Hebrew and English Lexicon of the Old Testament*. Lafayette, IN: AP&A, 1981.
BECNT	Baker Exegetical Commentary on the New Testament
BHQ	*Biblia Hebraica Quinta Edition: The Twelve Minor Prophets*. Edited by Adrian Schenker et. al. Stuttgart: Deutsche Bibel Gesellschaft, 2010.
BHS	*Biblia Hebraica Stuttgartensia*. Edited by Karl Elliger and Wilhelm Rudolph. Stuttgart: Deutsche Bibelgesellshaft, 1997.
BibSem	The Biblical Seminar
BSac	*Bibliotheca Sacra*
BST	Bible Speaks Today
BZAW	Beihefte zur Zeitschrift für die alttestamentliche Wissenschaft
CEB	Common English Bible
CEV	Contemporary English Version
COS	*The Context of Scripture: Canonical Compositions, Monumental Inscriptions, Archival Documents from the Biblical World*. Edited by William W. Hallo. 3 vols. Leiden: Brill, 2003.
CSB	Christian Standard Bible
CSMS	Canadian Society for Mesopotamian Studies
CTR	*Criswell Theological Review*
DSS	Dead Sea Scrolls
EBC	Everyman's Bible Commentary
ESV	English Standard Version
GKC	*Gesenius' Hebrew Grammar*. Edited by Emil Kautzsch. Translated by A. E. Cowley. 2nd ed. Oxford: Clarendon, 1910.
GNT	Good News Translation
HALOT	*Hebrew and Aramaic Lexicon of the Old Testament*. Ludwig Koehler and Walter Baumgartner. Revised by Walter Baumgartner and Johann Jakob Stamm. Translated and edited by M. E. J. Richardson. 5 vols. Leiden: Brill, 2000.
HSM	Harvard Semitic Monographs
HSS	Harvard Semitic Studies

HTR	Harvard Theological Review
IBHS	*An Introduction to Biblical Hebrew Syntax.* Bruce K. Waltke and M. O'Connor. Winona Lake: Eisenbrauns, 1990.
ICC	International Critical Commentary
ISBE	*International Standard Bible Encyclopedia.* Edited by Geoffrey W. Bromiley. Rev. ed. Vol. 3. Grand Rapids: Eerdmans, 1986.
ISV	International Standard Version
ITC	International Theological Commentary
JBL	*Journal of Biblical Literature*
JBQ	*Jewish Biblical Quarterly*
JETS	*Journal of Evangelical Theological Society*
JNES	*Journal of Near Eastern Studies*
Joüon	Paul Joüon. *A Grammar of Biblical Hebrew.* Translated by Takamitsu Muraoka. 2 vols. Subsidia Biblica 27. Rome: Gregorian Biblical Press, 2011.
JPS	Jewish Publication Society
JSOT	*Journal for the Study of the Old Testament*
JSOTSup	Journal for the Study of the Old Testament Supplement Series
JSS	*Journal of Semitic Studies*
JTS	*Journal of Theological Studies*
KJV	King James Version
LXX	Septuagint
MT	Masoretic Text
NAC	New American Commentary
NASB	New American Standard
NET	New English Translation
NICNT	New International Commentary on the New Testament
NICOT	New International Commentary on the Old Testament
NIDOTTE	*New International Dictionary of Old Testament Theology and Exegesis.* Edited by Willem A. VanGemeren. 5 vols. Grand Rapids: Zondervan, 2012.
NIGTC	New International Greek Testament Commentary
NIV	New International Version
NIVAC	New International Version Application Commentary
NKJV	New King James Version
NPNF¹	*Nicene and Post-Nicene Fathers*, Series 1
NRSV	New Revised Standard Version
OTL	Old Testament Library
OTWSD	*Old Testament Word Study Dictionary.* Warren Baker and Eugene Carpenter. Chattanooga: AGM Publishers, 2018.
PRSt	*Perspectives in Religious Studies*
RSV	Revised Standard Version
RTR	*Reformed Theological Review*
SAAB	*State Archives of Assyria Bulletin*
SBL	Society of Biblical Literature
SBLDS	Society of Biblical Literature Dissertation Series
SJOT	*Scandinavian Journal of the Old Testament*

SSN	Studia Semitica Neerlandica
ST	*Studia Theologica*
SubBi	Subsidia Biblica
TDOT	*Theological Dictionary of the Old Testament*. Edited by G. J. Botterweck, H. Ringgren, and H. J. Fabry. Translated by J. T. Willis, G. W. Bromiley, and D. E. Green. 16 vols. Grand Rapids: Eerdmans, 1974–2006.
TLOT	*Theological Lexicon of the Old Testament*. Edited by Ernst Jenni and Claus Westermann. Translated by Mark E. Biddle. 3 vols. Peabody, MA: Hendrickson, 1997.
TOTC	Tyndale Old Testament Commentaries
TWOT	*Theological Wordbook of the Old Testament*. Edited by R. Laird Harris. Chicago: Moody, 1980.
TynBul	*Tyndale Bulletin*
TZ	*Theologische Zeitschrift*
VT	*Vetus Testamentum*
VTSup	Vetus Testamentum, Supplements
WBC	Word Biblical Commentary
YLT	Young's Literal Translation
ZAW	*Zeitschrift für die alttestamentliche Wissenschaft*

HABAKKUK

INTRODUCTION OUTLINE

1 Author
2 Date
3 Historical Background
    3.1 The Neo-Assyrian Empire: Late Eighth Century BC
    3.2 Struggle for Dominion: Early Seventh Century BC
    3.3 The Assyrian War Machine's Stall: Late Seventh Century BC
    3.4 A Narrow Window of Freedom in Josiah's Reign:
        627–609 BC
    3.5 The Neo-Babylonian Empire: Late Seventh Century BC
    3.6 Habakkuk's Prophecy Fulfilled: Early Sixth Century BC
    3.7 World Dominion: A Theological Reflection
4 Religious Background
    4.1 Judah's Religious, Social, and Moral Depravity
    4.2 Prophets of the Seventh Century BC
5 Text
6 Literary Characteristics of Habakkuk
    6.1 Genre: Poetic Prophecy
        6.1.1 Habakkuk's Use of Prophetic Subgenres
        6.1.2 Habakkuk's Use of Poetry
        6.1.3 Habakkuk's Use of Psalmody
    6.2 The Structure of Habakkuk
        6.2.1 A Survey of Diverse Structural Divisions
        6.2.2 Structure and the Theological Message of Habakkuk
        6.2.3 The Possibility of Macro-chiasm in Habakkuk
        6.2.4 Habakkuk as a Literary Triptych
            6.2.4.1 Chiastic Features in the Central Panel
            6.2.4.2 Parallelism in the Side Panels
            6.2.4.3 Advantages of the Proposed Literary
                      Triptych
        6.2.5 Outline of Habakkuk

INTRODUCTION

Why? Sometimes the question rises from the pit of the stomach, from an ache somewhere deep in the soul. Over the course of a lifetime, few escape it. It can erupt in an instant when an unexpected phone call knocks you to your knees. It can surface slowly after weeks or months or years of unrelenting pain. This one-syllable word wells up in the yawning chasm of profound loss; it wafts upward from the smouldering rubble of shattered dreams. Traveling on the heels of a pandemic sweeping the planet, it has been whispered behind masks in every language under the sun. The question *Why?* is often coupled with another: *How long?*

For Habakkuk, these questions emerged from a heart rubbed raw by violence and social injustice. Was God not aware of the evil and suffering surrounding him? If so, then why didn't he do something? And why wasn't God answering the prophet's hoarse cries for help?

Where do you turn when life has gone off the rails and God doesn't seem to hear your prayers—or even make sense? Refusing to give up or give in to hopeless despair, Habakkuk immersed himself in God's Word and persistent prayer. In time he received answers to some of his questions, but also something far better: a glimpse of God's mission and the presence of the Lord himself. Habakkuk emerged from this encounter with a new perspective and, surprisingly, a heart full of praise. An unthinkable crisis still loomed on the horizon, but a transformed Habakkuk could now walk through it with faith, assured by the presence of a sovereign God. Prayer did not change the prophet's circumstances, but prayer did change the prophet.

This brief prophetic book allows us to eavesdrop on a conversation between a seventh-century-BC prophet and the Lord of Armies. The interchange was not meant to stay private. In fact, the Lord answered the singular prophet with a plural address. Furthermore, God instructed Habakkuk to record the vision carefully for others to read. God's message to and through the prophet was for the nation of Judah, for Babylon, and for the world.

That same message has continued to reverberate, speaking to countless generations ever since. We may find ourselves surprised by just how contemporary Habakkuk's questions and setting sound. The book's movement from theodicy to theophany reads like a case study in contemporary apologetics. It is certainly a corrective to shallow anthropocentric, "health and wealth" faith. As we read this brief book, we may discover a new perspective for our own present circumstances. May we also, like Habakkuk, encounter the Lord himself.

1 AUTHOR

We know little about Habakkuk the man. The derivation and meaning of his name are uncertain. Identified as "Habakkuk" in 1:1 and 3:1, the prophet's name may refer to a kind of plant, as in the Assyrian word *ḥambakūku*. If so, the foreign loanword speaks to the invasive reach of Assyria's influence into Judah. On the other hand, the name may derive from a Hb. verb *ḥābak*, meaning to "clasp or embrace," which can refer to embracing a person (Gen 29:13) or folding one's arms (Eccl 4:5). Interestingly, the book of Habakkuk closes with the recognition that the prophet's hands would likely be empty. The advancing Babylonian troops would strip away all the plant-based staples of Israel's diet: fig trees, grapevines, olive trees, and grains (3:17). Still, the prophet held out an open hand, relinquishing to the Lord his possessions—including the means of his own daily sustenance. Faced with certain destruction of all he once held dear and perhaps even his own life, Habakkuk resolved to cling only to the Lord.

The OT uses three Hb. words to denote the office or role of a prophet: *ḥōzeh* ("one who beholds or perceives a vision"), *ro'eh* ("a seer," an archaic word for prophet), and by far the most common, *nābîʾ* ("a prophet," one who speaks on another's behalf).[1] The opening verse refers to Habakkuk as a prophet (*nābîʾ*) who saw/perceived (*ḥāzḥāzâ*) a prophetic oracle, or literally, "a burden" (*maśśāʾ*).[2]

Primarily, a prophet served as a spokesperson for the Lord, delivering God's message to his people.[3] The role of a prophet included the denouncement of religious and social sins,[4] a call to repentance,[5] and a warning of impending judgment if the people did not respond.[6] Sometimes prophetic literature also offered hope for future restoration.[7] A prophet often proclaimed that the one true God reigns as sovereign Lord over all the earth; he marshals the nations to accomplish his own purposes.[8]

The book of Habakkuk is unique in that it is missing several of these typical prophetic features. We do not find the expected phrase so prominent in other prophetic literature: "Thus says the Lord."[9] The prophet himself apparently initiated this dialogue with God. The voice that expressed righteous anger against oppression belonged not to the Lord but to Habakkuk: Why didn't God do something about such evil? The usual prophetic call to repentance is also missing. As the Lord revealed to this late-seventh-century-BC prophet, certain judgment was already set in motion both for Judah and, in turn, for the nation invading her. Habakkuk prayed on the people's behalf that the Lord "remember mercy" in his wrath (3:2).

Habakkuk's encounter with God resulted in his appointment as a prophet. His dialogue with God became a message for others as it was recorded, disseminated, and preserved for future generations. The book of Habakkuk served notice that God himself was about to unleash judgment on wayward Judah for her stubborn rebellion. It also

---

[1] E.g., *ḥōzeh* (2 Sam 24:11; 2 Kgs 17:13; 1 Chr 21:9; Isa 29:10); *roʾeh* (1 Sam 9:9; 11, 18; 1 Chr 26:28; Isa 30:10); and *nābîʾ* (Num 12:6; Deut 18:15; 1 Sam 3:20; 1 Kgs 18:22; Jer 7:25; Hag 1:1; Zech 1:1).

[2] See *maśśāʾ* in the discussion of Hab 1:1.

[3] For discussion of the prophetic call and role, see C. Hassell Bullock, *An Introduction to the Old Testament Prophetic Books*, 2nd ed. (Chicago: Moody Press, 2007), 13–44; Johannes Lindblom, *Prophecy in Ancient Israel* (Philadelphia: Fortress, 1962), 89–90, 105–219; Gary V. Smith, "Prophet, Prophecy," *ISBE* 3:986–1004.

[4] Isa 5:8, 11–12, 18–23; Amos 2:4–8; Zeph 3:1–5.

[5] Isa 1:16–20; Hos 14:1–3; Amos 5:4–6, 14–15; Zeph 2:1–3.

[6] Isa 5:5–7; Amos 9:8–10; Zeph 1:4–7.

[7] Isa 4:2–6; Hos 14:4–7; Amos 9:11–15.

[8] Isa 5:26–30; 7:17–20.

[9] Isa 7:7; Jer 35:13; Ezek 25:3; Amos 5:16; Hag 1:2; Zech 8:2; Mal 1:4.

offered hope that after the sovereign Lord of Armies accomplished his purposes through the Babylonians, he would judge that pagan nation as well. Additionally, Habakkuk pointed the way forward for the remnant—a life of faith and worship before the God of glory.

The apocryphal book, Bel and the Dragon, narrates a legendary story that drops the prophet Habakkuk into an account of Daniel facing a den of lions (vv. 31–42). While Habakkuk was carrying food to reapers in Judah, an angel instantly transported the prophet to Babylon. There Habakkuk gave the food to Daniel, sustaining him during his ordeal. This fictional narrative portrays Habakkuk as carrying soup, bread, and wine in a field of grain; this is the same prophet who resolved to trust God even if the Babylonian onslaught decimated all sources of food in Judah. Additionally, the first verse of the Old Greek version of the story purports that Habakkuk was a member of the tribe of Levi.[10]

Beyond fanciful speculation, can anything be known about Habakkuk other than the barest of details revealed in the superscription: his name and his identification as a prophet? Francis I. Andersen calls the book of Habakkuk "an intensely personal testament."[11] Noting that the prophetic "I" seldom appears in the canonical prophetic books, Donald Gowan observes, "[T]he person of the prophet is more prominent in this book than any other except for that of his contemporary, Jeremiah."[12] Michael Floyd suggests that this "autobiographical first-person perspective" dominates the entire book and promotes the audience's identification with the prophet.[13] Habakkuk serves as an example of transformation, having come to recognize God's involvement in the crisis he faced.[14] Given the unique autobiographical

---

[10] Bel and the Dragon, *A New English Translation of the Septuagint*, International Organization for Septuagint and Cognate Studies (Oxford: Oxford University Press, 2007), 1025. A similar legend in a later pseudepigraphal work (first-century AD) claims Habakkuk hailed from the tribe of Simeon. See Charles Cutler Torrey, *The Lives of the Prophets: Greek Text and Translation* (Philadelphia: SBL, 1946), 43.

[11] Francis I. Andersen, *Habakkuk*, AB 25 (New York: Doubleday, 2001), 11.

[12] Donald E. Gowan, *Theology of the Prophetic Books: The Death and Resurrection of Israel* (Louisville: John Knox, 1998), 91.

[13] Michael H. Floyd, *Minor Prophets Part 2*, The Forms of the Old Testament Literature 22 (Grand Rapids: Eerdmans, 2000), 86–87. Brevard Childs, *Introduction to the Old Testament as Scripture* (Philadelphia: Fortress, 1979, 2011), 451, contends that Habakkuk has an "autobiographical framework."

[14] Floyd, *Minor Prophets*, 86.

elements of the book, searching for further possible insights into the prophet's character may prove worthwhile.

Habakkuk seems to have been more philosopher than prophet. Surrounded by violence and social injustice, he thought deeply and wrestled with difficult questions about God. Habakkuk was a man of prayer and felt a level of intimacy with the Lord. He was not afraid to be honest and transparent. He laid his questions and confusion before God and waited. When the Lord responded with a glimpse of his mission and a theophany revealing his powerful presence, the prophet was left breathless in awe.

Habakkuk's heightened interest in music may also hint of a Levitical background. The book contains laments and closes with a prayer that includes musical notations and terminology normally found in the psalms (*Shigionoth* in Hab 3:1; cf. Psalm 7; *Selah* in Hab 3:3, 9, 13; cf. Psalm 3). The closing instructions—"for the choir director: on stringed instruments"—suggest that the passage was sung in community (Hab 3:19). Some scholars therefore argue that Habakkuk had an official prophetic-cultic role similar to that of the temple prophets described in 1 Chr 25:1–8.[15] Others argue that Habakkuk's role of prophet-priest is unlikely.[16] Perhaps it is best to remain open to the possibility of Habakkuk as a temple prophet while recognizing there is not enough evidence for a definitive conclusion.[17] Although questions abound regarding the prophet's relationship to Psalm 3,[18] that psalm beautifully anticipates the global worship he prophesied about in Hab 2:14 and 3:3. It also exemplifies the rejoicing the prophet embraced amid unimaginably difficult circumstances (3:17–18).

---

[15] J. H. Eaton, *Obadiah, Nahum, Habakkuk, Zephaniah*, Torch Bible Commentaries (London: SCM Press, 1961), 24–26. The Chronicler reports that when Josiah led the nation to renew observance of the Passover in 622 BC, he commissioned the Levitical singers to stand at their stations in the temple. Second Chronicles 35:15 refers to David's earlier command that the sons of Asaph, Heman, and Jeduthan "were to prophesy accompanied by lyres, harps, and cymbals" (1 Chr 25:1). Even if Habakkuk was not a part of this group of Levites, he likely would have been aware of this renewed interest in prophetic worship.

[16] O. Palmer Robertson, *The Books of Nahum, Habakkuk, and Zephaniah*, NICOT (Grand Rapids: Eerdmans, 1990), 37–38. Andersen, *Habakkuk*, 19, observes that asserting the book of Habakkuk is prophetic liturgy based on the claim that the prophet was a temple official—or vice versa—is circular reasoning.

[17] Ralph L. Smith, *Micah-Malachi*, WBC 32 (Waco: Word Books, 1984), 93.

[18] See the discussion below under "Text."

Finally, a careful reading of Habakkuk reveals that the prophet was saturated not only in worship but also in God's Word. The book shows influence from all three parts of Hebrew Scripture: the Law, the Prophets, and the Writings. For example, as Habakkuk longed for God's salvation, his poetry echoes with imagery from passages exalting the Divine Warrior (Exod 15; Deut 32–33; Josh 10; Judg 5). Habakkuk 2:14 is reminiscent of Isa 6:3 and 11:9: "For the earth will be filled / with the knowledge of the LORD's glory, / as the water covers the sea." Likewise, the prophet seems to have been well acquainted with the psalms (e.g., Pss 11:4; 72:19; 77:16, 19). Habakkuk 3:19b is likely a quotation from Ps 18:33 // 2 Sam 22:34: "[H]e makes my feet like those of a deer / and enables me to walk on mountain heights!"

The contrast between Psalm 18 and Habakkuk's personal situation may have even added fuel to the prophet's initial despair. As someone steeped in Scripture, Habakkuk must have thought he had a biblical worldview. The Lord would rescue him and rout his enemies just as he had done for David (Ps 18:3, 6, 17–19; 37–40, 42; 47–48). When the prophet called to the Lord in his distress, he expected the Lord to hear from his holy temple (Ps 18:6; cf. Hab 2:20). Instead, Habakkuk's desperate pleas seemed to fall on deaf ears (Hab 1:2). Since the Lord ignored the cries of his enemies, did that mean God counted Habakkuk among them (Ps 18:41)? Rather than causing foreign nations to cringe and tremble, the Lord was summoning the Babylonians to punish the Judeans (Ps 18:44–45; cf. Hab 1:6). Whereas Ps 18 opens with the declaration, "I love you, LORD, my strength," Habakkuk found it difficult to understand God, much less declare his love for him. Struggling perhaps with the dissonance between Ps 18 and his own experience, Habakkuk turned to the Lord for answers. By the close of the book, the transformed prophet was able to declare, "The LORD my Lord is my strength" (3:19). Habakkuk had learned to live by faith.

2 DATE

Because nothing in the text of Habakkuk supplies a definitive date for his oracle, proposals cover a wide range of possibilities.[19] Most scholars date the book to somewhere near the close of the seventh

---

[19] Some outliers on the spectrum locate the book's backdrop in the fourth-century-BC campaigns of Alexander the Great, or even as late as 161 BC in the Maccabean period.

century BC.[20] The discussion centers around a few clues found in 1:4–17.

The strongest evidence for dating Habakkuk is in v. 6. God's answer to the prophet's complaint about social evils was this shocking announcement:

> [5] Look at the nations and observe—
> be utterly astounded!
> For I am doing something in your days
> that you will not believe
> when you hear about it.
>
> [6] Look! I am raising up the Chaldeans,
> that bitter, impetuous nation
> that marches across the earth's open spaces
> to seize territories not its own (Hab 1:5–6).

The news that the Chaldeans (i.e., Babylonians) would set their sights on Judah seems to have been an astonishing surprise.[21] Some scholars believe this alarming statement necessitates a date before the Babylonians emerged as a nation bent on expansion—somewhere in the reign of the wicked Manasseh (697–642 BC)[22] or in the early reign of Josiah, before his religious reforms took root (640–626 BC).[23] But hints of a Babylonian invasion were not entirely new. As early as 703 BC, Isaiah had prophesied to Hezekiah that the Babylonians would cart off all of Jerusalem's treasures (2 Kgs 20:12–19). In that same

---

[20] Most proposals fall in the span of approximately 609–597 BC. See, for example, Elizabeth Achtemeier, *Nahum-Malachi*, Interpretation (Louisville: John Knox, 1986), 32; Andersen, *Habakkuk*, 27; David W. Baker, *Nahum, Habakkuk, and Zephaniah: An Introduction and Commentary*, TOTC 27 (Downers Grove: IVP Academic, 2009), 43; Thomas Renz, *The Books of Nahum, Habakkuk, and Zephaniah*, NICOT (Grand Rapids: Eerdmans, 2021), 210. Others narrow the window to approximately 609–605 BC: D. Waylon Bailey, "Habakkuk," in *Micah, Nahum, Habakkuk, Zephaniah*, NAC 20 (Nashville: B&H, 1999), 260; F. F. Bruce, "Habakkuk," in *The Minor Prophets*, ed. Thomas Edward McComiskey (Grand Rapids: Baker Academic, 1993), 834; Robertson, *The Books of Nahum, Habakkuk, and Zephaniah*, 37.

[21] The Chaldeans came into power in Babylon under Nabopolassar, whose Neo-Babylonian dynasty lasted from 626 to 539 BC.

[22] Richard D. Patterson, *Nahum, Habakkuk, Zephaniah* (Richardson, TX: Biblical Studies Press, 2003), 110, sets the date just before Ashurbanipal's western campaigns in 652 BC. Patterson, 109, also notes his dating would accord with a Jewish tradition in *Seder Olam* that links Habakkuk to Manasseh's reign.

[23] Andrew E. Hill and John H. Walton, *A Survey of the Old Testament*, 3rd ed. (Grand Rapids: Zondervan, 2009), 661; Bullock, *An Introduction to the Old Testament Prophetic Books*, 220–21.

century, the prophet Micah foretold the destruction of the city of Jerusalem and the temple by Babylon (Mic 3:12; 4:10; cf. Jer 26:18–19).

Perhaps Habakkuk's astonishment arose not only from the identification of the invaders as the Babylonians but also from the announcement that the Lord himself was behind this imminent attack against his own people. Just when Judah had finally shrugged off the yoke of submission to Assyria, God declared he was setting another in its place. Furthermore, the Lord's preservation of Jerusalem in the past led many to believe the "temple of the LORD" granted the city immunity from invasion (Jer 7:4). The proclamation the Lord himself was raising up a foreign army to besiege them must have shaken the prophet to his core.

Marvin Sweeney suggests yet another factor behind the astonishment. Judah and the Babylonians had been allies since Hezekiah received Merodach-baladan's envoys in the waning years of the eighth century BC—a partnership intended to oppose the Assyrians' advance under Sennacherib. In Habakkuk's day a century later, King Josiah died on the battlefield in 609 BC when he tried to support the Babylonian Nabopolassar by blocking the Egyptians from coming to the aid of the Assyrians in their last-ditch battle against the Babylonians. When the Babylonians defeated the Egyptians at the battle of Carchemish in 605 BC, Judah would have expected to be treated as an ally. Instead, they were treated as "a hostile vassal state"—an astonishing turn of events in a brief period of time.[24]

The phrase "in your days" (Hab 1:5) implies this judgment would play out during Habakkuk's generation. Following the Battle of Carchemish in 605 BC, Nebuchadnezzar forced Judah into subjugation. The Babylonian king again marched on Jerusalem, besieging the city in 597 BC. A second siege begun in 588 BC resulted in Jerusalem's destruction in 586 BC. The time frame required by "in your days" seems to rule out a date earlier than 626 BC.

Another possible clue is the description of the Babylonians as already in the process of a terrifying land grab (1:6–11). This would suggest that the date was some time after the Babylonian advance against Assyria began. The first major city, Ashur, fell in 614 BC; Calah and Nineveh, in 612 BC; and the last city, Haran, in 610 BC. For the

---

[24] Marvin A. Sweeney, *The Twelve Prophets Volume 2: Micah, Nahum, Habakkuk, Zephaniah, Haggai, Zechariah, Malachi*, ed. David W. Cotter, Berit Olam Studies in Hebrew Narrative & Poetry (Collegeville, MN: Liturgical Press, 2000), 465.

pronouncement in vv. 5–6 to be "breaking news" to Habakkuk, however, it must have preceded the Battle of Carchemish in 605 BC, when the Babylonians defeated the Egyptians and the last of the Assyrians. In the aftermath of that combat, no one would have been surprised that the Babylonians would continue to march into Syria-Palestine.

Some commentators date Habakkuk's first lament (1:2–4) before 605 BC but propose a date from 597 BC to 586 for the second lament (1:12–17).[25] Andersen, however, argues that the description of 1:15–16 "does not have the flavor of a recent horrifying experience still in memory."[26] Rather, 1:12–17 anticipates the Babylonian conquest, and the passage expresses the prophet's desire that the Lord alter his plans. Andersen concludes that nothing in the second lament requires a later date than the first.

A final factor affecting the dating of Habakkuk is the identification of "the wicked" in 1:4 and 1:13. In vv. 2–4, the prophet lamented the social oppression of his day, the violence and injustice perpetrated by "the wicked" against "the righteous" people of Judah. Some scholars identify "the wicked" in vv. 4 and 13 as foreigners. Those who claim "the wicked" in v. 4 were the Assyrians[27] must explain why Habakkuk would then jump to the defense of those who had long oppressed his people: "Why are you silent / while one who is wicked [i.e., Babylon, v. 5] swallows up / one who is more righteous than himself?" (1:13). Likewise, the proposal that "the wicked" in vv. 4 and 13 both refer to the Babylonians[28] must explain how God was raising up the Babylonians if they were already present in Judah.

---

[25] Robert B. Chisholm Jr., *Handbook on the Prophets* (Grand Rapids: Baker Academic, 2002), 433; J. J. M. Roberts, *Nahum, Habakkuk, and Zephaniah*, OTL (Louisville: John Knox, 1991), 82–84; Smith, *Micah-Malachi*, 95. Floyd, *Minor Prophets*, 87, indicates a bit longer span, from 610 to 550 BC.

[26] Andersen, *Habakkuk*, 17.

[27] Walter Dietrich, "Three Minor Prophets and the Major Empires: Synchronic and Diachronic Perspectives on Nahum, Habakkuk, and Zephaniah," in *Perspectives on the Formation of the Book of the Twelve: Methodological Foundations, Redactional Processes, Historical Insights*, ed. J. Wöhrle, J. Nogalski, and R. Albertz, BZAW 433 (Berlin: de Gruyter, 2012), 151–52. Robert I. Vasholz, "Habakkuk: Complaints or Complaint?" *Presbyterion* 18/1 (1992): 50–52, suggests "the wicked" in both Hab 1:2–4 and 1:12–17 are the Assyrians, whom God would use the Babylonians to judge. Vasholz's proposal thus places Habakkuk before Nabopolassar's rise to power in 626 BC. Cf. Eaton, *Obadiah, Nahum, Habakkuk, Zephaniah*, 82, 87–94.

[28] Marvin A. Sweeney, "Structure, Genre, and Intent in the Book of Habakkuk," *VT* 41.1 (1991): 74, argues that the wicked in Hab 1:2–4 were the Babylonians, and 1:5–11 simply amplifies their description.

The text, however, offers evidence that "the wicked" in 1:4 came from within the community. Verse 4 uses covenantal language to describe the results of these wrongs: "This is why the law [Hb. *tôrâ*] is ineffective / and justice [Hb. *mišpāṭ*] never emerges. / . . . justice [Hb. *mišpāṭ*] comes out perverted."[29] The prophet appears to describe "the wicked" as Judeans who had wronged their fellow countrymen, indicating "the wicked" of v. 4 were domestic rather than foreign.[30] In v. 13, however, "the wicked" were the Babylonians God would use as his agent (v. 6) to chastise the wickedness among his own people.

If "the wicked" in 1:4 were in fact Judeans oppressing their brothers, the observation that Habakkuk did not include religious idolatry in his list of their wrongs (1:2–4) suggests that the setting is sometime after Josiah's religious reforms began in 628 BC and gained further momentum in 622 BC (cf. 2 Kgs 22–23; 2 Chr 34). This prophet who mocked idol worship among the Babylonians (Hab 2:18–19) would have condemned rampant idolatry among his own people if he lived in Manasseh's day.

Some scholars point out that the wickedness described in 1:2–4 was more characteristic of Jehoiakim's day than the final days of Josiah's reign.[31] These social ills correspond with Jeremiah's description of the son's reign in contrast to that of his father who "administer[ed] justice and righteousness" (Jer 22:13–17). If this view is correct, then it would push the earliest date to sometime after Josiah's death in 609 BC. It is not inconceivable that Josiah's religious reforms—though genuine for the godly king—may have been only surface deep for some, especially given the unchecked wickedness of his grandfather Manasseh's six-decade reign. The rapidity with which the Judeans shook off moral constraints after the death of Josiah suggests that the nation's religious commitment during his two-decade religious reform may have been primarily external.

Based on these clues, the earliest date for Habakkuk would be after the Babylonians had destroyed the cities of Assyria (614–610 BC) and likely after the death of Josiah in 609 BC. The latest date would occur before the Battle of Carchemish in 605 BC. The approximate brackets for dating the book of Habakkuk are 609–605 BC.

---

[29] Achtemeier, *Nahum-Malachi*, 34–35.

[30] Andersen, *Habakkuk*, 19.

[31] Heath A. Thomas, *Habakkuk*, The Two Horizons Old Testament Commentary (Grand Rapids: Eerdmans, 2018), 25–26.

3 HISTORICAL BACKGROUND

3.1 THE NEO-ASSYRIAN EMPIRE: LATE EIGHTH CENTURY BC

Habakkuk's generation witnessed a momentous shift in players on the political stage of the ancient Near East. For more than a century, the Assyrians had dominated the map as the first empire intent on ruling the world.[32] Ascending to the throne in 745 BC, Tiglath-pileser III ("Pul" in 2 Kgs 15:19) had reenergized the Neo-Assyrian Empire. After shoring up his authority at home, Tiglath-pileser (745–727 BC) turned his attention toward Syria-Palestine, where he collected exorbitant "tribute" from kings like Menahem of Israel (2 Kgs 15:19–20). His actions underscore the goal of the Assyrian Empire, which was not only to enlarge its territory but also "to extract as much wealth as possible from outlying areas."[33] At first it was in Assyrian interests to offer a degree of independence to small client states so they could pay taxes. But when these vassal kings grew weary of the unrelenting taxation and rebelled, Assyrian kings answered with overwhelming force. Repeated rebellions eventually resulted in the incorporation of these regions into Assyrian provinces ruled by a governor under Assyrian control.[34]

A militaristic nation, Assyria had a reputation for brutal warfare that proved to be an effective psychological weapon.[35] If an enemy would not surrender, severe punishment served as a warning to others. As siege machines battered a city into submission, escapees were beheaded, flayed alive, or impaled on stakes—all while fellow citizens looked on with horror from city walls. To ensure that the vanquished would be incapable of a subsequent uprising, the Assyrians leveled houses, salted fields, and cut down orchards.[36] Once a besieged city

---

[32] Marc Van de Mieroop, *A History of the Ancient Near East, ca. 3000–323 BC*, 3rd ed., Blackwell History of the Ancient World (Malden, MA: Blackwell, 2016), 229.

[33] Christopher B. Hays and Peter Machinist, "Assyria and the Assyrians," in *The World around the Old Testament: The People and Places of the Ancient Near East*, ed. Bill T. Arnold and Brent A. Strawn (Grand Rapids: Baker Academic, 2016), 45.

[34] Van de Mieroop, *A History of the Ancient Near East*, 250–51.

[35] Hays and Machinist, "Assyria and the Assyrians," 62, observe that Assyria's militaristic propaganda was so effective that it has long swayed modern scholars to propagate what may be an oversimplistic stereotype of the Assyrians. The authors note that recent scholarship has produced a portrait that tempers Assyrian aggression with "a nuanced and savvy administration that was bent on maximizing wealth and consolidating power more than wreaking havoc."

[36] Van de Mieroop, *A History of the Ancient Near East*, 248.

fell, they uprooted survivors and sent them into exile, resettling the land with captives from other nations.

The northern kingdom of Israel experienced Assyrian cruelty firsthand. After the death of Tiglath-pileser, King Hoshea of Israel withheld the expected annual tribute. Shalmaneser V (726–722 BC) responded with a ruthless siege on Samaria that lasted three years. When the capital city finally fell in 722, both Shalmaneser V and his successor Sargon II (721–705 BC) claimed responsibility for her capture. The Assyrians sent more than twenty-seven thousand Jewish survivors into exile and resettled Samaria with refugees from other places (2 Kgs 17:3–7, 24).[37]

In 701 BC, Sennacherib (704–681 BC) mounted a campaign against the southern kingdom of Judah. After a horrific siege on the city of Lachish, Sennacherib marched up through the foothills, intent on tightening a similar noose around Jerusalem. In his royal account of the campaign, the Assyrian king boasted that he pillaged forty-six cities, took captive 200,150 citizens of Judah, and "locked up [Hezekiah] within Jerusalem, his royal city, like a bird in a cage."[38] Only divine intervention in response to the prayers of King Hezekiah and the prophet Isaiah spared the city of Jerusalem a fate similar to that of Lachish (2 Kgs 18:13–19:37; Isa 36–37; 2 Chr 32:1–23). Though the Assyrians allowed Hezekiah to retain his throne, however, they exacted a heavy tribute from the Judean king (2 Kgs 18:14–16).

When Sennacherib moved the Assyrian capital to Nineveh the following year, he decorated the walls of his newly constructed palace with friezes memorializing his brutal siege against Lachish.[39] While the depictions may have leaned toward hyperbole, they were effective propaganda intended to give potential rebels pause. The horror of Assyrian atrocities must have lingered long in the collective memory of Judah. All her inhabitants longed to see the demise of the Assyrian Empire.

---

[37] Hays and Machinist, "Assyria and the Assyrians," 48. Sargon also conquered Urartu, Assyria's northern neighbor, in 714 BC and repeatedly had to deal with rebellions in Babylon (p. 49).

[38] "Sennacherib's Siege of Jerusalem (2.119B)," COS 1:303.

[39] Large sections of these wall reliefs are now on display in the Lachish Room of the British Museum, London. For a description of these panels and the archaeological remains of the battle at Lachish, see Ephraim Stern, The Assyrian, Babylonian, and Persian Periods (732–332 B.C.E.), vol. 2 of Archaeology of the Land of the Bible, ABRL (New York: Doubleday, 2001), 5–6.

	Assyria	Babylonia	Israel	Judah	Prophets
	Significant dates, people, and events leading up to the fall of Jerusalem				
728 BC	Tiglath-pileser III	*Assyria seizes throne*			
725	Shalmaneser V		Hoshea		
722	Sargon II		*Samaria falls*		
703	Sennacherib	Merodach-baladan		Hezekiah	Isaiah/Micah
689		*Babylon destroyed*		Manasseh	
680	Esarhaddon	*Babylon rebuilt*			
669	Ashurbanipal	Shamash-shuma-ukin		Amon	
648		*Babylon recaptured*		Josiah	Nahum
627	*Ashurbanipal dies*	Nabopolassar		*Josiah's reforms*	Zephaniah
612	*Assyria collapses*				
609				Jehoahaz	Habakkuk
605		Nebuchadnezzar		Jehoiakim	Jeremiah
597		*Besieges Jerusalem*		Jehoiachin	
586		*Destroys Jerusalem*		Zedekiah	

3.2   STRUGGLE FOR DOMINION: EARLY SEVENTH CENTURY BC

Other nations who suffered under Assyrian domination assuredly felt the same way—perhaps none more so than the Babylonians. In 728 BC, Tiglath-pileser III stamped out a revolt and claimed the Babylonian throne for himself; he was the first Neo-Assyrian king to do so. The Babylonian kings list shows that for the next hundred years subsequent Assyrian kings followed his lead. Their names stand out prominently amid other names marked by affixes honoring the Babylonian gods Marduk and Nabu.[40] A pattern also emerges from the list. Babylonians saw the death of an Assyrian king as a chance to throw

[40] Van de Mieroop, *A History of the Ancient Near East*, 313.

off—however briefly—the yoke of Assyrian rule.[41] Sennacherib had to deal repeatedly with Babylonian uprisings as Babylonian rule changed hands seven times during his reign.[42]

The first biblical hint of an earthshaking shift in power players surfaces in 2 Kgs 20:16–18.[43] Hearing of Hezekiah's illness and recovery, the Babylonian king Merodach-baladan sent envoys bearing letters concerning an alliance with Judah against Sennacherib. Instead of exalting the Lord for his miraculous healing, Hezekiah proudly paraded all his treasures before the Babylonian delegation. When Isaiah heard about Hezekiah's pride and misplaced trust, he pronounced the following prophecy:

> Hear the word of the Lord: "Look, the days are coming when everything in your palace and all that your fathers have stored up until today will be carried off to Babylon; nothing will be left," says the Lord. "Some of your descendants—who come from you, whom you father—will be taken away, and they will become eunuchs in the palace of the king of Babylon." (2 Kgs 20:17–18)

Isaiah's prophecy was fulfilled a century later when the Babylonians began the first of several punitive campaigns against Judah (605–604; 598–97; 588–86 BC). At the time the prophet uttered these words, however, it is unlikely anyone in the ancient Near East could have imagined the aggressors would be the Babylonians rather than the Assyrians.

---

[41] Sandra Richter, "Eighth-Century Issues: The World of Jeroboam II, the Fall of Samaria, and the Reign of Hezekiah," in *Ancient Israel's History: An Introduction to Issues and Sources*, ed. Bill T. Arnold and Richard S. Hess (Grand Rapids: Baker Academic, 2014), 342.

[42] Van de Mieroop, *A History of the Ancient Near East*, 270–73, observes that during the reigns of the six major Neo-Assyrian kings, the city of Babylon endured twenty transitions in power.

[43] Cf. Isa 39:1. In all likelihood, the events in 2 Kgs 20 chronologically preceded the previous two chapters' account of Sennacherib's invasion in 701 BC. The Babylonian king, Merodach-baladan, must have intended to form alliance with Judah ahead of the Assyrian onslaught. Additionally, some of the treasures Hezekiah showed the Babylonians must have placated the invading Assyrians (2 Kgs 18:15–16).

Van de Mieroop, *A History of the Ancient Near East*, 358–59, appends the Babylonian king list, which identifies Merodach-baladan as Marduk-apla-iddina II (721–10; 703 BC). Hays and Machinist, "Assyria and the Assyrians," 48–49, note that the Babylonian had successfully wrested the throne from Sargon II and reigned for a decade before Sargon snatched it back in 710 BC. Not surprisingly, Merodach-baladan attempted the same feat after Sennacherib became king in 704 BC. This time, however, his success lasted only a few months.

Although most of Assyria's opponents made sporadic attempts to escape her clutches, the Assyrians somehow managed to retain control. Merodach-baladan's rebellion against Sennacherib was short-lived, but others like him repeatedly attempted to break free.[44] Finally, Sennacherib resorted to a siege against Babylon lasting fifteen months. When the city fell in 689 BC, Sennacherib completely destroyed it. According to his inscriptions, he not only burned and leveled the city, but he also dug a canal through it to render it unrecognizable in the future.[45] Babylon's prospects looked bleak. A survey of the political landscape in 689 BC might have labeled Babylonia as the least likely to survive, much less to usurp Assyria's role as the dominant player in the ancient Near East.

Still, the Assyrians seemed to recognize that Babylonia had an enduring uniqueness in Mesopotamia that stretched back over a thousand years. The Assyrians themselves owed a significant debt to this "cultural lodestar [of] the ancient Near East," in the areas of both literature and religion.[46] As a result of this residual influence, the Assyrians often extended unusual privileges to Babylon—for example, granting them a special tax status as a site of religious significance for all of Mesopotamia.[47] In recognition of Babylon's importance, Esarhaddon (680–669 BC) rebuilt the city with the aim of integrating it into the Assyrian Empire. His solution to the perennial Babylonian problem was to appoint one son, Ashurbanipal, as the king of Assyria, and another son, Shamash-shuma-ukin, as the king of Babylonia.[48]

Meanwhile the Assyrian war machine continued to roll across the map of the ancient Near East. Esarhaddon set his sights on Egypt, capturing the Nile Delta and taking a tenuous hold on the city of Memphis in 671 BC. Mentioned in the Bible only once (2 Kgs 19:37), Esarhaddon included "Manasseh, king of the city of Judah" in the list of foreign kings tasked with supplying building materials for a palace

---

[44] Sennacherib drove Merodach-baladan into the marshes of southern Babylonia in 703 BC and immortalized this "victory" in sculpture reliefs at Nineveh—now on display in the British Museum, London.

[45] Hays and Machinist, "Assyria and the Assyrians," 51.

[46] David S. Vanderhooft, "Babylonia and the Babylonians," in *The World around the Old Testament: The People and Places of the Ancient Near East*, ed. Bill T. Arnold and Brent A. Strawn (Grand Rapids: Baker Academic, 2016), 119. The Babylonian literary legacy includes the Code of Hammurabi, the Gilgamesh Epic, and *Enuma Elish*.

[47] Hays and Machinist, "Assyria and the Assyrians," 68.

[48] Van de Mieroop, *A History of the Ancient Near East*, 273.

in Nineveh.[49] Manasseh's surprisingly long reign (698–644 BC) is further evidence that Judah remained a loyal vassal, for the most part, during Assyria's expansion southward into Egypt. After the death of Esarhaddon, his son Ashurbanipal (669–627 BC) renewed the conquest of Egypt, pushing all the way up the Nile into Upper Egypt, capturing Thebes in 663 BC. This expansion meant that Assyrian dominion stretched from western Iran to the Mediterranean Sea, from Anatolia to Upper Egypt.[50] Under Ashurbanipal the Assyrian Empire had reached its zenith.

3.3   THE ASSYRIAN WAR MACHINE'S STALL: LATE SEVENTH CENTURY BC

Though the shadow of their influence appears monolithic on a map, the Assyrians seriously overextended their reach. Ironically, their phenomenal military success contributed to their downfall. The Assyrians' infamous brutality had fomented a deep resentment, prompting vassal states to break free whenever possible. Uprisings on multiple fronts soon revealed fatal fault lines all over the map. In the mid-650s, Ashurbanipal mounted a brutal offensive in retaliation to Elam's rebellion in the east. In the same time period, Egypt cast off Assyrian control once and for all.[51] Back home, Esarhaddon's dream of a united Assyria and Babylonia ruled by two brothers collapsed into civil war. Ashurbanipal fought for four years before the Assyrians finally recaptured Babylon yet again in 648 BC.[52]

In this same year and against this backdrop Josiah, grandson of the infamously wicked King Manasseh, was born in Jerusalem. Six years later, his grandfather died after a record-setting fifty-five year reign.[53]

---

[49] Erle Leichty, *The Royal Inscriptions of Esarhaddon, King of Assyria (680–669 BC)*, vol. 1 in *The Royal Inscriptions of the Neo-Assyrian Period* (Winona Lake: Eisenbrauns, 2011), 23. James Bennett Pritchard, ed., *Ancient Near Eastern Texts Relating to the Old Testament*, 3rd ed. (Princeton: Princeton University Press, 1992), 294, observes that according to a later inscription list, Manasseh also supplied tribute and troops to support Ashurbanipal's campaign against Thebes in 663 BC.

[50] Van de Mieroop, *A History of the Ancient Near East*, 246.

[51] Hays and Machinist, "Assyria and the Assyrians," 54.

[52] Van de Mieroop, *A History of the Ancient Near East*, 273–74.

[53] Second Kings 21:1 reports that Manasseh reigned for fifty-five years. That span may have included an initial ten-year coregency with his father, Hezekiah. Chronicles adds an unusual footnote to the reign of Manasseh. Evidently the king provoked both the Lord and the Assyrians, who "captured Manasseh with hooks, bound him with bronze shackles, and took him to Babylon" (2 Chr 33:11). Humbled and repentant, Manasseh later returned to Jerusalem, instituted a

Josiah's father Amon ruled only two years before being assassinated by his servants—possibly an indication of a brief struggle between pro- and anti-Assyrian factions (2 Kgs 21:23).[54] Ancient records contain no mention of Assyrians in Syria-Palestine after 645 BC.[55] The once-great power player had withdrawn from Judah by the time eight-year-old Josiah (640–609 BC) ascended the throne of Judah. For nearly a century, Judah had tread cautiously as a vassal state under the ominous cloud of the Assyrians. If the empire rallied, might they once more set their sights on Judah?

When Ashurbanipal died in 627 BC after a forty-two-year reign, there was no clear line of succession, and the resulting internal instability added to the nation's precipitous decline. Additionally, because the Assyrians had always taken the military offensive, they never anticipated the need to defend their homeland.[56] This ruthless nation, who had honed the military art of siege to a fine edge, now experienced the horror of their own military practices. Poorly fortified cities fell like dominoes before a combined onslaught of Medes and Babylonians: Ashur in 614 BC; Nineveh and Calah, 612 BC; Haran, 610 BC. The victors unleashed a deep-seated resentment in their destruction.[57] Assyria, the once-great empire that had engulfed the ancient Near East with terror and foreboding, simply vanished from the map.

The destruction of Assyria was celebrated by all who had endured her unbridled brutality, and that included just about everyone. The

---

degree of religious reform, and began to build up fortifications in Jerusalem and Judah (2 Chr 33:12–17).

[54] Brad E. Kelle, "Judah in the Seventh Century: From the Aftermath of Sennacherib's Invasion to the Beginning of Jehoiakim's Rebellion," in *Ancient Israel's History: An Introduction to Issues and Sources*, ed. Bill T. Arnold and Richard S. Hess (Grand Rapids: Baker Academic, 2014), 367.

[55] Stern, *The Assyrian, Babylonian, and Persian Periods*, 4.

[56] Sarah C. Mellville, "A New Look at the End of the Assyrian Empire," in *Homeland and Exile: Biblical and Ancient Near Eastern Studies in Honour of Bustenay Oded*, ed. Markham J. Geller et al., VTSup 130 (Leiden: Brill, 2009), 194. Melville, p. 186, notes that the Assyrians' hazardous miscalculation is understandable: their heartland had remained "invasion-free" for over five hundred years.

[57] Van de Mieroop, *A History of the Ancient Near East*, 286, describes how the soldiers took the time to search the wall reliefs for depictions of Sennacherib and Assurbanipal. Once found, they defaced them by gouging out the kings' eyes and ears before burning the palaces to the ground. The results can be seen on Lachish relief panel 12 in the British Museum, London. "Sennacherib—Lachish Relief Inscription 2.119C," *COS* 1:304, notes the inscription on the panel identifies the seated figure as "Sennacherib, king of the universe, king of Assyria."

prophet Nahum, writing a few decades before Habakkuk, anticipated the empire's destruction with longing:

> King of Assyria . . .
> All who hear the news about you
> will clap their hands because of you,
> for who has not experienced
> your constant cruelty? (Nah 3:18–19)

3.4 A NARROW WINDOW OF FREEDOM IN JOSIAH'S REIGN: 627–609 BC

The biblical passages reporting Josiah's reign are 2 Kgs 22:1–23:30 and 2 Chr 34:1–35:27.[58] The primary concern of these texts is Josiah's religious reform (see below). The second half of Josiah's reign, and the lead-up to Habakkuk's book, straddled this tense transition between the demise of the Neo-Assyrian Empire and the simultaneous emergence of the Neo-Babylonian Empire. Josiah must have looked on warily as the waning years of Assyria played out during his reign.

The death of Ashurbanipal in 627 BC occurred after Josiah initiated his religious reforms. Scholars have debated whether some of Josiah's reforms—for example, his destruction of northern shrines and his inclusion of people from northern territories in the Passover (2 Chr 34:6–7; 35:17–18)—imply Judean expansion during this period. Archaeological and inscriptional evidence supporting this theory is inconclusive.[59] Whatever the extent of their borders, the citizens of Judah must have breathed a collective sigh of relief as the Assyrian Empire drew its final breaths. After nearly a century of appeasement, the nation was finally free from foreign oppressors.

This window of freedom did not remain open long.[60] God already pronounced the imminent destruction of Judah but promised it would not happen until after Josiah's death (2 Kgs 22:15–20; 2 Chr

---

[58] Although Nahum, Zephaniah, and Jeremiah prophesied during the time of Josiah, none mention his reign or religious reform specifically. Jeremiah does reference Josiah's death in 22:10–12.

[59] Kelle, "Judah in the Seventh Century," 372–75.

[60] The outside limits of this freedom are 627–609 BC. Kelle, "Judah in the Seventh Century," 376–77, observes that the window may have closed as early as 616 BC when Psammetichus I led the Egyptian army into Mesopotamia in support of the Assyrians. Nevertheless, since Psammetichus had operated as an Assyrian ally for most of his reign, Assyria may have seamlessly handed over control of Judah to Egypt as they withdrew from the area. If so, the window may have never even opened.

34:22–28). The wait was not long, though, since other nations hungrily watched for opportunities to fill the growing void of power left by the retreating Assyrians. In 609 BC, Egyptian Pharaoh Neco II marched through the Jezreel Valley on his way to shore up a remnant Assyria, allies in the face of Babylonia's relentless march westward. Perhaps delaying the inevitable, Josiah confronted Neco at Megiddo, and the Egyptian killed him (2 Kgs 23:28–30; 2 Chr 35:20–27). Neco subsequently deposed and exiled Josiah's newly crowned heir, Jehoahaz. Neco replaced him with another of Josiah's sons—Jehoiakim (609–598 BC)—and extracted a large tribute from his new vassal.

With the death of Josiah, nothing stood between Judah and God's judgment. Despite Egypt's expansionist plans for the Levant, the next imperial powerhouse was already emerging on the scene. The immediate setting for the Lord's pronouncement to Habakkuk probably falls in this transitional period, just after Josiah's death.

3.5 THE NEO-BABYLONIAN EMPIRE: LATE SEVENTH CENTURY BC

The swift collapse of the Neo-Assyrian Empire is mirrored in reverse by the simultaneous rise of the Neo-Babylonian Empire.[61] When Assyrian leadership fell into disarray, the first Neo-Babylonian king, Nabopolassar (626–605 BC), leaped at the chance to rid Babylon of Assyrian control forever. In 616 BC, he launched an attack on Assyria from the south. Soon after, the Medes, led by King Cyaxares, engaged Assyrian armies on an eastern front. The Medo-Babylonian coalition swept relentlessly across the heartland of Assyria, felling her proud cities one after the other. (Habakkuk 1:6–11, 14–17 paints a graphic description of the Babylonian advance.) Nabopolassar not only succeeded in securing Babylon's independence; he also established Babylonian dominance in Mesopotamia and most of former Assyria.

It was Nabopolassar's son, however, who initiated the "full-throated imperialism" of Babylonia that came to rival that of the Assyrians.[62] Before he even ascended the throne, Nebuchadnezzar II (604–562 BC) crushed the Assyrian remnant and the Egyptian army

---

[61] Vanderhooft, "Babylonia and the Babylonians," 111–12, points out that Babylon—listed as a provincial city as early as the Ur III dynasty of the third millennium BC—had blossomed into a significant cultural center under her most famous king, Hammurabi (1792–1750 BC), whose influence generated the golden age of the Old Babylonian period.

[62] Vanderhooft, "Babylonia and the Babylonians," 127.

led by Neco at the Battle of Carchemish in 605 BC (Jer 46:1–26). Having curtailed Egyptian influence in Syria, Nebuchadnezzar extended Babylonia's dominion from the Upper Euphrates to the Nile, and from the Persian Gulf to the eastern Mediterranean. In essence, Nebuchadnezzar's program of expansionism led him to adopt roughly the same map as the former Assyrian Empire. He acquired her former territories but with far fewer military campaigns than the Assyrians. The resulting outcome, however, turned out to be far more destructive:

> Unlike the previous Assyrian imperial system, which strived to create a network of semi-independent provinces, the Babylonian concept was quite different: their entire focus was on the welfare of the city of Babylon and its immediate surroundings, while the periphery was largely neglected, with negative consequences for those living in those territories.[63]

Nebuchadnezzar adopted the Assyrian practice of exacting heavy annual tribute from all the peoples within his empire's vast footprint. The Assyrians funneled some of these resources to build capital cities reflecting the Assyrian ideal that their human monarch was king of the universe. An Assyrian king's palace always overshadowed any other temples. In contrast, Nebuchadnezzar rebuilt Babylon as a cosmic religious center on behalf of Marduk, king of the universe.[64] Though Babylonian kings wielded great power, they stood in the shadow of their pantheon. The architectural plan of Babylon bears out this ideal. The temple complex formed the central hub of the city, whereas the royal palace and its famed hanging gardens sat deferentially to the side.[65] Whether or not Herodotus visited Babylon in person, the ancient Greek historian described the grandiose beauty of the city in great detail.[66] Archaeological excavations likewise bear witness to the

---

[63] Stern, *The Assyrian, Babylonian, and Persian Periods*, 303.

[64] Paul-Alain Beaulieu, "Nebuchadnezzar's Babylon as World Capital," CSMS 3 (2008): 10, explains that the Babylonian literary epic *Enuma Elish*, composed at the end of the second millennium BC, recounts how Marduk conquered the dragon Tiamat and created the world from her dismembered body. Crowned as king by the rest of the gods, Marduk founded Babylon as the center of the universe, his own dwelling place, and the home of the gods.

[65] Beaulieu, "Nebuchadnezzar's Babylon as World Capital," 9. Although there were many temples in Babylon honoring various gods, chief among them stood those built to the glory of Marduk: the Esagil Temple and the Etemenanki ziggurat.

[66] Herodotus, *The History*, trans. David Grene (Chicago: University of Chicago Press, 1987), 80–81.

enormity of the city and its extensive walls. Part of the massive Ishtar gate, with its breathtaking, blue-glazed tiles and artistic reliefs of bulls and dragons, has been reconstructed and is on display in the Pergamon Museum in Berlin.

Although Nebuchadnezzar succeeded in restoring Babylon as the consummate paradigm of an ancient Sumerian city-state ideal, he struggled to lead an empire on the same level as his Assyrian predecessors.[67] Whereas the Assyrian pattern had been to rebuild conquered cities and repopulate them with other deported peoples, Nebuchadnezzar's singular focus on Babylon meant that he left in his wake a trail of abandoned cities and ruined provinces. This would hold true in the Levant as well, where the only archaeological remains of Babylonian dominance are widespread destruction levels.[68]

3.6   HABAKKUK'S PROPHECY FULFILLED: EARLY SIXTH CENTURY BC

As shocking as the Lord's pronouncement must have originally sounded to Habakkuk, the reality of the Babylonian threat became apparent to everyone in Judah. Of the period following Egypt's defeat at Carchemish in 605 BC, the Babylonian Chronicles report Nebuchadnezzar marched south throughout Syria-Palestine to secure vassals and collect tribute. In 604 BC, his army destroyed the Philistine city of Ashkelon, leaving it in ruins until the Persian period.[69] Not surprisingly, Jehoiakim, king of Judah, switched his allegiance from Egypt to Babylonia. He remained loyal for three years before he rebelled against Nebuchadnezzar, possibly emboldened by Egypt's successful rebuff of a Babylonian incursion in 601 BC (2 Kgs 24:1).[70]

In her final two decades, Judah's allegiance wavered between Egypt and Babylonia. Nebuchadnezzar's dominance in Syria-Palestine during these years must have created a tense internal struggle within Judah. Biblical passages imply an extremely stressful polarization since Judah's political leadership seemed to align with Egypt, while prophets like Jeremiah and Habakkuk counseled submission to Babylonia

---

[67] Beaulieu, "Nebuchadnezzar's Babylon as World Capital," 5–12.

[68] Stern, *The Assyrian, Babylonian, and Persian Periods*, 308–9.

[69] Albert Kirk Grayson, *Assyrian and Babylonian Chronicles*, Texts from Cuneiform Sources 5 (Locust Valley, NY: J. J. Augustin, 1975), 100. Nebuchadnezzar likely deported Daniel and his three friends during this same campaign.

[70] Kelle, "Judah in the Seventh Century," 380–81.

(Jer 22:13–19; 26:1–24).[71] The author of Kings records the Lord himself summoned raiders from the Transjordan to join forces with the Babylonians. They were to remove Judah from the Lord's presence in payment for all the sins of Manasseh because "he had filled Jerusalem with innocent blood" (2 Kgs 24:2–4).

Jehoiakim's rebellion was not only ill-advised, but also short-lived. Nebuchadnezzar mounted the first siege against Jerusalem in 597 BC. It is unclear exactly when Jehoiakim died, leaving his throne to his eighteen-year-old son—Josiah's grandson—Jehoiachin. The young king quickly surrendered, and Nebuchadnezzar deported him, along with ten thousand others, including his mother, wives, servants, officials, seven thousand soldiers, and one thousand skilled craftsmen. Nebuchadnezzar placed Jehoiachin's uncle, twenty-one-year-old Zedekiah, on the throne (2 Kgs 24:10–18).

Against the warning of Jeremiah (Jer 27–29), Zedekiah rebelled against Babylonia. Nebuchadnezzar brought his entire army to besiege Jerusalem a second time (588–586 BC). After eighteen months the city ran out of food. When the attackers breached the walls, Zedekiah attempted to escape. The Babylonian army caught up with him near Jericho. They slaughtered Zedekiah's sons before his eyes, blinded him, bound him with chains, and sent him to Babylon. The invaders burned the temple, the king's palace, and the rest of Jerusalem. They carted off all the temple utensils and marched off most of the survivors to Babylon. Only the poorest of the land remained behind under Gedaliah, the governor appointed by Nebuchadnezzar. Even this last flicker of hope died out with the assassination of Gedaliah. Just as the Lord had warned through his prophets, all of Judah went into exile (2 Kgs 25:1–26; 2 Chr 36:11–21; Jer 52:4–34). The Babylonians had come and conquered. Jerusalem lay in ruins, waiting for the day of disaster to dawn on their enemies (Hab 3:16).[72] The Lord's shocking pronouncement to the prophet Habakkuk had come to pass.

---

[71] Kelle, "Judah in the Seventh Century," 381. Robert D. Haak, Habakkuk, VTSup 44 (Leiden: Brill, 1992), 130–49, dates Habakkuk to Jehoiakim's reign. He takes a unique approach, however, arguing that Habakkuk was a supporter of the deposed Jehoahaz, the legitimate "righteous" king as opposed to the pro-Egyptian Jehoiakim, "the wicked" king. Haak's theory requires that the prophetic text maintain a consistent pro-Babylonian stance throughout, which he supplies in his own translation (p. 130).

[72] That day would come when Cyrus the Great led Persian forces to defeat the Babylonian army at Opis in 539 BC. Soon afterward, Cyrus captured Babylon with little resistance. Cyrus,

3.7   WORLD DOMINION: A THEOLOGICAL REFLECTION

As the Neo-Assyrian wave crested and fell across the map of the ancient Near East, the Neo-Babylonian wave surged behind it, and yet a third wave from Persia began to build in the distance. Perhaps the only thing more shocking than the violent thunder of each of these mighty waves was how quickly an empire's dominance dissipated as another rose to take its place.

Where does it come from—this compelling drive to sweep over the face of the earth and rule it? In some sense it is a warped distortion of that first great commission: "Be fruitful, multiply, fill the earth, and subdue it. Rule the fish of the sea, the birds of the sky, and every creature that crawls on the earth" (Gen 1:28). Instead of filling the earth with image bearers who worship God and reflect his character, these human rulers exalted themselves rather than serve the one true God. They craved glory and wanted to make a name for themselves. They gobbled up the earth's peoples, lands, resources, and wealth for themselves. A small nation like Judah, seemingly untethered between the troughs, had no hope but to be swept away by the pounding waves.

This is where the role of the prophets was so crucial. The prophets proclaimed that the true King of the universe is none other than the One who created it. As early as Isaiah, the Lord explained that the king of Assyria was merely an instrument he used to judge Israel and punish Judah:

> [T]he Lord will certainly bring against them
> the mighty rushing water of the Euphrates River—
> the king of Assyria and all his glory.
> It will overflow its channels
> and spill over all its banks.
> It will pour into Judah,
> flood over it, and sweep through,
> reaching up to the neck;
> and its flooded banks
> will fill your entire land, Immanuel!
> (Isa 8:7–8)

---

an instrument of God's providence, issued a pronouncement the following year, allowing the Jewish exiles to return to Judah.

A just God would not allow nations who opposed him to go unpunished. As the prophet Nahum declared, a day of calamity would come for the Assyrians, too: "[The Lord] will completely destroy Nineveh / with an overwhelming flood, / and he will chase his enemies into darkness" (Nah 1:8). Similarly, even though God would use Babylonia to discipline Judah, Babylon would face judgment in turn: "'Babylon is captured; / Bel is put to shame; / Marduk is terrified.' / Her idols are put to shame; / her false gods, devastated. . . . The sea has risen over Babylon; / she is covered with its tumultuous waves" (Jer 50:2; 51:42).

Habakkuk was greatly troubled to hear that the Lord intended to use a pagan nation like the Babylonians to judge his own people. He asked, "Why are you silent / while one who is wicked swallows up / one who is more righteous than himself?" (Hab 1:13). The Lord, however, realigned Habakkuk's thinking:

> Is it not from the LORD of Armies
> that the peoples labor only to fuel the fire
> and countries exhaust themselves for nothing?
> For the earth will be filled
> with the knowledge of the LORD's glory,
> as the water covers the sea, (Hab 2:13–14).

Despite their arrogant ambitions, nations like Assyria and Babylonia were simply tools God used to accomplish his mission. Although he would also bring these nations to justice for their own violence and idolatry, the sovereign Lord used them to purge Judah of her wicked ways. Out of this purified remnant would come his Son, who would establish his own worldwide kingdom, comprised of citizens representing every tongue and tribe on the globe (Rev 5:8–9; 7:9–10). As the Creator, his ultimate goal is to fill every inch of the earth with the knowledge of his own glory, as the waters cover the sea. Other waves followed these: the Persians, the Greeks, and the Romans. The Lord accomplished his mission not in spite of these pagan kings bent on ruling the world; rather, he used their labor to set the stage for the birth of the King and the inauguration of his own kingdom.

The choppy sea has not stilled since the closing of the canon. Wave after wave of nations has continued to break upon the world's shore in quest of immortality and glory. British colonialism set out to rule the world's seas, and the modern missionary movement launched aboard its ships. Various Asian communist regimes bent on rooting out Christianity produced a tempered-steel faith that thrived in persecution. A failed Arab Spring and ISIS designs for an Islamic caliphate have precipitated an unprecedented spiritual harvest among Muslims. Even the drive of capitalism intent on staking flags emblazoned with corporate logos on every corner of the map has contributed to the spread of the name of the incarnate Logos, Jesus Christ. The risen Lord gave his followers a second global commission—to "make disciples of all nations" (Matt 28:19). Despite secular rulers bent on conquering the world, God is still able to use them for his own purposes—to spread the gospel to the ends of the earth and cover the world in praise.

4   RELIGIOUS BACKGROUND

4.1   JUDAH'S RELIGIOUS, SOCIAL, AND MORAL DEPRAVITY

When Habakkuk heard God's plans for judgment, he questioned how the Lord could use a nation as treacherous and wicked as Babylonia to chastise his own people. Modern readers might wonder what Judah could have done to deserve complete destruction and exile; however the waywardness of God's people, however, was not a new development. The Israelites' history of disobedience extended all the way back to their beginnings as a nation. Jeremiah, a contemporary of Habakkuk, outlined the Lord's case against his people:

> [W]hen I brought your ancestors out of the land of Egypt, I . . . [gave] them this command: "Obey me, and then I will be your God, and you will be my people. Follow every way I command you so that it may go well with you." Yet they didn't listen or pay attention but followed their own advice and their own stubborn, evil heart. They went backward and not forward. Since the day your ancestors came out of the land of Egypt until today, I have sent all my servants the prophets to you time and time again. However, my people wouldn't listen to me or pay attention but became obstinate; they did more evil than their ancestors. (Jer 7:22–26)

The religious reforms of King Hezekiah (715–687 BC) temporarily checked the moral free fall of Judah, even though the reform lasted only a short while. Sadly, Hezekiah failed to do the one thing that might have spared the nation future destruction. Even with God's gracious extension of his life by fifteen years and the miraculous delivery of Jerusalem from the Assyrians, Hezekiah did not raise his son Manasseh to know and fear the Lord.

After his father died, Manasseh quickly returned Judah to the pagan ways of his grandfather, Ahaz. As the longest reigning king in either Israel or Judah, Manasseh set a course for Judah that led the nation into gross apostasy. He adopted the detestable practices of the surrounding cultures. He rebuilt the high places and built altars to Baal; he set up an Asherah pole within the Lord's temple and in the courtyard built altars to all the stars. Manasseh practiced witchcraft and sorcery and even sacrificed his own son. In addition to these sins, the writer of Kings records that "Manasseh also shed so much innocent blood that he filled Jerusalem with it from one end to another" (2 Kgs 21:16). Far more dangerous than any external enemy, Judah's own spiritual and moral depravity proved to be her downfall. Although Habakkuk contains only a few hints about the moral condition of Judah, the prophet Jeremiah provides a thorough assessment of the nation's religious decline.

The nature of God's covenant relationship with his people made the nation's stubborn rebellion all the more shocking. In times past the Lord described his bond to his people in terms of the most intimate relationships known to humanity, that of husband-wife and parent-child. Speaking through Jeremiah, however, the Lord now described them as a rebellious, adulterous wife, who "lay down like a prostitute" on "every high hill / and under every green tree" (Jer 2:20). They had become rebellious children, who "say to a tree, 'You are my father,' / and to a stone, 'You gave birth to me'" (Jer 2:27). The Hb. word for "abandon" (ʿāzab) echoes mournfully throughout the first half of Jeremiah (1:16; 2:13, 17, 19; 5:7, 19; 9:13; 16:11 [2x]; 17:13; 22:9). Because God's people had abandoned him for mute, lifeless, useless idols, he would abandon his house and hand "the love of my [his] life over to her enemies" (Jer 12:7).

Idolatry in Judah was not limited to a few. The community's widespread complicity demanded that the Lord's wrath would be equally extensive:

> Don't you see how they behave in the cities of Judah and in the streets of Jerusalem? The sons gather wood, the fathers light the fire, and the women knead dough to make cakes for the queen of heaven, and they pour out drink offerings to other gods so that they provoke me to anger. . . . Therefore, this is what the Lord

GOD says: "Look, my anger—my burning wrath—is about to be poured out on this place, on people and animals, on the tree of the field, and on the produce of the land. My wrath will burn and not be quenched. (Jer 7:17–20)

Because of her abominable practices, the Lord determined to remove Judah from his presence, and nothing would dissuade him—not even the prayers of his prophet.[73]

Jeremiah catalogs a long list of other spiritual maladies stemming from this underlying sin of abandoning the Lord. The people had defiled God's land, and their leaders quit asking, "Where is the Lord?" (Jer 2:7–8). They looked to nations like Egypt and Assyria rather than trusting God for salvation (2:18). Judah failed to learn from Samaria's example or to heed the warning of the Deuteronomic curses (3:6; cp. Deut 28).). Refusing to acknowledge their guilt, they contradicted the Lord: "Harm won't come to us" (Jer 2:35; 5:12). Even many prophets prophesied falsely; the priests ruled "by their own authority" (5:31). Pronouncing God's Word "contemptible," they no longer found "pleasure in it" (6:10). The religious leaders treated the "people's brokenness superficially" and promised peace when there was none (6:14). Going through the motions of religiosity, the people of Judah rejected the Lord's instructions and broke the Sabbath (6:20; 7:21). Treating the temple as a charm of immunity, they defiled the Lord's house with idols (7:4, 30). They even burned their children as sacrificial offerings to Baal (7:31; 19:4–5).

Recent archaeological finds dating to the historical period discussed above (late eighth century to early sixth century BC) reflect this same syncretistic portrait of Judah. The evidence—including "the remains of sanctuaries, *bamôt* ('open sacred high places'), as well as altars and figurines or other vessels"—points to what Ephraim Stern calls "Yahwistic paganism."[74] A comparison of these cultic objects with those from other nations in Palestine during the same time period suggests the main difference lies in the names of the chief national gods: "Yahweh in Judah, Qos in Edom, Milkom in Ammon, Ba'al

---

[73] The Lord repeatedly instructed Jeremiah *not* to pray that God would spare Judah (Jer 7:16; 11:14; 14:11–12; cf. 15:1).

[74] Stern, *The Assyrian, Babylonian, and Persian Periods*, 200.

in Phoenicia, etc."[75] The archaeological evidence suggests Judah had indeed become just like the nations that surrounded her.

Of particular interest is the preponderance of small clay figurines representing a female, usually associated with the fertility goddess Astarte. The mold-made heads are all alike. The handmade bodies are simple "pillars" with exaggerated breasts supported by the goddess's hands. A second popular type of Astarte figurine is completely handmade with a head pinched from clay. Stern observes the widespread distribution of these figurines indicates this religious cult was practiced virtually in all towns throughout Judah at this time. Half of the 822 figurines found in Judah came from Jerusalem; some were located near the temple area. Since these figurines are all from Judah, they likely were understood to represent Yahweh and his female consort, Astarte.[76] William G. Dever points out that these eighth-to-seventh-century-BC figurines, which he relates to the "Mother-goddess" cult of the ancient Near East, have been found exclusively in domestic contexts and tombs. He concludes, "[T]hey are undoubtedly talismans to aid in conception and childbirth, rather than idols in the true sense, designed for sanctuary usage."[77] Perhaps, however, these figurines were just the sort of detestable "household idols" Josiah tried to eradicate from the land of Judah (2 Kgs 23:24).

Apparently, Josiah's attempts to eliminate syncretistic elements and centralize worship in Jerusalem were never successful. They may have temporarily driven Judah's pagan idolatry out of sight since Habakkuk's mockery of idols was directed at the Babylonians rather than his fellow citizens (Hab 2:18–19). In the opening verses, however, the prophet's lament of the violence, oppression, and injustice in

---

[75] Stern, *The Assyrian, Babylonian, and Persian Periods*, 201.

[76] Importantly, the Lord has no consort. Stern, *The Assyrian, Babylonian, and Persian Periods*, 206–8. Male figurines depicted on horseback, though fewer in number, have a similarly widespread distribution throughout Judah.

[77] William G. Dever, "Material Remains and the Cult in Ancient Israel," in *The Word of the Lord Shall Go Forth: Essays in Honor of David Noel Freedman in Celebration of His Sixtieth Birthday*, ed. Carol L. Meyers and M. O'Connor (Winona Lake: Eisenbrauns, 1983), 574. Jeffrey H. Tigay, *You Shall Have No Other Gods: Israelite Religion in the Light of Hebrew Inscriptions*, HSS 31 (Atlanta: Scholars Press, 1986), 91, explains that the figurines "have large breasts or pregnant bellies" and lack the typical symbols of divinity from non-Israelite sites: "headdresses, papyrus stalks, and lotus blossoms, or animals beneath their feet." Based on his analysis of inscriptional evidence, Tigay, p. 40, concludes that "there existed some superficial, fetishistic polytheism and a limited amount of more profound polytheism in Israel," but he cautions against quantifying their prevalence.

Judah reveals that the reforms proved only surface deep. As shocked as Habakkuk was to hear the Lord was raising up a pagan nation to judge his own people, he must have noticed that most of the descriptions of the Babylonians in the five woe oracles could have just as easily fit the inhabitants of Judah (Hab 2:6–19). As a result of Judah's syncretism, she became like the pagan nations, hurtling down a path headed toward certain judgment.

Since their hearts were far from God, their actions failed to reflect his character. In addition to their spiritual apostasy, Jeremiah laid bare the moral decay of the nation in Habakkuk's day. Judah had descended to a shocking level of violence and destruction: they shed the innocent blood of the poor and the prophets (Jer 2:30, 34). Instead of taking up the case of the marginalized, they grasped every opportunity to exploit and brutalize the poor, widows, and the fatherless, the resident aliens and slaves (5:28; 7:6; 22:3; 34:11). "From the least to the greatest," everyone made a "profit dishonestly" (6:13). Even King Jehoiakim forced laborers to work and withheld wages, building his palace through extortion (22:13). They practiced treachery, speaking peaceably with friends while inwardly setting a trap or ambush against them (5:26–27; 9:8). They lusted after one another's wives and committed adultery (5:7–8). Truth had perished; lies abounded; the courts ignored justice (7:28, 9:3; 21:12). Meanwhile, the privileged had grown powerful, rich, fat, and sleek (5:27–28).

This is the same kind of nation Josiah had inherited years earlier when he ascended the throne in 640 BC as an eight-year-old child. According to the Chronicler, Josiah began to seek the Lord at age sixteen. Four years later he started cleansing Judah of her pagan altars in high places (2 Chr 34:3–7).[78] Both Kings and Chronicles record that in 622 BC, Josiah's restoration of the temple led to the discovery of "the book of the law."[79] When the king heard the contents read aloud, he

---

[78] The year was 628 BC. These initial religious reforms began on the cusp of the political sea change with Ashurbanipal's death the following year and Nabopolassar's rise to power in 626 BC.

[79] This "book of the law" was likely Deuteronomy. Each king should have been familiar with it as he was commanded to write out his own copy and read from it daily (Deut 17:18–20). Inconceivably, this portion of the Torah had been "lost," so that at the very least Josiah was unaware of all its contents (2 Kgs 22:8, 11). Deuteronomy contained the curses/sanctions God would enact against his people if they forsook him to follow other gods: drought, famine, pestilence, war, defeat, and exile. When Josiah heard it read, he realized that the nation had incurred God's impending wrath.

tore his clothes and wept before the Lord because he recognized Judah was ripe for judgment. The scroll served as further impetus for Josiah's far-reaching religious reforms, including a covenant renewal ceremony and a reinstitution of the Passover celebration (2 Kgs 23:4–24; 2 Chr 34:8–35:19). Josiah's humility and repentance pleased the Lord, and he informed the godly king that the judgment would not occur during his lifetime (2 Kgs 22:18-20).

Tragically, Josiah's reforms ended abruptly with his premature death at the hands of Pharaoh Neco II in 609 BC. Josiah's reformation, which lasted roughly twenty years, was too little, too late. Although his reforms were admirable, they must have been primarily external and cosmetic. They did not last beyond his death, and they failed to make any impact on how the nation lived out their faith in community. In fact, the description of the extent of the reforms reveals just how endemic and deeply rooted idolatry was in Judah. The measure of Judah's depravity was full. Destruction and exile were necessary in order to spare a remnant in order to save the world. Still, God was faithful to warn his people through his messengers, the prophets.

4.2 PROPHETS OF THE SEVENTH CENTURY BC

The tectonic shift in power from the Assyrians to the Babylonians triggered a surge in prophetic activity during the latter half of the seventh century BC. Speaking through the prophet Nahum (c. 650 BC), the Lord announced that judgment loomed for the arrogant Assyrians.[80] Although God had shown mercy and spared Nineveh in the days of Jonah, he "will never leave the guilty unpunished" (Nah 1:3). Nineveh, a "city of blood, / totally deceitful, / full of plunder, / never without prey," would be completely destroyed (3:1). Nahum shows that the all-powerful Lord is both good and just: he fights for those who take refuge in him and against those who oppose him (1:2, 7).

The prophet Zephaniah (c. 627 BC) warned of a global judgment including not only the Assyrians but also the people of Judah. This day of the Lord would come upon Jerusalem because of the pagan practices during the days of Manasseh and Amon. Zephaniah recorded a list of gods that were syncretistically worshiped alongside the Lord,

---

[80] The outer perimeters for the dating of Nahum are his backward glance at the fall of Thebes in 663 BC (Nah 3:8–11) and the actual fall of Nineveh in 612 BC. Nahum's presentation of Assyria at the height of its power likely dates the book to around 650–640 BC.

including Baal, the starry hosts, and Milcom (Zeph 1:4–5, 9). This prophet, who may have been related to royalty (1:1), had the difficult task of announcing to his peers that judgment was coming for them as well (1:8). Three times he begged them to seek the Lord and repent before it was too late (2:1–3). Yet his was not a message of unrelenting doom. Zephaniah closes with a beautiful picture of restoration in 3:14–20.

Lamenting the spiritual decline of his day, Habakkuk cried out for God to do something about the violence and oppression perpetrated by his own people. Much to the prophet's dismay, the Lord announced he was doing something by raising up the Babylonians to judge his wayward people. But the Babylonians were not exempt from judgment themselves. Having glimpsed the reality of a God who comes to save his own, Habakkuk committed to wait patiently for the day of distress to dawn on the pagan nation. Although the book of Habakkuk contains no call to repentance, at least two decades passed before Jerusalem fell to the Babylonians. In answer to the prophet's prayer in Hab 3:2, God showed mercy even in wrath.

Jeremiah had the longest ministry of the seventh-century-BC prophets (c. 627–580 BC). Called as a young man in the thirteenth year of King Josiah, Jeremiah may have had an influence on the religious reforms of that king of Judah. Regardless, as a result of his long ministry, Jeremiah saw Josiah's reforms swept aside in the wake of his wicked descendants. Like Habakkuk, Jeremiah prophesied that Babylon would be the instrument the Lord would use to judge his own people. He endured persecution for his faithful service, and he witnessed his prophecies play out in the horrific destruction of both Jerusalem and the temple. Even so, the Lord promised through Jeremiah not only "to uproot and tear down, / to destroy and demolish," but also to "build" up and "plant" (Jer 1:10; 24:6). God would preserve a remnant; he would return them to the land and to himself.

5   TEXT

Study of the Minor Prophetic texts has long been enhanced by versions that predate the Masoretic Text (MT; ca. AD 1000), including, for example, the Septuagint (LXX) and its various Old Greek referents, the Syriac Peshitta, and the Targum Jonathan. The discovery of multiple manuscripts in the Dead Sea Scrolls (DSS) added to our understanding of Habakkuk.[81] Discovered at Naḥal Ḥever in 1952, the earliest surviving Greek scroll of the Minor Prophets (8ḤevXIIgr) dates between 100 and 50 BC.[82] The manuscript contains several portions of Habakkuk (1:5–11, 14–17; 2:1–8, 13–20; 3:9–15).[83]

The DSS also produced Hebrew manuscripts of the Minor Prophets. The massive cache of fragments discovered in 1952 in Qumran Cave 4 included pieces of eight Hebrew manuscripts. Unfortunately, the poorly preserved 4QXII[g]—which contains fragments from several of the Minor Prophets—includes only one possible verse from Habakkuk.[84] A better-preserved Hebrew scroll of the Minor Prophets also surfaced in 1952, at another cave eleven miles south of Qumran in Murabba'at Wadi. A proto-Masoretic text, Mur 88 "varies only in minor details from the text and the form and structure of the mediaeval MT."[85] The manuscript dates to c. AD 50–100 and includes Hab 1:3–2:11 and 2:18–3:19.[86]

Another significant DSS find was the 1947 discovery of the Habakkuk Pesher in Qumran Cave 1. This ancient commentary on Habakkuk adds another layer to the textual history of the book. Labeled 1QpHab, the *pesher* ("interpretation") presents a portion of the Hebrew text, followed by commentary interpreting the text in light of the Qumran sect's first-century-BC context.[87] The ancient commentator sometimes follows the Hebrew text, but in other instances he prefers a variant

---

[81] For an example of how these various manuscripts might impact the study of Habakkuk, see Michael B. Shepherd, *A Commentary on the Book of the Twelve*, Kregel Exegetical Library (Grand Rapids: Kregel Academic, 2018), 311–50. Shepherd begins each new section of Habakkuk with his own translation of the text. Within the text he brackets alternate translations of variants along with corresponding citations from the MT, LXX, Syriac Peshitta (Syr), Targum Jonathan (Tg Jon.), Latin Vulgate (Vg.), Barberini (Barb.), and DSS (1QpHab; 8ḤevXIIgr). See also the discussion of the text in Haak, *Habakkuk*, 1–10.

[82] Russell Fuller, "The Text of the Twelve Minor Prophets," *Currents in Research* 7 (1999): 87. Fuller points out that Dominique Barthélemy, the original editor, and Emmanuel Tov have shown that the Naḥal Ḥever scroll is "a *recension* of the LXX, that is, a conscious revision of the LXX to bring the Greek translation closer to [an extant] Hebrew text." See Emmanuel Tov, *The Greek Minor Prophets Scroll from Naḥal Ḥever: 8ḤevXIIgr*, Discoveries in the Judean Desert, 8 (Oxford: Clarendon Press, 1990), 145–53.

[83] Andersen, *Habakkuk*, 23.

[84] Russell Fuller, "The Twelve" in *Qumran Cave 4, X: The Prophets*, ed. Eugene Ulrich et al., Discoveries in the Judean Desert XV (Oxford: Clarendon, 1997), 272.

[85] Fuller, "The Text of the Twelve Minor Prophets," 89.

[86] Andersen, *Habakkuk*, 23.

[87] The commentator, for example, understood the "Chaldeans" (Hb. *kaśdim*) in Hab 1:5 to be the Romans (*Kittim*) of his day. His interpretation of Habakkuk's prophecy pointed to unnamed contemporaries: "the Teacher of Righteousness," "the Wicked Priest," and "the Man

reading from what some scholars postulate may belong to the Septuagint *Vorlage*.[88] The commentator's ideological presuppositions and purposes are not that helpful in establishing the biblical text. Qumran scholar William Brownlee determined a large percentage of the 125 variants from the MT are orthographic in nature.[89] His list of fifty-six "principal variants" include, for example, articles added (5); conjunctions added (8) or omitted (3); and verbs with different root (3), stem (5), number (2), or tense (3). Brownlee concludes, "[I]n all cases of doubt, the safer criterion would be to follow the MT."[90]

The Qumran *pesher* comments only on Habakkuk 1 and 2. The uniqueness of chap. 3 and its apparent intentional omission from the Habakkuk Pesher[91] generated much scholarly debate concerning its compositional history. Scholars offered a variety of explanations for its absence.[92] Some cited the omission as evidence that chap. 3 was a later addition to the book, but Brownlee judged their arguments inconclusive.[93] Other major manuscripts of the Minor Prophets dating to roughly the same time—the Wadi Murabba'at Scroll (Mur 88) and the Naḥal Ḥever Scroll (8HevXIIgr)—contain portions from all three chapters of Habakkuk.

In contrast to the pesher of Habakkuk 1–2, a later Greek manuscript contains chap. 3 alone. This Barberini Codex is a unique Greek translation of that single chapter independent of the LXX. Composed sometime before mid-third century AD, the translation is attested by

---

of the Lie." The commentator exhorted the religious community to remain faithful and not lose heart in their waiting for God's judgment.

[88] Bruce, "Habakkuk," 835.

[89] William H. Brownlee, *The Text of Habakkuk in the Ancient Commentary from Qumran*, *JBL* Monograph Series 11 (Philadelphia: Society of Biblical Literature and Exegesis, 1959), 96.

[90] Brownlee, *The Text of Habakkuk in the Ancient Commentary from Qumran*, 113. See also pp. 108–13.

[91] The commentary concludes after line 4 of column 13. The remainder of column 13 and all of column 14 are left blank. See photographs of the Habakkuk Pesher scroll in the digital DSS collection on the Israel Museum, Jerusalem website: dss.collections.imj.org.il/habakkuk.

[92] Timothy Lim, *The Earliest Commentary in the Prophecy of Habakkuk* (Oxford: Oxford University Press, 2020), 11, dismisses the typical explanations for omission—that the pesherist lost interest or left the work unfinished. He contends instead that the pesherist's copy of Habakkuk simply did not contain chap. 3 and that the commentary reaches a fitting conclusion. F. F. Bruce, "The Dead Sea Habakkuk Scroll," *The Annual of Leeds University Oriental Society* 1 (1958/59): 5, likewise sweeps aside the notion that the psalm genre of chap. 3 did not lend itself to the commentator's purposes since the DSS include a Psalm Pesher. Bruce, pp. 5–6, proposes that the commentator simply considered "Habakkuk's 'prayer' . . . to be a separate work, quite distinct from his 'oracle.'"

[93] Brownlee, *The Text of Habakkuk*, 91–95.

six medieval manuscripts. The author who composed this well-written manuscript typically made changes to Hebrew idioms and syntax that might have otherwise proved unusual or awkward for Greek readers.[94]

The debate regarding the authenticity and integrity of chap. 3 extends even to the dating of the liturgical markings of the psalm. Some scholars argue the markings were a significant part of the original composition.[95] Others believe they were added to the psalm when it was taken from its context for liturgical use.[96] Still others believe the markings point to the psalm's existence in a liturgical collection before its adoption as a fitting ending to Habakkuk.[97] We are not likely to discover which of these scenarios is true, but even so, determining their veracity does not change the content of the psalm.

The archaic language, imagery, and style of Hab 3:3–15 led scholars to speculate the psalm originated early in Israel's history.[98] Theodore Hiebert, for example, concludes that "[t]he original text, linguistic features, literary form, historical allusions, and religious motifs all suggest that this poem was composed in the premonarchic era as a recitation of the victory of the divine warrior over cosmic and earthly enemies."[99] Hiebert contends that this ancient "Hymn of Triumph" was appended "to the Habakkuk corpus by postexilic editors of the prophets who were caught up in the apocalyptic fervor of their era."[100] For Hiebert, the obvious conclusion is that although the poem may shed light on its original historical context or the postexilic period, it has nothing to do with Habakkuk.[101]

Andersen observes the same archaisms as Hiebert but draws a different conclusion. The "intense personal character" of the poem convinces Andersen of both its authenticity and "integral place in the prophecy as a whole": "[Habakkuk] did pray this prayer."[102] Ander-

---

94 Joshua L. Harper, *Responding to a Puzzled Scribe: The Barberini Version of Habakkuk 3 Analyzed in the Light of Other Greek Versions* (New York: Bloomsbury, 2015), 128.

95 Watts, "Psalmody in Prophecy," 222.

96 Roberts, *Nahum, Habakkuk, and Zephaniah*, 148.

97 Theodore Hiebert, *God of My Victory: The Ancient Hymn in Habakkuk 3*, HSM 38 (Atlanta: Scholars Press, 1986), 141–42.

98 For specific examples, see 6.1.3: "Habakkuk's Use of Psalmody."

99 Hiebert, *God of My Victory*, 1. Hiebert maintains his conclusions confirm the suspicions of an "earlier generation of scholars."

100 Hiebert, *God of My Victory*, 1.

101 Hiebert, *God of My Victory*, 2.

102 Andersen, *Habakkuk*, 260. Like other scholars, Andersen, p. 259, cites shared vocabulary and content in chaps. 1–2 and 3 as support for unity of the text. He also observes that,

sen maintains that, although Habakkuk did not compose the ancient psalm, he affixed the poem as a fitting conclusion to his work, enclosing it in a personal, contemporary framework (3:1–2, 16–19).[103]

There is also a possibility that chap. 3 is a deliberately archaized poem. Andersen acknowledges that "there is little or no trace of archaic spelling" in 3:3–15.[104] The theophanic imagery and language of ancient hymns resonated with Habakkuk as indicated by his quotation of Ps 18:33 (Hab 3:19). He may have intentionally adopted their language and imagery to compose a fresh, archaized song of victory expressing theophanic revelation (3:3–15). John Goldingay and Pamela Scalise observe, "We do not know whether this is indeed simply a vision Habakkuk received or whether the Holy Spirit inspired him consciously to construct a prophecy in the form of a vision report that utilizes the form and the language of accounts of Yahweh's coming with which he and his readers would be familiar."[105] The prophet's response recorded in 3:16 indicates that his experience was much more profound than simply reworking an ancient hymn.

In summarizing research on Habakkuk in the 1990s, Oskar Dangl observed most exegetes—like Andersen—regard chap. 3 as "an authentic work of the prophet."[106] Roberts concurs: "Without it, the book remains a fragment with no resolution of the prophet's laments, and with no vision for the prophet to record as he had been commanded to do (2:2). There is no justification for treating Habakkuk 3 as an independent piece or for denying its traditional attribution to Habakkuk."[107] The argument that chap. 3 is a later addition to

---

ironically, Hiebert's research on inclusion in chap. 3 demonstrates the entire book exhibits a shared literary structure as well.

[103] Andersen, *Habakkuk*, 260. See W. F. Albright, "The Psalm of Habakkuk," in *Studies in Old Testament Prophecy*, ed. H. H. Rowley (Edinburgh: T&T Clark, 1950), 8–9; Hiebert, *God of My Victory*, 140–41. For redactional analyses of Habakkuk 3, see Nogalski, *Redactional Processes*, 180; and John E. Anderson, "Awaiting an Answered Prayer: The Development and Reinterpretation of Habakkuk 3 in its Contents," *ZAW* 123/1 (2011): 57–71.

[104] Andersen, *Habakkuk*, 285. He also points out that although "modern" spelling does not prove the poem is not archaic, it does indicate that these verses were not "copied unchanged from a *written* version of this poem."

[105] John Goldingay and Pamela J. Scalise, *Minor Prophets II*, Understanding the Bible Commentary Series (Grand Rapids: Baker, 2009), 81.

[106] Oskar Dangl, "Habakkuk in Recent Research," *Currents in Research: Biblical Studies* 9 (2001): 145. Roberts, *Nahum, Habakkuk, and Zephaniah*, 148–49, argues, "There is no justification for treating Habakkuk 3 as an independent piece or for denying its traditional attribution to Habakkuk."

[107] Roberts, *Nahum, Habakkuk, and Zephaniah*, 149.

Habakkuk loses ground considering the psalm's integral relation to the rest of the book.

Did Habakkuk compose the hymn, or did he simply borrow it? Were the notations added later when Habakkuk's poetry was set to music by someone else? Or did another hand insert the hymn as a fitting conclusion to Habakkuk's message? The answers must allow that the psalm perfectly fits both the message and the structural parallels of the rest of the book. As we will see, the intentional parallels between Panel I (1:1–2:5) and Panel III (3:1–19) underscore this integrity.[108] In addition, in considering the extant text, we must continually seek to understand the purpose and function of the hymn in its context, and determine why the prophet included it here.

The Hebrew text of Habakkuk includes several challenges, particularly in chap. 3. Based on the plethora of scholars' suggested emendations, Andersen has dubbed it "the most rewritten chapter in the Hebrew Bible."[109] Hiebert, however, observes, "One might expect from a difficult text such as this a profusion of interpretations and proposals. But such, ironically, is not the case. What might almost be called a consensus has emerged regarding the form and content of Habakkuk 3."[110] In addition to difficult passages, other challenges in Habakkuk include several *hapax legomena* (obscure words used once in the Hebrew Bible; e.g., 1:4, 1:9; 2:11; 3:4) and ambiguous or missing nouns/pronouns (e.g., 1:5; 2:4). However, despite the nine centuries that lay between them, the text of Habakkuk in MurXII and the MT are virtually identical.[111] This "faithful preservation of an ancient text" compels some scholars to urge restraint in relying on emendations to solve the difficulties in the MT.[112]

A comparison of NT quotations highlights some of the differences between the MT and the LXX. When the NT quotes Habakkuk, it always follows the LXX rather than the MT (see, for example, Hab 1:5 in Acts 13:41; and Hab 2:4 in Rom 1:17, Gal 3:11, and Heb 10:38).[113]

---

[108] See 6.2.4: "Habakkuk as a Literary Triptych."

[109] Andersen, *Habakkuk*, 264.

[110] Hiebert, *God of My Victory*, 81. Hiebert, of course, steps outside the consensus with his proposal regarding the postexilic addition of chap. 3 to the Habakkuk corpus.

[111] Andersen, *Habakkuk*, 265.

[112] Andersen, *Habakkuk*, 264–68; Christopher R. Lortie, *Mighty to Save: A Literary and Historical Study of Habakkuk 3 and Its Traditions*, Arbeiten zu Text und Sprache im Alten Testament 99 (St. Ottilien: EOS, 2017).

[113] Smith, *Micah-Malachi*, 96.

6 LITERARY CHARACTERISTICS OF HABAKKUK

6.1 GENRE: POETIC PROPHECY

The role of a biblical prophet was more forthteller than foreteller. God spoke through the prophets to show his people how far they had strayed from their covenant relationship with him. True prophets held forth God's Word—in particular, the covenant blessings and curses outlined in Leviticus 26 and Deuteronomy 28–30—to warn the people of judgment, to encourage them to repent, and to give them hope for a restored relationship if they would turn back to God. Many of the prophets' predictions for the future reflected the consequences of community obedience or disobedience. But at times the Lord would also reveal specific predictions about those future consequences—both in their own day (e.g., Hab 1:5–6) and in a day far in the distance (e.g., Hab 3:3–15).

The book of Habakkuk falls under the overarching genre of poetic prophecy. "Prophecy" describes the basic content of the prophet's message, while "poetic" describes how he used language to relay his message. Like most prophetic books, Habakkuk also contains a number of different subgenres under both of these headings.

6.1.1 Habakkuk's Use of Prophetic Subgenres

Prophecy typically contains three different categories of pronouncement: announcements of judgment, oracles of salvation, and a call to repentance.[114] Some of the minor prophetic books contain all three, but Habakkuk is primarily an oracle of judgment. Although chap. 3 hints at a future salvation, even that hope is set in the context of judgment. Nowhere in the book is there a stated call to repentance. Judah's failure to heed previous prophetic calls to turn back to God meant her opportunity to repent was coming to an end. The nation stood condemned; judgment was imminent. Even so, history reveals that the Babylonian attack on Judah came in stages (604, 597, and 588–586 BC). Arguably, the Lord's patience allowed individuals time to heed Habakkuk's warning and follow his example of exercising faith in God.

---

[114] Richard Alan Fuhr and Gary E. Yates, *The Message of the Twelve: Hearing the Voice of the Minor Prophets* (Nashville: B&H Academic, 2016), 29.

The book of Habakkuk opens with a lament, a subgenre of the prophetic category of judgment. Often found in the Psalms, a lament opens with a cry to God, a complaint describing a particular evil, and possibly even questions about God's failure to address the situation. A lament often concludes with a petition for help, a statement of confidence in God, and a promise to praise him.[115] In Hab 1:2–4, the prophet voiced his outrage over the violence, injustice, and strife perpetrated by his fellow citizens. Overwhelmed, he questioned God's seeming inaction or lack of concern. When the Lord revealed he was using the Babylonians to execute judgment, Habakkuk responded with a second lament, in which he questioned how God's actions corresponded with his divine character (1:12–13). Although these two laments do not include the remaining standard elements, Habakkuk's concluding psalm contains all three: a prayer for help, a declaration of confidence in God, and a vow to rejoice in the Lord (3:2–19).

Judgment oracles typically include both accusation and announcement of judgment.[116] Perhaps because Habakkuk had already enumerated Judah's sins in his lament, the Lord immediately announced judgment. He described the advancing Babylonian army in terse statements designed to strike terror in those listening: "Their horses are swifter than leopards / and more fierce than wolves of the night. / Their horsemen . . . fly like eagles, sweeping to devour" (1:8). Like other judgment oracles, the Lord's announcement introduced a component of *lex talionis* or retributive justice.[117] Like the Judeans, who were guilty of injustice, oppression, and violence, their attackers were guilty of the same (1:7, 9). Just how closely they mirrored each other's sins became even clearer in another prophetic subgenre—the taunt song.

---

[115] Leland Ryken, *A Complete Handbook of Literary Forms in the Bible* (Wheaton: Crossway, 2014), 113.

[116] Fuhr and Yates, *The Message of the Twelve*, 30.

[117] Aaron Chalmers, *Interpreting the Prophets: Reading, Understanding, and Preaching from the Worlds of the Prophets* (Downers Grove: IVP Academic, 2015), 101. *Lex talionis* is a Latin phrase meaning "law of retaliation." Basically, the term refers to retributive justice where the punishment fits the crime in kind and degree. The list of examples in Mosaic law (Exod 21:23–27) is often summed up by one particular example: "an eye for an eye." The principle of *lex talionis* was a safeguard against the harsh overretaliation displayed in Gen 4:23–24. The pronouncements of woe in the middle panel contain a sense of irony or "poetic justice" in that the perpetrators' punishment to some degree mirrored their offenses.

Translated in 2:6 as "taunt," the Hb. noun *māšāl* is a "proverb" sometimes translated as a "song of jest, mocking" when used in parallel with *məlîṣâ* ("mockery") as it is here.[118] Taunts in the Bible usually occur in a military setting. Consider Goliath's mockery of David in 1 Sam 17:43–44 and David's reply in vv. 45–47. Isaiah 14:4 labels what follows (Isa 14:4b-21) as a "song of contempt about the king of Babylon." Another example of an extended taunt is the speech by Sennacherib's royal spokesman recorded in 2 Kgs 18:19–35. Since combatants relied on their respective gods to save them, taunts often conveyed a religious aspect as well. Isaiah 44:6–20 is, in fact, a taunt song against those who fabricate idols but fail to see the result as merely the work of their own hands.

Habakkuk 2:6a introduces a "taunt" song consisting of "mockery and riddles" about the "arrogant man" described in 2:4–5. Although the text does not specifically identify the recipients, the context suggests the mockery took aim at the Babylonians. Some of the charges best fit the uncircumcised Babylonians, who "plundered many nations" and committed "violence against lands, cities, / and all who live in them"—"countries [who] exhaust[ed] themselves for nothing"[119] (Hab 2:8, 13, 17). Likewise, the Babylonians were guilty of the idolatry condemned in 2:18–19.

Ironically, many of the other charges could have just as easily applied to the people of Judah. They too were guilty of greed, violence, immorality, and amassing wealth dishonestly (Hab 2:6b, 8–9, 15). Although Josiah's recent reforms had removed the external trappings of Judah's idolatry, for many the reforms had merely driven their idolatry behind closed doors. They had certainly fallen short of affecting a change of heart in how the people treated one another. The Lord intended that the Hebrews would squirm as they heard the charges leveled at the Babylonians. The law of retaliation or *lex talionis* was at play.[120] God chose the Babylonians to mete out judgment against his own people. The people of Judah would suffer the same evils they had perpetrated on others. In response to Habakkuk's complaint God

---

[118] *HALOT*, 648. See also Luis Alonso Schökel, *A Manual of Hebrew Poetics*, SubBi 11 (Rome: Editrice Pontificio Istituto Biblico, 1988), 8–9.

[119] *HALOT*, 513, indicates that the term for "countries" (Hb. *lə'ummîm*) is "archaic or archaising." In the plural, *lə'ummîm* usually stands for nations other than Israel (BDB, 522).

[120] Carol Dempsey, "Harrowing Woes and Comforting Promises," in *The Book of the Twelve and the New Form Criticism*, ed. Mark J. Boda, Michael H. Floyd, and Colin M. Toffelmire, ANEM 10 (Atlanta: SBL Press, 2015), 104.

would use the wicked Babylonians to punish them, the Lord reassured the prophet this pagan nation would one day face judgment as well.

The central panel of Habakkuk (2:6–19) is a woe oracle, another subgenre of judgment. Introduced by the Hb. interjection *hôy* (Eng. "Woe!"; "Alas!"), a woe oracle literally declared woe on the guilty party, followed by a description of the accusations against them.[121] Most woe oracles occur in prophetic literature, including Isaiah (21x) and Jeremiah (8x). Other instances of woe oracles in the Book of the Twelve include Amos 5:18, 6:1; Mic 2:1; Nah 3:1; Zeph 2:5; 3:1; Zech 2:6–7; 11:17. The five pronouncements of woe in Habakkuk are in 2:6, 9, 12, 15, and 19, and serve as a structural guide. The word "woe" repeatedly rings like a death knell in the center of Habakkuk—for both the Babylonians and the wayward Hebrews.

6.1.2 Habakkuk's Use of Poetry

English readers may not immediately appreciate the subtleties of poetry in the Prophets. Unlike English poetry, biblical Hebrew verse rarely has rhyme or "easily discernible meter."[122] Instead, it has a free rhythm that flows naturally from its orality and the influence of Hebraic psalms.[123] Hebrew poetry has much in common with ancient Syrian verse and shares some characteristics with Assyrian and Babylonian poetry.[124] The primary criterion of poetry is a "linguistic richness [that] must not be confused with mere elaboration or ornamentation. Often the 'simplest' poems are the most complex linguistically."[125]

---

[121] Although the similar interjection *'ôy* is also often translated as "woe," *TLOT* 1:357, notes it is sharply distinct "in grammatical and semantic usage" since the interjection is almost "always followed by a particular person or group of persons introduced by . . . and a causal clause." E.g., "Woe to you, Moab" (Num 21:29).

[122] Adele Berlin, *The Dynamics of Biblical Parallelism*, The Biblical Resource Series (Grand Rapids: Eerdmans, 2008), 4. Berlin, p. 4n, lists several metric studies, noting that scholars are divided over the presence of meter and how to measure it.

[123] F. W. Dobbs-Allsopp, *On Biblical Poetry* (New York: Oxford University Press, 2015), discusses this topic in chap. 2, "The Free Rhythms of Biblical Poetry." For Schökel's theory of Hebrew accentual rhythm and a brief synopsis of other theories on Hebrew poetic rhythm, see Schökel, *A Manual of Hebrew Poetics*, 36–47.

[124] Wilfred G. E. Watson, *Traditional Techniques in Classical Hebrew Verse*, JSOTSup 170 (Sheffield: Sheffield Academic, 1994), 15.

[125] Stephen A. Geller, "Were the Prophets Poets?" in *"The Place Is Too Small for Us": The Israelite Prophets in Recent Scholarship*, ed. R. P. Gordon, Sources for Biblical and Theological Study 5 (Winona Lake: Eisenbrauns, 1995), 157.

Poetry is well suited for persuasion—the ultimate goal of prophecy—because metaphoric language is engaging, powerful, and memorable. Rich imagery and gripping figures of speech captivate the imagination and convey emotion. Poetry expresses ideas succinctly and communicates abstract thoughts clearly—even concepts about God.[126] Since God is transcendent, human expression of divine revelation relies on the language of analogy and symbol.[127] If a prophet like Habakkuk were to attempt to express the inexpressible, it is natural that he would turn to poetry.

Like other prophetic poets, Habakkuk used figures of speech to craft his message, including metaphor (2:16), simile (2:14), animation (2:11), personification (2:5), and anthropomorphism (3:6).[128] A low degree of correspondence between the objects compared adds to the level of freshness or alarm while a high degree of correspondence allows for a greater development of the comparison.[129] Low correspondence, for example, allowed Habakkuk to produce this interesting metaphor: "the law is paralyzed" (1:4 NIV). A familiar topic like fishing yielded an extended metaphor describing how the Babylonians caught people in their nets (1:14–17). The prophet also used a variety of other literary devices, including merism (3:3), hyperbole (1:8), and rhetorical questions (3:8).[130]

In addition to figures of speech, another hallmark of Hebrew poetry is parallelism.[131] By placing two lines of poetry (sometimes more) side by side, the poet draws on the connection between them. The correspondence between the lines may yield clarification or ambiguity—sometimes both simultaneously.[132] Consequently, that ambi-

---

[126] D. Brent Sandy, *Plowshares and Pruning Hooks: Rethinking the Language of Biblical Prophecy and Apocalyptic* (Downers Grove: InterVarsity, 2002), 60.

[127] Schökel, *A Manual of Hebrew Poetics*, 128–29.

[128] Schökel, *A Manual of Hebrew Poetics*, 122–25, differentiates between "animation" (inanimate objects—like stones and rafters—exhibit human characteristics) and "personification" (abstract qualities—like Wisdom, or Death and Sheol—act like people in society).

[129] G. B. Caird, *The Language and Imagery of the Bible* (Grand Rapids: Eerdmans, 1997), 155.

[130] For discussion of various poetic devices, techniques, and structural patterns in Hebrew poetry, see Schökel, *A Manual of Hebrew Poetics*; Wilfred G. E. Watson, *Classical Hebrew Poetry: A Guide to Its Techniques*; JSOTSup 26 (Sheffield: JSOT Press, 1986); and Watson, *Traditional Techniques in Classical Hebrew Verse.*

[131] Berlin, *The Dynamics of Biblical Parallelism*, 7, argues that "biblical poetry is characterized by a high incidence of terse, balanced parallelism."

[132] Berlin, *The Dynamics of Biblical Parallelism*, 98–99. Berlin observes, "Redundancy and ambiguity . . . are locked in an eternal struggle in parallelism."

guity causes the audience to slow down and ponder the message to comprehend it fully.[133] In Habakkuk we find examples of semantic parallelism (2:13), contrast/antithetic parallelism (3:13), and even a powerful example of climactic parallelism (3:17). Chiasm appears at both the sentence level (3:3) and a macro-level (2:6–19).

Repetition is another characteristic of Hebrew poetry. As in English poetry, repetition may occur on the level of sounds, whether through assonance (repeating vowels) or consonance (repeating consonants).[134] In Hab 2:18, for example, the repeated sounds in the Hebrew words translated "mute idols" (ʾĕlîlîm ʾillǝmîm) in NKJV draw attention to the irony of gods that cannot speak. Likewise, the repetition in 1:5 in the phrase "doing something" (pōʿal pōʿēl) underscores that the Lord intended to address the sins Habakkuk lamented in the previous verses.

Repetition may occur on the level of words or phrases. Reading Habakkuk in Hebrew reveals an interesting Semitic pattern of repetition. Basically, the prophet occasionally repeats a word using a different form of the same root. The repetition draws attention to the word and emphasizes it. Since this repetition does not read as well in English, the examples are harder to spot in translation. A literal translation of Hab 1:5, for example, reads: "Astound yourselves; be astounded." The CSB attempts to approximate this by adding an adverbial modifier: "[B]e utterly astounded." Others, like the ESV, translate the word and add a synonym: "[W]onder and be astounded." The ISV repeats the same word twice: "Be astounded! Be really astounded!" All of these translations recognize Habakkuk's repetition of the verb added a level of intensity to the shocking thing that God was about to reveal. Other examples of repetition include cognate accusatives[135] (e.g., "doing a deed," 1:5; "forming his form," 2:18) and infinitive absolutes that function as adverbs of emphasis[136] ("To come it will come" = "It will certainly come," 2:3).

Repetition also occurs on the level of refrains. Habakkuk 2:8b is a refrain repeated verbatim in 2:17: "[B]ecause of human bloodshed and violence / against lands, cities, and all who live in them." The repetition of these grievous charges against the Babylonians indicates their

---

[133] Chalmers, *Interpreting the Prophets*, 109.
[134] Berlin, *The Dynamics of Biblical Parallelism*, 103.
[135] GKC §117p.
[136] GKC §113w.

fate is sealed. The word "violence" (Hb. *ḥāmās*) recalls 1:2, where Habakkuk used the same word to describe the wicked of Judah. The implication is that their fate is likewise sealed.

6.1.3 Habakkuk's Use of Psalmody

The third chapter of Habakkuk is a prayer expressed as a psalm. Both the superscription and subscription of this chapter contain instructions for the choir director incorporating this psalm into worship. Psalm 7 is the only other psalm that begins with a similar superscription (in the singular): "A *Shiggaion* of David." Fifty-five psalms also include instructions for the "choir director."

Habakkuk's psalm fits in the category of a victory song celebrating military triumph. Other ancient victory psalms in the OT include the Israelites' song celebrating the defeat of the Egyptians (Exod 15:1–18); Moses's hymn of instruction at the end of his life (Deut 32:1–43); Joshua's account of the Israelite victory over the Amorites (Josh 10:12–13); Deborah's song rejoicing over the defeat of the Canaanites (Judg 5:1–31); and finally, David's psalm of thanksgiving for his deliverance from Saul (2 Sam 22:1–51 // Ps 18:1–50).

These ancient Hebrew songs share certain archaic literary features. Based on his comparison of several of these hymns, David Freedman posits that "the early Israelites had a strong sense of meter . . . more precise than the commonly accepted accentual system."[137] Wilfred Watson observes several other common archaisms, including both grammatical and stylistic criteria.[138] Describing the unusual verbal syntax in Hab 3:3–15, alternating prefixes and suffixes to describe past narrative, Hiebert notes that this archaic practice prompted D. A. Robertson's suggestion that the hymn dates to somewhere between the thirteenth and tenth centuries BC.[139] Hiebert also contends that the imagery of Yahweh's appearing in the southeast (3:3–7) echoes the "old war songs" where God "marches out from a sanctuary in the

---

[137] David N. Freedman, "Archaic Forms in Early Hebrew Poetry," *ZAW* 72 (1960): 107.

[138] Watson's catalog of archaisms in *Classical Hebrew Poetry*, 39, includes grammatical criteria, such as archaic spellings (fewer vowel letters), the use of *yqtal* as a past tense, and the use of ה as a relative pronoun, as well as stylistic criteria like *yqtl-qtl-qtl-yqtl* parallel sequences and staircase parallelism. Watson shares a chronological table dating several ancient songs: 1150 BC (Exod 15; Judg 5; Ps 29); 1000 BC (Deut 32; Hab 3; Job, Ps 18); 900 BC (Ps 78; Deut 33; Gen 49; Num 23–24); 600 BC (Hab).

[139] Hiebert, *God of My Victory*, 77–79.

southeast to fight for his people."[140] Scholars remain divided over whether the archaisms in chap. 3 indicate Habakkuk incorporates one of the oldest poems in the Bible or if the prophet purposefully added it to convey his vision in a familiar, antiquated format.

All these Hebrew songs of deliverance pay tribute to God as the main actor in the military battle.[141] Although they celebrate the Lord's rescue of his people, deliverance comes in the context of judgment. In Habakkuk 3 both people and place tremble before the Lord of Hosts, the Cosmic Warrior. All people fall prostrate before this God. Whether this act of submission means judgment or salvation depends on whether the person is rightly related to the God of glory.

The memorable poetry found in Habakkuk demonstrates the prophet's skillful crafting of his message to capture the audience's attention. The prophet used it to convey both a somber warning and an encouragement. God will establish his dominion over the whole earth. He judges the wicked, but he delivers those who faithfully trust in him.

6.2   THE STRUCTURE OF HABAKKUK

Although scholars may use different labels, they generally agree Habakkuk contains three basic literary components: (1) dialogue/lament, (2) a series of woe oracles, and (3) a concluding prayer/psalm. Even a cursory reading of Habakkuk reveals a diversity of literary genre.

After an introductory superscription, the prophet expresses a complaint to God, lamenting the injustices of society and the wicked who surround the righteous (1:2–4). His questions—"How long?" and "Why?"—challenge God for his seeming inactivity. God announces he is raising up the Babylonians to punish his people for those sins (1:5–11).

God's response provokes a second complaint: How can God allow the wicked to swallow up those more righteous than themselves (1:12–17)? The prophet stubbornly waits to see what answer his reproof provokes (2:1). The Lord answers by commanding the prophet to write down the vision because it will come to pass (2:2–3). The arrogant,

---

[140] Hiebert, *God of My Victory*, 90.
[141] Ryken, *A Complete Handbook of Literary Forms in the Bible*, 207.

who are never satisfied, will falter and fall, while the righteous will live by faith (2:4–5).

A series of five woe oracles follows, condemning the wicked (2:6–19). Although the oracles do not identify a specific enemy, several indicators suggest an international power like the Babylonians. Ironically, Judah has been guilty of some of these same sins as well. In the first two woes, the punishment appears to be the natural outcome of the actions of the wicked. The third and subsequent woes, however, reveal it is the Lord of Armies who administers justice. This section closes with the Lord's command that the whole world "be silent in his presence" (2:20).

Chapter 3 opens with a superscription introducing the "prayer of the prophet Habakkuk" and musical instructions for the psalm that follows (3:1). The prophet voices a petition for God to "revive" his work and to "remember mercy" in wrath (3:2). The psalm that follows draws from a wealthy store of imagery typically found in victory songs (see Exod 15; Deut 32–33; Josh 10, Judg 5; and Ps 18 // 2 Sam 22). It describes a theophany portraying the Lord as a divine warrior (3:3–15), who comes to defeat the wicked and deliver his own. The prophet concludes his prayer psalm humbled and trembling in awe. He voices a moving declaration of his faith in God despite the looming crisis. Even if he were to lose everything, Habakkuk resolves to rejoice in the Lord. The sovereign Lord is his strength. God is with him. He enables the prophet to walk on the heights, and that is enough (Hab 3:17–19). Habakkuk moves from the problem of theodicy to the praise of theophany. In his initial complaint, the prophet struggled to understand the justice of God in view of the prosperity of the wicked at the expense of the righteous. By the book's end, divine revelation and an encounter with God have utterly changed the prophet's perspective. He stands as an example of those who walk with God and live by faith.

6.2.1 A Survey of Diverse Structural Divisions

The book of Habakkuk contains an eclectic assortment of material, making it difficult to determine its structure. Scholars agree neither on the precise boundary between the first two components, nor on how all three fit together to form the macrostructure of the book. In 1979, Brevard Childs concluded most scholars reached a consensus, arguing the structure of Habakkuk consists of three divisions: Hab 1:1–2:4(5);

2:6–20; and 3:1–19.[142] Childs's proposal reveals the uncertainty about the boundary between the first and second divisions. (See the chart below.[143])

CHILDS'S STRUCTURE					
1:1–2:4(5)				2:6–20	3:1–19
COMPLAINTS AND THE DIVINE RESPONSE				A Series of Woe Oracles	Concluding Psalm
1:2–4	1:5–11	1:12–17	2:1–4(5)		
First Complaint	Divine Response	Second Complaint	Divine Answer		

Since Childs's statement, similar tripartite structural proposals have located the beginning of the second section at 2:1,[144] 2:2,[145] 2:4,[146] and 2:6.[147]

Childs's declaration of consensus proved premature since many scholars have subsequently proposed various forms of a two-part structure for Habakkuk. The argument for a bipartite structure rests primarily on the book's two superscriptions: the "Pronouncement" (*maśśāʾ*) of Habakkuk in 1:1 and the "Prayer" (*təpillâ*) of Habakkuk in 3:1. Marvin Sweeney stands as an example of those who base the structure of Habakkuk on these superscriptions.[148] (See chart below.[149])

---

[142] Childs, *Introduction to the Old Testament as Scripture*, 448.

[143] The chart is adapted from Kei Hiramatsu, "The Structure and Structural Relationships of the Book of Habakkuk," *The Journal of Inductive Biblical Studies* 3.2 (2016): 120.

[144] Floyd, *Minor Prophets*, 81–82; Robertson, *The Books of Nahum, Habakkuk, and Zephaniah*, 44–45; Grace Ko, *Theodicy in Habakkuk*, Paternoster Biblical Monographs (Milton Keynes: Paternoster, 2014), 23–24.

[145] Roberts, *Nahum, Habakkuk, and Zephaniah*, 82.

[146] Shepherd, *A Commentary on the Book of the Twelve*, 316.

[147] Carl E. Amerding, "Habakkuk," in *Daniel–Minor Prophets*, EBC 7 (Grand Rapids: Zondervan, 1985), 495; Bailey, "Habakkuk," 257; Dong-Weon Lim, "Structural Analysis of the Book of Habakkuk," *Korean Journal of Christian Studies* 72 (2013): 71.

[148] Sweeney, "Structure, Genre, and Intent in the Book of Habakkuk," 65.

[149] The chart is adapted from Hiramatsu, "The Structure and Structural Relationships of the Book of Habakkuk," 121. Hiramatsu notes that his own presentation follows "Sweeney's

Not surprisingly, others who propose a two-part structure may subdivide the two sections differently.[150]

SWEENEY'S STRUCTURE									
1:1–2:20 Habakkuk's Pronouncement					3:1–19 Habakkuk's Prayer				
1:1	1:2–2:20 Pronouncement				3:1	3:2–19a Prayer/Petition			3:19b
	1:2–4	1:5–11	1:12–17	2:1–20		3:2	3:3–15	3:16–19a	
Superscription	First Complaint	Divine Response	Second Complaint	Report of Second Divine Response and Explanation	Superscription	Introduction	Theophany Report	Conclusion	Instruction to the Choirmaster

Like many others, both Kei Hiramatsu and Dong-Weon Lim point out the importance of inclusion in their structural/rhetorical analyses of Habakkuk.[151] The most important of these is the one that envelops the entire book. Habakkuk opens with the prophet's accusation, "[Y]ou do not listen" (1:2), and closes with the prophet's declaration, "I heard" (3:16). Hiramatsu observes that these uses of the Hb. word šāmaʿ form a "contrastive inclusio" bracketing the entire book. Whereas Habakkuk initially challenged that God needed to hear him, by the book's end, the prophet came to an understanding he needed to hear God—and he did.[152] A third occurrence of šāmaʿ ("I have heard"

two-part structural understanding of the book," but he focuses on how "Climax with Causation and Contrastive Inclusio" show movement between the two parts.

[150] Mária Eszenyei Széles, *Wrath and Mercy: A Commentary on the Books of Habakkuk and Zephaniah*, ITC (Grand Rapids: Eerdmans, 1987), 7; Patterson, *Nahum, Habakkuk, Zephaniah*, 118; Bruce, "Habakkuk," 837; Bullock, *An Introduction to the Old Testament Prophetic Books*, 212; Thomas, *Habakkuk*, 17; Renz, *The Books of Nahum, Habakkuk, and Zephaniah*, 199; S. D. Snyman, *Nahum, Habakkuk, and Zephaniah: An Introduction and Commentary*. TOTC 27 (Downers Grove: IVP Academic, 2020), 53.

[151] Berlin, *The Dynamics of Biblical Parallelism*, 3, 132, explains that *inclusio*—the repetition of words or phrases in "the first and last lines of a text"—serves to frame a text, giving it cohesion and unity. Watson, *Classical Hebrew Poetry*, 283, calls inclusion "an envelope figure" that may delimit a stanza within a poem.

[152] Hiramatsu, "The Structure and Structural Relationships of the Book of Habakkuk,"

in 3:2) forms a second inclusio with 3:16, framing the psalm in chap. 3. Significantly, both instances of Habakkuk's "hearing" occur after the Lord's command in 2:20: "Silence!" These inclusions based on "hearing" draw attention to the transformation that occurred in the life of the prophet.

Other uses of inclusio in Habakkuk help delimit the structural subdivisions within the outer panels. Lim notes that the first round of dialogue in chap. 1 begins and ends with the names of two "diametrically opposed deities": *Yahweh*, the covenant name for God (1:2), and *ʾĕlôâ*, the god of the Babylonian who worships his own strength (1:11).[153] He also notes that an inclusio delineates Habakkuk's second complaint with questions and temporal markers: "Are you not from eternity . . . ?" (1:12) and "Will they . . . continually slaughter? (1:17).[154] In the third panel, inclusio brackets subsections with geographic place-names (3:3, 7) and imagery of the Divine Warrior's horses trampling the sea (3:8, 15).

Hiebert, in his literary structural analysis of chap. 3 observes that "inclusion is the primary stylistic device with which the poet has given shape to the poem."[155] His words could just as easily apply to all three chapters: "Very often inclusion operates not only as a single circle uniting the beginning and end of a literary unit but as a series of concentric circles carefully fashioned to produce a cyclic structure in which many layers of inclusion may be found. This inclusive structure operates at every level of the poem."[156] Clearly, inclusio plays an important role in the structure of the entire book.

A variety of other factors produced a wide array of structural outlines for Habakkuk. The view that the entire book is an interactive dialogue between the prophet and the Lord has yielded slightly different structures and labels for Robert Chisholm, as well as John Goldingay and Pamela Scalise.[157] The book's dialogical interchange

---

127–28.

[153] Dong-Weon Lim, "Rhetorical Analysis of the Book of Habakkuk," *Korean Journal of Christian Studies* 72 (2013): 25.

[154] Lim, "Structural Analysis of the Book of Habakkuk," 73.

[155] Hiebert, *God of My Victory*, 59.

[156] Hiebert, *God of My Victory*, 76.

[157] Chisholm, *Handbook on the Prophets*, 433–34, labels chap. 3 as "Habakkuk's Response." Similarly treating the entire book as dialogue, Goldingay and Scalise, *Minor Prophets II*, 47, divide chap. 3 into three sections: "Habakkuk's plea to Yahweh" (vv. 1–2); "A vision of Yahweh's coming" (vv. 3–15); and "Habakkuk's response" (3:16–19).

between the prophet and the Lord prompted David Fuller to develop a model of discourse analysis using the framework of Systemic Functional Linguistics.[158] Reading Hab 2:2 as a prose speech introduction on the level of the two superscriptions, Loren Bliese divides Habakkuk into three sections that consist of seven poems each—"the number of fullness."[159] Ben Y. Leigh argues that the frame of Habakkuk is a lament psalm (Psalm "H") broken into two portions by the literary insertion of material for rhetorical purpose: "AXB; A for a lament-cry, X for a literary insertion, B for a response of faith."[160] Finally, Gert T. M. Prinsloo contends ancient paragraph markers (*petuchot* and *setumot*) reveal a macrostructure that challenges traditional interpretations of the book.[161]

6.2.2 Structure and the Theological Message of Habakkuk

The matter of the structure of this brief prophetic book remains unsettled. But is it really necessary? A careful structural analysis is important not just because it yields an appropriate outline for the book but because it contributes to understanding the theological message of the text.

So, where do most scholars locate the primary message of Habakkuk? Thomas calls 2:2–5 "the key to unlocking the book" and claims v. 4 is "the heart of the teaching of Habakkuk."[162] Smith observes, "There is no more important passage in Habakkuk than this one [2:1–5], and few in the OT are more significant."[163] David Prior contends that 2:4 contains "the core of Habakkuk's vision," and Mária Eszenyei Széles labels v. 4 as "the centerpiece, the heart, of the whole

---

[158] David J. Fuller, *A Discourse Analysis of Habakkuk*, SSN 72 (Boston: Brill, 2020), 1–2. Fuller, p. 15, divides the text into four layers of discourse: (1) the superscriptions, (2) the announcement/quotation formula of 2:1–2a ("a narrative aside"), (3) traditional subdivisions of remaining text with the exception of the fourth layer, and (4) the woe oracles (2:6b-20). His analysis explores mode, field, and tenor in each of the various speech discourses.

[159] Loren F. Bliese, "The Poetics of Habakkuk," *Journal of Translation and Textlinguistics* 12 (1999): 47. Bliese, pp. 67–71, analyzes these individual poems metrically and notes several features of peak prominence.

[160] Ben Y. Leigh, "A Rhetorical and Structural Study of Habakkuk" (Ph.D. diss., Golden Gate Baptist Theological Seminary, 1992), 186–87. The three structural divisions are A 1:2–4, X 1:5–3:15, and B 3:16–19.

[161] Gert T. M. Prinsloo, "Reading Habakkuk in the Light of Ancient Unit Delimiters," *Theological Studies* 69.1 (2012): 3–4.

[162] Thomas, *Habakkuk*, 104, 107.

[163] Smith, *Micah–Malachi*, 105.

prophecy."[164] Narrowing the field even more, Robertson suggests that 2:4b is "the central message of Habakkuk," and "[it] summarizes the essence of the Christian gospel."[165] The canonical significance of 2:4b—quoted three times in the NT (Rom 1:17; Gal 3:11; Heb 10:38)—has influenced the selection of Hab 2:4 as the central message of the book, but is there structural evidence for this conclusion?

Ernst Wendland seems to think so. He declares Hab 2:4b to be "the thematic core of Habakkuk's entire message" and "the semantic kernel" that shapes "the structure, style, content, and purpose" of the book.[166] He sets out to demonstrate how the three Hb. words in 2:4b govern "the compositional interaction of progression and cohesion" of Habakkuk.[167] Using a two-part structure—problem (1:1–2:1) and solution (2:2–3:19)—Wendland proposes the following structural-thematic parallels[168]:

I.   A. *Superscription* (1:1)
      B. Habakkuk's first *complaint*: Why does God allow injustice to go unpunished? (1:2–4)
      C. God's *response*: The Babylonians will punish Judah and all nations. (1:5–11)
      D. Habakkuk's second *complaint*: Why use the wicked to judge? (1:12–17)
      E. Habakkuk rests his case (*transition*): How will God respond? (2:1)

II.   F. God's *response*: A vision will pronounce judgment on Babylon. (2:2–5)
      G. A *taunt* against Babylon: Five woes declared on the unjust nation (2:6–20)
      H. *Psalm* of Habakkuk: Praising God's past deliverance and a faith-filled response

---

[164] David Prior, *The Message of Joel, Micah, and Habakkuk*, BST (Downers Grove: IVP, 1998), 253; Széles, *Wrath and Mercy*, 30.

[165] Robertson, *The Books of Nahum, Habakkuk, and Zephaniah*, 181, 185.

[166] Ernst R. Wendland, "'The Righteous Live by Their Faith' in a Holy God: Complementary Compositional Forces and Habakkuk's Dialogue with the Lord," *JETS* 42.4 (1999): 591.

[167] Wendland, "'The Righteous Live by Their Faith' in a Holy God," 591. Italics original.

[168] Wendland, "'The Righteous Live by Their Faith' in a Holy God," 591. I have abbreviated Wendland's statements following the colons. His indentions highlight the parallel themes. Wendland's two-part structure is different from that of Sweeney and others who divide Habakkuk according to the superscriptions in 1:1 and 3:1.

Wendland explains that the two middle segments E (2:1) and F (2:2–5) "act as a structural pivot between the two unequal, but thematically balanced halves."[169] Although his statements are parallel, the unbalanced structure does not readily reflect the natural flow of dialogue.

Similarly, David Dorsey proposes a chiastic structure to demonstrate the centrality of Habakkuk's message in 2:4b. The term *chiasm* (or *chiasmus*) is a literary device which incorporates symmetry on either side of a central element. The second half of a verse, a passage, or even a whole book mirrors the first half, presenting parallel elements in reverse order.[170] Dorsey explains the central "pivot point" often has no parallel, and it is "the natural location for the turning point, climax, high point, or centerpiece, since it marks the point where the composition reverses order."[171] Old Testament writers used this literary feature in order to aid memory, enhance aesthetic beauty, emphasize literary coherence, and highlight comparison, contrast, or illustration.[172] Although a symmetrical chiastic structure may seem foreign to modern readers, it was a common feature in ancient literature.[173] Dorsey's seven-part outline centers around the message found in 2:1–5:[174]

a   Habakkuk's first complaint: How long must I wait for your justice? (1:2–4)
   b   Yahweh's first answer: The powerful army of Babylon is coming.(1:5–11)
      c   Habakkuk's second complaint: How can you allow the wicked to destroy those more righteous (1:12–17)
         d   CENTER: Wait, for in the end the wicked will be punished, but the righteous will live by faith. (2:1–5)

---

[169] Wendland, "'The Righteous Live by Their Faith' in a Holy God," 591.

[170] The name for the device comes from the Greek letter *chi* (X), which graphically illustrates this inverted symmetry.

[171] David A. Dorsey, *The Literary Structure of the Old Testament: A Commentary on Genesis-Malachi* (Grand Rapids: Baker Books, 1999), 31.

[172] Dorsey, *The Literary Structure of the Old Testament*, 31.

[173] J. W. Welch, ed., *Chiasmus in Antiquity: Structures, Analyses, Exegesis* (Hildesheim: Gerstenberg, 1981), 9.

[174] Dorsey, *The Literary Structure of the Old Testament*, 308. Dorsey's statements have been slightly abbreviated. Each of his statements include numerous bulleted subpoints not included here.

      c′ Yahweh's answer to second complaint: "woes": The
          wicked will be punished; wrongs will be righted.
          (2:6–20)
     b′ Yahweh's final answer: the coming of a more powerful
        army of Yahweh, defeat of Babylon; rescue of Israel
        (3:1–15)
  a′ Habakkuk's final resolution to first complaint: I will wait for
     God's help; he is my source of joy. (3:16–19)

Despite Dorsey's claim that 2:4 falls "at about the midpoint of the
book,"[175] his structure is just as unequal as Wendland's: the second
half of his proposed chiasm (c′b′a′) is twice as long as the first half
(abc). Although Dorsey expresses his proposed structure in symmetrical concepts, the two halves are not symmetrical.

    Timothy Lim observes that Hab 2:3–4 falls not at the center of
Habakkuk, but at the center of the Qumran pesher—the ancient commentary on the first two chapters of Habakkuk alone. He writes,

> The turning point [of the pesher] occurs at Hab. 2:3–4, precisely
> when the prophet announces the coming of a second vision and the
> fate of the wicked and righteous. Habakkuk 2:1–4 forms the cen-
> tre of the prophecy, and it is also the pivotal point of the pesher-
> ist's interpretation. The third chapter of Habakkuk is absent, but
> the pesher is coherent and complete, the work of a sophisticated
> reader of the biblical text.[176]

The ancient Qumran commentator evidently recognized the significance of this passage located at the center of Habakkuk's first two
chapters and made it the central focus of his interpretation as well.
Habakkuk 2:4 is at the center of the pesher, but that means it is not
the structural center of all three chapters of Habakkuk.

    Some researchers locate the central message of Habakkuk some-
where other than Hab 2:1–5. Though Fuller does not tie a central message to a specific text, his detailed discourse analysis reveals a linear
progression of shifts: from a focus on the prophet, Yahweh, and evil
things; to the Babylonians in a spotlight role; to Yahweh acting upon
the Babylonians. He then detects "a radical shift" in chap. 3, where

---

[175] Dorsey, *The Literary Structure of the Old Testament*, 306.
[176] Lim, *The Earliest Commentary on the Prophecy of Habakkuk*, 3.

Yahweh assumes "the most dominant position linguistically."[177] Fuller observes,

> Significantly, this power is not exercised over merely the enemies of the prophet, but the nations, earth, and seas as a whole. *It is as if the prophet received the interaction of YHWH and the earth in the woe oracles and greatly expanded upon this.* . . . Therefore, when the chain interaction is surveyed throughout the pericopae of the book of Habakkuk, the book starts with the prophet portraying himself and YHWH linked with evil things, and ends with the prophet portraying YHWH in connection with numerous extensions of his power and with the entire earth as an object under his control.[178]

Although Fuller locates a profound shift in chap. 3, he at least perceives that the interaction between the Lord and the earth originated somewhere in the woe oracles.

Mark Allen Hahlen calls 2:1–5 the "hermeneutical center of the book." Still, like Fuller, Hahlen notes that "chapter [3] carries forward the climactic shift of attention away from the wicked and toward Yahweh with an attendant shift in tone from accusation to confidence."[179] Unlike Fuller, Hahlen astutely locates the origin of this shift in the third woe, a location that he views as "highly significant in the structure and thought of the *hôy* oracle series. Its middle position within the series gives it a structural importance upon which the content capitalizes."[180] He explains that the first two woes show "the outworking of a *lex talionis* system of justice" where the evildoer reaps what he sows, but the Lord is noticeably absent. In the middle of the third oracle, however, "Yahweh suddenly emerges . . . as the impetus behind the reversal of fortunes."[181] From the third woe onward, the Lord is

---

[177] Fuller, *A Discourse Analysis of Habakkuk*, 302. To detect major shifts in mode, field, and tenor, Fuller, p. 299, traces chain interaction, transitivity, and mood through the various speeches in Habakkuk. He observes that in chap. 3, "YHWH is by far the most significant entity" and concludes that the alignment of all three categories is a "far more striking" correlation of the Lord's domination than in the previous speeches (p. 305).

[178] Fuller, *A Discourse Analysis of Habakkuk*, 301. Italics added.

[179] Mark Allen Hahlen, "The Literary Design of Habakkuk" (Ph.D. diss., The Southern Baptist Theological Seminary, 1992), 186.

[180] Hahlen, "The Literary Design of Habakkuk," 105.

[181] Hahlen, "The Literary Design of Habakkuk," 183.

no longer passive or absent; he is personally involved, administering judgment and, ultimately, salvation.

Bliese is another example of someone who locates the central teaching of Habakkuk outside of 2:1–5. His detailed poetic analysis locates the structural "center of the book" at the conclusion of the second woe (v. 11) because "the last line is one of the two center lines of the book, being the 50th from the beginning."[182] Bliese then makes the following observations regarding the third woe:

> This chiastic poem [2:12–14] has features which recommend it as the central high point of the book. Its first line is the other 50th line of the 100 in the book. The divine name "LORD of hosts" comes in the first line of the peak. This is significantly the only occurrence in the book. . . . The peak is a rhetorical question giving it emphasis. It relates to the main question of the book regarding God's ultimate control and his holiness in setting things right. The last line is clearly a climax with the change from despair to "the earth will be filled with the knowledge of the glory of the Lord."[183]

The importance of the third woe clearly stands out. Somewhat surprisingly then, Bliese moves away from these findings to locate the "peak" of the entire book in the doxology of the fifth woe (2:20) because of its "climactic emphasis."[184] Observing that the word "holy" occurs only once in each of the three sections (1:12; 2:20; 3:3), Bliese claims—somewhat arbitrarily—that "this unique structural pattern serves to point out the main teaching of the book."[185] His conclusion seems to contradict his own research suggesting the third woe might be "the central high point of the book."[186] Even scholars who locate the central message of Habakkuk outside of the middle woe sometimes note the heightened significance of 2:13–14, which demands further investigation.

---

[182] Bliese, "The Poetics of Habakkuk," 58–59.

[183] Bliese, "The Poetics of Habakkuk," 59.

[184] Bliese, "The Poetics of Habakkuk," 67.

[185] Bliese, "The Poetics of Habakkuk," 49.

[186] Bliese, "The Poetics of Habakkuk," 59.

6.2.3   The Possibility of Macro-chiasm in Habakkuk

As part of his groundbreaking work on chiasmus, Nils Lund argued as early as 1934 that chiasmus is the key to unlocking the structure of Habakkuk based on "parallelism of thought."[187] In fact, H. H. Walker and Lund claimed that Habakkuk was the first book-length poem revealed to have "closely knit chiastic structure throughout" and painstakingly attempted to map out chiasm in every single strophe of the book.[188] Walker and Lund divided Habakkuk into three sections—I, II, and I'—with the following strophe subdivisions:

I	II	I'
A (1:1–4)	K (2:5c–8)	A (3:1–2)
B (1:5–11)	L (2:9–13)	B (3:3–7)
C (1:12–13)	K' (2:14–17)	C (3:8–10b)
B' (1:14–17)	L' (2:18–20)	B' (3:10c–15)
A' (2:1–5b)		A' (3:16–19)

Walker and Lund's proposed chiastic structure recognizes the parallels inside each of the outer sections; for example, the similarities between I:B and I:B' (descriptions of the Babylonian invaders) and between I':B and I':B' (descriptions of the Divine Warrior).

Since Walker and Lund's proposal in 1934, a proliferation of other proposals for the structure of Habakkuk have surfaced, yet no one appears to follow their lead.[189] Their proposal failed to convince others, possibly because of some of the following issues:

---

[187] H. H. Walker and Nils Lund, "The Literary Structure of the Book of Habakkuk," *JBL* 53.4 (1934): 355–70.

[188] Walker and Lund, "The Literary Structure of the Book of Habakkuk," 355. Since Lund, creating outlines based on chiastic structure has become popular among biblical scholars, so much so that there is a danger in seeing chiasm where there is none. While a chiasmus is clearer when it is a micro-chiasm spanning only a few lines (e.g., Hab 1:12a), the longer a passage is, the more difficult it is to identify macro-chiasm. For this reason, some scholars argue against macro-chiasm, maintaining that chiastic structures should be limited to no more than fifteen verses. For a concise discussion of this subject and a defense of macro-chiasm, see Wayne Brouwer, "Understanding Chiasm and Assessing Macro-Chiasm as a Tool of Biblical Interpretation," *Calvin Theological Journal* 53.1 (2018): 99–127. To guard against overreaching claims, Craig Blomberg, "The Structure of 2 Corinthians," *CTR* 4.1 (1989): 5–7, has outlined nine criteria for recognizing an extended chiasmus. Working through a rigorous list of criteria helps avoid the twin pitfalls of excessive imagination and scrapping the possibility of macro-chiasm altogether.

[189] Intriguingly, Ko, *Theodicy in Habakkuk*, 80, makes the passing comment, "[T]he whole 'woe oracles' section from 2:6b to 2:19" has a chiastic structure of AB // B'A'—which is the opposite of Lund's KLK'L'. Ko does not mention what function this central chiastic structure serves. Elsewhere, p. 71, she states, "The divine promise that the righteous will live by his faithfulness

1. Part I: The subdivision of the first part muddies the clear
   back-and-forth dialogue between the prophet and Yahweh. A
   more natural division would retain the conversational repartee
   of Habakkuk's questions and Yahweh's answers.

2. Part I': The authors admit, "The dividing line between C and
   B' is not clear."[190] By separating Habakkuk's questions into
   strophe C, their proposal ignores the obvious inclusio brack-
   eted by 3:8: "[I]s your fury against the sea / when you ride on
   your horses" and 3:15: "You tread the sea with your horses, /
   stirring up the vast water."

3. Part II: Walker and Lund acknowledge they "had to do much
   puzzling over many details" before settling on "an alternating
   order of strophes" for this middle section (KLK'L').[191] The
   decision to divide the five woes into four strophes, however,
   is a less than satisfying solution. Crowding the second and
   third woes into one strophe (L) ignores the natural paragraph
   breaks. Even worse, this stutter-step division at the center of
   the book obscures both the chiastic turn and the intended
   focus of the entire chiastic structure. The separation of 2:13
   (end of L) and 2:14 (beginning of K'), results in more of a leap
   than a pivot.

4. Parts I and I': For the entire book to be a macro-chiasm,
   the structure of these outer panels would also have to be
   inverted; for example, IABCDE // I'E'D'C'B'A'. Although
   Walker and Lund claimed to find chiasm *within* each of the
   outer panels (IABCB'A' and I'ABCB'A'), their framework fails
   to adequately articulate the detailed parallelism and symmetry *between* the two outer panels, where each subdivision
   in the outer panels matches the corresponding subdivision
   in the opposite panel (e.g., IABCB'A' // I'ABCB'A'). The
   authors mention only a few parallels found in both parts I
   and I' before concluding that "the third portion of the book
   was conceived as the parallel and the completion of the first

---

becomes the turning point of the book." In other words, Ko locates the turning point at 2:4b
rather than in the chiastic center of the woe series.

[190] Walker and Lund, "The Literary Structure of the Book of Habakkuk," 359.

[191] The authors offer no explanation of why they used the labels KLK'L' instead of EFE'F',
nor do they address the deviation from the typical chiasm, which would have been KLL'K'.

part."[192] Walker and Lund's proposal of macro-chiasm for the entire book is unconvincing.

5. Part II: Walker and Lund apparently recognized that 2:13–14 falls at the center of both the series of woes and, by extension, the book itself. Unfortunately, however, they do not comment on the theological significance of the verses or explain what function their proposed chiastic structure serves.

According to Watson, finding a chiastic pattern in a poem is "largely a preliminary." The crucial next steps seek to determine how it articulates or structures the whole and what function it serves.[193] In short, why did the author place it there? Watson describes two broad categories of chiastic patterns: (1) structural functions—including opening or closing stanzas, linking components of a poem, or indicating the midpoint of a poem; and (2) expressive functions—including merism, reversal of an existing state, emphatic negation, and strong contrast or antithesis.[194] He further explains that chiasmus at the midpoint may be "the hinge or turning-point in a poem, or its climax."[195] Because there is a marked shift in the tone of Habakkuk and a corresponding turnaround in the prophet's perspective, the possibility of a midpoint chiasm that expresses reversal must be considered to discover the role of the third woe in the book's structure and theology.

The middle woe causes problems for many scholars. William Hayes Ward maintains this "remarkable succession of quotations" is "the late addition of one who was not himself an original and authoritative prophet, but a scribe."[196] Regarding 2:14, Ward declares it has no "particular bearing on the subject, but is merely a pious reflection thrown in at hazard."[197] Robert's analysis of the third woe considers 2:14 "a partial and somewhat garbled quotation of Isa.11:9"; furthermore, 2:13a and 14 are glosses made by someone who "did not

---

[192] Walker and Lund, "The Literary Structure of the Book of Habakkuk," 360. The parallels Walker and Lund mention are the similarities between lines in I:B (1:5–11) and I':B (3:3–7), the "disconnected reference to the sea" in both I:B' (1:14–17) and I':B' (3:10c-15), and the "two pairs of cohortative imperfects" in I:A' (2:1–5b) and I'A' (3:16–19).

[193] Watson, *Traditional Techniques in Classical Hebrew Verse*, 368.

[194] Watson, *Traditional Techniques in Classical Hebrew Verse*, 369.

[195] Watson, *Traditional Techniques in Classical Hebrew Verse*, 370.

[196] William Hayes Ward, "Habakkuk," in *A Critical and Exegetical Commentary on Micah, Zephaniah, Nahum, Habakkuk, Obadiah and Joel*, ICC (Edinburgh: T&T Clark, 1974), 16.

[197] Ward, "Habakkuk," 17.

interpret, much less understand, the whole text."[198] He contends that "to interpret Hab. 2:5–20 as a unified composition, one must bracket out such secondary glosses that confuse the argument."[199] Andersen entertains the possibility 2:14 "does not belong at all."[200] Though he suspects "from Yahweh ṣĕbāʾôt" (2:13a) to be a gloss, he inexplicably declares elsewhere, "'Isn't this—Behold!—from Yahweh Sebaoth?' with its arresting language and the impressive title for God, must be regarded as the climax of the entire set and the key theological statement of the whole."[201]

Significantly, the issues these scholars raise regarding the third woe also function as markers for chiasm. Lund observed these same elements often appear in the center of a chiastic structure: (1) quotations, (2) divine names, and (3) a shift in thought before resuming the original thread.[202] The woe oracles in Habakkuk contain these and more of Lund's "laws governing chiastic structures," including (4) a central turning point, (5) the presence of frame passages (2:8b, 17b), and (6) echoes from the middle that recur in the extremities.[203] The presence of all these elements calls for a careful exploration of a chiastic structure—at least in the series of woes. Any proposed chiastic outline must also meet Craig Blomberg's criteria for macro-chiasm, which include (1) the outline must solve structural problems that "more conventional outlines fail to resolve"; (2) the outline must retain the natural paragraph breaks of the passage; (3) the corresponding halves must contain verbal/grammatical parallelism and conceptual/structural parallelism, and (4) the chiastic center must have theological gravitas

---

[198] Roberts, *Nahum, Habakkuk, and Zephaniah*, 123–24.

[199] Roberts, *Nahum, Habakkuk, and Zephaniah*, 124.

[200] Andersen, *Habakkuk*, 242. Even the *BHS* apparatus suggests that 2:14 may be an addition.

[201] Andersen, *Habakkuk*, 243, 227.

[202] Nils Lund, *Chiasmus in the New Testament: A Study in Formgeschichte* (Chapel Hill: University of North Carolina Press, 1942), 41. Ian Thomson, *Chiasmus in the Pauline Letters*, (Sheffield: Sheffield Academic, 1995), 27, clarifies that the shift can be the introduction of "a new or unexpected idea" and labels it "shift and reversion." Roland Meynet, *Treatise on Biblical Rhetoric* (Boston: Brill, 2012), 291, verifies Lund's observations regarding the presence of quotation in the center—whether direct, explicit, implicit, or allusion. He also explains, p. 290, "The function of the question at the centre [of a concentric construction], always a riddle, is to get the reader to reflect for himself and give his own answer."

[203] Lund, *Chiasmus in the New Testament*, 40–41. Realizing that there needed to be guidelines for detecting chiasm, Lund listed several "laws" drawn from his observations of chiastic structures.

worthy of its central, climactic position.[204] Although the entire book of Habakkuk fails to meet these criteria for chiasm, there is compelling evidence for chiasm in the central section of the book.

6.2.4 Habakkuk as a Literary Triptych

A careful analysis of Habakkuk reveals that its structure is analogous to a literary triptych.[205] (See chart below.) The book contains three panels, labeled respectively, I, II, and III: Panel I—dialogue (1:1–2:5), Panel II—woe oracles (2:6–20), and Panel III—prayer/psalm (3:1–19). Even though they are different genres, the two outer panels are parallel (I // III), as indicated by the superscriptions and the labels for the subdivisions: I A:B:C:D // III A′:B′:C′:D′. Sandwiched between these outer panels, the middle panel (II) contains the woe oracles arranged in a chiastic structure, indicated by the indentations of the subdivision labels: E:F:G:F′:E′. The parallelism of the outer panels (I A:B:C:D // III A′:B′:C′:D′)—on either side of the chiasmus—affords Habakkuk the opportunity to exploit this symmetry for his purposes, emphasizing the contrast between the two outer panels and highlighting the reversal in the chiastic centerpiece. The contrast also helps explain the transformation that takes place in the life of the prophet. The chiastic structure of the middle panel thus suggests a concentric structure for the entire triptych. The basic structure of Habakkuk looks like this:

---

[204] Blomberg, "The Structure of 2 Corinthians," 5–7.

[205] I developed the idea of a literary triptych based on the ancient practice of using wooden writing tablets—possibly like those prescribed in Hab 2:2. These wax-covered tablets were often hinged together to form diptychs or polyptychs. The three-panel structure of Habakkuk readily suggests a literary triptych—especially since the focal point of the triptych would be the chiasm located in the central panel. (See the discussion of "tablets" in this volume's commentary on Hab 2:2.) Byron Curtis, "The *Maśʾot* Triptych and the Date of Zechariah 9–14," in *Perspectives on the Formation of the Book of the Twelve*, BZAW 433 (Berlin: de Gruyter, 2012), 191, compares his "*Maśʾot* Triptych" to "a three-paneled painting or altarpiece." The vivid imagery of Habakkuk is especially fitting as an altarpiece since the central panel provides glimpses of God's global sanctuary and heavenly temple (2:14, 20). Having experienced the theophanic presence of God in chap. 3, the prophet invites people of faith from all generations to join him in praise of the God whose glory fills the heavens and the earth. See "A Theological Altarpiece" below.

Proposed Concentric Literary Triptych												
PANEL I: DIALOGUE				PANEL II: WOE ORACLES					PANEL III: PRAYER/PSALM			
Superscription (1:1)				2:6–8	2:9–11	2:12–14	2:15–17	2:18–20	Superscription (3:1)			
1:2–4	1:5–11	1:12–17	2:1–5						3:2	3:3–7	3:8–15	3:16–19
A First Complaint	B First Divine Response	C Second Complaint	D Second Divine Response	E First Woe	F Second Woe	G Third Woe	F′ Fourth Woe	E′ Fifth Woe	A′ Humble Petition	B′ Divine Warrior Arrives	C′ Divine Warrior Fights	D′ Joyful Submission

6.2.4.1   Chiastic Features in the Central Panel

Perhaps the most striking feature of the proposed outline is the label indentations in the middle panel, which serve to indicate a chiastic structure for the series of woe oracles. In contrast to Walker and Lund's structure, which divided the five woe oracles into four subdivisions (KLK′L′), the proposed structure (E:F:G:F′:E′) represents the natural paragraphing of the five woe oracles with a five-part division. The third woe functions as the centerpiece of both the middle panel and the entire book. It is also the location of most of the chiastic structure markers.

Even an initial reading of the center panel of Habakkuk reveals an unusual literary feature. Habakkuk 2:17b is a repetition of 2:8b: "because of human bloodshed / and violence against lands, cities, / and all who live in them."[206] These repeated lines serve as a refrain at the end of the first and fourth woes, bracketing the middle three woes and alerting the reader to a possible chiastic structure. As Walker and

---

[206] These lines are the same in Hebrew, but because the second refrain also has an additional introduction (2:17a), it is a "variant refrain," which—according to Watson, *Classical Hebrew Poetry*, 295—is much more frequent than "strict" refrains. Watson's observation that refrains rarely occur at the beginning of a poem, may help explain why the first refrain is delayed

Lund observed, this repetition is "a rare phenomenon [that] must signify two fixed points in unravelling the composer's scheme."[207] The refrains have the effect of highlighting the central importance of the third woe (2:12–14), which lies at the middle of this frame passage.[208] The fact that the third woe also contains key words that echo the refrain—bloodshed (Hb. *dāmim*), city (Hb. *qiryâ*), and earth (Hb. *ereṣ*)—further heightens its significance since there is often parallelism at the extremities and middle of a chiasm.[209]

Closer examination of panel II reveals structural, verbal, and conceptual parallelism in both halves of the chiasm in this series of woes. (See the following page.) As the structural labels on the left show, the corresponding subdivisions E // E′ and F // F′ display chiastic structural parallelism. The verbatim semantic parallels include the two refrains and their echoes in II:G (italicized in bold) and the initial phrasing of the woe statements (in bold). Other semantic parallels between corresponding subdivisions are indicated with capital letters.[210]

---

until after the first woe saying, and the second refrain follows suit, appearing just before the final woe saying.

[207] Walker and Lund, "The Literary Structure of the Book of Habakkuk," 358.

[208] According to Thomson, *Chiasmus in the Pauline Letters*, 27, a "frame passage" works as "a spring-board from which to launch into the chiasmus."

[209] A literal translation of the Hb. refrain in 2:8b and 2:17b makes the repetition more obvious: "because of bloods [*dāmim*] of man and violence against the earth [*ereṣ*], the city [*qiryâ*], and all who dwell in it."

[210] Some of these Hb. words are not exact repetitions; but as the English translation reveals, they are from the same semantic domain. Because the Hb. word *qûm* (v. 6; "arise") is related to *yəqûm* ("what exists, what lives"; Terry Brensinger, "קוּם," *NIDOTTE* 2:513), it is parallel to *ʿûr* (v. 19; Eng. "be awake, stir"; *HALOT*, 802; "come alive" CSB). Because the Hb. terms *yāqaṣ* (v. 7) and *qîṣ* (v. 19) are related (*HALOT*, 431), both are translated "wake up" in English. The words "shame" (Hb. *bōšet*) and "disgrace" (Hb. *qālôn*) are synonyms ("Shame, disgrace, humiliation, scorn," *NIDOTTE* 5:170).

E Question 1: Won't **ALL OF THESE** [taunt, mock, and ridicule] him?
THEY WILL SAY
1st Woe: **Woe to him who . . . LOADS HIMSELF WITH GOODS!**
Question 2: Won't your creditors suddenly **ARISE** and . . . **WAKE UP?**
Lex Talionis: **ALL THE PEOPLES** [you plundered] will plunder you.
Refrain: *because of human bloodshed*
and violence against lands [Hb. *ereṣ*; "earth"],
cities [Hb. *qiryâ*; "city"], *and all who live in them.*

F 2nd Woe: **Woe to him who** [places his nest on high]
to escape the grasp [Eng. **PALM**; Hb. *kap*] **OF DISASTER!**
Lex Talionis: You have planned **SHAME** for your house; . . .
the stones [and rafters] will cry out.

G 3rd Woe: **Woe to him who** builds a city with *bloodshed*
and founds a *town* [Hb. *qiryâ*] with injustice!
Question/ *Lex Talionis:* Is it not—[behold!]—from the LORD of Armies that
the peoples labor only to fuel the fire?
Chiastic Pivot: For the *earth* [Hb. *ereṣ*] will be filled
with the knowledge of the LORD's glory,
as the water covers the sea.

F' 4th Woe: **Woe to him who** gives his neighbors drink. . . . in order to
look at their nakedness!
Lex Talionis: You will be filled with **DISGRACE** instead of glory.
The cup in **the LORD'S RIGHT HAND** will come to you
and utter **DISGRACE** will cover your glory.
Refrain: *because of human bloodshed*
and violence against lands [Hb. *ereṣ*; "earth"],
cities [Hb. *qiryâ*; "city"], . . . *and all who live in them.*

E' Question 1: What use is a carved idol after its craftsman carves it?
Idols . . . **CANNOT SPEAK.**
5th Woe: **Woe to him who SAYS** to wood: **WAKE UP!**
Or to mute stone: **COME ALIVE!**
Question 2: Can it teach?
Look! It may be **PLATED WITH GOLD AND SILVER,**
yet there is no breath in it at all.
Lex Talionis: Let **THE WHOLE EARTH** [including worshipers of mute idols]
be **SILENT!**

All four of the outer subdivisions of the chiasmus (E:F:F':E') contain a statement of *lex talionis* or retributive justice: the plunderer
becomes the plundered; the ill-gotten house testifies against its builder;
the one who exposes others is exposed; and the worshiper of mute

idols is silenced by the Lord. In the middle strophe (G), it is the question that expresses a sense of retributive justice: Is it not from the Lord that the labor of the bloodstained builder only fuels the fire? This central strophe suddenly diverges from the rest, however, with the stunning announcement that "the earth will be filled / with the knowledge of the Lord's glory, /as the water covers the sea." Habakkuk 2:14 is exactly the kind of surprise that a chiasm typically generates. After this "shift and reversion," the series of woes continues.[211] The prime subdivisions in the middle panel exhibit the expected inverted verbal and conceptual parallelism (E // E′; F // F′). (See chart below.)

Inverted Chiastic Parallelism in the Woe Series	
E: First Woe Saying (2:6–8A)	**E′: Fifth Woe Saying (2:18–20)**

a: ALL OF THESE [nations/peoples; 2:5]
b: they will take up a TAUNT . . .
    with MOCKERY and RIDDLES
    THEY WILL SAY . . .
c: Woe to him who
    LOADS HIMSELF WITH GOODS
d: Won't your creditors suddenly ARISE
    and those who disturb you WAKE UP?
	d′: Woe to him who says to wood: WAKE UP!
	    Or to mute stone: COME ALIVE!
	c′: [An idol] may be
	    PLATED WITH GOLD/SILVER
	b′: SILENCE! before him [Hb. *Has! mipānāyw*]
	a′: ALL THE EARTH [Hb. *kāl-hā'āreṣ*]

F: Second Woe Saying (2:9–11)	**F′: Fourth Woe Saying (2:15–16)**

a: Woe to the one who . . . [attempts] to
    escape THE PALM [Hb. *kap*] OF DISASTER
b: You have planned SHAME for your house
	b′: You will be filled with disgrace
	a′: THE CUP IN THE LORD'S RIGHT HAND will
	    come around to you

In the first set of parallel woes, the cacophony of the nations and peoples (v. 6) is silenced when the Lord hushes "all the earth" with a single word (v. 20). The imagery of the one who "loads himself with goods" (v. 6) echoes in the idol "plated with gold and silver" (v. 19). In stark contrast to the victims who will "arise" and "wake up" (v. 7), the mute idol cannot "wake up" and "come alive" because it has no breath in it (v. 19). In the second parallel pair of woes, the imagery of the palm of disaster (v. 9) parallels "the cup in the Lord's right hand" (v. 16), and the words "shame" and "disgrace" are synonyms.

Again, as Watson explains, identifying chiasmus in a passage is just the first step; we must also discover how it functions. The first line of the third woe (2:12) falls in the exact midpoint of the woe oracles

---

[211] Thomson, *Chiasmus in the Pauline Letters*, 27, uses this term to describe the "shift" that occurs in the center of a chiasm because it implies that after the shift, "the original thought is resumed."

and of the entire book. It thus fills the structural function of indicating the midpoint of the poem. The third woe also fills the expressive
function of indicating "a reversal in state of being."[212] At the book's
beginning, the world appeared to be a place where the wicked could
surround and devour the righteous with impunity. The Lord appeared
ignorant or uncaring or impotent to stop them, and the prophet questioned how the Lord could make no distinction between the wicked
and the righteous. The final answer to his questions surfaces in the
midpoint of the book. Wickedness will not go on forever. The Lord
of Armies will himself administer justice and build his own kingdom,
where "the earth will be filled / with the knowledge of the LORD's
glory / as the water covers the sea" (2:14). This revelation is worthy of
serving as the theological climax of the poem.

All the violence, all the arrogance and mockery, all the exhausting
labor of the peoples described to this point in Habakkuk are for naught.
Everything is simply stubble that will be consumed by fire. Verse 13
contains the answer the prophet had longed to hear: God is actively at
work bringing about justice for those who are being devoured by the
wicked. As the shift in the middle of the third woe clearly reveals, the
basis of justice centers on God: "Is it not—[behold; Hb. *hinnê*]—from
the LORD of Armies . . . ?" The Babylonians, attempting to establish
their dominion over city (*qiryâ*) and land (*ereṣ*) by bloodshed (*dāmîm*),
were merely pawns in the hand of the sovereign Lord of Armies. God
appointed them to punish his own wayward people. From this point
on in Habakkuk, the Lord of Armies is establishing his dominion over
all the earth (*ereṣ*). One day the entire globe will be engulfed with the
knowledge of his glory.

The concentric structure in the center of Habakkuk helps explain
the contrast between the outer panels. The chiastic center located in
vv. 13–14 provides the reason for the contrast, and it helps explain the
transformation in the prophet as well. The material in Habakkuk that
precedes this shift is anthropocentric: it is the perception of life from
a human-centered worldview. Although Habakkuk counted himself
among the righteous (1:4), he used a morality ladder to do so: "I am
more righteous than they!" But when God announced the Babylonian
invasion, Habakkuk complained that the wicked Judeans below him
on the ladder must be several rungs above those wicked Babylonians

[212] Watson, *Traditional Techniques in Classical Hebrew Verse*, 369.

(1:13). Confused by his human perspective, the prophet grappled with God to understand why the Lord would tolerate the wicked. The central panel of woes reveals that the Lord will judge all moral depravity that results from a worldview not based on true knowledge of the Lord.

Following the chiastic shift, the remainder of the book is thoroughly theocentric. Though the passage reverts to the list of woes, the last two woes declare that the cup of wrath is in the Lord's hand, and the Lord unmasks idols as false gods. From 2:13–14 on, the book of Habakkuk is all about God from God's perspective. This revelation—and the corresponding theophanic vision—is the reason the prophet can live by faith (2:4b). Habakkuk received a precious glimpse of God's mission to restore all things. Faith is not the end goal. For now it is the penultimate goal. One day faith will become sight. The whole world will be filled to overflowing with the knowledge and experience of the presence of God in all his glory. This understanding helped Habakkuk reframe his perspective on his current circumstances. The vision of God in his glory resulted in trust and praise.

John Breck explains how a chiasm works as a "rhetorical helix" to communicate the "real meaning or essential message of the text." He observes, "*The resultant concentric or spiral parallelism, with progressive intensification from the extremities inward, produces a helical movement that draws the reader/hearer toward the thematic center.*"[213] With Breck's diagram as a template, the helical structure of concentric parallelism in the middle panel would look something like the chart on the next page.[214]

[213] John Breck, *The Shape of Biblical Language: Chiasmus in the Scriptures and Beyond* (Crestwood, NY: St. Vladimir's Seminary Press, 1994), 58, 339. Italics in original.
[214] Breck, *The Shape of Biblical Language*, 42. Arrowheads added to Breck's template.

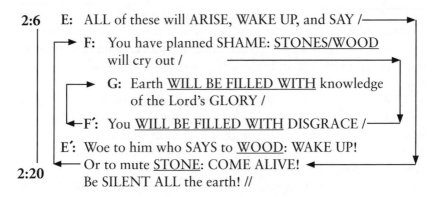

2:6 E: ALL of these will ARISE, WAKE UP, and SAY /⟶

F: You have planned SHAME: STONES/WOOD will cry out /

G: Earth WILL BE FILLED WITH knowledge of the Lord's GLORY /

F′: You WILL BE FILLED WITH DISGRACE /⟶

E′: Woe to him who SAYS to WOOD: WAKE UP!

2:20 Or to mute STONE: COME ALIVE! ⟵

Be SILENT ALL the earth! //

Figure 1: Rhetorical Helix in the Series of Woes

A chiasm requires following two lines of thought concurrently. The vertical line on the left side of the diagram indicates a linear reading of the passage (2:6–20). At the same time, the passage reads concentrically by tracing the spiraling path through the text on the right side: E-E′; F-F′; G. This spiral reading helps explain why the underlined verbal parallels ("stones," "wood," and "will be filled with" fall outside the chiastic complements.[215] Breck observes that a concentric reading involves a "'what's more' principle" that is, "[a] heightening effect occurs from the first parallel . . . strophe to its prime complement."[216] This "progressive intensification," which moves from the outer strophes inward, "produces a helical movement that draws the reader/hearer toward the thematic center."[217] After hearing about the "shame" and "disgrace" of the wicked, the reader arrives at the startling antithesis: "the LORD's glory" will fill the earth (2:14).

Breck further points out that "[c]hiastic units are framed by inclusion." Intriguingly, the woe oracles are framed by an inclusio: "all of these" (2:6) and "all the earth" (2:20 NIV), and 2:13–14 falls at the center of these. Although Lim did not include this inclusio with the others he observed, he notes Hab 2:14 introduces "a sudden temporary shift of mood" where "[t]he emotional pressure built up from the three woe oracles finds a vent" that prepares readers to "brace" for

---

[215] In v. 16, the wicked "will be filled" comes from śabaʿ ("to eat one's fill of"; *HALOT*, 1303), whereas, in v. 14, the earth "will be filled" comes from mālēʿ ("to be filled"; *HALOT*, 583). As indicated by the CSB translation, they are from the same semantic domain. The wicked will be satiated with disgrace, but—what's more—creation will be filled with the glory of the Lord.

[216] Breck, *The Shape of Biblical Language*, 42, 338.

[217] Breck, *The Shape of Biblical Language*, 339.

the "final two blows of the oracles."[218] This is just the kind of significant pause or interlude Dorsey mentions as one of the functions of a
chiasmus.[219] Habakkuk 2:14, however, does not provide mere temporary relief from a series of unrelenting woes. This pause emphasizes
the significance of Hab 2:13–14 as the theological centerpiece of the
book.

6.2.4.2 Parallelism in the Side Panels

The chiastic pivot in the center of the middle panel has a powerful
effect on all that follows. By the end of Habakkuk, there has been
a total inversion of worldview. Every single subdivision in panel III
reflects a total reversal in perspective. The clue to this inversion surfaces in 2:13–14, which contains intentional verbal echoes from the
side panels as well:

> Is it not—[behold!; Hb. *hinnê*; 1:5; 2:4, 19]—from the LORD of
>   Armies [1:6–11; 3:3–15]
> that the peoples [3:16] labor only to fuel the fire
> and countries exhaust themselves for nothing?
> For the earth [1:6; 3:3–4, 9, 12] will be filled [3:3] with the
>   knowledge [3:2] of the LORD's glory ["splendor"; 3:3]
> as the waters [3:8–15] cover the sea [1:14–17].

Verbal parallels not only cluster in the chiastic center; they also
reverberate across the symmetrical subdivisions of the outer panels.
An examination of the parallelism between the two side panels uncov-
ers a corresponding symmetry between each of the four subdivisions.
Both outer panels begin with superscription titles introducing the sections as "The pronouncement that the prophet Habakkuk saw" (1:1)
and "A prayer of the prophet Habakkuk" (3:1), along with instructions for singing panel III as a psalm.

The following chart depicts parallels between corresponding sections of the outer panels of the literary triptych.

---

[218] Lim, "Rhetorical Analysis of the Book of Habakkuk," 29. See the discussion of inclusion
in 6.2.1: "A Survey of Diverse Structural Divisions."

[219] Dorsey, *The Literary Structure of the Old Testament*, 41.

Parallelism in the Side Panels

	I: A (1:2–4)	III: A′ (3:2)
SETTING	Prophet in prayer	Prophet in prayer
ACTIONS	He accuses the Lord of not listening.	He's heard the report about the Lord.
	Why won't the Lord do something?	He stands in awe of the Lord's deeds.
	He asks three questions.	He makes three petitions.
COMPLAINT	"[T]he wicked restrict the righteous; . . . justice comes out perverted."	
SHIFT		"In . . . wrath remember mercy!"
	I: B (1:5–11)	**III: B′ (3:3–7)**
SETTING	"earth's open spaces"	"the heavens, and the earth"
ACTORS	The Babylonian soldiers	The Divine Warrior
ATTENDANTS	Horses—like wild animals	Plague and pestilence
ACTIONS	They "come from distant lands."	ʾĔlôâ comes from southern mountains.
	They march across the earth.	He stands and shakes the earth.
	Look at the nations; be astounded.	He looks and startles the nations.
	They build siege ramps.	Age-old mountains crumble; hills sink.
	They sweep by like the wind and pass.	His pathways are ancient.
	Their strength is their god (ʾĕlôâ).	His power is hidden in his hand.
	They are guilty.	He is the Holy One.
COMPLAINT	All of them come to do violence, to seize territories not their own.	
SHIFT		"His splendor covers the heavens, and the earth is full of his praise."
	I: C (1:12–17)	**III: C′ (3:8–15)**
INTRO	Prophet questions Lord's inaction	Prophet questions target of Lord's wrath
SETTING	The sea	The rivers, sea, deep, heavens, earth
ACTORS	Babylonian fishermen vs. nations	The Divine Warrior vs. Babylonians
WEAPONS	Hook, dragnet, fishing net	Bow and arrows, spears
ACTIONS	Lord made men "fish" with no ruler.	Lord slays the ruler of the wicked.
	Babylonians pull them up with a hook.	He pierces the enemy's head with his own spears.

Parallelism in the Side Panels (cont.)		
	They gather victims in a net like food.	Warriors stormed out to scatter/devour.
	They sacrifice to continue ruling the sea.	The Lord rules over earth, sky, and sea.
COMPLAINT	Lord is silent while wicked swallow the righteous: Will they continually slaughter nations without mercy?	
SHIFT		The Lord crushes the leader of wicked; he comes to save his people/his anointed.
	I: D (2:1–5)	**III: D' (3:16–20)**
SETTING	Prophet in prayer on lookout tower	Prophet in prayer on mountain heights
PARALLEL FORMS	2 cohortatives:[220] I will stand . . . I will station myself!	2 cohortatives: I will celebrate in the Lord; I will rejoice!
ACTIONS	Petulant prophet expects reply.	Chastened prophet quakes before God.
	Wait for vision's appointed time!	He will wait for invaders' day of distress.
	Wicked people without integrity will fall.	The Lord enables the prophet's feet to scale mountains.
PORTRAIT	A wicked man	The prophet, righteous by faith
	His enlarged appetite is like Sheol.	Trusting God, even if he loses all sources of food.
	Like Death, he is never satisfied.	The prophet is content to rejoice in the Lord.
COMPLAINT	The Babylonian Empire is set on gathering and devouring all nations.	
SHIFT		God of salvation will sustain his people and restore his dominion over the land.

The contrasts between the parallel subdivisions in the outer panels are significant. The reader naturally wonders what brought about this reversal. The epicenter of the shift lies in the heart of the central

---

[220] Walker and Lund, "The Literary Structure of the Book of Habakkuk," 360, likewise point out the corresponding occurrence of double pairs of cohortative imperfect Hebrew verbs in 2:1 (I:D; "I will stand"; "I will station myself") and 3:18 (III:D; "I will celebrate"; "I will rejoice"). GKC §108a notes the added suffix (-āh) indicates an "emphatic statement of fixed determination." The cohortative verb form does not appear elsewhere in Habakkuk.

panel. The theological message tucked away in the third woe creates concentric circles that reach the outermost extremities of the entire book.

6.2.4.3 *Advantages of the Proposed Literary Triptych*

In summary, the structure of the book of Habakkuk is a three-panel literary triptych, in which concentric parallelism emanates from the heart of the middle panel and results in a contrasting parallelism that cascades down each of the outer panels. This proposed structure helps solve several riddles in Habakkuk that have sparked much debate.

1. **Where is the proper division between the dialogue and the series of woes?**

   The outer panels close with a contrasting pair of portraits: a wicked man (2:4–5) vis-à-vis the faithful prophet (3:16–19). The insatiable appetite of a wicked man—like the Babylonian emperor—leaves him always hungry for more:
   "He gathers all the nations to himself;
   he collects all the peoples for himself" (2:5).
   In contrast, the man of faith—even in deprivation—finds his contentment in a relationship with God. He trusts in the Lord to restore dominion over his land:
   "[H]e makes my feet like those of a deer
   and enables me to walk on mountain heights!"
   Without 2:5, the parallel portrait is incomplete.

   Furthermore, Luis Alonso Schökel's discussion of Psalm 51 as a two-scene literary diptych provides further support for this division. He notes, "One word from each scene has escaped to the other side to serve as a link."[221] The same thing happens at the hinge between panels I and II, where the twice-repeated "all" at the bottom of the first panel (2:5) "escapes" to sound a third time (2:6) at the top of the second panel.[222]

---

[221] Schökel, *A Manual of Hebrew Poetics*, 197.
[222] Similarly, the word "Yahweh" ("LORD") serves as a hinge between the second panel (2:20) and the third panel (32..

2. **Why does the fifth woe saying appear to be out of order?**

    This structure recognizes that the first woe saying opens in 2:6 with a rhetorical question. It then becomes clear that in the chiasm, the final woe stands parallel to the first. The fifth woe opens with a rhetorical question (v. 18), followed by a pronouncement of the fifth "woe" (v. 19).

3. **Why does the third woe saying seem random and out of place?**

    Understanding the chiastic structure of the middle panel helps explain that the oddities of the third woe are markers of chiasm. The quotations, the surprising shift in thought and reversion, and the echoes from the frame passage are not evidence of a gloss that should be bracketed out; rather, they are expected indicators that signal the main message of the entire book and the answer to the prophet's questions.

4. **If there is chiasm in the middle panel, how should it be properly divided?**

    Walker and Lund struggled to untangle this riddle before they decided on an alternating four-strophe chiasm: K:L:K':L'. If they had understood the nature of chiasm results in a helical reading—as discussed above—they might have avoided awkwardly dividing the five woes into four strophes. A five-part division is necessary to retain the natural paragraphing: E:F:G:F':E'.

5. **What is the benefit of locating the central teaching of Habakkuk in 2:13–14 rather than 2:4?**

    Wendland admits that his proposal centered on 2:4b results in "two unequal, but thematically balanced halves," and it initially appears to be anthropocentric.[223] In contrast, the beginning of the third woe falls in the exact physical center of the book. Recognizing the corresponding theological centrality of 2:13–14 grounds the crucial teaching of 2:4 in the theocentric mission of God. As Wendland recognizes, the reliability of the Lord of Armies in 2:13—and, I would add, his mission— grounds the truth of 2:4b.

---

[223] Wendland, "'The Righteous Live by Their Faith' in a Holy God," 591,6.1.

6. Is there unity in the book of Habakkuk?

The detailed parallelism and symmetry skillfully woven across all three panels point to the artistry and comprehensive unity of the entire book of Habakkuk.

Although the proposed literary triptych structure provides possible solutions for some riddles, it raises at least one more: **What is the proper terminology for the structure of the central panel: is it chiasm or concentric parallelism?** Unfortunately, scholars do not appear to have reached a consensus regarding the terminology and definitions for these literary devices.

A brief survey shows that scholars are divided over whether chiasmus includes an odd or even number of elements. Walker and Lund's article claims that both odd- and even-numbered chiastic patterns are present in Habakkuk.[224] In his discussion of *narrative* patterns of structure, S. Bar-Efrat presents the following clarifying labels:[225]

A A′	(parallel pattern)
A X A′	(ring pattern)
A B B′ A′	(chiastic pattern)
A B X B′ A′	(concentric pattern)

Scholars that follow Bar-Efrat (1980) chronologically do not appear to follow his lead.[226]

Breck (1994), for example, argues that "the uniqueness of chiasm, as distinct from other forms of parallelism, lies in its focus upon a

---

[224] Walker and Lund, "The Literary Structure of the Book of Habakkuk," 355.

[225] S. Bar-Efrat, "Some Observations on the Analysis of Structure in Biblical Narrative," *VT* 30 (1980): 170.

[226] Schökel (1988), *A Manual of Hebrew Poetics*, 55, 200, defines chiasmus as "inversions of position" and remarks that Lund "applies the term chiasmus to what today we call concentric structure." Schökel explains, "A *concentric* structure is one where words are repeated in inverse order on both sides of a central point. . . . Others see it as a kind of augmented chiasm" (p. 192, italics in original). His own examples of concentric structure include both odd- and even-numbered elements: ABC X CBA or ABCDDCBA. Blomberg (1989), "The Structure of 2 Corinthians 1–7," 6, treats both odd- and even-numbered patterns under the heading of chiasmus. Angelico-Salvatore Di Marco (1993), "Rhetoric and Hermeneutic—on a Rhetorical Pattern: Chiasmus and Circularity" in *Rhetoric and the New Testament: Essays from the 1992 Heidelberg Conference*, ed. Stanley E. Porter and Thomas H. Olbricht, Library of New Testament Studies (New York: Sheffield Academic, 1993), 479, laments the "lack of unanimity in terminology" and observes that the term "chiasmus"—which he describes as "(a-b-x-b-a, or, a-b-b-a)"—is "simpler" to use than "concentric structure." Watson (1994), *Traditional Techniques in Classical Hebrew Verse*, 367, notes that in considering chiasmus over longer passages, "a great deal of variety is possible and . . . the term 'chiastic' can be interpreted in quite different ways."

pivotal theme, about which the other propositions of a literary unit are developed."[227] Maintaining that the center may consist of one focal statement (e.g., ABCB′A′) or two—or more—parallel lines (e.g., ABB′A′), Breck claims that the pivot is the "essential characteristic of genuine chiasmus," and the best description of it is "concentric parallelism."[228] His definition of chiasm thus includes both odd- and even-numbered elements.

Some scholars have questioned the legitimacy of the entire enterprise of detecting a chiastic structure in a longer passage. Stanley Porter and Jeffrey Reed (1998) dismiss most of the guidelines and controls others have put forward to rein in the search for chiasm in every text.[229] Porter and Reed argue that "[b]ecause one cannot proffer macro-chiastic analyses recognized by the ancients," "the burden of proof, therefore, rests on those who claim that . . . [any ancient writing] is structured as a 'grand' or macro-chiasm."[230] The authors conclude that macro-chiasmus is "a problematic model" for literary analysis of any ancient text.[231] Despite their strong cautionary words, proposals for chiastic structures of biblical texts continue to abound.

Avoiding the term "chiasmus" altogether, Roland Meynet (2012) makes clear distinctions between three types of total symmetry in their simplest forms.

1. "*Parallel composition* [is the] bi-member segment with four terms equally spread out among the two members and in direct relation to them, according to the plan a b | a′b′"; (2) "*Mirror composition* [is the] bimember segment with four terms spread equally among the two members and in direct relation with them,

---

[227] Breck, *The Shape of Biblical Language*, 18. Italics in original.

[228] Breck, *The Shape of Biblical Language*, 19.

[229] Stanley E. Porter and Jeffrey T. Reed, "Philippians as a Macro-Chiasm and Its Exegetical Significance," *New Testament Studies* 44 (1998): 214–21.

[230] Porter and Reed, "Philippians as a Macro-Chiasm and Its Exegetical Significance," 222.

[231] Porter and Reed, "Philippians as a Macro-Chiasm and Its Exegetical Significance," 231. Against Porter and Reed, Di Marco, "Rhetoric and Hermeneutic—on a Rhetorical Pattern," 483, argues that "the same circular-concentric procedures" have been detected in recent and ancient extrabiblical literary works" as well as "in other arts and sciences." He further argues that because language circularity appears to be "a linguistic universal" (p. 485), it may be "*unconscious-implicit*"—and thus "more real precisely because it is unconscious" (p. 487, italics in original). Although Di Marco, p. 481, sees "a distinction between chiasmus-circularity in sentences or short compositions," he suggests "great structures in a whole work . . . might [also] be entirely structured in a concentric-circular way."

according to the plan a b | b′a′″"; and (3) *"Concentric composition* [is the] segment with five terms of which four correspond inversely according to the plan a b | x | b′a′."[232]

By definition, parallelism and mirror composition require an even number of units; whereas concentric composition requires an odd number of units. Although some scholars would label the last two terms as "chiasmus," Meynet distinguishes between the two.

Despite Meynet's careful definitions, his terminology has not convinced subsequent scholars. Brouwer (2018), for example, notes that chiasm most often contains a center, unparalleled element that expresses "the most significant idea intended by the author."[233] The term "chiasmus" appears to be both irrepressible and resistant to careful definition.

More important than assigning a label is determining how the structure functions. The central panel of the literary triptych in Habakkuk contains clear evidence of structural, verbal, and conceptual parallelism—the latter two being inverse. All of this serves to underscore the prominent position of the middle woe in Hab 2:12–14. These verses at the midpoint of the book contain multiple indicators that the passage is the theological key and the answer to the prophet's questions. According to Meynet's definitions, the middle panel is a concentric composition because it has an odd number of strophes: II:E:F:G:F′:E′. Because it exhibits concentric parallelism, according to Breck's definitions, it could also be called a chiasm. The middle woe serves as the crucial pivot that reveals the reason for the contrastive parallels between the two outer panels I:A:B:C:D // III:A′:B′:C′:D′. In the commentary sections that follow, the term "chiasm" will serve as a shorthand way of communicating the general understanding of a concentric parallelism with chiastic features.

Meynet illustrates the significance of concentric parallelism with an apt analogy, in which he compares concentricism to the central branch of the *men'ôrâ* lampstand described in Exodus 25—a candlestick with seven branches. He writes,

> Its heavier decoration is a sign of its importance. But it is not the decoration that performs the function of this central branch,

---

[232] Meynet, *Treatise on Biblical Rhetoric*, 130–31. Italics in original.
[233] Brouwer, "Understanding Chiasm," 100n.

it is the fact that the other branches "come out" "from" it, are attached to it. The central branch, therefore, . . . has an articulating function. That is what provides cohesion for everything and makes it a unique object, a unified whole. . . . The interpretation must start from there; at least, it is the thing on which it must concentrate its attention.[234]

The commentary that follows demonstrates that Hab 2:12–14 serves just such a central role in the structure and interpretation of the entire book.

6.2.5 Outline of Habakkuk

I.   Habakkuk's Dialogue with God (1:1–2:5)
     A. Habakkuk's First Complaint (1:2–4)
     B. God's First Response (1:5–11)
     C. Habakkuk's Second Complaint (1:12–17)
     D. God's Second Response (2:1–5)
     EXCURSUS 1: The New Testament Use of Habakkuk 2:4
II. God Pronounces Judgment on the Wicked (2:6–20)
     A. Woe 1 (2:6–8)
     B. Woe 2 (2:9–11)
     C. Woe 3 (2:12–14)
     D. Woe 4 (2:15–17)
     E. Woe 5 (2:18–20)
III. Habakkuk's Prayer (3:1–19)
     A. Habakkuk's Humble Petition (3:2)
     B. The Divine Warrior Arrives (3:3–7)
     C. The Divine Warrior Fights (3:8–15)
     D. Habakkuk's Joyful Submission (3:16–19)

7   HABAKKUK'S PLACE IN THE BOOK OF THE TWELVE

7.1   THE BOOK OF THE TWELVE

Early Hebrew and Greek manuscript evidence suggests by the close of the second century BC, the twelve books of the Minor Prophets may have been grouped together as the "Book of the Twelve" in the same order as the later Masoretic Text. Talmudic tradition seems to indicate

---

[234] Meynet, *Treatise on Biblical Rhetoric*, 350.

that the twelve books attained special status as both one volume and as separate books.[235] The Christian tradition reflects the same unique status of these prophetic books. Consistently grouping the Twelve together, Christians still numbered them as individual books.

The past few decades witnessed an outpouring of interest in the Book of the Twelve—both regarding the individual books and the collection as a whole.[236] Mark Boda observes that earlier studies focused on the development of the books, in particular exploring how the various layers were patched together by various redaction processes.[237] Later research focused on the unity of the Twelve and reading the books in view of their final literary form.[238] Since 2000, some suggest scholarly interest has shifted back again to redaction analyses.[239]

The entire premise that the Book of the Twelve is a book rather than a collection is not without its detractors. David Petersen prefers to refer to the Minor Prophets as a "thematized anthology" rather than a book.[240] Ehud ben Zvi argues strongly against the idea that collect-

---

[235] James Nogalski and Marvin A. Sweeney, eds. *Reading and Hearing the Book of the Twelve* (Atlanta: SBL Press, 2000), ix.

[236] For a survey of research on Habakkuk in the 1990s, see Dangl, "Habakkuk in Recent Research," 131–68. For a survey of research since 2000, see Barry A. Jones, "The Seventh-Century Prophets in Twenty-First Century Research," *Currents in Biblical Research* 14 (2016): 129–75. Jones observes "a broad and increasing pluralism of methods, goals, and outcomes" in the recent research on Nahum, Habakkuk, and Zephaniah. He therefore sees "consensus concerning methods and results" as "an increasingly remote goal" (p. 130).

[237] Mark J. Boda, *Exploring Zechariah: The Development of Zechariah and Its Role within the Twelve*, ANEM 16 (Atlanta: SBL Press, 2017), 193–94. For an example of this diachronic redaction approach, see James D. Nogalski, *Literary Precursors to the Book of the Twelve*, BZAW 217 (New York: de Gruyter, 1993). Nogalski conjectures that there are multiple redaction layers present in Habakkuk. In the initial dialogue section, for example, he proposes the existence of an original Wisdom literature layer questioning the prosperity of the wicked (1:2–4, 12a, 13–14, and 2:1–5a), which redactors expanded by adding commentary on the Babylonians (1:5–11, 12b, 15–17; 2:5b–6). See also James Nogalski, *Redactional Processes in the Book of the Twelve* BZAW 218 (Berlin: de Gruyter, 1993), 136–46.

[238] For examples of this synchronic approach, see Paul House, *The Unity of the Twelve* (Sheffield: Sheffield Academic, 1990); Terence Collins, "The Scroll of the Twelve," in *The Mantle of Elijah: The Redaction Criticism of the Prophetical Books*, BibSem 20 (Sheffield: JSOT Press, 1993), 59–87; Nogalski and Sweeney, *Reading and Hearing the Book of the Twelve*. See also James W. Watts and Paul R. House, eds., *Forming Prophetic Literature: Essays on Isaiah and the Twelve in Honor of John D. W. Watts*, JSOTSup 235 (Sheffield: Sheffield Academic, 1996).

[239] Jones, "The Seventh-Century Prophets in Twenty-first Century Research," 129. For Jones's own approach of using textual criticism to discover the literary history of the Twelve, see Barry Alan Jones, *The Formation of the Book of the Twelve: A Study in Text and Canon*, SBLDS 149 (Atlanta: Scholars Press, 1995).

[240] David L. Petersen, "A Book of the Twelve?" in *Reading and Hearing the Book of the Twelve*, ed. James D. Nogalski and Marvin A. Sweeney (Atlanta: SBL Press, 2000), 10.

ing these texts into one scroll produces a unified book. (1) Although other literary collections existed in ancient Israel, evidence falsifies the claim that the scroll must be read as a unit. (2) The lack of a fixed order of the twelve books raises questions about their being understood as a single literary work. (3) Although there are thematic links, allusions, and quotations in these books, the same also surface outside the Twelve in both other prophetic and nonprophetic texts. (4) The titles (superscriptions/incipits) of these twelve books place them on the same level as separate prophetic books, namely Isaiah, Jeremiah, and Ezekiel. (5) No heading or superscription introduces the Book of the Twelve as a unified literary unit.[241]

Even if one rejects the claim that the Book of the Twelve is a literary unit, the twelve books still may exhibit "a unity of a different nature." Ben Zvi explains:

> Rather than assuming a unified book that is read and redacted as such, it is perhaps better to focus on the common repertoire of a relatively small social group consisting of educated writers and readers within which and for which prophetic—and other "biblical"—books were written, at the very least in their present form. Such a focus is likely to uncover a (largely) shared discourse, a common linguistic heritage, implied "intertextuality," and shared literary/ideological tendencies.[242]

There are benefits in reading these twelve prophetic books both as individual books and as a plurality since together they trace the unfolding relationship between the Lord and Israel and her neighbors.[243]

The ordering of the twelve books raises a question about what factors played a role in their final arrangement. Although the order of the last six books of the Twelve is the same in both the Hebrew MT and the ancient Greek LXX, the sequence of the first six books is different.[244] Chronology accounts for the ordering of the six books whose

---

[241] Ehud ben Zvi, "Twelve Prophetic Books or 'The Twelve': A Few Preliminary Considerations" in *Forming Prophetic Literature: Essays on Isaiah and the Twelve in Honor of John D. W. Watts*, ed. James W. Watts and Paul R. House, JSOTSup 235 (Sheffield: Sheffield Academic, 1996), 130–38.

[242] ben Zvi, "Twelve Prophetic Books or 'The Twelve,'" 155.

[243] Christopher R. Seitz, *Prophecy and Hermeneutics: Toward a New Introduction to the Prophets* (Grand Rapids: Baker Academic, 2007), 214–16, lists several potential benefits of reading the Twelve as a whole.

[244] The LXX order of the first six books is Hosea, Amos, Micah, Joel, Obadiah, Jonah. The

superscriptions contain specific historical allusions: Hosea, Amos, Micah, Zephaniah, Haggai, and Zechariah. Within the Twelve, the books are arranged in approximate chronological groupings: eighth, seventh, and sixth centuries BC. Within the centuries, however, the order appears to be more fluid.[245] A chronological arrangement of the seventh-century prophets, for example, should be Nahum (c. 645 BC), Zephaniah (c. 625 BC), followed by Habakkuk (c. 609–605 BC).[246] Why, then, does the present order of both the MT and LXX place Habakkuk in the middle?

Other factors besides chronology may have influenced the order of Nahum-Habakkuk-Zephaniah. Petersen suggests the predominant theme of the Twelve is the "day of the Lord." He observes that more than just a phrase, "the day of Yahweh" [yôm Yahweh] is a liminal moment when Yahweh will act as regent, often in a military manner. The day is ambiguous; it can offer weal or woe, depending on the historical circumstance.[247] Although Habakkuk does not contain this exact phrase, in Hab 3:16 the prophet resolves to wait for the yôm ṣārâ, the "day of distress" coming upon the nation invading Judah. This is the same wording found in Nah 1:7–8: "The Lord is good, / a stronghold in a *day of distress*; / he cares for those who take refuge in him. / But he will completely destroy Nineveh / with an overwhelming flood, / and he will chase his enemies into darkness" (emphasis added). Both Nah 1:7 and Hab 3:16 come at the end of hymns that present Yahweh as a powerful, avenging Divine Warrior. Thus, the two hymns possibly form an inclusio bracketing the beginning of Nahum with the ending of Habakkuk. While some scholars interpret this as evidence of an editorial hand, it may simply be that the preexisting parallelism influenced the placement of Habakkuk after Nahum instead of Zephaniah. In fact, Zephaniah, which also opens with a similar theophanic

---

difference involves the placement of Joel, Obadiah, and Jonah. The length of the books may even have been a factor in the ordering of the LXX, as the first five books move from longest to shortest. See Petersen, "A Book of the Twelve?" 6, and Jones, *The Formation of the Book of the Twelve*, 2–13.

[245] Sweeney, "Sequence and Interpretation in the Book of the Twelve" in *Reading and Hearing the Book of the Twelve*, ed. James D. Nogalski and Marvin A. Sweeney (Atlanta: SBL Press, 2000), 62.

[246] Robertson, *The Books of Nahum, Habakkuk, and Zephaniah*, 29–30.

[247] Petersen, "A Book of the Twelve?" 9. Petersen also notes that ten of the twelve books include the phrase—the exceptions being Jonah and Nahum—but even then, the day is implicit in Nah 1:7.

poem, expands this anticipated "day of distress" awaiting Nineveh (Nah 1:7–8) and Babylon (Hab 3:16) to a "day of the Lord" (Zeph 1:7, 15), which brings judgment on a global scale that includes Jerusalem (Zeph 1:7–18). Certainly, all three of these seventh-century prophetic books share this common theme. Perhaps the "out of order" sequence of Nahum-Habakkuk-Zephaniah reflects the compiler's interest in showing God metes out judgment to Assyria, to Babylon, to the whole earth—including Jerusalem—before he graciously grants restoration.

Another possible factor in ordering is the thematic transition between the ending of Nahum (the destruction of Assyria) and the beginning of Habakkuk (the coming of Babylon). Nogalski includes the following catchwords among those that link Nah 3:1–19 and Hab 1:5–17: *nation, horse, horsemen, devour, captives, kings, fortress,* and *strength.* He believes these similarities demonstrate an intentional for-mulation of "a heightened parallel" between the vanquished Assyri-ans and the advancing Babylonians.[248] Though Nogalski's proposal is interesting, these similarities may well be attributed to the common theme of war in the ancient Near East rather than intentional editorial techniques. The shared military theme may have been a factor, how-ever, in the compiler's placement of Habakkuk just after Nahum.

7.2   THEMES SHARED BY HABAKKUK AND THE TWELVE

Habakkuk shares certain themes with other books in the anthology of the Twelve. First, in addition to sharing a historical setting in the seventh century BC, Nahum, Habakkuk, and Zephaniah display dra-matic coherence. Paul House suggests that "dramatic literary princi-ples may link [these] adjoining books."[249] He concludes his analysis of speech types in this group by noting these similarities: all three prophetic books use alternating speakers to present their message, verbal markers to underscore speeches, and similar patterns of divine-prophetic address.

Though Nahum and Zephaniah are more alike in their phrasing, two speech types are unique to the middle prophetic book. Habak-kuk questions God directly (1:2–3; 1:12–2:1) and praises God directly

---

[248] Nogalski, *Redactional Processes in the Book of the Twelve,* 147–48.
[249] Paul R. House, "Dramatic Coherence in Nahum, Habakkuk, and Zephaniah," in *Forming Prophetic Literature: Essays on Isaiah and the Twelve in Honor of John D. W. Watts,* ed. James W. Watts and Paul House (Sheffield: Sheffield Academic, 1996), 196.

(3:2–19).[250] The result of this dramatic interchange deepens the reader's understanding of God's character. He is regal, merciful, kind, just, wrathful, and forgiving. Though the Lord reveals his plans "alongside" his messengers Nahum and Zephaniah, he treats Habakkuk—though not his equal—as a "dialogue partner, even his intimate friend."[251] Even an initial reading of Habakkuk sounds rather like a play as one listens to the dialogue and follows the repeated directions of the Lord to "Look!" The unfolding drama invites the reader to understand God in a new light and to see himself in the prophet who moves from burdensome questions to profound faith.

Second, Habakkuk shares a "Call to Silence" with Zephaniah and Zechariah.[252] Although the message of Habakkuk is largely conveyed through dialogue between the prophet and the Lord, the theme of silence in Habakkuk starts as a whisper and slowly builds. The prophet laments the seeming silence of the Lord in the face of wickedness (Hab 1:13). Former victims wake up and find a voice to accuse those who plundered them (2:6–7). Mute, inanimate building stones and timbers testify against dishonest builders (2:11). In contrast, wood and stone idols remain speechless (2:18–19). In 2:20, however, the theme reaches a crescendo: "But the LORD is in his holy temple; / let the whole earth / be silent in his presence."

Most English translations do not convey the strength of the interjection which should carry imperatival force: "Keep quiet!" or "Silence!"[253] This Hb. word "*Has!*" is probably onomatopoeic, much like the English word "Hush!"[254] Six other passages where the same interjection appears call for silence before an important person (Moses, a king, the Lord) or a weighty event (the reading of the Law, disastrous judgment).[255] After the Lord calls for silence in Hab 2:20, the prophet speaks once more but only in reverent prayer and praise (Hab 3:2–19). Now it is the prophet who listens: "LORD, I have heard the report

---

[250] House, "Dramatic Coherence in Nahum, Habakkuk, and Zephaniah," 200–201.

[251] House, "Dramatic Coherence in Nahum, Habakkuk, and Zephaniah," 202–4.

[252] Mark J. Boda, "A Deafening Call to Silence: The Rhetorical 'End' of Human Address to the Deity in the Book of the Twelve," in *Exploring Zechariah: The Development of Zechariah and Its Role within the Twelve*. ANEM 16 (Atlanta: SBL Press, 2017), 193–217.

[253] *HALOT*, 253, describes it as an "order to keep sacred silence."

[254] BDB, 245.

[255] See Num 13:30; Judg 3:19; Zeph 1:7; Zech 2:13 in relation to persons and Neh 8:11; Amos 6:10 in relation to events. See John N. Oswalt, "הַס," *NIDOTTE* 1:1024.

about you; / Lord, I stand in awe of your deeds" (Hab 3:2); "I heard, and I trembled within; / my lips quivered at the sound" (Hab 3:16).

Boda has researched instances in the Twelve in which humans address God, either directly or indirectly.[256] He notes that following Habakkuk, "there is a paucity of direct human address to the deity in the remainder of the Book of the Twelve."[257] There is none in Zephaniah and Haggai. In Zechariah, the prophet speaks with angels to ask for clarification on the visions, but the only challenge to the Lord comes from an angel who asks, "How long?" (Zech 1:12). The indirect address to the Lord in Zech 11:5b is a flippant remark by abusive leaders, who inappropriately attribute their ill-gotten gains to God. Although Malachi frequently records humans speaking to God, Boda labels them as "inappropriate" challenges the Lord immediately refutes (Mal 1:2, 6–7; 2:14, 17; 3:7–8, 13).[258] Boda maintains the last four Minor Prophets contain few instances in which humans address God; those that do occur are all inappropriate, save one, which is actually spoken by the Lord himself.[259] Boda concludes the command to silence in Hab 2:20 results in a veritable cessation of human address to deity in the Book of the Twelve.

The Lord's "Call to Silence" in Hab 2:20 forcefully reverberates in the next two prophetic books, as well. After announcing judgment on those who worship idols, the Lord commands, "Be silent in the presence of the Lord God, / for the day of the Lord is near" (Zeph 1:7). When he proclaims that he will once more choose Jerusalem, the Lord declares, "Let all humanity be silent before the Lord, for from his holy dwelling he has roused himself" (Zech 2:13). Boda explains, "The reason for the silencing of human address is the enduring sin of the people and their lack of response to Yahweh's message to the people. This disqualifies both cries for help as well as theodicy."[260] These three calls for silence suppress all further human challenges that cast doubt on God's character and activity.

Although the reader might expect proper human address to the Lord to return in the postexilic prophets (Haggai-Malachi), it does

---

[256] Boda, "A Deafening Call to Silence," 193–217.

[257] Boda, "A Deafening Call to Silence," 210.

[258] Boda, "A Deafening Call to Silence," 214. One could make the case that the significant amount of backtalk contained in these verses lessens Boda's argument for "paucity of direct human address to the deity" in the books following Habakkuk.

[259] Boda, "A Deafening Call to Silence," 210–11.

[260] Boda, "A Deafening Call to Silence," 213.

not. As Malachi makes abundantly clear, the Lord has grown weary of the people's harsh words flung in his direction (Mal 2:17; 3:13). He does, however, overhear and remember the words spoken about him by those who rightly revere him (Mal 3:16–18). The MT placement of Malachi at the close of the Hebrew Bible effectively shuts down both inappropriate address to God and all prophetic communication.[261] Following the Book of the Twelve, centuries of silence pass before the heavens break open with the glorious angelic pronouncement concerning the Messiah's birth—"good news of great joy that will be for all the people" (Luke 2:10).[262]

Third, Habakkuk shares a unique symmetry with the book of Jonah.[263] Both prophets directly address the Lord and wrestle with theodicy. Jonah challenges God's concern for the evil Assyrians; Habakkuk cannot understand how God could use the wicked Babylonians to judge his own wayward people. Both books contrast worthless idols with the sovereign Lord who dwells in his holy temple. The sea plays a role in both books. The Lord causes a fish (*dāg*) to swallow (*bālaʿ*) Jonah, sparing him from the great depths (Jonah 1:17). Habakkuk accuses the Lord of allowing the wicked to swallow (*bālaʿ*) the righteous, whom he has made like the fish (*dāg*) of the sea to the delight of the Babylonian "fishermen" (Hab 1:13–14). Both prophets praise God with a psalm of thanksgiving in trying circumstances (Jonah from the belly of the fish; Habakkuk facing the prospect of an empty belly). Both psalms contain direct and indirect address to God, which may indicate liturgical use.[264]

These two prophetic books also display noticeable contrasts. Despite his ordeal, the prophet Jonah shows limited growth. Initially, he refused to proclaim judgment among the Assyrians. Even the prayerful penitence of the Gentile sailors failed to persuade the reluctant prophet that the people of Nineveh deserved an opportunity for mercy. Jonah sulked when the Ninevites repented, and the Lord spared

---

[261] Boda, "A Deafening Call to Silence," 200.

[262] Boda observes that the three commands to silence addressed to all peoples of the earth find their counterpart in three calls to joy addressed to the Daughter of Zion. See Zeph 3:14–15; Zech 2:10; 9:9. Ultimately, what makes both repentance and joy possible is the coming of the promised King. See Boda, "A Deafening Call to Silence," 214.

[263] Seitz, *Prophecy and Hermeneutics*, 242–44.

[264] The liturgical notations in Hab 3 are clear evidence of congregational use. James Limburg, *Jonah: A Commentary*, OTL (Louisville: John Knox, 1993), 64–66, maintains that the alternation between first- and second-person address to the deity in psalms also points to a liturgical use in a congregational setting.

the great city. The Lord's mercy toward his enemies made the sullen prophet "angry enough to die" (Jonah 4:9).[265] In contrast, Habakkuk's encounter with the Lord had a powerful impact on the prophet, who displayed transformation over the course of the book. His complaints shifted to resolute trust and rejoicing even as unimaginably difficult circumstances began to emerge on the horizon. Essentially, the two prophets posed mirror questions. Habakkuk asked, "Why do bad things happen to good people?" while Jonah wondered, "How can good things happen to bad people?" (Both questions are based on a sliding morality scale. The better question might be "How can a holy God extend mercy to any of us?") Jonah fumed at the answer he received; Habakkuk learned to trust. God's mission is far greater than either prophet could have imagined. The Lord's concern and salvation extend beyond the borders of Israel to the far ends of the earth.

Finally, several of the Minor Prophets share a common theme of agricultural fertility. For those living in an agrarian society in ancient Israel, life was closely tied to a short list of staple foods. For the Israelites these were the seven staples enumerated in Deut 8:8: wheat, barley, (grape)vines, figs, pomegranates, olive oil, and honey. Drought or war could quickly tip the fragile balance of life-sustaining harvests. This is particularly true of the unique geography of Israel. Unlike Egypt's Nile River or Mesopotamia's Tigris and Euphrates, Israel had no major river to rely on for irrigation in the hill country. God intentionally placed his people in a land that depended on regular rainfall and ultimately on the Lord to provide it. The cause and effect of rain and harvests relied on an underlying cause-and-effect pattern of obedience to God. Speaking through the prophets, the Lord declared that he was the source of their food supply, as well as the one who could withhold it.

Even a cursory reading of Hosea, the first of the Twelve, shows how central this theme is. The Lord, who had wed Israel to himself, accused her of spiritual adultery when she ran after other gods in search of food. Israel failed to recognize that it was the Lord "who

---

[265] Before judging Jonah too harshly, we should remember that unlike Habakkuk, Jonah had to offer his enemies mercy face-to-face. No doubt he would have preferred to proclaim imprecatory psalms rather than grace. When the Lord's stay of judgment on Nineveh expired, Nahum declared that the whole world would applaud the demise of the cruel Assyrians (Nah 3:19). Similarly, Habakkuk vowed to wait for "the day of distress" to come on the invading Babylonians in turn.

gave her **the grain, the new wine, and the fresh oil**" (Hb.: *dāgān, tīrôš, yiṣhār*; Hos 2:8).[266] He therefore declared, "I will take back my **grain** in its time / and my **new wine** in its season . . . / I will devastate her vines and fig trees" (Hos 2:9, 12). But once the relationship was restored, he promised, "I will respond to the sky, / and it will respond to the earth. / The earth will respond to **the grain, / the new wine, and the fresh oil**" (Hos 2:21–22). Despite God's promises, Israel continued to run after other gods: "They slash[ed] themselves for **grain and new wine**"; they refused to offer wine or bread to the Lord (Hos 7:14; 9:4). The Lord pronounced judgment against Israel. Even then, he begged them to repent and return. Once restored, "[t]he people will return and live beneath his shade. / They will grow grain / and blossom like the vine" (Hos 14:7). Hosea links agricultural fertility to God's engagement with Israel in terms of relationship, rebellion, rejection, and restoration.

The theme of agricultural abundance is not limited to Hosea. Joel also uses fertility imagery extensively, including similar terms: "grain, new wine, fresh oil."[267] This threefold phrase appears in Hag 1:11 as well. Although these Minor Prophets may have borrowed from one another, they may have used stock formulaic phrasing reflected in biblical texts outside of their ranks. The threefold list first appears in Num 18:12, in reverse order: "I am giving you [priests and Levites] all the best of the **fresh oil, new wine, and grain**, which the Israelites give to the LORD as their firstfruits."[268]

The same list occurs several times in Deuteronomy, in the same order as in Hosea, Joel, and Haggai. Like Hosea, Deuteronomy uses the language of agricultural fertility to describe God's engagement with Israel in terms of relationship, rebellion, rejection, and restoration. The first two instances fall in the context of covenantal relationship:

---

[266] Emphasis added to highlight the verbatim phrasing parallels both here and in the chart below: **grain, new wine, and fresh oil**. This survey of agricultural fertility language in the Book of the Twelve and in Deuteronomy is representative and not exhaustive.

[267] Nogalski, "Joel as the Literary Anchor for the Book of the Twelve," in *Reading and Hearing the Book of the Twelve*, ed. James D. Nogalski and Marvin A. Sweeney (Atlanta: SBL Press, 2000), 100, claims this wording may indicate "redactional implantation." Nogalski, *Redactional Processes*, 176–78, also argues that Hab 3:17 is a redactional insertion drawn from Joel 1–2.

[268] Two of these three catchwords also appear in Gen 27:28, where Isaac conferred on Jacob the blessing of abundant grain and new wine. See also Ps 4:7.

He will love you, bless you, and multiply you. He will bless your offspring, and the produce of your land—your **grain, new wine, and fresh oil** (Deut 7:13).

If you carefully obey my commands I am giving you today, to love the LORD your God and worship him with all your heart and all your soul, I will provide rain for your land in the proper time . . . and you will harvest your **grain, new wine, and fresh oil** (Deut 11:13–14).

The next three occurrences in Deuteronomy also are in the context of right relationship: eating the tithe of firstfruits before the Lord with rejoicing (Deut 12:17–18; 14:23, 26b) and providing sustenance for the Levites (Deut 18:4).[269]

Agricultural Motif in the Book of the Twelve and Deuteronomy			
RELATIONSHIP	REBELLION	REJECTION	RESTORATION
Hos 2:8; 11:4	Hos 2:5; 7:14; 13:6	Hos 2:9, 12; 8:7; 9:2, 4	Hos 2:14–15, 22; 14:4–7
		Joel 1:4–9; 10–12; 16–20	Joel 2:14, 18, 24; 3:18
	Amos 4:4–5; 6:4–6	Amos 4:6–9; 5:11, 22; 6:7; 7:1–2	Amos 9:13–14
	Mic 2:11; 3:3, 5	Mic 6:14–15	Mic 4:4
		Nah 2:2b	Nah 2:2a
		Hab 3:17	
		Zeph 1:13; 2:11	Zeph 2:7; 3:13
		Hag 1:6, 9–11; 2:16–19a	Hag 2:19b
	Zech 7:5–7	Zech 11:9	Zech 3:10; 8:12; 9:15–17; 10:1
	Mal 1:8, 12–14; 3:8	Mal 2:2–3	Mal 3:10–11
Deut 7:13; 11:14; 12:17–18; **14:23; 18:4**; 32:12–14	Deut 32:15, 38	**Deut 28:51**	Deut 30:9; 33:28

---

[269] The other OT occurrences of this threefold phrase describe usury assessments (Neh 5:11), provisions for Levites from tithes (Neh 10:37–39; 13:5, 12; 2 Chr 31:5), and the abundant riches the Lord gave to Hezekiah (2 Chr 32:28). Jeremiah 31:12 refers to grain, new wine, and fresh oil in the context of restoration.

A distinct shift to rebellion and rejection occurs in Deuteronomy 28, a passage outlining covenantal blessings and curses.[270] If the Israelites obeyed the Lord, he would abundantly bless their produce and livestock. If they disobeyed, however, the Lord would decimate their produce and livestock through disease, drought, pests, and marauding foreign invaders. Moses warned, "They will leave you no **grain, new wine, fresh oil**, young of your herds, or newborn of your flocks until they cause you to perish" (Deut 28:51). The purpose of this terrifying rejection was redemptive. If God's rebellious people returned with all their hearts and obeyed him, the Lord promised to make their offspring, livestock, and produce "prosper abundantly" (Deut 30:9). Deuteronomy closes with a preview of restoration: "So Israel dwells securely; / Jacob lives untroubled / in a land of grain and new wine; / even his skies drip with dew" (Deut 33:28). The twelve prophets were steeped in this rich tradition of biblical imagery highlighting their dependence on God even for their daily sustenance.

As the above chart shows, Habakkuk (in italics) is unique among the Twelve that contain imagery of agricultural fertility. All the Minor Prophets using this agricultural motif to express the people's relationship with God, their rebellion, and/or the Lord's redemptive rejection, also used it to point to the hope of the restoration. Habakkuk, however, did not. He alone used the agricultural motif only in terms of rejection. That is precisely what makes his statement in Hab 3:17–18 so powerful:

> Though the fig tree does not bud
> and there is no fruit on the vines,
> though the olive crop fails
> and the fields produce no food,
> though the flocks disappear from the pen
> and there are no herds in the stalls,
> yet I will celebrate in the LORD;
> I will rejoice in the God of my salvation!

Rather than reciting the list of grain, new wine, and fresh oil, Habakkuk worked through a more expansive list. He eliminated every possible source of food. Food was considered a reward for walking in

---

[270] Deuteronomy, the "rediscovered" book that impacted Josiah's reform, may have played a role in Habakkuk's understanding of covenantal blessings and curses.

right relationship with God (Deut 7:13; 11:14). God intended his people to share and enjoy it in his presence with rejoicing (Deut 12:17–18; 14:23, 26b). But Habakkuk clearly understood the implications of the advancing Babylonian army. He was familiar with the curses outlined in Deuteronomy. He knew impending disaster would leave his homeland thoroughly ravaged. There would likely be no food. The judgment incited by the wicked would fall on the righteous as well. Through the eyes of faith, however, the prophet was still able to trust and even rejoice in the Lord.

7.3   HABAKKUK'S PLACE IN THE PLOTLINE OF THE TWELVE

In his theology of God's character in the Book of the Twelve, House proposes a plotline that describes the overall unity of these diverse prophetic texts. He suggests the book's first readers must have recognized familiar themes took precedence over specific chronological sequence. According to his analysis, the first six prophetic books (Hosea, Joel, Amos, Obadiah, Jonah, Micah) focus on warning; the next three (Nahum, Habakkuk, Zephaniah), on judgment; and the final grouping (Haggai, Zechariah, Malachi), on renewal.[271] The conflict that plays out in the Twelve concerns God's goal "to forge Israel into a faithful nation" and secondarily, "to redeem all the peoples of the world."[272]

House further describes the plotline of the Book of the Twelve as a "U-shaped comic framework."[273] He takes his cue for this structure from Northrop Frye's literary analysis of the Bible:

> Prophecy in the Bible is a comprehensive view of the human situation, surveying it from creation to final deliverance . . . . [T]he prophet sees man in a state of alienation caused by his own distractions, at the bottom of a U-shaped curve. . . . It postulates an original state of relative happiness, and looks forward to an eventual restoration of this state, to, at least, a "saving remnant."[274]

---

[271] Paul R. House, "The Character of God in the Book of the Twelve," in *Reading and Hearing the Book of the Twelve*, ed. James D. Nogalski and Marvin A. Sweeney (Atlanta: SBL Press, 2000), 126–27.

[272] House, *The Unity of the Twelve*, 117–18.

[273] House, *The Unity of the Twelve*, 123.

[274] Northrop Frye, *The Great Code: The Bible and Literature* (New York: Harcourt Brace Jovanovich, 1982), 128–29.

Frye explains,

> This U-shaped pattern . . . recurs in literature as the standard shape of comedy, where a series of misfortunes and misunderstandings brings the action to a threateningly low point, after which some fortunate twist in the plot sends the conclusion up to a happy ending. The entire Bible, viewed as a "divine comedy," is contained within a U-shaped story of this sort"[275]

Although Frye's explanation of this literary term makes sense, in reference to the Bible or prophetic literature in particular, "comedy" or "comic" sounds jarringly alien. Perhaps "optimistic" is a more appropriate term to describe this U-shaped structure.[276] In contrast to the pessimistic downward trajectory of tragedy, House's proposed plotline of the Book of the Twelve is optimistic because of its final upward sweep: the promise and hope of a restored remnant.

The first six of the Twelve form the initial downward descent of the U. They make clear that "God's dispute with Israel comes, not because of a single transgression, but because of a long-term, deep-seated rejection of Yahweh's person and covenant."[277] Although these six prophecies warn of punishment for sin, "Nahum, Habakkuk, and Zephaniah move beyond the description of sin to specific threats about the coming Day of the LORD."[278] Nahum announces Assyria's annihilation; Habakkuk records both the Babylonians' appointment to conquer Judah and their subsequent demise. The reader of the Twelve is left with an unsettling question: Is the Lord's concern for all nations—including his own people—utterly exhausted? House observes, "Habakkuk marks the apex of the conflict between the Lord and the world. If no further word comes, the final decision of God is

---

[275] Frye, *The Great Code*, 169.

[276] Yair Zakovitch, "∩ and U in the Bible," in *Tragedy and Comedy in the Bible*, Semeia 32 (Decatur, GA: Scholars Press/SBL, 1984), 113–14. Because of the historical nature of the Book of the Twelve, Donald K. Berry, "Malachi's Dual Design: The Close of the Canon and What Comes Afterward," in *Forming Prophetic Literature: Essays on Isaiah and the Twelve in Honor of John D. W. Watts*, ed. James W. Watts and Paul House (Sheffield: Sheffield Academic, 1996), 300, prefers to describe it as an "open-ended epic" rather than a comedy or tragedy. Although this characterization avoids the awkwardness of applying Greek dramatic terms to the Bible, "epic" loses the U-shape altogether.

[277] House, *The Unity of the Twelve*, 118.

[278] House, "The Character of God in the Book of the Twelve," 129.

to totally devastate the universe."[279] According to House, Habakkuk concludes with the tension unresolved.

Following Habakkuk, Zephaniah completes the U-turn and "begins the journey upwards."[280] Although the book of Zephaniah opens with a prophecy of horrifying judgment on a global scale (1:2–18), it concludes with a vision of a glorious future where both the Lord and his restored remnant rejoice in each other with singing (3:9–20). Zephaniah declares that a "multinational remnant of faithful persons" will remain "to serve the Creator and to inherit blessings."[281] This promise hints at the dénouement that plays out in the final three of the Twelve.[282] Perhaps this concluding upswing explains why Zephaniah follows Habakkuk because it anticipates the remnant's physical return to Jerusalem, the setting of Haggai-Malachi.

The change in chronological order for thematic purposes places Habakkuk in the unique position at the bottom of the proposed U-shaped plotline of the Twelve.[283] But Habakkuk is not without hope. House makes the following observation about Hab 2:12–14, the passage I labeled as a chiastic pivot in the center of Habakkuk:

> In many respects Hab 2.12–14 provides the climax of Hosea-Habakkuk. First, 2.12 proclaims the fate of all who attempt to abuse others (cf. Amos 1.3–2.3) to achieve their own wicked goals, which summarizes the concerns of Hosea, Amos, etc. Second, 2.13 demonstrates the sovereignty of God over the whole process of sin, punishment, and restoration described in the Twelve. Despite all the nations have done to rebel against Yahweh, their rebellion amounts to a mere useless exhaustion of energy. God can and will punish those who exalt themselves against their Lord. Third, 2.14 explains the purpose and end result of all Yahweh's work in creation. What is sin but the rejection of the knowledge of God (cf. Hos. 4.6)? Punishment results from a struggle against God's reign, and restoration remains the ultimate result of all Yahweh's efforts.

---

[279] House, *The Unity of the Twelve*, 119. Perhaps "nadir" would be a better fit than "apex."

[280] House, *The Unity of the Twelve*, 151.

[281] House, "The Character of God in the Book of the Twelve," 129.

[282] House, *The Unity of the Twelve*, 119.

[283] The discussion of Habakkuk's unique place in the above chart lends credence to his observation. Of all the Minor Prophets who describe God's judgment and rejection of his people in terms of agricultural demise, Habakkuk alone does not also describe the restoration in terms of abundant fruitfulness.

Renewal is as inevitable a result of punishment as punishment is of sin. Here the whole message of the Twelve hangs in the balance.[284]

These prophetic verses serve not only as the chiastic center within the book of Habakkuk itself, but—according to House—they also capsulize the U-turn in the Book of the Twelve.

House's proposed plotline for the Book of the Twelve is intriguing, but it also raises some questions. As others have noted, his plotline can seem oversimplistic since individual books on both sides of the U contain pronouncements of sin, judgment, and restoration at the same time.[285] The overall U-shape of the Twelve appears convincing enough until the postexilic prophets reveal a strong undertow pulling toward the same sinful practices that resulted in the destruction of Jerusalem and the exile. Malachi is anything but a comic, happy ending as evidenced by the stubborn taproot of sin and the people's shocking backtalk to God. The Book of the Twelve—and the English OT—ends on a somber note with the threat of a curse (Mal 4:6). Although the exile preserved a remnant who returned and restored Jerusalem, it failed to transform the people and achieve the glorious restoration envisioned by the prophets.

A better solution understands the place of Habakkuk and the Twelve in the metanarrative of the Bible. Habakkuk 2:12–14 anticipates the upswing of not only the Minor Prophets but also the marvelous conclusion of the entire Bible and the fulfillment of God's mission—the global kingdom hinted at in 2:14.

8 HABAKKUK'S PLACE IN THE CANON

Although the Book of the Twelve may not have an intentionally developed, unified plotline, the structure follows an "implied narrative."[286] The books in this prophetic collection reflect the overarching plotline of the entire Bible from Genesis to Revelation. This prophetic section of the history of Israel is part of a larger story that moves forward

---

[284] House, *The Unity of the Twelve*, 146–47.

[285] For example, Petersen, "A Book of the Twelve?" 9; Aaron Schart, "Reconstructing the Redaction History of the Twelve Prophets: Problems and Models," in *Reading and Hearing the Book of the Twelve*, ed. James D. Nogalski and Marvin A. Sweeney (Atlanta: SBL Press, 2000), 38–39.

[286] Norman K. Gottwald, "Tragedy and Comedy in the Latter Prophets," in *Tragedy and Comedy in the Bible, Semeia* 32 (Decatur, GA: Scholars Press/SBL, 1984), 83.

according to the purposes of God. A number of biblical-theological scholars communicate the Bible's storyline in four acts: Creation, Fall, Redemption, and Restoration.[287]

8.1 THE FOURFOLD BIBLICAL PLOTLINE

The description in Hab 2:14 expresses God's goal from the beginning of creation. The *missio Dei* lies in the nexus of God, people, and place, and the first time these three converge is in the garden of Eden. In the first recorded words spoken to humans, God gave the "first 'Great Commission.'"[288] He commanded Adam and Eve to "be fruitful" and "multiply" and "fill the earth" with image bearers, who would "rule" as his representatives (Gen 1:27–28). These worshipers were to walk with the Lord and cover the earth with his praises. The original garden sanctuary would expand until the entire earth became a sanctuary—God's dwelling place—enveloped in the glory of God.[289]

Habakkuk 2:14 beautifully articulates God's mission statement that awareness of his glory will fill every person and every place: "For the earth will be filled with the knowledge of the LORD's glory, as the water covers the sea." Habakkuk spliced together two concepts in this verse. The first describes the glory of God's most holy presence, as in the seraph song of Isa 6:3: "Holy, holy, holy is the LORD Almighty; / the whole earth is full of his glory" (NIV). The second is in Isa 11:9: "[T]he earth will be filled with the knowledge of the LORD / as the waters cover the sea" (NIV).[290] Although the whole earth is presently filled to some degree with the glory of God, not everyone recognizes or even acknowledges the Lord. One day, however, the world will be filled with those who know him. By weaving these two concepts together, Habakkuk added something significant. On that day, the

---

[287] Bruce Riley Ashford and David P. Nelson, for example, expound these four plot movements in "The Story of Mission: The Grand Biblical Narrative," in *Theology and Practice of Mission: God, the Church, and the Nations*, ed. Bruce Riley Ashford (Nashville: B&H, 2011), 7–16. Several other contributors to this volume also use the same fourfold framework as the outline of various missional topics.

[288] G. K. Beale, *The Temple and the Church's Mission: A Biblical Theology of the Dwelling Place of God*, ed. D. A. Carson, New Studies in Biblical Theology 17 (Downers Grove: InterVarsity, 2004), 117.

[289] For graphic diagrams illustrating each of the stages of the fourfold biblical plotline, see Susan Maxwell Booth, *The Tabernacling Presence of God: Mission and Gospel Witness* (Eugene: Wipf & Stock, 2015), 231–33.

[290] See also Num 14:21; Ps 72:19.

world will overflow with the knowledge of the unmediated glory of God, and all its inhabitants will live life awash in an ocean of his most holy presence.

With the advent of the fall, however, humanity veered off course. Adam and Eve welcomed sin into the world, and the consequences were catastrophic. Relationships between God, people, and place were irrevocably broken as a result of their rebellion. The Lord evicted the couple and their descendants from his unmediated presence. Spiritual and physical death have plagued every generation since.

As the OT narrative documents, the fall of humanity was not a freefall. God continually intervened as his original mission shifted to a rescue mission. Ironically, the means to the rescue is the same as the end goal: God's dwelling among his people, his mediated presence made manifest in the holy of holies. At Sinai, for example, God took up residence in the tabernacle, filling it with his glory. Later the Lord took up residence in the temple, filling it with his glory. Tragically, however, the Israelites became like the world around them instead of becoming like the Lord who placed his sanctuary in their midst.

Habakkuk's context reflects the tragic consequences of the fall in nearly every line of the first two chapters. The prophet cried out in anguish over the violence, oppression, wrongdoing, conflict, and strife among his own people (1:2–4). The descriptions of the Babylonians revealed their callous cruelty, exposed their hidden sins, and mocked their idolatry (1:6–11, 13–17; 2:4–20). Yet God announced he would use the Babylonians to judge his own people before judging this pagan nation (1:5–6a). Habakkuk could not suppress his surprise that the Lord would use such a wicked nation to do his work (1:13).

The prophet had cause to be concerned. If the Babylonians besieged Jerusalem and destroyed the temple, it would spell disaster for God's mission. But Hab 2:14 showed the prophet that nothing can stop the mission of God—not Assyria, not Babylon, not even the waywardness of God's own people (cf. 1 Sam 2:10; Ps 2). Many years before, Micah pronounced the destruction of Jerusalem and the temple—a message Jeremiah reiterated to Habakkuk's generation (Mic 3:12; Jer 26:6–9, 18). The Babylonians' efforts to carve out an empire were merely fuel for the fire (Hab 2:13). These pagan troops were an instrument in God's hand; the destruction of the temple and exile were next steps in God's mission. He would use the Babylonians to preserve a remnant of his people, through whom he would bring the promised Messiah.

Even so, neither the return from exile nor the rebuilt temple altered the downward trajectory of the OT plotline.

God promised to send a deliverer who would rescue people from their sin on account of his great love. Beginning with Gen 3:15, murmurs of a Messiah echo throughout the OT, increasing in volume in the prophetic books.[291] Although Habakkuk does not contain a specific prophecy concerning the coming Messiah, the theophany of chap. 3 contains a purpose statement for the Divine Warrior's appearance: "You come out to save your people, / to save your anointed. / You crush the leader of the house of the wicked / and strip him from foot to neck" (Hab 3:13). The word "anointed" (Hb. *māšîaḥ*) in this context likely refers to the Davidic king of Judah (cf. 1 Sam 2:10; Ps 2:2; 28:8). Even so, the reference recalls the promised deliverer who would come through David's lineage. Willem VanGemeren points out other messianic hints in chap. 3. He says,

> The hymn of Habakkuk is a celebration of the power, glory, and victorious nature of our God. His are the "victorious chariots" (3:8; lit. "chariots of salvation," *yᵊšûʿâ*), and his is the deliverance (*yēšaʿ*, v. 13, 2x; NIV "deliver . . . save") of his "messianic" community (NIV "anointed one," v. 13; Ps. 28:8). He is their Savior (3:18; lit. "the God of my salvation," *yišʿî*).[292]

Although these verses respond to Habakkuk's cry for salvation in 1:2, the NT believer cannot help but hear faint salvific echoes of the one whose name in Hebrew is *Yeshua*: "He will save." Only in the NT does the extent of God's rescue mission become clear. Yeshua, Jesus, is the "Coming One," the deliverer through whom God is reconciling both people and place to himself.

This story of redemption spans the bulk of Scripture, from Genesis 3 all the way to the end of Revelation. Habakkuk could not have dreamed it, but God the Son stepped into human flesh in order to dwell

---

[291] Sidney Greidanus, *Preaching Christ from the Old Testament: A Contemporary Hermeneutical Method* (Grand Rapids: Eerdmans, 1999), 248, observes that as early as the third century BC, the Septuagint and Jewish Targums understood Gen 3:15 as a reference to the coming messianic victory over Satan. Fuhr and Yates, *The Message of the Twelve*, 58, identify the key messianic texts in the Book of the Twelve as Hos 3:5; Amos 9:11–15; Mic 5:2–6; Hag 2:20–23; and Zech 3:8–10; 6:10–15; 9:9–10; 12:8–14.

[292] Willem A. VanGemeren, *Interpreting the Prophetic Word: An Introduction to the Prophetic Literature of the Old Testament* (Grand Rapids: Zondervan, 1990), 172–73.

among his people, revealing the glory of God the Father. Jesus Christ is the true sanctuary, the meeting place between God and humanity that the former tabernacle and temple merely anticipated (John 1:14, 18; 2:19–22). He is the once-for-all sacrifice, "the Lamb of God, who takes away the sin of the world" (Heb 10:10; John 1:29). Through Christ's death, burial, and resurrection, God made a way for forgiven sinners to enter into the most holy presence of God. Joel's prophecy was fulfilled: God began pouring out his Spirit on all kinds of people who call upon the name of the Lord (Joel 2:28–32). These believers, incorporated in Christ, are themselves now the temple—the dwelling place of God—as they glorify God in their lives and worship (1 Cor 6:19–20; 2 Cor 6:16–18). The indwelling Spirit enables them to fulfill the second Great Commission: making "disciples of all nations" (Matt 28:19–20). As a result of the expanding church, the knowledge of the glory of the Lord is increasing over the earth, a preview of the eventual fulfillment of Hab 2:14.[293]

The final element of the biblical plotline is restoration. On the last day, Jesus will return as the King of glory. He will crush the head "of the house of the wicked," and he will "save [his] people" and restore both heaven and earth (Hab 3:13). The new creation will be a sanctuary where God's most holy presence fills both people and place. God's dwelling will be with his people for all eternity, and the knowledge of his glory will fill the earth—every compass point and every human heart—"as the waters cover the sea"—just as Habakkuk foretold (Hab 2:14; cf. 3:3b).

Although Habakkuk longed for a historical deliverance from Babylon, his psalm in chap. 3 anticipates God's ultimate eschatological deliverance of the true remnant.[294] Habakkuk's theophanic vision provides a glimpse of God's glory as the Divine Warrior Incarnate exerts his dominion over the world. He stands and shakes the earth; he marches across the land and tramples down the nations; he treads upon the sea. The Lord reclaims the high places littered with pagan altars and Asherah poles, pathetic human attempts staking a claim for gods made in their own image. This terrain will now be under his firm control. The God of glory makes Habakkuk's feet "like those of a deer," enabling him "to walk on" the heights as well (v. 19). The humbled

---

[293] See also 2 Cor 4:4, 6.
[294] Daniel C. Timmer, "The Twelve," in *A Biblical-Theological Introduction to the Old Testament: The Gospel Promised*, ed. Miles V. Van Pelt (Wheaton: Crossway, 2016), 331–32.

prophet is confused no more. Even if the coming Babylonians destroy everything—and they will—the God of glory is with him. Despite his circumstances, Habakkuk worships. He says, "I will celebrate in the LORD; I will rejoice in the God of my salvation" (Hab 3:18).

Revelation 7:9 shows that among the vast multitude of worshipers gathered before the Lamb will be people representing every tongue and tribe and nation—including Chaldeans/Babylonians (Hab 1:6) from across the ages. Abraham who hailed from "Ur of the Chaldeans" (Gen 15:7), will join the magi who knelt before the infant Jesus (Matt 2:1–12; cf. Dan 5:7–12), alongside twenty-first-century believers from Iraq and Iran. All will bow before the Lord of glory. God's mission is much bigger than propping up the struggling nation of Judah. It was beyond the ability of his prophet to fathom. Habakkuk spoke more than he knew. The Lord of Armies is redeeming the cosmos.

8.2   THE SHAPE OF THE BIBLICAL PLOTLINE

Since the days of Aristotle's *Poetics*, scholars have sought to analyze the structure of dramatic narratives. Figure 2 below depicts a common version of a narrative plotline.[295] Figure 3 below flips this familiar pyramid on its head to yield the V-shaped plotline that more closely resembles the overarching plotline of the biblical story.

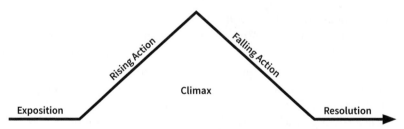

Figure 2: The Shape of Most Narratives

---

[295] This figure is a simplified version of a plotline pyramid developed by Gustav Freytag in 1896, based on Aristotle's work on tragedies. See *Freytag's Technique of Drama: An Exposition of Dramatic Composition and Art*, trans. Elias J. MacEwan, Classic Reprint Series, 2nd ed. (London: Forgotten Books: 2017), 114–15.

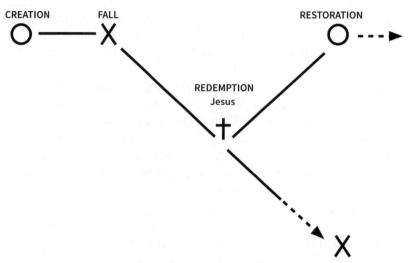

Figure 3: The Shape of the Biblical Narrative

The creation narrative in Genesis 1–2 introduces this setting: God, people, and place in perfect "peace" (Hb. *shālôm*), represented by the circle. The rebellion of Genesis 3, represented by the X, plunges all creation on a downward trajectory that nothing seems able to alter: neither tabernacle nor temple, neither exile nor return of a remnant. Only in the NT does the plotline of the Bible make an abrupt V-turn at the cross.[296] The atoning death and resurrection of the promised Messiah, the incarnate Son of God, make the redemption and restoration of all creation possible. When Christ returns and restores all things, the plotline has a grand and glorious ending, which, ironically, is only just the beginning. By virtue of God's mission to redeem his creation, the entire Bible reflects the same optimistic upswing that shapes the overall "comedic" tone of the prophetic collection.

Nevertheless, the narrative of Scripture does not have a "happily ever after" ending for everyone. As Habakkuk and the rest of the Twelve indicate, two endings are depicted in the overall biblical narrative. By the close of Habakkuk, the prophet recognized despite his former misgivings (1:2–4, 13), that the Lord would defeat the wicked and deliver those who belong to him (2:4, 2:13–14; 3:13). Malachi's

---

[296] This abrupt turn explains why the biblical plotline more closely resembles a V-shape rather than the U-shaped plotline proposed by House, *The Unity of the Twelve*, 123.

description of how God distinguishes between the wicked and the righteous has even clearer eschatological overtones:

> For look, the day is coming, burning like a furnace, when all the arrogant and everyone who commits wickedness will become stubble. The coming day will consume them . . . not leaving them root or branches. But for you who fear [God's] name, the sun of righteousness will rise with healing in its wings, and you will go out and playfully jump like calves from the stall. You will trample the wicked, for they will be ashes under the soles of your feet on the day [God is] preparing. (Mal 4:1–3)

These OT prophetic passages foreshadow NT teaching. Although God will welcome the righteous home into his presence in the new heaven and earth, he will cast the wicked into outer darkness and eternal destruction away from his presence—as represented by the second X in the biblical narrative graphic (Matt 22:13; 2 Thess 1:9).

More than resembling a U or even a V, the biblical plotline is actually Y-shaped, with dual outcomes. The chiasmus of Habakkuk reflects this duality as well:

> Is it not from the LORD of Armies
> that the peoples labor only to fuel the fire
> and countries exhaust themselves for nothing?
> For the earth will be filled
> with the knowledge of the LORD's glory,
> as the water covers the sea. (Hab 2:13–14)

In the end, God's perfect justice is served. Those who refuse to acknowledge God and only serve their own desires will face a just outcome—albeit one tragic for them. Nevertheless, the Bible is not a tragedy. It is more like a movie in which the conquering superhero defeats the enemy and restores peace. No critic would label a movie a tragedy simply because its "bad guy" received a just sentence.

The Lord answers Habakkuk's prayer: in wrath, he remembers mercy (Hab 3:2). He sets all things right by punishing abuse, oppression, and injustice. He conquers humanity's ancient foe and slays death forevermore. For believers, he dries every tear; he erases sin and sorrow, grief and pain. One look at the King transforms his redeemed people into the image of the Son (see 1 John 3:2). Best of all, the Lord welcomes them home to a new heaven and earth overflowing with the glory of the Lord as the waters cover the sea.

When we view the plotline chronologically, Habakkuk is situated to the left of the cross. The prophet looked around him and saw evidence of a world out of control, plummeting toward certain judgment. At the same time, through prophetic revelation, Habakkuk was able to catch a glimpse of righteous judgment, deliverance, and restoration. What he saw through the eyes of faith reframed his perspective and gave him courage to trust and praise God amid his dismal circumstances.

Though the biblical plotline follows the story of Israel and her neighbors, it also traces the outline of all human history. This is our story. Unlike Habakkuk, today's generation is situated to the right of the cross, somewhere along the dashes of the descending "broken" arrow. At the same time, believers who have made that V-turn (by repentance and faith) are in Christ, on the ascending arrow. In other words, we are living life in the middle, a challenging place to be. Pressing in on every side is a broken world on a collision course with judgment. In contrast to Habakkuk, believers today have much more of the story in view, including a clearer glimpse of its glorious ending. Following the prophet's example, we need to allow that vision to reframe our perspective on our present circumstances through the eyes of faith.

The prophet Habakkuk stands as an excellent model of what that persevering faith looks like in real life. His message inspires believers living in the middle to stand in awe before a holy God and trust in his sovereign purposes, to praise him even in the face of suffering, to wait for him and walk in his strength. The author of Hebrews also looked to Habakkuk to encourage his readers facing persecution:

> For yet in a very little while,
> the Coming One will come and not delay.
> But my righteous one will live by faith;
> and if he draws back,
> I have no pleasure in him.
> But we are not those who draw back and are destroyed, but those who have faith and are saved. (Heb 10:37–38)

Until that day comes, the righteous have a reason for their faith. It rests in a God who will accomplish his mission to flood the whole earth with knowledge of his glory.

9 A THEOLOGICAL ALTARPIECE

The vivid imagery of Habakkuk makes it easy to conceive of the book as not only a literary triptych[297] but also a painted, three-paneled altarpiece that those that played a central role in churches of the Middle Ages. This metaphor helps us trace the theology of Habakkuk as it develops through these unfolding scenes.

9.1 PANEL I: THEODICY

The Revelation of God

Imagine what seems only a heavy wooden panel on the left of our altarpiece swings open on its hinges, revealing four paintings on its other side; hanging beneath them are these carefully lettered words: "The pronouncement that the prophet Habakkuk saw" (superscription, 1:1). The Lord is a God who reveals himself and his ways. The four paintings beneath this title illustrate a theodicy—the prophet's struggle to understand the justice of God in view of his circumstances.

1. The Seeming Inactivity of God in View of Human Depravity

The first painted scene (I:A, 1:2–4) presents the prophet on his knees, plagued by the injustices of his fellow citizens, agonizing over God's silence and inaction. He complains: "Because the wicked restrict the righteous, justice comes out crooked!" Habakkuk is all too aware of the fallen nature of humanity.

2. The Sovereignty of God over the Nations

Although God may seem absent, he hears his people's prayers and sees the evil of their days. In the second painting (I:B, 1:5–11), the Lord instructs the prophet to look at the nations and behold how he is already at work. The scene portrays a divine deed the prophet and his contemporaries will find hard to believe. The Lord has summoned the Babylonians, who march relentlessly across open plains toward

---

[297] See 6.2.4: "Habakkuk as a Literary Triptych."

Jerusalem. God knows the inner thoughts of this arrogant army. Bent on violence, they plan to erect siege ramps. Though they boast in their own strength as their god, they are clueless. They are agents of a sovereign God who rules over the nations and directs them to fulfill his purposes.

3. The Character of God and the Problem of Evil

The prophet falls back on what he knows of God in painting three (I:C, 1:12–17). The Lord is eternal, yet he is personal—a Rock to his people. He is a covenant-keeping God. God's holiness means he cannot tolerate wrongdoing; he is too pure to look at evil. The prophet is incredulous, asking, Why does God tolerate the treacherous? How can he remain silent when the wicked swallow up those more righteous than they? Based on his comments in vv. 4 and 13, he includes himself among those who are righteous. Habakkuk describes the actions of the Babylonians in the third scene: masters of the sea, they pull up leaderless human "fish" with hooks and nets, rejoicing in their bountiful catch, offering pagan sacrifices to ensure ongoing success. Habakkuk cries out in consternation: "Will God allow this evil to go on unchecked forever?"

4. The Response of God to the Wicked and the Righteous

In the fourth painting (I:D, 2:1–5), the prophet mounts his guard post, determined to see how the Lord responds to his complaint. God graciously condescends to answer the prophet, revealing his plans for the future. He commands him to wait for a vision of the end that will eventually come. He instructs the prophet to record it carefully on tablets so that others may read it as well. He offers Habakkuk a preview: The arrogant will falter and perish, but those made righteous by faith will live. The first panel incorporates the portrait of a person who surely fits Habakkuk's profile of the wicked. Guzzling wine, the swollen man tries to satiate his enlarged appetite with all the nations and all the peoples he can gather, but he is never satisfied. Ironically, he is just as ravenous as Sheol and Death, who will eventually consume him. Notably, the scene offers no corresponding depiction of someone who fits the profile of a righteous man.

9.2 PANEL II: JUDGMENT

1. God Must Address the Universal Injury of Sin

The central panel reveals a series of five paintings that demonstrate, contrary to the prophet's accusation, the Lord will not allow sin to go unpunished. God is just, and in each scene he metes out justice with a pronouncement of woe on the wicked. In the center of the first painting here (II:E, 2:6–7) stands a man laden down with plunder and spoils from all the nations and peoples he has subdued. His victims suddenly awake and arise, reversing the tables to plunder him. An uproar erupts as the peoples and nations accuse the plunderer with taunts, mockery, and riddles. God hears the cries of the victims of injustice; he takes up their cause and confronts their oppressors. Woe will come to the plunderer.

An engraved plate beneath the first painting lists the charges against the wicked: "[B]ecause of human bloodshed and violence against lands, cities, and all who live in them" (2:8). God keeps a record of humanity's sins. The wicked transgress against both people and place.

2. The Sinner Cannot Hide from God

The subject of the second painting (II:F, 2:9–11) is a magnificent house set high on a ridge, supposedly out of the reach of retribution. Nevertheless, its builder, who wiped out many peoples to gain his wealth, cannot escape judgment. The stones and rafters of his refuge will testify against him. His blueprints for safety turn out to be house plans for shame; the wicked cannot hide their sin from God or escape his justice. Woe will come to the one who profits at others' expense.

3. The Dual Destinies of Humanity

The middle painting (II:G, 2:12–14) depicts not just one house but a whole city full of houses painted in dark red hues. Woe will come to the one who builds with bloodshed. The Lord announces, "Is it not [behold!] from the LORD of Armies / that the peoples labor only to fuel the fire / and countries exhaust themselves for nothing?" (2:13). One day the works of the wicked, and ultimately the wicked themselves, will be fuel for judgment fire. Sin always brings judgment, and the Lord of heaven's armies will not fail to administer justice. In the bottom half of the painting, just beneath the city of blood, billowing waves of translucent gold begin to rise. The Lord proclaims the final outcome: "For the earth will be filled / with the knowledge of the LORD's glory, / as the water covers the sea" (2:14). Following the great conflagration, a restored earth will be flooded with the knowledge of the glory of God. This is the essence of God's mission from the beginning. The earth will be a global sanctuary where God dwells among his redeemed people from every tongue and tribe and nation. They will know him and rejoice in his glory. Nothing can thwart the fulfillment of God's mission, not even humanity's darkest sins.

Significantly, the tone of the entire triptych shifts in the middle of this scene. In contrast to the darkness of the first half of the triptych, the second half is suddenly suffused with light. Though the paintings that follow retain dark hues of judgment, the glorious light that emanates from the centermost picture appears to spill over. Up until 2:14, the triptych depicts the prophet's attempt to understand God's activity in the world from a human perspective. From this point on, however, the triptych reveals an understanding of God's activity in the world from heaven's perspective.

4. God Will Expose the Sinner

The setting of the fourth painting (II:F′, 2:15–16) depicts an opulent residence similar to the one in the second painting. This owner intends to use his house as a trap, getting his neighbors drunk so he can exploit them for his own despicable perversions. Nevertheless, God knows, and the Lord will snuff out the man's glory and cover him with disgrace. Woe will come to the predator who exploits his neighbors' vulnerability. The host will himself be exposed and forced to drink the bitter cup of judgment from the Lord's own right hand.

Under the fourth painting, a second engraved plate repeats the former charges against the wicked (2:8), adding their transgressions against plants and animals (2:17). God sees and cares for all his creation. He takes note when sinners harm anything he has created.

5. God Must Address the Universal Guilt of Sin

The final painting (II:E′, 2:18–20) of the middle panel contains faint echoes of the first. The focal point is an idolater bowing before the work of his hands: mute idols, carefully plated with gold and silver. He implores his idols to wake up and come alive. He begs them to speak, but there is no breath in wood and stones. The idolater is surrounded by a vast crowd that includes all those who are guilty of setting their highest affections on something or someone other than

God. The polemic is palpable. The so-called gods of the peoples and the nations are not gods at all. Woe will come to the one who worships a lifeless idol. Ultimately, the wicked transgress against the living God. The Lord Almighty is in his holy temple, a sanctuary that encompasses not only the heavens but also the entire earth. He therefore silences the clamoring of all the nations and peoples with just one syllable: "Hush!" His command in v. 20 silences the prophet and the altarpiece viewer as well. All humans stand guilty before a holy God.

9.3 PANEL III: THEOPHANY

Prayer and Worship

The righthand third and final panel swings open wide. The title at its top (superscription, 3:1) mirrors the same careful font of the others: "A prayer of the prophet Habakkuk," followed by musical directions for praise. In light of the central panel, prayer and praise are the only proper human response before the Lord in his holy temple.

1. God's Wrath and Mercy

The setting of the first painting (III:A′, 3:2) once again pictures Habakkuk kneeling in prayer. His focus now is on the Lord rather than the circumstances of his former complaint (I:A, 1:2–4). The prophet's questions have been silenced. He is left with humble petitions, including the request that God temper his wrath with mercy. Although the Lord often tempers his wrath this way, he will not leave the guilty unpunished. God fights for justice and will restore all things.

2. God Comes in Power and Glory

The second painting (III:B′, 3:3–7) depicts God's arrival from the south, as he strides across the earth, reclaiming his global sanctuary. The glory of God covers the heavens, and the earth resounds with his praises. His coming resembles the dawning sun advancing across the face of the earth. The amazing scene pictures age-old mountains crumbling and ancient hills bowing low before him. Both people and place tremble before the God who made them. The glory and power of the Divine Warrior pictured here form a sharp contrast to the corresponding painting in the first panel (I:B, 1:5–11), where the Babylonians gloried in their military might as they galloped across the earth's open plains.

3. God Comes to Judge and to Save

The third painting (III:C′, 3:8–15), like its parallel in the first panel, focuses on the waters. Habakkuk's final trio of questions concerns the object of God's anger. Does the Lord direct his wrath at the rivers or the sea? All nature is subservient to God and serves as his arsenal. Brilliant streaks of lightning pierce the darkness. The Divine Warrior marches across earth and sea, reclaiming that which rightfully belongs to him. Habakkuk receives his answer: God's anger is directed against the wicked. He comes to thresh the nations and to crush the leader of their household. God also comes to save his people and his anointed. Though this scene could just as easily depict a victory from the distant past or the defeat of the Babylonian "masters" of the sea (I:C, 1:12–17), the entire panel has an eschatological tone. On the last day, God will destroy all that is evil, and he will deliver his people. This painting offers encouraging news: Though there are none righteous, the Lord will still come to save those he calls "my people."

4. The Response of the Faith(ful)

The final painting (III:D′, 3:16–19) is a portrait of the prophet, over-whelmed by all he has seen and heard. His face, however, reflects a quiet resolve to wait for the fulfillment of the vision and pronouncements. In the scene Habakkuk is holding his hands open before the Lord. Although he may lose everything—even his daily sustenance—he will have the Lord, and the Lord is enough. Surprisingly, the prophet's face radiates joy as he relies totally on the Lord's strength to sustain him.

9.4   THE ALTARPIECE AS A WHOLE: A REFLECTION

Having considered all the paintings separately, the viewer should step back to take in the altarpiece as a whole. The portrait of the prophet on the bottom right is a vivid contrast to the portrait of the wicked man on the bottom left. Is Habakkuk, then, the example of a righteous man the viewer expected to find?

Searching the triptych for clues, the viewer finds his gaze drawn once more to the central panel. There the top and bottom paintings clearly portray the global scope of sin. Although all peoples have been victims of sin (II:E), they are also all guilty of sin (II:E′). None are righteous; all are silenced before a holy God. The second (II:F) and fourth (II:F′) paintings indicate that sinners cannot hide from God; they will be exposed, and a cup of judgment awaits each one. Although the Lord addresses injustices in the present, the middle painting (II:G) hints at the eschaton. The wicked and their works will be consumed by the fire of judgment. How, then, can anyone be saved?

Against the somber backdrop of the entire altarpiece, a brilliant swath of color running across the bottom of the central painting stands out as a beacon of hope. It expresses God's mission to dwell with his people forever in a global sanctuary filled with worshipers who rightly acknowledge his glory. How can anyone participate in this glorious worship? The preview of Hab 2:4 anticipates a dual outcome: Not only will the wicked falter and perish, but those righteous by faith will live. After the close of the first panel, Habakkuk no longer makes a claim to righteousness based on his own faithfulness. The final painting of the triptych reveals him to be an example of a man who trusts in the Lord; he is thus righteous by his faith that is demonstrated by his faithfulness. Habakkuk could not have expressed how God could declare such a one righteous. He only knew that somehow the Lord had answered his humble petition to show mercy in the midst of wrath.

New Testament believers have a better understanding of the cost of that mercy. The depths of God's love meant that he would give his only Son, so that whoever believes in him would not perish, but live (see John 3:16). The "vision to come" became "the Coming One": the righteous One fulfilled the justice required by flagrant sin. Christ would leave the safety of his Father's house to bear the shame of sinners (II:F), he would drink down the cup of wrath that awaited the offender (II:F′), and he would shed his own blood for the citizens of the city built by blood (II:G). God would then raise his Son to life, so that those who trust in him might also be raised to life.[298] The Lord makes it possible for his people to enter into the glorious worship of the global sanctuary by faith.

Habakkuk 2:13–14 forms the theological centerpiece of the entire triptych. This chiastic pivot capsulizes the answer to Habakkuk's questions regarding the wicked and the righteous. It also takes the preview of v. 2:4—which hints of the dual outcomes that await individuals—and amplifies it, providing a brief but tantalizing glimpse of the cosmic scale of the dual destinies that will be inaugurated at the

---

[298] See the discussion below on Hab 1:5–6 and 2:4.

eschaton. Habakkuk 2:14 also articulates the mission of God that has existed since the dawn of creation.

On the eve of the Babylonian invasion and the destruction of Jerusalem, the book of Habakkuk is understandably somber. The next phase of God's mission required drastic measures to preserve the lineage that would lead to the Messiah. Even so, this momentary but glorious glimpse of God's purposes for humanity provides hope. The Lord is presently at work in the world, administering justice and setting things right behind the scenes. His ultimate intention for humanity, however, is life in his presence. One day "the earth will be filled / with the knowledge of the LORD's glory, / as the water covers the sea." Believers who know and have experienced the mercy and glory of God will joyfully take their places in the new heavens and earth and praise his name forever. The beautifully crafted theological altarpiece that is the book of Habakkuk welcomes viewers to trust and worship the God of glory now.

COMMENTARY

1   HABAKKUK'S DIALOGUE WITH GOD (1:1–2:5)

1.1   SUPERSCRIPTION (1:1)

The first panel of the literary triptych opens with a superscription in v. 1.[1] This superscription offers only the barest of introductions to both the author and the book of Habakkuk. The opening verses of prophetic books often provide a few more details about a prophet, such as his occupation or family lineage, or possibly his geographical or chronological setting. Here, however, the emphasis is clearly on the content rather than the carrier.[2]

> [1] The pronouncement that the prophet Habakkuk saw.

1:1   Verse 1 contains three words that relate to the role of a prophet as described in the OT. The first of these is "pronouncement" (Hb. *maśśāʾ*, "load, burden"), a term that occurs in the superscriptions of Nahum and Malachi and in portions of Zechariah (9:1; 12:1). Derived from the verb for "to carry" or "lift up," the word sometimes translates as "burden" (KJV, NKJV).[3] Approximately half of the OT occurrences of the word refer to an actual "burden" or "load" carried by an animal (Exod 23:5), or a person (Num 4:27), or metaphorically, as an emotional weight or responsibility (Deut 1:12). The other half includes twenty-seven occurrences in a prophetic context.[4] In this setting, the word sometimes translates as "oracle" (NASB, ESV). Delivering a prophetic pronouncement from God is a weighty responsibility, and the context frequently involves a heavy word of judgment. Isaiah, for example, uses the word *maśśāʾ* to announce judgment against Babylon (Isa 13:1), and several other foreign nations.[5] Pronouncing judgment must have been even more burdensome for prophets like Habakkuk, whose messages included judgment against their own people. Another possible meaning derived from the root "to lift" is "to raise one's voice, make a statement."[6] Still, the etymology is tentative, and the two definitions of *maśśāʾ*—"burden" and

---

[1] For an explanation of the literary triptych, see 6.2.4 "Habakkuk as a Literary Triptych" as well as the commentary on Hab 2:2 below.

[2] See "Author" in the Introduction.

[3] *HALOT*, 639.

[4] Walter C. Kaiser, "מַשָּׂא," *TWOT* 2:602.

[5] See Isa 14:28; 15:1; 17:1; 19:1; 21:1, 11, 13; 22:1; 23:1.

[6] *HALOT*, 639.

"pronouncement"—may simply be unrelated homonyms.[7] The CSB translation indicates that Habakkuk received a prophetic "pronouncement" from God.

A second word in v. 1 describes Habakkuk's role as "prophet" (Hb. nābî'). Some of the functions of a prophet become clear from the passages that apply this same term to early figures. Abraham, for example, interceded on behalf of another (Gen 20:7); Aaron delivered the words from God (Exod 7:1); Miriam led women to worship through music (Exod 15:20); Deborah pronounced legal judgments (Judg 4:4); and the Lord confirmed Samuel's words as his own (1 Sam 3:19–20).[8] The activities of later prophets were varied. They included "[e]cstatic raptures elicited by the Spirit, the communication of actual divine sayings, legal and repentance preaching, inquiries and intercessions addressed to Yahweh, [and] wondrous deeds."[9] A prophet's primary job aimed to communicate God's message to its intended recipients. Although Habakkuk is unique among the writing prophets—in view of his interactive dialogue with the Lord—he does inquire of God (Hab 1:2–3, 13, 17; 2:1; 3:8) and intercedes on behalf of others (Hab 3:2). He also receives a vision from the Lord, along with the command to write it down to communicate it clearly to others (Hab 2:2).

Habakkuk is the first prophetic book to include the term nābî' or "prophet" in the superscription "title." Some see this label as evidence of Habakkuk's status as a temple-prophet.[10] This argument loses some ground, however, considering that two subsequent postexilic prophetic

---

[7] Since the etymological discussion of maśśā' has reached an impasse, Michael Floyd, "The מַשָּׂא (maśśā') as a Type of Prophetic Book," JBL (2002): 401–22, argues for the adoption of Richard Weis's rhetorical definition of maśśā': "a prophetic reinterpretation of a previous revelation" (p. 409). Floyd's rationale for such an analysis, however, is more convincing than his results. Weis focused his rhetorical analysis on the single narrative description of the term in 2 Kgs 9:25–26 (pp. 410–11). Just because this one narrative contained a previous revelation, Weis—and Floyd—extrapolated that every occurrence of the maśśā' "genre" requires a previous revelation. Applying this rhetorical definition to the term in Hab 1:1, Floyd, pp. 413–15, concludes that Hab 1:5–11 must be a previous revelation, which Habakkuk mentions as a flashback. Floyd, Minor Prophets, 99, maintains that the genre of Hab 1:2–17 should be described as a "Prophetic Complaint about the Fulfillment of an Oracle." David Cleaver-Bartholomew concurs in "An Alternative Approach to Hab 1, 2–2, 20," SJOT 17 (2003): 206–25. Still, this argument based on a single narrative in 2 Kings seems strained.

[8] J. Jeremias, "נָבִיא," TLOT 2:703.

[9] Jeremias, TLOT 2:698.

[10] Scholars who hold this view include Lawrence Boadt, Jeremiah 26–52, Habakkuk, Zephaniah, Nahum, Old Testament Message 10 (Wilmington: Michael Glazier, 1982), 165–67; Eaton, Obadiah, Nahum, Habakkuk, Zephaniah, 24–26, 81–82; Lindblom, Prophecy in Ancient Israel,

books, Haggai and Zechariah, follow suit (Hag 1:1; Zech 1:1). Others conjecture the term was often avoided because of its association with false prophets.[11] Although Habakkuk's contemporary, Jeremiah, condemned false prophets (e.g., Jer 23:9–40; 28:1–17), he considered himself to be a prophet, called and commissioned by God to be his spokesman (Jer 1:5; 20:2).

The third term in Hab 1:1 relating to prophetic function is the word translated "saw" (Hb. *ḥāzâ*). The OT often refers to a prophet as a "seer" (Hb. *ḥōzeh*), one who sees a vision or revelation from God (e.g., 2 Sam 24:11).[12] In Hebrew as in English, there is a close relationship between seeing and perception. Habakkuk 1:1 contains something of a mixed metaphor—a pronouncement that the prophet saw rather than heard. The very first verse introduces themes of hearing and seeing that weave throughout this prophetic book.[13] God opened Habakkuk's eyes and allowed the prophet to see—and hear—his message on a spiritual plane.

The superscription clearly identifies Habakkuk as filling the role of prophet in multiple ways. At first glance, it appears that the book of Habakkuk—and its unfolding dialogue—begins with Habakkuk's questions. But—as always—God was the one who called Habakkuk to be a prophet. He gave him both a spiritual burden for the brokenness that surrounded him and the "burden" of addressing it through prophetic pronouncement. At a time when the nation was far from him, the Lord still chose to reach out and communicate a powerful vision to those who stood on the brink. The terrible judgment awaiting Judah was redemptive in nature. Through it, the Lord would preserve

---

254; Sigmund Mowinckel, *"Zum Psalm des Habakuk,"* TZ 9.1 (1953): 3–4; Otto Eissfeldt, *The Old Testament, An Introduction* (Oxford: Basil Blackwell, 1965), 422.

[11] Roberts, *Nahum, Habakkuk, and Zephaniah*, 86, points out that "a problematic reading of Amos 7:14" has led some scholars to make a sharp distinction between "the professional cult prophets—the 'false prophets'—and the non-professional, independent, classical prophets—the 'true' prophets." Roberts argues that there is little scriptural evidence for how prophets—false or true—made a living. The test of authenticity was not how a prophet made a living, but the fulfillment of his prophecies (Jer 28:9).

[12] *HALOT*, 301.

[13] The OT contains other passages that pair "seeing" and "hearing" to express revelation. Sheri L. Klouda, "The Dialectical Interplay of Seeing and Hearing in Psalm 19 and Its Connection to Wisdom," *BBR* 10.2 (2000): 192, concludes that "the dialectical interplay" between the two senses provides "a plausible organizational framework" for Psalm 19 and "accounts for the wisdom overtones of the psalm" as well. See also Francis Landy, "Vision and Voice in Isaiah," *JSOT* 88 (2000): 19–36.

and purify a remnant of his people. Habakkuk's calling as a prophet, his vision, and his pronouncement of God's message all started with a sovereign God who desires to reveal himself to his people.

1.2 HABAKKUK'S FIRST COMPLAINT (1:2–4)

The first panel of Habakkuk reports a dialogue between the prophet and the Lord. Surprisingly, the first set of questions comes from the prophet. In the past, reports of the Lord's speech punctuated the prophetic books with great regularity. Formulaic phrases like "The word of the Lord came to X" and "This is what the Lord says" occur so often that the reader begins to find them repetitive. In the prophetic books the message comes from the Lord to and through the prophet. Ezekiel 2, for example, captures this prophetic essence:

> He said to me, "Son of man, stand up on your feet and I will speak with you.". . . [A]nd I listened to the one who was speaking to me. He said to me, . . . "I am sending you to them, and you must say to them, 'This is what the Lord GOD says.' Whether they listen or refuse to listen . . . they will know that a prophet has been among them." (Ezek 2:1–5)

In contrast to all the other prophetic books, Habakkuk contains none of these standard phrases. Habakkuk 2:2 uses the closest thing to a formulaic introduction: "The LORD answered me." Even though this verse introduces reported speech from God, the Lord spoke in reply to Habakkuk's anguished plea for an answer. The Lord stooped to dialogue with this prophet who cried out in frustrated confusion.

There is no preface to Habakkuk's comments, no preamble of worship, no polite address. Habakkuk's situation was so painful he could simply hold back no longer. Dropping all formality and propriety, Habakkuk launched into a complaint that seems to adopt an accusatory tone. He felt God's silence in the face of evil and suffering suggested that he was inactive or indifferent.[14]

The same questions have reverberated across the generations, down to our own. A friend recently asked me, "If the gospel is true,

---

[14] A sampling of OT passages indicates similar sentiments were not infrequent: Pss 10:1, 11; 13:2; 22:1–2; 44:23–26; 69:17; 88:14; 102:1–2, 10; Isa 8:17; 63:11–15. Other passages reveal that the Lord intentionally abandoned his people for a time: Deut 32:20; 2 Kgs 17:23; 23:27; Isa 63:10; Mic 3:4.

then why isn't the world getting better? Does it mean that God doesn't see or care? Is he ineffectual? Powerless to do something? If God is supposed to be omniscient and omnipotent, then why do things go on like this?" Though my friend is likely unfamiliar with the seventh-century-BC prophet, her questions echo those of Habakkuk.

1.2.1   How Long Must I Cry for Help? (1:2)

> 2 *How long, LORD, must I call for help*
> *and you do not listen*
> *or cry out to you about violence*
> *and you do not save?*

1:2 The first words Habakkuk uttered reveal the weight of his despair: "How long?" This distressing situation was not new. His question, however, was not "How long will this suffering continue?" Instead, his query took a personal tone: "How long must I call for help and you do not listen or save?"[15] The prophet was hurt by the Lord's seeming indifference. Confused, Habakkuk brought his complaint directly to the Lord—Yahweh, the God of the covenant.

This opening section of Habakkuk resembles a lament that might be more at home in the Psalms than in the Prophets.[16] The question "how long?" sounds familiar. A similar question, with the same Hb. phrasing, plaintively resounds in Ps 13:1–2:

> How long, LORD? Will you forget me forever?
> How long will you hide your face from me?
> How long will I store up anxious concerns within me,
> agony in my mind every day?
> How long will my enemy dominate me?

---

[15] Andersen, *Habakkuk*, 125, argues that the prophet's prayer is not a lament but rather a complaint "driven by one mood—moral outrage and perplexity." Thomas, *Habakkuk*, 67, however, proposes a definition of lament that includes complaint: "[L]*ament is a kind of prayer that voices a complaint to God about distress, and it is uttered to persuade God to act on the sufferer's behalf*" (italics in original). Thomas's "Excursus: The Power of Lament Prayer," 67–76, underscores the place of lament prayer in the lives of believers: "Lament prayer is not God-denying language but God–affirming language that reveals a radical faith in God and a firm understanding of our dependence upon him for all things" (p. 76).

[16] For a discussion of lament, see 6.1.1: "Habakkuk's Use of Prophetic Subgenres."

A survey of the seven other occurrences of this same Hb. construction is revealing. In three instances the phrase occurs in speech between humans (Job 18:2; 19:2; Ps 62:3); one, in the context of the Lord's judgment of Philistia (Jer 47:6). In the remaining three examples, however, it is the Lord himself who demanded, "How long?" When the Israelites searched for manna on the Sabbath, the Lord asked Moses, "How long will you refuse to keep my commands and instructions?" (Exod 16:28). When they balked at entering Canaan, he asked, "How long will these people despise me? How long will they not trust in me despite all the signs I have performed among them?" (Num 14:11). And when the next generation failed to possess the land, Joshua expressed the Lord's frustration: "How long will you delay going out to take possession of the land that the LORD, the God of your ancestors, gave?" (Josh 18:3).[17] Fully a third of the occurrences express the Lord's weariness with his disobedient people. In the NT Jesus echoed his Father's frustration: "You unbelieving generation, how long will I be with you? How long must I put up with you?" (Mark 9:19; cp. Matt 17:17). Habakkuk was not informing God of something he did not know. The Lord was fully aware of Judah's wickedness. Habakkuk's heartfelt cry—"How long?"—could have just as easily expressed the Lord's frustration with their rebellion. God's seeming silence was part of his redemptive judgment on a people who had abandoned him.[18]

God's silence, however, drove the prophet to complain. His repeated cries for help failed to elicit God's response.[19] Habakkuk felt a tension between what he knew about God and his current experience.[20] He was familiar with Scripture passages giving assurance that the Lord would answer the cries of his people (e.g., Isa 58:9; Jonah 2:2; Pss 5:3; 119:147). At the same time, the Lord would refuse to answer the pleas of his enemies, who were unlikely to ask anyway (Ps 18:41; Job 36:13). Psalm 18:6 expresses it well: "I called to the LORD in my distress, / and I cried to my God for help. / From his temple he

---

[17] This first group of "how long?" examples, including Hab 1:2, are ʿad-ʾānāh. Two other related Hb. constructions—ʿad-meh or ʿad-mātay—are also translated in English as "How long?" Two of these occurrences ask about a situation like Habakkuk's: How long will the wicked insult the righteous? How long will they gloat about their oppression of the weak? (Pss 4:2; 94:3). Two other instances ask how long the Lord will be angry and hide his face (Pss 79:5; 89:46).

[18] 2 Kgs 24:20. See too Deut 29:24–28, but also 30:1–10.

[19] J. F. Sawyer, "ישׁע," *TDOT* 6:443, notes that the verb šûaʿ (Eng. "to cry for help")—found only in the intensive *piel* stem—probably refers to "a succession of cries."

[20] Thomas, *Habakkuk*, 65, calls this tension "a theological conundrum."

heard my voice, / and my cry to him reached his ears." Habakkuk was familiar with this psalm since he later quotes Ps 18:33 in Hab 3:19. In keeping with what he knew from Scripture, Habakkuk needed help, so he called on the God who helps. Yet nothing happened.

The prophet reinforced his appeal and called out, "Violence!" This Hb. noun (*ḥāmās*) occurs sixty times in the OT, six of them in Habakkuk (1:2, 3, 9; 2:8, 17 [2x]);[21] the prophet's book has the highest concentration of the word "violence" in the OT for its size.[22] The word refers primarily to physical violence but includes social injustices or "psychological anguish" inflicted on another.[23] In OT usage, the word almost always refers to human sinfulness and never to natural disasters such as a "violent" earthquake.[24] Habakkuk's cry of "violence" would command the Lord's attention. It is a one-word cry for help that prompts both a visceral reaction and a quick response.[25] Continually the prophet cried out to God and repeatedly came up empty.[26] His desperate tone edges on accusation: You do not listen; you do not save.

What response had Habakkuk anticipated from the Lord? He expected the Lord to save (Hb. *yāšaʿ*) his people in their distress.[27] Almost without exception, the word *yāšaʿ* inherently evokes theological associations, "with Yahweh as subject and his people as object."[28] In times past, God had raised up deliverers like Moses, judges, and kings to save his people (Exod 2:17; Judg 2:18; 1 Sam 9:16; 2 Sam 3:18). Even so, God himself is always the one who saves, though he sometimes works through human agents (Neh 9:27). Habakkuk knew that besides the Lord, "there is no Savior," for foreign gods cannot save, nor can idols (Isa 43:11–12; 46:6–7). With salvation so closely tied to God, the Israelites even incorporated the word into a title describing

---

[21] According to *Collins Dictionary*, in Arabic the word *ḥāmās* means "zeal." "Hamas" is also an acronym for the Islamic Resistance (Armed) Movement founded in 1987 with the purpose of establishing an Islamic state in Palestine.

[22] In comparison, *ḥāmās* occurs six times in Ezekiel and four times in Jeremiah.

[23] I. Swart and C. Van Dam, "חָמַס," *NIDOTTE* 2:174.

[24] R. Laird Harris, "חָמַס," *TWOT* 1:297.

[25] Consider the kind of cry in view in Deut 22:27.

[26] Habakkuk was not the only one who cried out to God only to find his pleas for help went unanswered. Job complained bitterly of the same (Job 19:7; 30:20), as did the poet who penned the fall of Jerusalem (Lam 3:8).

[27] Sawyer, *TDOT* 6:443, notes that the noun "salvation" (Hb. *yᵉšûʿāh*) comes from this root, as do fourteen proper names in the OT, including the name Jeshua, "a late form of 'Joshua' through dissimilation." See, for example, Ezra 4:3; Neh 10:9.

[28] Sawyer, *TDOT* 6:444.

him "the God of my (or our) salvation."[29] Scripture declares that the
Lord will save not only "his anointed" (Ps 20:6) but also the poor, the
helpless, the faithful aged, the crushed in spirit, and the needy who
trust in God (Pss 34:6; 72:13; Isa 46:4; Pss 34:18; 86:1–2). No wonder
Habakkuk cried to the Lord and trusted him to intervene and save his
people from their troubles. What the prophet failed to consider was
that Judah stood under God's judgment for their entrenched rebellion;
the Lord, therefore, had finally refused to step in and save them from
themselves (cf. Deut 28:29). Habakkuk's unanswered pleas for deliverance resonate with Christ's own cry from the cross: "My God, my
God, why have you abandoned me?" (Matt 27:46; Mark 15:34). Just
before dying, Jesus quoted the opening line of Ps 22, where the suffering psalmist—like Habakkuk—felt abandoned when his cries for
deliverance were met with silence:

> My God, my God, why have you abandoned me?
> Why are you so far from my deliverance [Hb. *yəšûʿātī*; my
>   salvation]
> and from my words of groaning?
> My God, I cry by day, but you do not answer,
> by night, yet I have no rest. (Ps 22:1–2)

The similarities between this psalm and Jesus's passion compelled NT
writers to mine the entire hymn repeatedly for quotations and allusions.[30] Close parallels appear between the violence and humiliation
perpetrated on both the psalmist and the suffering King (vv. 6–8; 12–
18). Psalm 22, however, ends not in desperation, but in victory and
praise because, ultimately, the Lord answered the psalmist:

> You answered me! . . .
> You who fear the LORD, praise him! . . .
> For he has not despised or abhorred
> the torment of the oppressed.
> He did not hide his face from him
> but listened when he cried to him for help. (vv. 21, 23–24)

---

[29] For "God of my salvation," see 2 Sam 22:47; Pss 18:46; 25:5; 27:9; 51:14; 88:1; Mic 7:7. For
"God of our salvation," see Pss 65:5; 79:9; 85:4; 1 Chr 16:35.

[30] The "Index of Quotations" in the UBS Greek New Testament, 5th ed., 858, lists four NT
quotations from Ps 22 (v. 1 in Matt 27:46; Mark 15:34; v. 18 in John 19:24; and v. 22 in Heb 2:12).
The "Index of Allusions and Verbal Parallels," p. 872, lists an additional twenty NT passages.

Ironically, the Messiah's rescue came not through deliverance *from* death but through deliverance *beyond* death—in the resurrection. God's apparent abandonment resulted in vindication for his anointed and gained salvation for all who seek his face. God may appear to abandon, but he does not; he may appear to be silent, but he is not. Behind the scenes and in the silence, the Lord is steadily accomplishing his mission to save "[a]ll the ends of the earth" and "[a]ll the families of the nations" (Ps 22:27). God the Son left the glories of heaven and came to rescue the world. Understanding that the Lord willingly embraced the depths of human anguish to secure our salvation should comfort those who trust in him—even in seasons of suffering and seeming silence.[31]

1.2.2   Why Do You Ignore Injustice? (1:3–4)

> [3] *Why do you force me to look at injustice?*
> *Why do you tolerate wrongdoing?*
> *Oppression and violence are right in front of me.*
> *Strife is ongoing, and conflict escalates.*
> [4] *This is why the law is ineffective*
> *and justice never emerges.*
> *For the wicked restrict the righteous;*
> *therefore, justice comes out perverted.*

1:3–4   God's lack of response to Habakkuk's first question prompted a second question: "Why?" As in every generation, suffering invariably elicits a cry for understanding or explanation. Here, the prophet, unable to reconcile apparent divine inactivity in the face of so much evil, suggested since the Lord did not seem to hear, perhaps he did not see. The first two lines of v. 3 are parallel, pairing two Hb. verbs, *rāʾâ* ("to see") and *nābaṭ* ("to look at"). The verb stem (*hiphil*) of both terms denotes "causative" action; the first verb could be translated as "show" or "reveal" (i.e., "you allow me to see"); and similarly, for the second verb, "consider, look."[32] Because the second clause does not contain the first common singular suffix "me," some translations read it as an elliptical expression where the substantival

---

[31] See 1 Pet 3:18; 4:1–2.
[32] *HALOT*, 1161, 661.

object has been omitted.[33] These translations indicate this by inserting "me" in italics: e.g., "And make *me* look at destitution?" (NASB).[34] The (*hiphil*) stem of the second verb may also relate to "considering/ acknowledging, i.e., a careful, sustained, and favorable contemplation."[35] Habakkuk suggested that God did not just glance at wrongdoing; he gazed at it and did nothing. Thus, the CSB translates the second clause as "you tolerate wrongdoing."[36]

Habakkuk and the Lord both witnessed the same ongoing situation.[37] Whereas the prophet reacted in horror, the Lord seemed to ignore it or—even worse—tolerate it. Verse 3 continues to expound on the theme of "seeing" introduced in v. 1. Habakkuk could not help but look and see evil because, as he complained, it was "right in front of [him]."[38] Why was God forcing the prophet to look at these wrongs if he himself was not doing anything about them? Why was the Lord looking but failing to respond? Habakkuk might well echo the plea from the psalmist's lament, urging the Lord to action: "Look down from heaven and *see*" (Ps 80:14; emphasis added).

Were Habakkuk's questions presumptuous? Aron Pinker argues since the "why" is rhetorical rather than inquisitive, the prophet was indeed presumptuous: "Do not bother with [showing me] this. I know it all." Pinker also cites the Midrash as evidence of insolence: "There were four who prayed and spoke harshly to the Lord out of their love for Israel: Jeremiah, Habakkuk, David, and Moses."[39] Although the prophet's complaint conveys a bit of an edge, charges of presumption and insolence seem too harsh. Habakkuk's complaint aligns with lament psalms that ask similar questions.[40] By asking "how long," Habakkuk envisioned an indeterminate future time when God would

---

[33] GKC §117g.

[34] See also KJV, NKJV. The Syriac Peshitta suggests making this form first person: "I see, observe."

[35] Jackie A. Naudé, "נבט," *NIDOTTE* 3:8.

[36] Like the CSB, the NIV translates the verb as "tolerate"; the ESV, "idly look at"; and the NET, "put up with."

[37] Both verbs are active imperfects, which may imply continuing or incomplete action. The prophet's previous question—How long?—also implies a persistent problem that the Lord hadn't yet addressed, despite his many pleas.

[38] In Hos 7:2 the Lord used similar phrasing to describe the evil perpetrated by his own people: "right in front of my face."

[39] Shocher Tov 90:2 cited in Aron Pinker, "Was Habakkuk Presumptuous?" *JBQ* 32 (2004): 29–30.

[40] See Pss 6:3; 10:1; 13:1–2; 22:1; 42:9; 43:2; 79:5; 82:2; 89:46; 94:3.

address these wrongs.[41] His "why" questions acknowledged though the Lord was not responsible for the wrongdoing the prophet witnessed, his inaction was "an exacerbating factor" making the situation unbearable.[42] Even so, the motivation behind his questions was faith. Andrew Davies observes, "'Why' would be a soul-destroying question if the answer went back to any inability on God's part. Only because they know God is all powerful and has chosen, for whatever purpose, to withdraw from the people, can Israel dare to ask questions such as 'when,' 'how long' and 'why.'"[43] Only in the context of an intimate relationship based on trust did Habakkuk dare to ask these hard questions.

The prophet summarized what he saw. Habakkuk used six synonyms for "wrongdoing" within only four lines of poetry (v. 3), and their cumulative weight lends credence to his level of desperation. The first of these is "injustice" (Hb. ʾāwen), an intentional harm that results in "disastrous calamity."[44] These evildoers often targeted the marginalized members of the covenant community. According to Ps 5:5, God hates all those who do such things. The second is "wrongdoing" (Hb. ʿāmāl). With the connotation of toilsome labor, this word can also suggest "injustice"—the suffering a worker of evil afflicts on another.[45] Everywhere the prophet looked, he saw "oppression" (Hb. šōd) and "violence" (Hb. ḥāmās). Šōd, often translated as "destruction" or "havoc," occurs primarily in the Prophets.[46] This is the second of six times the word "violence" occurs in Habakkuk (cf. 1:2). These two nouns are sometimes paired together as they are here, but in reverse order: "violence and oppression / destruction" (Jer 6:7; 20:8; Ezek 45:9; Amos 3:10). Together, they express a stereotype: "death and destruction."[47]

---

[41] See Andrew Davies, "My God . . . Why? Questioning the Action and Inaction of YHWH in the Psalms" in *Why? . . . How Long?: Studies on Voice(s) of Lamentation Rooted in Biblical Hebrew Poetry*, ed. LeAnn Snow Flesher, Carol J. Dempsey, and Mark Boda (New York: Bloomsbury, 2014), 58.

[42] Davies, "My God . . . Why?" 62.

[43] Davies, "My God . . . Why?" 64.

[44] R. Knierim, "אָוֶן," *TLOT* 1:62.

[45] S. Schwertner, "עָמָל," *TLOT* 2:926.

[46] E.g., Isa 59:7; 60:18; Jer 48:3; Hos 7:13; 9:6; 10:14.

[47] *HALOT*, 1418.

The final two words carry legal connotations: *rīb* and *mādôn*.[48] Goldingay and Scalise observe, "They insinuate that the wrongdoers are able to use the law to wrong other people who are less adept at working the legal system."[49] Furthermore, Habakkuk saw no relief in sight because "strife" (Hb. *rīb*) was ongoing.[50] As Exod 21:18 indicates, this quarreling was not limited to words but could spill over into physical violence resulting in bodily harm.[51] The "conflict" (Hb. *mādôn*) would escalate. Proverbs 17:14 observes, "To start a conflict is to release a flood." With these last two words in place, the series of synonyms is linked together in Hb. with a series of five conjunctions ("and"): injustice and wrongdoing . . . and oppression and violence . . . and . . . strife and conflict. The escalated tension conveyed through the cumulative range of these three sets of word pairs causes the reader to sense the evil of Habakkuk's day threatened to collapse onto the prophet.

Much of the blame for the injustices of this era fell at the feet of Judah's king, Jehoiakim: "Those who held subordinate positions of power in the land—governors and judges—took their cues from him."[52] Jeremiah corroborates the social injustices perpetrated on those who lived on the fringes of society. The privileged often exploited widows, orphans, foreigners, and the poor. The weeping prophet cataloged an even more specific list of sins committed by his fellow citizens: dishonest gain, extortion, treachery, deception, adultery, and

---

[48] *HALOT*, 1225, 548.

[49] Goldingay and Scalise, *Minor Prophets II*, 54.

[50] As Schökel, *A Manual of Hebrew Poetics*, 166–68, observes, Hebrew poetry frequently uses "economical" grammatical phenomena like ellipsis and concision, where "two equal words or phrases depend on the same word." Watson, *Classical Hebrew Poetry*, 304, lists parts of speech that may perform this "double-duty" role: pronouns, suffixes, nouns, verbs, prepositions, particles, and other expressions. Building on this characteristic of Hebrew poetry, Andersen, *Habakkuk*, 99, explains that readers must therefore search the nearby context for functional items that play a "double duty" role. Andersen goes on to claim that "the literal translation 'and there is strife,' is mistaken." Instead, he proposes the idiom: "'I had a lawsuit,' literally, 'And it was to me a *rîbʾ* (*wayĕhîlîrîb*). The usual *lî* ["to me"] is missing from Hab 1:3" (p. 100). Based on possible forensic connotations of the terms *rīb* and *mādôn*, Andersen contends Habakkuk may be saying, "'I have a quarrel' (that is, with Yahweh)." Habakkuk was no longer concerned with the human perpetrators of oppression; instead, "God must now bear responsibility for the spread and perpetuation of evil," as well as the "ineffective" *tôrâ* and twisted *mišpāṭ* (pp. 118–19). Andersen concludes, "Habakkuk's prayer is nothing but questions and outright accusation of God. It has gone beyond complaint. It is an indictment" (p. 125). Andersen's argument, although possible, seems to place a great deal of weight on the presumption of a missing possessive pronoun.

[51] G. Liedke, "ריב," *TLOT* 3:1234.

[52] Bruce, "Habakkuk," 844.

shedding the blood of both prophet and poor.[53] The knowledge those responsible for this oppression were Judeans was especially galling. The hollowness of Judah's religious practices came to light in how they treated one another.

All these wrongs appeared to render the law ineffective. The Hb. word *tôrâ* ("instruction" or "law") has a broad meaning that "encompass[es] history, regulations and their interpretation, and exhortations."[54] Eventually the word "Torah" came to describe the first five books of the OT. It is also the word that describes the book of the law rediscovered in the temple in Josiah's day (2 Kgs 22:8, 11; 23:24).[55] Jeremiah repeatedly rebuked the Israelites for forsaking the law, and for failing to walk according to God's law and his statutes (Jer 16:11; 26:4; 32:23; 44:10, 23).[56] Here in Habakkuk, v. 4 refers to "the law" in light of its moral regulations and the abuses of social injustice. In the face of overwhelming wickedness, the law no longer worked; it "gr[ew] numb."[57] Helpless, unable to function as it should, the law dropped to its knees, "paralyzed" (NIV, ESV).[58] For the same reason, justice (Hb. *mišpāṭ*) was unfairly administered as the result of governmental corruption. Proper sentences or judgments failed to materialize. When justice finally emerged, it no longer resembled equity and fairness because the wicked had manipulated and twisted it. Although the court system may be the prophet's focus, "this lack of justice, no doubt, permeated every aspect of life—legal, social, ethical, moral,

---

[53] See section 4.1: "Judah's Religious, Social, and Moral Depravity."

[54] John E. Hartley, "תּוֹרָה," *TWOT* 1:404.

[55] Roberts, *Nahum, Habakkuk, and Zephaniah*, 90, maintains that this is a reference to the same *tô* scroll "that fueled Josiah's reform."

[56] G. Liedke and C. Petersen, "תּוֹרָה," *TLOT* 3:1421.

[57] Or possibly "it [grew] cold" as Jacob's heart did when he heard that Joseph was alive (Gen 45:26). See "פּוג," *HALOT*, 918. Thomas, *Habakkuk*, 77–83, observes that though the law was not salvific, it was a gift from a gracious God, instructing God's covenant people in how they were to "live missionally in God's world, as his ambassadors among the nations" (pp. 80–81). The *tôrâ* itself was not defective; the defect noted by Habakkuk stemmed from "Israel's lack of faith."

[58] Marshall D. Johnson, "The Paralysis of Torah in Habakkuk I 4," *VT* 35.3 (1985): 257–66, sees the wicked in 1:4 as the Babylonians, and 1:5–11 as an intensification of the complaint in 1:2–4 (p. 261). He thus argues that "the paralysis of the law" refers to God's failure to fulfill the *tôrâ* promises found in Deuteronomy. Johnson calls the prophet Habakkuk "a disillusioned Deuteronomist, one who had believed that the Josianic reform along Deuteronomic lines would clear the way for the fulfillment of God's promises recorded in that law code" (p. 264). Contrary to Johnson, if the wicked in 1:4 are Judeans guilty of the apostasy described by Jeremiah, then God's judgment announced in 1:5–11 is the fulfillment of his promise to bring curses of foreign military invasion and exile in order to purify a remnant (cf. Deut 28:49–52, 63–64).

and religious."[59] This failure was particularly egregious because "doing justice" is one of the three basic things the Lord requires of humanity (Mic 6:8).

Where there is righteousness, there is justice. Both should flow on forever, like a never-ending stream (Amos 5:24). Justice and righteousness often appear together in Scripture as a hendiadys—a pair of words closely associated with each other, linked together by "and," that express one idea (see for example, Pss 89:14; 99:4; Isa 28:17; 33:5; Jer 22:3). The incongruity grieved the prophet: the righteous failed to receive the justice they were due because the wicked surrounded them—pressing in on all sides with evil intent.

Whom did Habakkuk characterize as "righteous" and "wicked"? The root behind the word "righteous" originally conveyed the idea of "straight" and eventually evolved to describe a norm—conforming to God's moral and ethical standards based on his character.[60] The "righteous" are upright and just, in right relationship with both God and fellow man. Declining in number, the righteous Judeans felt surrounded by the wicked.[61] The identity of the wicked is crucial to understanding the historical context of Habakkuk. Some scholars argue "the wicked" in 1:4 were the Assyrians, whom the Babylonians would soon destroy since the prophet does not clearly identify them.[62] Others claim the wicked in 1:4 and 1:13 refers to the Babylonians.[63]

---

[59] D. David Garland, "Habakkuk," in *Hosea-Malachi*, Broadman Bible Commentary 7 (Nashville: Broadman Press, 1972), 252.

[60] Harold G. Stigers, "צַדִּיק," *TWOT* 2:753.

[61] Roberts, *Nahum, Habakkuk, and Zephaniah*, 90, suggests that the prophet Jeremiah experienced this constriction firsthand (Jer 12:6; 18:20, 22–23; 20:7–10).

[62] For example, Seitz, *Prophecy and Hermeneutics*, 212; Boda, *Exploring Zechariah*, 157–58; and Dietrich, "Three Minor Prophets and the Major Empires," 147–56.

[63] Martin Sweeney, "Structure, Genre, and Intent in the Book of Habakkuk," *VT* 41.1 (1991): 73–78; Sweeney, *The Twelve Prophets*, 455; and Cleaver-Bartholomew, "An Alternative Reading of Hab 1 and 2," 206–25. Haak, *Habakkuk*, 107–11, proposes an elaborate historical-critical theory, in which he identifies "the righteous man" as the deposed Jehoahaz, and "the wicked man" as Jehoiakim and those who support him. For a similar view, see Eduard Nielsen, "The Righteous and the Wicked in Habaqquq," *ST* 6.1 (1953): 71.

Literary critics who argue that Habakkuk contains multiple text layers dating from different historical periods naturally conclude that the labels "righteous" and "wicked" describe different entities at different times. The Qumran community that produced the earliest commentary on this prophetic book, *Pesher Habakkuk*, believed that these terms pointed to specific identities fulfilled in their own day: "The Wicked Priest" and his followers, who opposed "the Teacher of Righteousness" and his followers. See William H. Brownlee, *The Midrash Pesher of Habakkuk*, SBL 24 (Missoula, MT: SBL, 1979). See also James VanderKam and Peter Flint, *The Meaning of the Dead Sea Scrolls: Their Significance for Understanding the Bible, Judaism, Jesus, and Christianity*

Ralph Smith concludes, "There is nothing in this passage that points to a foreign nation."[64] Much more convincing is identifying the wicked in 1:4 as citizens of Judah who strayed far from God's moral and ethical standards. Habakkuk's use of the covenantal terms *tôrāh* and *mišpāṭ* suggests a Hebrew identity for the wicked in 1:4. The OT frequently attests to the presence of impious evildoers among God's own people (e.g., Num 16:26; Pss 12:8; 37:32; 101:8; Prov 21:27; Jer 5:26). The prophets repeatedly warned that the Lord would hand both Israel and Judah over to their enemies. Their abandonment of the covenant and oppression of their fellow countrymen were the reasons the Lord was raising up the Babylonians to judge the wicked among his own people.[65] This initial contrast between these antonyms—the righteous and the wicked—is a major theme that winds throughout the rest of Habakkuk.

This prophet found himself surrounded by oppression, and he could have grown accustomed to it. Although it would have been difficult to ignore, he could have endlessly bemoaned the loss of social mores and shrugged his shoulders in indifference. But Habakkuk's horrified reaction and grief reflected the heart of God. The prophet could not ignore evil, and he could not believe God would ignore it either. So he brought his questions and confusion to the Lord. Habakkuk wanted the Lord to respond and set things right.

As God's chosen people, the Israelites were to be a light to the nations, a people whose lifestyle was consistent with the Holy God dwelling among them in the Jerusalem temple. The same is true of Christians today (see 1 Pet 2:9). Believers are tasked with manifesting the presence of the indwelling Holy Spirit to a lost and broken world. Tragically, all too often the same sins that characterize the world are present in the church. As OT prophets like Habakkuk pointed out, how we treat the most vulnerable of society—widows and orphans, single moms, the newly arrived immigrant, the poor, the unborn, the

---

(San Francisco: HarperSanFrancisco, 2002), 282–86. VanderKam and Flint, 284–85, conclude that since the Teacher was a priest with claims to "legal and interpretive authority," who was attacked by the "Wicked Priest," he may have "acted as high priest in the years 159–152 BCE when, according to the received list, there was no high priest in Jerusalem."

[64] Smith, *Micah-Malachi*, 342. Smith explains that those who identify the wicked as foreign nations base their claims on the fallacious argument that the wicked in 1:4 and in 1:13 must be the same entity.

[65] The authors of Kings and Chronicles came to the same conclusion: the Lord raised up the Babylonians to judge the wickedness among his own people (cf. 2 Kgs 24:2–4; 2 Chr 36:15–21).

elderly—is often a far better indicator of character than outward religiosity. Similarly, in the NT, John questioned how anyone can say they love God and not be moved to action by compassion to meet the needs of the marginalized (1 John 3:17).

When wrongs are right in front of us, it is easy to become desensitized to them. Our own society is rife with examples: bullying, racism, domestic abuse, gun violence, pornography, sex trafficking, homelessness, and substance addiction. As in Habakkuk's day, the list is long. Many watch evil play out on screens for entertainment, convincing themselves it can't be harmful if it isn't real. Many conveniently rename evil to reframe it: for instance, "sin" becomes "shortcoming" and "euthanasia," "medical assistance in dying." The law seems to be paralyzed. The wicked outnumber the righteous. Caught in a riptide of a cultural sea change, we may become social media warriors, adding to the strife without making a difference. We may march and chant for change, only to despair when our paltry efforts seem ineffective, or worse, devolve into more violence and more injustice. Or maybe we rail against heaven, wondering if we have more compassion than God himself because if we were in charge, we would do something to make things right. If that thought occurs to us, it is our thinking that is off the mark, not God.

1.3 GOD'S FIRST RESPONSE (1:5–11)

God was not offended by Habakkuk's confusion and his sincere questions. The Lord did not rebuke the prophet; instead, he condescended to reply to the prophet's desperate pleas. God responded to the prophet's first complaint in 1:5–11. He affirmed Habakkuk's horror and grief over the wickedness among his own people. God himself was already at work behind the scenes, bringing the perpetrators of injustice to judgment. God was in the process of judgment and restoration, fulfilling his divine mission.

1.3.1 Look, I Am Doing Something! (1:5)

> [5] *Look at the nations and observe—*
> *be utterly astounded!*
> *For I am doing something in your days*
> *that you will not believe*
> *when you hear about it.*

1:5 The Lord's response to Habakkuk was alarming. The prophet had accused God of forcing him to see wickedness (1:3a), yet the Lord himself seemed to overlook the evil, or worse, "tolerate" it (1:3b). Complaining that wrongdoing was right "in front of" him everywhere he turned (1:3c), Habakkuk expressed his dissatisfaction from his narrow perspective. God issued two imperatives in order to shift the prophet's perspective to a more encompassing view of the situation.[66] Using the same two verbs in the same order as Habakkuk used them in 1:3, the Lord commanded, "*Look* at the nations and *observe.*"[67] Not only was the Lord well aware of Habakkuk's catalog of evils, but he also perceived them so much more deeply that his own solution seemed overwhelming.[68] Raising the prophet's eyes to the horizon allowed him to see from God's vantage point.

Although not readily apparent in English, the plural imperatives imply a wider audience: "[You all] look; [you all] observe." Thus, this revelation was not for Habakkuk alone; the Lord intended that the prophet share this warning with Judah.[69] As James Bruckner observes, "Habakkuk begins with a domestic problem, and Yahweh answers with an international issue."[70] God instructed the people of Judah to focus their attention on the nations (Hb. *gôyim*), a word that usually described the Gentile peoples surrounding the Israelites.[71]

The Lord's revelation was shocking. Two imperative forms occur in tandem in 5b—both from the Hb. root *tāmâ*, meaning "be astounded, dumbfounded, bewildered."[72] The first of these (*hithpael*) forms is reflexive ("astonish yourselves"), and the second is tolerative ("let yourselves be astonished").[73] This Semitic pattern of repetition

---

[66] Andersen, *Habakkuk*, 141, astutely observes, "The purposes of God for one person or one nation can be understood only in terms of the whole world. This means that God alone understands it all, while humans get glimpses."

[67] Italics added. Patterson, *Nahum, Habakkuk, Zephaniah*, 139, points out that נָבַט ("look/observe") serves as a "literary hook between the first two sections" and appears in the next section as well (v. 13). He also notes two other hooks between these sections: מִשְׁפָּט (justice) and חָמָס (violence).

[68] Robertson, *The Books of Nahum, Habakkuk, and Zephaniah*, 141.

[69] This shift in person and imperatives also indicates a new speaker.

[70] James Bruckner, *Jonah, Nahum, Habakkuk, Zephaniah*, NIVAC (Grand Rapids: Zondervan, 2004), 210.

[71] The word *gôyîm* appears several times in Habakkuk: 1:5, 6, 17; 2:5, 8; 3:6, 12.

[72] Ronald F. Youngblood, "תָּמַה," *TWOT* 2:972.

[73] According to GKC §54.3, the *hithpael* form is primarily a reflexive of *piel*; therefore, it has an intensive meaning.

suggests a strong emphasis. The CSB captures this intensification with the use of an adverb: "be *utterly* astounded."[74] Although an initial reading of Hab 1:5 might seem to convey a sense of wonderment, a survey of the OT usage of this Hb. term shows the verb *tāmâ* often accompanies judgment and always conveys a sense of fear.[75]

The Lord's impending activity referenced in v. 5 would result in widespread shock. The Hb. word order is unusual, beginning with the accusative, "a work" (Hb. *pōʿal*) followed by a participle from the same root (Hb. *pōʿel*) "I am working" (CSB: "I am doing something"). This construction in Hb., called a *cognate accusative*, functions to show emphasis on the work itself rather than the agent.[76]

The ESV translates the line "I am doing a work"; the KJV and NKJV, "I will work a work."[77] Although the phrasing sounds a bit awkward in English, the repetition underscores the idea that despite Habakkuk's complaint about God's inactivity in the face of suffering, the Lord was already acting, having set justice in motion by summoning the Babylonians. The Hb. root of the verb *pāʿal* ("work") can describe both good and evil deeds, but when God is the subject, the deeds can only be good because God himself is righteous.[78] This explains why God's activity described in the following verse (1:6) was so shocking. From the Judeans' perspective, God was doing something evil by raising up a foreign nation to judge his own people. Even in judgment, however, the Lord's actions are always righteous.[79] The

---

[74] Other translations, like the ESV, translate the word and add a synonym: "wonder and be astounded." The ISV, however, repeats the same word twice: "Be astounded! Be really astounded!" All of these recognize that Habakkuk's repetition of the word added a level of intensity to the shocking thing God was about to reveal.

[75] See Gen 43:33; Job 26:11; Ps 48:5; Eccl 5:8; Isa 13:8; 29:9; Jer 4:9. Warren Baker and Eugene Carpenter, "תְּמַהּ," *OTWSD*, 1231, observe the related Aramaic word *təmâ*—found only in Dan 4:2, 3; 6:27—does convey a sense of wonder at the works of God.

[76] *IBHS* §10.2.1g.

[77] The original Hb. is "a work I am working."

[78] When a person is the subject of the verb, the deeds are often evil. Paired with the Hb. word *ʾāwen* (Eng. "injustice"; cf. Hab 1:3), the phrase becomes formulaic: "evildoers" or "workers of iniquity" (e.g., Ps 59:2).

[79] J. N. Boo Heflin, *Nahum, Habakkuk, Zephaniah, and Haggai* (Grand Rapids: Zondervan, 1985), 84, explains, "Obviously God was not responsible for the violence and cruelty practiced by the Babylonians. He did not inspire these attitudes and actions. Likewise, He did not force the Babylonians to assume the role of world conqueror. That was their own goal. In 'raising up the Babylonians,' God allowed them to do what they themselves wanted to do, but He used it for His purposes." Achtemeier, *Nahum—Malachi*, 38, imagines the Lord's response: "'If that is what you want,' God says in so many words, 'all right, you can have it. I give you over to your evil. You can wallow in it, and the very evil that you do will become my punishment of you.'"

initial phase of this judgment was already underway, and God would accomplish it soon: "in [Habakkuk's] days." The prophet's generation would see this work of God unfold before them. What follows in v. 6 was so astounding they would not be able to believe it even when they were told.[80]

The apostle Paul quoted Hab 1:5 (from the LXX) in the context of preaching to the Jews and God-fearers in the synagogue at Antioch of Pisidia (Acts 13). He explained that the residents and rulers of Jerusalem failed to recognize Jesus although they heard the prophets read every Sabbath. Jesus was crucified and buried, but God raised him from the dead as these Scriptures foretold.[81] Everyone who believes in him is justified and receives forgiveness from sin. Paul added the following warning:

> So beware that what is said in the prophets does not happen to you:
> **Look, you scoffers,[82]**
> **marvel [Gk. *thaumazō*] and vanish away,[83]**
> **because I am doing [Gk. *ergazomai*] a work [Gk. *ergon*] in your days,**
> **a work that you will never believe [Gk. *pisteuō*],**
> **even if someone were to explain it to you.** (Acts 13:40–41)

---

[80] Andersen, *Habakkuk*, 144, notes, "This 'deed' of God constitutes a crisis of faith for the believer, not an invitation to faith for the unbeliever."

[81] In the verses leading up to the Hab 1:5 quotation, Paul references God's "raising" Jesus from the dead four times: *egeirō* (Acts 13:30, 37) and *anistēmi* (Acts 13:33, 34). Louw and Nida's *Greek Lexicon* §23.94, includes these two synonyms in the same semantic domain along with *exegeirō*: "to cause someone to live again after having once died—'to raise to life, to make live again.'"

[82] Paul's quotation of Hab 1:5 as addressing "scoffers" (Gk. οἱ καταφρονηταί) reflects the LXX, which—along with the DSS, and Syriac versions—reads "treacherous people" (Hb. בֹּגְדִם; *bōgədim*) rather than "at the nations" (Hb. בַּגּוֹיִם; *baggôyim*). The same term appears in Hab 1:13 ("those who are treacherous") and the verb in 2:5 ("betrays"). The similarity in lettering may point to an accidental scribal substitution. Shepherd, *A Commentary on the Book of the Twelve*, 316, suggests, however, that "it is also plausible that the MT reading is an intentional attempt to soften the harshness of the reading reflected by the LXX." Unfortunately, the 1QpHab text is fragmentary in this exact spot, but the commentary on this verse refers to בוגדים three times. Shepherd, 316, concludes that "Habakkuk 1:5 serves to issue an initial warning against unbelief to the readership." Paul passed on this same warning to his audience in Pisidian Antioch (cf. Acts 13:41).

[83] Nothing in the MT corresponds to the phrase "and vanish away/be destroyed" in the LXX, as quoted here by Paul.

Paul took God's fearful work of judgment in Hab 1:5 and applied it to God's wonderful work of justification. Christ's work on the cross, however, was also in the context of judgment since God's own Son took upon himself the judgment that sinful humanity deserved. This action, which may have appeared to be "evil," was an indescribable act of love that purchased the pardon of all who by grace believe (Acts 13:39). Perhaps this later work of God in the gospel was even more astonishing than the announcement of judgment in Habakkuk's day. Paul admonished his hearers not to become like those who scoff at God's work, refusing to believe even when someone explains the resurrection to them—as Paul had just done. Despite Paul's warning, most of the Jews in Pisidian Antioch rejected his message and stirred up persecution. Many Gentiles, however, believed, and the word of God spread throughout the whole region.

Paul, familiar with the Prophets, understood how they pointed to the Messiah—just as Jesus had taught the two disciples on the road to Emmaus (Luke 24:25–27). By the Holy Spirit's direction, Paul recognized God's amazing work culminated in the crucifixion and resurrection of the Savior. Although Paul stopped short of quoting Hab 1:6, he had just described Jesus as "the one God raised up" [Gk. *egeirō*] (Acts 13:37). This word comes from the same root found in the LXX version of Hab 1:6: "I am raising up" [Gk. *exegeirō*].[84] Paul may have recognized God's work of "raising up" the Babylonians at the end of the seventh century BC in some strange way anticipated the far more marvelous work of God's raising Jesus from the dead.[85]

Intriguingly, Jesus's teaching in John 5:17–30 contains several of these same echoes that originated in Hab 1:5–6. Jesus explained that just as his Father is "working" [Gk. *ergazomai*], he also is working [Gk. *ergazomai*] (John 5:17). The Father will show the Son even "greater works" [Gk. *ergon*] so that they might "be amazed" [Gk. *thaumazō*] (v. 20, cf. 28). This astonishing work is that the Father

---

[84] In 1 Cor 6:14, Paul used both forms to refer to the resurrection of Christ and that of believers: "God raised up [Gk. *egeirō*] the Lord and will also raise us up [Gk. *exegeirō*] by his power." The only other NT occurrence of *exegeirō* is Rom 9:17, where Paul refers to God's raising up Pharaoh for his purposes (Exod 9:16)—as he would later raise up the Babylonians (Hab 1:6). The LXX often translated the *hiphil* stem of *qûm* with (*ex*)*egeirein* (e.g., Judg 2:16; Hab 1:6; Zech 11:16). See S. Amsler, "קום," *TLOT* 3:1141.

[85] Amsler, *TLOT* 3:1141, notes the *hiphil* stem of *qûm* expands its meaning: "to set (something that has fallen) up (again)," and in both Hos 6:2 and Isa 26:19, *qûm* appears parallel to *ḥyh*—"to live/come to life again."

"raises [Gk. *egeirō*] the dead" (v. 21), giving eternal life to those who believe [Gk. *pisteuō*] (v. 24). Jesus said, "Do not be amazed [Gk. *thaumazō*] at this [the healing of a disabled man], because a time is coming when all who are in the graves will hear his voice and come out . . . to the resurrection of life . . . [or] the resurrection of condemnation" (vv. 28–29). The marvelous work causing believers to be astounded is the resurrection of Christ from the dead and the subsequent resurrection of humanity—some to eternal life and others to judgment. The concentration of these same words in a similar conceptual context at least raises the possibility that Jesus, like Paul, recognized the work mentioned in Hab 1:5 pointed to the resurrection.

We can learn much through Habakkuk's experience. Although the prophet had been unable to perceive it, God was already at work in his day, purifying a remnant of his people through whom the Messiah would come. Sometimes we, too, can feel overwhelmed by the injustice and evil of our day. We cry out to heaven with heavy hearts; but for all appearances, God seems to be silent, strangely unaware, or uncaring. Habakkuk reminds us that God always sees, and he is actively working to make all things right in the end. We must cling to that assurance by faith, knowing things get darker before the dawn.

The Lord has a cosmic, eternal perspective. He sees everything in far greater detail on a global scale. The evil of Habakkuk's day was not news to him. God called him to look and observe from a broader perspective. Justice was imminent, but the prophet had to wait for it. Although it may seem like God is inactive in the present, he is marshalling justice on a grand scale. Like Habakkuk, we are focused on our own immediate context. Contrary to the vacuous tenets of Moralistic Therapeutic Deism, God doesn't exist to make us happy or make us nice.[86] This is his world, his story, his mission. He is accomplishing his

---

[86] Christian Smith and Melinda Lundquist Denton, *Soul Searching: The Religious and Spiritual Lives of American Teenagers* (New York: Oxford University Press, 2005), 162–63, coined the phrase "Moralistic Therapeutic Deism" (MTD) to describe the "de facto dominant religion among contemporary U.S. teenagers" based on the results of the massive National Study of Youth and Religion (2002–2005). The authors summarize the "creed" of MTD drawn from their findings:
1. A God exists who created and orders the world and watches over human life on earth.
2. God wants people to be good, nice, and fair to each other, as taught in the Bible and by most world religions.
3. The central goal of life is to be happy and to feel good about oneself.
4. God does not need to be particularly involved in one's life except when God is needed to resolve a problem.

eternal purposes. They may make us personally uncomfortable—to say the least—but God is administering justice and bringing about righteousness through a glorious restoration on a grand, global, eternal scale.

1.3.2   I Am Raising Up the Babylonians (1:6)

> [6] Look! I am raising up the Chaldeans,
> that bitter, impetuous nation
> that marches across the earth's open spaces
> to seize territories not its own.

1:6   In Hb., verse 6 opens with an interjection: "Behold, me!" The word "behold," from Hb. *hinnê*, frequently introduces a prophetic announcement of judgment.[87] In this instance it is combined with a first-person suffix indicating divine speech, followed by a participle. The construction underscores it was God himself who intervened in human history.[88] The OT often uses the (*hiphil*) stem of the verb "raising up" (Hb. *qûm*) to indicate God's appointment of people for a specific task: judges (Judg 2:16), priests (1 Sam 2:35), prophets (Amos 2:11), and kings (1 Kgs 14:14).[89] Although the word conveys God's sovereign provision for leaders in Israel, it also refers to his raising up someone to enact judgment against his own people. Amos used the Hb. phrase 150 years earlier to warn the Israelites of impending judgment resulting in the northern kingdom's destruction by Assyria: "But look, I am raising up a nation / against you, house of Israel"

---

5. Good people go to heaven when they die.

[87] The Hb. particle *hinnê* is often called the "particle of the outstretched finger"; in other words, it functions to instruct the reader to "pay attention" to whatever follows (*HALOT*, 252). The word "behold" may have initially entered prophetic speech as a report of a prophetic vision (e.g., Amos 7:1). The Prophets thus account for almost three-fourths of these occurrences, with Jeremiah responsible for almost half of them (sixty-three occurrences). See D. Vetter, "הִנֵּה," *TLOT* 1:380.

[88] GKC §116p, q, 147b. When the first-person suffix refers to a human, it is often an answer to a summons: "Here I am!" (e.g., 1 Sam 3:4; Isa 6:8; *HALOT*, 252). When followed by a participle, it is an announcement of what is about to occur. Allan Harman, "Particles: Exclamations," *NIDOTTE* 4:1029, notes that in 94 percent of these constructions, the subject is God, announcing a threat (Exod 9:18) or promise (Exod 34:11). These "emphatic particles . . . draw the special attention of the reader to something that is new or unexpected" (p. 1029).

[89] *HALOT*, 1088.

(Amos 6:14). The Lord would be the force responsible for stirring up and summoning "the Chaldeans."

The Chaldeans, an ancient people living in the time of the patriarchs, populated Abraham's homeland before God's calling (Gen 11:31; 15:7).[90] By the ninth century BC, the Chaldeans appeared as a well-established people located in the marshlands of the Tigris and Euphrates rivers in southern Babylonia.[91] A handful of Chaldeans had seized the opportunity of Assyrian weakness to ascend the Babylonian throne: Merodach-Baladan II (twice in the eighth century BC), Nabopolassar in 626 BC, followed by his son, Nebuchadnezzar II in 604 BC. By Habakkuk's time, the Chaldeans and Babylonians were virtually synonymous as proper names (see Isa 48:14, 20; Jer 51:24, 54).

The Lord characterized the Babylonians using poetic alliteration in Hebrew: *hammar wehannimhar* (lit., "bitter and impetuous").[92] Those words do reflect reality, since the years of Assyrian domination deeply embittered the Babylonians, and their nation was anxious to exact revenge. The Medo-Babylonian alliance hastily steamrolled across Assyria, decimating city after city: Ashur in 614 BC, Nineveh and Calah in 612, and Haran in 610. As impetuous as they were, the Babylonians took the time to identify and deface any depictions of the kings who had formerly oppressed them.[93]

Not content with crushing their longtime Assyrian nemesis, the Babylonians had already begun to march across the land aiming to take possession of territories that did not belong to them. The infinitive "to seize" (Hb. *lārešet*) in v. 6 implies "dispossession": ousting someone from his own land with the express intention of making it one's own inheritance.[94] This term often describes the "dispossession" of the Canaanites during the wilderness wanderings and the conquest.

---

[90] The English name more closely follows the Gk. spelling *chaldaioi* than the Hb. spelling *kaśdîm*. The DSS *Commentary on Habakkuk* identifies the "Chaldeans" with the historical "Kittim" of their day. VanderKam and Flint, *The Meaning of the Dead Sea Scrolls*, 281, observes that, depending on the scroll being read, "Kittim" refers to either Greeks or, more frequently, Romans. Because the word originally applied to Cyprians from the city of Citium, by extension it came to refer to any people who approached Israel from the west. In *Pesher Habakkuk*, the Kittim are likely the Romans since the commentary mentions "the Kittim sacrifice to their standards"—a Roman practice.

[91] Richard S. Hess, "Chaldea," *ABD* 1:886.

[92] Anthony Tomasino, "הָהַר," *NIDOTTE* 2:851.

[93] See 3.5, "The Neo-Babylonian Empire," in the Introduction.

[94] *HALOT*, 441.

The same infinitive appears in Deut 2:31, where the Lord dispossessed Sihon, king of Heshbon, and gave his land over to the Israelites to possess as their own inheritance.[95] Furthermore, the phrase "open spaces" (Hb. *merḥāb*) no doubt caught the attention of Habakkuk. This phrase derives from the same root as the place-name Rehoboth (Gen 26:22), a term describing the boundaries of land in Canaan promised by God as Israel's inheritance (cf. Exod 34:24; Deut 12:20; Isa 54:2).[96] Now he announced his intention to hand it over to another nation—in a reversal of the conquest.

The Lord further specified the Babylonians were coming to take possession of "dwelling places" (Hb. *miškānôt*). The word is likely more personal than the CSB translation of "territories."[97] In the plural, the word typically referred to the tents where humans resided (e.g., Num 24:5); but the Judeans were no longer a nomadic people. Perhaps a closer translation reflects the Babylonians advance to seize residences that were not their own.[98] The looming danger was literally close to home. *Miškān*, one of the terms in the ancient Near East designating a sanctuary of a deity, often refers to the tabernacle in the OT, synonymous with the Lord's dwelling place among the Israelites.[99] The temple had long since replaced the tent of the tabernacle.[100] Still, this word may have evoked the image of the holy sanctuary of the past—even more so when this prophecy would be read following the destruction of Jerusalem's temple. Verse 6 closes with a pair of homonyms emphasizing the Babylonians were not the rightful owners of these dwelling places: they are *"not* his" (Hb. *lōʾ-lō*; emphasis added).

---

[95] The land belonged to the Lord and was his to pass on to another when the sin of the previous "tenant" reached full measure. See Gen 15:16.

[96] *HALOT*, 634.

[97] According to *HALOT*, 647, the word *miškānōt* usually refers to the "abode" of individuals (Num 16:24) or a people (Isa 32:18).

[98] Andersen, *Habakkuk*, 150, conjectures that the word *miškānōt* underwent "a semantic shift with urbanization." As a metaphor it can describe "all the houses in a city" or "territories" without houses—as in Job 39:6 where the wild donkey makes "the salty wasteland his dwelling." Andersen, 150, concludes "the meaning in Hab 1:6 lies somewhere along this semantic spectrum—tents, houses, cities, (inhabited) regions."

[99] Richard E. Averbeck, "מִשְׁכָּן," *NIDOTTE* 2:1124–25.

[100] Several psalms use the plural form, *miškānōt*, in reference to the temple (Ps 43:3; 46:4; 84:1). Averbeck, *NIDOTTE* 2:1125, observes that these plural references may indicate "the various parts of the temple complex distributively" or "the complex as a whole as a plural of intensity or majesty."

Although some scholars observe the shock of the announcement in Hab 1:5–6 demands pushing the date of Habakkuk back a few decades, it is unnecessary.[101] The astonishing news focused on the Babylonians as the Lord's instrument of judgment. Just as the Lord graciously turned the land of Canaan over to the Israelites, now he was surrendering Judah into the hands of the Babylonians. Other OT passages likewise confirm the claim identifying the Lord himself as the force behind the imminent attack of the Babylonians against Judah (2 Kgs 24:1–4; Jer 37:6–10). The Babylonians would have been similarly surprised to discover their designs were not their own.

Habakkuk 1:5–6 underscores the truth that God is sovereign over the nations. He can move them like pawns in a board game, summon them to do his bidding, and accomplish his purposes. The prophet Isaiah frames this same truth with vivid imagery. Preceding the conquest of the northern kingdom, he warned, "On that day / the LORD will whistle to flies / at the farthest streams of the Nile / and to bees in the land of Assyria" (Isa 7:18). The prophet similarly warned Jerusalem as well: "He raises a signal flag for the distant nations / and whistles for them from the ends of the earth. / Look—how quickly and swiftly they come!" (Isa 5:26). Although the Lord is compassionate and slow to anger, once aroused, his judgment is terrifying. Trust in the temple rather than the Lord turned out to be misplaced trust.[102] The Lord would not even spare his own dwelling place. The looming destruction of Jerusalem and the temple was simply the next step in his mission to bring salvation not just to the Jews but to the whole earth.[103]

Imagine how terrifying Hab 1:5–6 would be if it were translated into our experience today. Tragically, for many people around the world, the task does not require imagination since they have recently experienced the horrors of war firsthand. Few countries escape the ravages of armed conflict for long. What if, after centuries of waiting, the Lord's patience reaches its limit? What if he announces that he is raising up a powerful foreign nation to invade and destroy your

---

[101] See "Date" in the Introduction.

[102] See Jer 7:1–20.

[103] In the NT, John 1:14 describes Jesus as the Word of God incarnate who tabernacled among his people. God would not spare him either but freely gave him up to justify us all (Rom 8:32–33). Both Testaments affirm that nothing can stop God from accomplishing his ultimate mission—to dwell in the midst of his purified people forever (Ezek 37:26–28; Rev 21:3–4).

country, to seize homes that are not their own—including yours? Could you trust that God must have a purpose behind his judgment?

A few years before his death, Billy Graham wrote the following in a prayer letter entitled "My Heart Aches for America":

> Some years ago, my wife, Ruth, was reading the draft of a book I was writing. When she finished a section describing the terrible downward spiral of our nation's moral standards and the idolatry of worshiping false gods such as technology and sex, she startled me by exclaiming, "If God doesn't punish America, he'll have to apologize to Sodom and Gomorrah."[104]

Consider how much further the world has plummeted into sin since Ruth Graham's death in 2007. Although God has repeatedly shown mercy, we cannot presume that he will continue to spare any nation indefinitely. If he did, he would owe Judah—and the prophet Habakkuk—an apology as well.

1.3.3   They Are Fierce and Terrifying (1:7–8)

> [7] *They are fierce and terrifying;*
> *their views of justice and sovereignty*
> *stem from themselves.*
> [8] *Their horses are swifter than leopards*
> *and more fierce than wolves of the night.*
> *Their horsemen charge ahead;*
> *their horsemen come from distant lands.*
> *They fly like eagles, swooping to devour.*

1:7   The Lord continued his description of the Babylonians.[105] The first adjective, translated as "fierce" (Hb. *ʾāyōm*), conveys an idea

---

[104] Billy Graham, "Billy Graham: 'My Heart Aches for America'" Billy Graham Evangelistic Association (July 19, 2012). Online: https://billygraham.org/story/billy-graham-my-heart-aches-for-america.

[105] The Hebrew text of 1:7–11 uses singular pronouns and pronominal suffixes to reference the singular antecedent "nation" in 1:5: "he," "him," "his," and "it." Roberts, *Nahum, Habakkuk, and Zephaniah*, 92, observes that "the lack of the neuter in Hebrew makes possible a certain fluidity between the nation, personified as a male, and the nation's king, as the embodiment of the character of the nation." Like most English translations, the CSB uses plural referents here: "they," "their," and "them." For examples of commentators' translations that retain singular referents, see Roberts, p. 91; and Shepherd, *A Commentary on the Book of the Twelve*, 314–15.

of arousing dread.[106] In its OT usage, the related noun describes things that instill terror, such as the snorting of a warhorse (Job 39:20), the teeth of Leviathan (Job 41:14), and the lion-like wrath of a king (Prov 20:2). The term also describes the panic descending on the surrounding peoples as the Lord accompanied the Israelites on their way into Canaan (Exod 15:16; 23:27; Josh 2:9). The second adjective, "terrifying" (Hb. *nôrāʾ*), describes the desert wilderness (Deut 1:19; 8:15; Isa 21:1) or a people to be feared, for instance, the Cushites (Isa 18:2, 7) or the Babylonians (Hab 1:7). Like the first adjective, the second also relates to the realm of supernatural fear. The word frequently refers to "the great redemptive acts of God"—like the exodus, as well as to God himself, his name, and his presence.[107] Both terms often describe the terror that descended on other nations as God led his people into the promised land; however, the roles were reversed in this context. God chose to use the invading Babylonians to ignite terror in the hearts of his own people, who continually disobeyed the Lord.

"Justice" and "sovereignty" belong to God. Because the Lord exemplifies true justice, all humanity should model this same characteristic (Ps 106:3; Mic 6:8).[108] When the source of justice is the sinful human heart, however, it results in injustice even among God's own people (Hab 1:4; Rom 3:10–12). The word translated in CSB as "sovereignty" (Hb. *śeʾēt*) conveys a sense of dignity or exaltation. In Gen 49:3, it describes the preeminence of Jacob's firstborn son. More appropriately, it describes the majesty of God (Job 13:11; 31:23).[109] All glory and honor belong to God. When the fallen human heart becomes the measure of what is right and just, the results are sure to come out skewed. Swollen with pride, the Babylonians considered themselves exalted and sovereign. They did not understand their fleeting success was due to sovereign God's plans and purposes. Ironically, the Lord planned to use the Babylonians to administer justice against his own people

---

Though the Judeans might view the Babylonian army as a monolithic force, from God's perspective, they were just one entity.

[106] M. V. Van Pelt and W. C. Kaiser Jr., "אָיֹם," *NIDOTTE* 1:377.

[107] Van Pelt and Kaiser, *NIDOTTE* 2:524.

[108] Robert D. Culver, "מִשְׁפָּט," *TWOT* 2:949.

[109] *HALOT*, 1301, suggests an alternative translation for v. 7b, in which the masculine singular suffix attributes "justice and sovereignty" to God rather than the self-affirming Babylonians (CSB). The alternative translation highlights the contrast between a terrifying enemy (v. 7a) and God's absolute control over her (v. 7b).

1:8   Verse 8 describes the Babylonian cavalry as formidable. For centuries ancient armies had harnessed horsepower to drive chariots, but the weaponization of horses themselves was a new tactical development in the art of warfare. Although reliefs dating to the twelfth century BC depict soldiers riding bareback, they lacked the control of the animal necessary for combat. An Assyrian eighth-century-BC bas-relief shows cavalrymen working in pairs: one soldier held both sets of reins while a second aimed his bow.[110] By the time of Ashurbanipal (668–626 BC), cavalry had overtaken the use of chariots in Assyrian warfare. Innovations in saddlery allowed individual riders to achieve secure seating, enabling them to shoot from a mounted position with precision.[111] These Assyrian improvements, likely borrowed from the Scythians, may have paradoxically contributed to their own demise. Nahum's poetic depiction of Nineveh's destruction at the hands of the Babylonians appears to include both chariots and cavalry (Nah 3:2–3). Later, Ezekiel warned the Lord would send Nebuchadnezzar against Tyre not only with a massive number of troops but also with chariots, cavalry, and horses "so numerous that their dust [would] cover [them]" as they "trample all [their] streets with [their] hooves" (Ezek 26:7–11). The Lord was assembling this same advanced army against Judah.

A series of animal metaphors in v. 8 amplifies the sense of terror aroused by the Babylonian army. Their approaching horses are "swifter than leopards." In the OT, leopards are noteworthy not only for their swiftness but also for their stalking prowess (Jer 5:6; Hos 13:7).[112] Verse 8 also describes the Babylonian horses as fiercer than wolves that prowl in the dark. The word translated "fierce" (from Hb. *ḥādad*) can refer to the literal sharpness of a sword (Ezek 21:9–11)

---

[110] John Keegan, *A History of Warfare* (Toronto: Vintage Books Canada, 1994), 177. Solomon, at the height of his reign, possessed "four thousand stalls for horses and chariots, and twelve thousand horsemen" (2 Chr 9:25). By 701 BC, however, when the Assyrians threatened Jerusalem, they taunted Judah for having to rely on Egypt's horses. Sennacherib's representative sarcastically offered to give Hezekiah two thousand horses, only to mock that he did not have the horsemen necessary to use them (see 2 Kgs 18:23–24 // Isa 36:8–9).

[111] Duncan Noble, "Assyrian Chariotry and Cavalry," *SAAB* 4.1 (1990): 65–66. See also Yigael Yadin, *The Art of Warfare in Biblical Lands*, vol. 1, trans. M. Pearlman (New York: McGraw-Hill, 1963), 4–5.

[112] Once considered common in Israel, the Judean (or Arabian) leopard ranged from the Negev and Sinai Peninsula to the Arabian Peninsula and typically fed on a wild mountain goat called an ibex (cf. Isa 11:6). Although Judean leopards are among the smaller leopard subspecies, larger leopards can reach speeds upwards of thirty-five miles per hour.

or the metaphorical keenness of a sharp-tongued enemy (Ps 57:4; Isa 49:2).[113] Ezekiel described Judah's government officials as bloodthirsty wolves, who tear their prey to pieces (Ezek 22:27). Because wolves possess powerful night vision, they are nocturnal predators. As in Hab 1:8, Zephaniah compared Judah's corrupt judges to evening wolves, observing they "leave nothing for the morning" (Zeph 3:3). The leaders of Judah acted like animals, preying on their own people, so the Lord vowed to punish Judah with an enemy (Babylon), whom he describes as "[a] wolf from arid plains," a leopard who "stalks their cities" (Jer 5:6). Not only are the Babylonian horses swift and fierce; they are also anxious to run.[114]

The second half of v. 8 shifts the focus from horses to their Babylonian riders.[115] The horsemen advanced with warhorses charging, coming from afar. As the crow flies, the distance between Babylon and Jerusalem was approximately six hundred miles (a thousand km).[116] Since the attack would come from the north, Jeremiah warned Judah's leaders when the snorting of the Babylonians' mighty steeds reached Dan—Israel's once northernmost city—the whole land would quake because "[t]hey come to devour the land and everything in it, / the city and all its residents" (Jer 8:16). Jeremiah 4:13 describes an advancing enemy as "swifter than eagles," as does the remarkably prescient prophecy found in Deut 28:49–52. Habakkuk 1:8 uses similar imagery, comparing the speed of the horsemen to eagles, "swooping to devour." When pursuing its prey, the golden eagle—native to Israel—folds its wings and power dives to surprise and kill its victim instantly. Incredibly, when swooping down from great heights, the golden eagle can reach speeds well over one hundred miles per hour.[117]

---

[113] P. J. M. Southwell, "חָדַד," NIDOTTE 2:24.

[114] Bailey, "Habakkuk," 306.

[115] The Hb. word pārāšāyw that occurs twice in v. 8 can refer to either "horse" or "horsemen" (HALOT, 977–78). BHS suggests that the duplicate wording may be a result of dittography. The deletion of one of the pārāšāyw duplicates finds support in a few MSS and in the Greek, Syriac, and Samaritan Pentateuch versions. Grace Ko, Theodicy in Habakkuk, 58, observes that the Hb. phrase behind "their horsemen charging" (ûphāšû pārāšāyw) is "brilliant." The onomatopoeia of these two similar-sounding words produces the rushing sound of fast-moving horses.

[116] The extreme conditions of the Arabian Desert, however, necessitated they take a northern route along the Fertile Crescent that lengthened the journey to over a thousand miles (that is, sixteen hundred km).

[117] Alice Parmelee, All the Birds of the Bible (New Canaan, CT: Keats, 1969), 118–19, 200. The Hb. word has alternatively been translated as "vultures" in the ISV, NET, and JPS. Here, however,

It is difficult for most modern readers to relate to the terror these animal metaphors must have triggered in Habakkuk's audience.[118] Habituation to humans, however, has led to terrifying wolf attacks in the Judean desert.[119] Intriguingly, modern armies have also tapped into these same animal metaphors.[120]

1.3.4 They Come for Violence (1:9–11)

9 *All of them come to do violence;*
   their faces are set in determination.
   They gather prisoners like sand.
10 *They mock kings,*
   and rulers are a joke to them.
   They laugh at every fortress
   and build siege ramps to capture it.
11 *Then they sweep by like the wind*
   and pass through.
   They are guilty; their strength is their god.

1:9   Verse 9 unmasks the motive of the Babylonian warriors. The whole army approached "to do violence." Ironically, the Hb. word *ḥāmās*, "to treat violently," echoes Habakkuk's own shouts of "Violence!" regarding the injustices committed by his fellow countrymen (1:2–3). The Lord's answer was a form of *lex talionis*—the law of

---

the image of an eagle diving after its prey seems more fitting than that of a vulture consuming carrion. See Amerding, "Habakkuk," 503.

[118] Research reported in 2004 indicates that the Judean leopard totters on the brink of extinction, with only eight such leopards reported in Israel, including two in the Judean desert. See Zafrir Rinat, "New Study Reveals Eight Leopards Remain in Israel," *Haaretz* (January 20, 2004). Online: https://www.haaretz.com/1.4830128.

[119] An expanding human population has also encroached on the habitat of the Arabian wolf in Israel, according to Nir Hasson, "Ten Attacks in Four Months: Brazen Wolves Preying on Children in Israel's South," *Haaretz* (September 22, 2017). Online: https://www.haaretz.com/israel-news/MAGAZINE-brazen-wolves-preying-on-children-in-southern-israel-1.5452359. Perhaps these recent campground encounters come closer to replicating the ancient world in which travel was usually by foot and temporary shelter was sought in tents.

[120] The legendary speed of leopards led the German army to christen their main battle tanks "Leopard 1" (1965–1979) and "Leopard 2" (1979 to the present). Likewise, the Israeli Defense Force has named its armored personnel carrier the "Wolf" because of its speed and maneuverability. The Israeli Air Force has incorporated its new F-35 stealth fighter jets into its "Golden Eagle Squadron." A news announcement that an attack was imminent from these Leopards, Wolves, and Eagles would strike fear into hearts of modern hearers.

reciprocal punishment: the perpetrators of violence, injustice, and oppression would meet a similarly violent end.

A survey of parallel translations and the extensive text critical notes in MT for v. 9 reveal the difficulty posed by the middle clause: "their faces are set in determination" (CSB). This clause contains a *hapax legomenon*—a word that appears only once in the OT. Suggested meanings for this obscure word (Hb. *məgammâ*) include "assembling,"[121] "totality,"[122] "to be full, abundant,"[123] and "horde; eagerness."[124] The term, in construct with "their faces," is modified by a second word (Hb. *qādîmâ*) meaning "the fore or front part," "east(-ward)" or, by extension, "an east wind."[125] OT references to an eastern wind reveal that it can bring locusts (Exod 10:13), wither vegetation (Ezek 17:10; Jonah 4:8), wreck ships (Ps 48:7), and deliver God's judgment (Isa 27:8). The CSB translation conveys the eager resolve of the soldiers, marching with determination. Various translations reflect a range of other possibilities: for example, "all their faces forward" (ESV); "Their horde of faces moves forward" (NASB); "Their faces are set *like* the east wind" (NKJV); and "Their hordes advance like a desert wind" (NIV). There is also the possibility both meanings—"face forward" and "like an east wind"—are intentional.[126]

---

[121] BDB, 170. Although acknowledging the meaning is uncertain, Dominique Barthélemy, *Preliminary and Interim Report on the Hebrew Old Testament Text Project*, vol. 5 (New York: United Bible Societies, 1980), 352, translates *məgammāt* as "the direction of."

[122] *HALOT*, 545.

[123] *HALOT*, 197; Andrew E. Hill, "מְגַמֶּה," *NIDOTTE* 2:837.

[124] "מְגַמֶּה," *OTWSD*, 568. Nogalski, *Redactional Processes in the Book of the Twelve*, 23, argues that "hordes" (Hb. *məgammāh*) is a catchword linking Habakkuk to the plague of locusts in Joel. This word, however, is too obscure to uphold such a claim. Ward, "Habakkuk," 9, pronounced it "untranslatable."

[125] *HALOT*, 1068. The translation as "east wind" is suggested by the readings in 1QpHab, the Targums, and the versions of LXX.

[126] David Toshio Tsumura, "Polysemy and Parallelism in Hab 1, 8–9," *ZAW* (2008): 198, argues that this is an example of "polysemous [multiple meanings] *Janus parallelism*." Cyrus H. Gordon, "New Directions," *The Bulletin of the American Society of Papyrologists* 15.1 (1978): 59, coined the literary term *Janus parallelism*—a reference to the two-faced Greek god that looks backwards and forwards—defining it as "the use of a singular word with two entirely different meanings: one meaning paralleling what precedes, and the other meaning, what follows." Tsumura, p. 198, observes the dual meanings of *qādîmâ* (in the middle line) fit both the previous and following lines:

All of them come for violence,
they all face forward/like an east wind;
they gather captives like sand.

With singleness of purpose, the Babylonians would "gather prisoners like sand." The reference to sand, along with the sweeping wind
in v. 11, reinforces a comparison of the advancing army to an east
wind, coming from the desert. This wind, however, is not the typical
sirocco-like wind (Arab. *hamsin*; Hb. *šarav*) that forms in the west
over the Sahara and flows in a northeasterly direction across Egypt
into Israel. Instead, this wind originates in the east over the Syrian
Desert before moving southwesterly into Israel.[127] In comparison to
the Babylonian troops blowing in from the east, their captives would
be insignificant grains of sand caught up by that wind and then carried
off into exile. The number of victims would be vast, ironically echoing
the Lord's promises to Abraham to make his descendants as numerous
as "the sand on the seashore" (Gen 22:17). David Baker observes this
metaphor of blessing from Genesis is here "turned on its head."[128]
As the prophet Isaiah warned, "Israel, even if your people were as
numerous / as the sand of the sea, / only a remnant of them will return.
/ Destruction has been decreed; / justice overflows" (Isa 10:22). The
claim of physical descent from Abraham was no guarantee of immunity from God's judgment.

1:10 The Babylonians displayed contempt for their opponents.
The word "mock" (Hb. *qālas*) means "to deride or make fun of people or things that deserve respect," such as a king (Hab 1:10) or a
prophet (2 Kgs 2:23),[129] showing blatant disregard for authority figures.[130] The participle translated "rulers" comes from the Hb. verb
rāzan, "meaning to be weighty, firm, reliable in judgment, as befitting
a dignitary."[131] Instead of honoring these dignitaries, the Babylonians
treated rulers as objects of derision. The behavior of the Babylonians
at Nineveh in 612 BC confirms this characterization. Before burning

---

Tsumura, 201, also suggests a second example of *Janus parallelism* exists in v. 8, where the
polysemous *pārāšāyw* carries the dual meaning of "his steeds" and "his horsemen."

[127] For example, Sharon Udasin, "Researchers stumped as dust storm persists in Israel
for third day," *The Jerusalem Post* (September 11, 2015), Online: https://www.jpost.com/Busi-
ness-and-Innovation/Environment/Researchers-stumped-as-dust-storm-persists-in-Israel-for-
third-day-415927. Garland, "Habakkuk," 254, explained the thinking behind the KJV translation:
"[T]heir faces shall sup up as the east wind." The invasion is so swift "the Chaldeans seem to
sup up the people or swallow them in the same way the east wind destroys all before it by its
scorching heat."

[128] Baker, *Nahum, Habakkuk and Zephaniah*, 52.

[129] *HALOT*, 1105.

[130] Tim Powell, "קָלַס," *NIDOTTE* 3:926.

[131] *HALOT*, 1210.

the palace to the ground, these conquerors searched the wall reliefs for Assyrian kings Sennacherib and Ashurbanipal in order to gouge out their eyes and ears. This grotesque mockery in art foreshadowed their later real-life actions against Zedekiah in 586 BC. When the last king of Judah tried to escape besieged Jerusalem, he was captured and brought before Nebuchadnezzar. The Babylonian king forced Zedekiah to watch the slaughter of his sons and all Judah's nobles before blinding him (Jer 39:6–7). In a sense this punishment carried a measure of retributive justice. The rulers and officials of Judah who repeatedly dared to mock God, his word, his covenant, and his prophets (Jer 20:7–8) would eventually find themselves the laughingstock of the surrounding nations (Ezek 22:4–5).

The Babylonians not only mocked kings and rulers; they also laughed at their defenses. For centuries fortresses based on Iron Age I casemate walls had formed an effective line of defense.[132] Iron Age II advances in warfare—like the battering ram—led to the construction of stronger, solid walls built on a stone base three to four meters thick, with brick superstructures reaching up to twelve meters in height. Archaeology shows that walls in this period used glacis (artificial slope that exposed attackers), recesses and salients (sections that jutted in and out), as well as bastions and towers. Details from Assyrian reliefs chronicling the destruction of Lachish reveal crenelated towers equipped with balconies and special wooden structures that held archers' shields in place. City gates also underwent strategic changes designed to contravene battering rams. They were smaller, more solid, and built with an angled approach.[133] John Oswalt observes, "Since fortified cities were so strong, it was a great temptation for the Israelites to put their trust in them instead of in their God. Thus, the prophets are at pains to show the folly of such trust . . . [for] God alone is mankind's stronghold" (cf. Ps 27:1; Jer 5:17).[134]

The Assyrians developed other innovations to compensate for these defensive improvements. The Lachish reliefs indicate Sennacherib (704–681 BC) made improvements to earlier Assyrian battering

---

[132] The spies' report of Canaan's "large and fortified cities" had melted the Israelites' hearts and frozen their advance in its tracks (Num 13:28). Even long after the Israelites conquered the land, the Iron Age I casemate walls of Jebus (Jerusalem) held them at bay until David's forces finally caught the city by surprise, using a water shaft to enter the stronghold (2 Sam 5:6–8).

[133] Yadin, *The Art of Warfare*, 322–27, 428–37.

[134] John N. Oswalt, "מִבְצָר," *TWOT* 1:123.

rams, lengthening the ramming rod, developing a smaller, prefabricated machine with easily assembled parts, and covering the entirety with leather. These siege machines used an existing path to approach and attack the city gates. Attempting to breach a wall, however, required the construction of an earthen ramp, paved with rocks or bricks.[135] The Assyrian reliefs also illustrate a wide range of other offensive modes of attack, including fully armored archers, slingmen, and shield bearers. Scenes depict soldiers wielding pikes and levers to breach the walls, others endeavoring to tunnel under them, and still others attempting to climb over them on ten-meter scaling ladders.[136] When these relatively sophisticated systems of offense and defense led to a standoff, a siege could ultimately prevail simply by starving the city into surrender. The citizens of Jerusalem were conscious of the horrors the city of Samaria had endured during the three-year siege by the Assyrians.[137]

1:11   The Babylonians are again compared to a wind sweeping through the land (v. 9).[138] Jeremiah used the metaphor of wind to describe God's judgment via a northern enemy who would besiege the cities of Judah: "A searing wind blows from the barren heights in the wilderness on the way to my dear people. It comes not to winnow or to sift; a wind too strong for this comes at my call. Now I will also pronounce judgments against them" (Jer 4:11–12). The Lord announced his intention in Hab 1:11 to use the Babylonians as the agent through whom his destructive "wind" would blow. An alternative translation by Bruce emphasizes a different aspect of wind: "Then they change course like the wind." Pointing to the Babylonians'

---

[135] Yadin, *The Art of Warfare*, 315. A literal translation of the phrase "build siege ramps" is "heap up dust." In context the word *dust* (Hb. *ʿāpār*) refers to loose soil, but it also theologically echoes humanity's origins from dust (Gen 3:19). The term often figuratively stands for death itself (e.g., Pss 22:16; 30:10). See G. Wanke, "עָפָר," *TLOT* 2:940.

[136] Yadin, *The Art of Warfare*, 316–18, 430–31.

[137] The Babylonians, as well, knew firsthand what a protracted siege involved. In 689 BC, the city of Babylon had fallen to the Assyrians after a grueling fifteen-month siege. The Babylonians, however, astutely learned the art of siege from their captors. Seventy-five years later, they turned the tables, destroying every major Assyrian stronghold with the Assyrians' own military innovations. By the time they turned their attention toward Judah, they were seasoned veterans. As impressive as Jerusalem's fortifications might have been, the Babylonians would laugh at them because they knew from experience they would eventually crumble.

[138] Andersen, *Habakkuk*, 158–59, observes that even without adding the preposition *k-*, *rûaḥ* can function as a simile. See also Andersen's "Excursus: Grammatical Gender of *rûaḥ*" (pp. 160–65).

temporary suspension of the Jerusalem siege in 588 BC (Jer 37:11), Bruce explains, "The reference is to a change in tactical or strategic planning."[139]

Intent on destruction, the Babylonian army typically swept through a country, creating a wide swath of carnage and wreckage. They did not follow the Assyrian paradigm of rebuilding cities and repopulating provinces to maintain streams of revenue. Instead, the Babylonians focused solely on the city of Babylon. Once they eliminated threats to her dominion, they simply abandoned and neglected the outlying territories of their empire. Archaeological remains testify to this same practice across the Levant. The only lasting mark the Babylonians would leave behind was a widespread level of destruction.[140]

The Lord, fully aware of the Babylonians' actions and the motivation behind them, pronounced them "guilty" (Hb. *'āšam*). This cultic term often implies moral or legal culpability, which among God's people includes covenant offenses.[141] Although the Babylonians were not guilty of breaking God's covenant, they were culpable for their delight in the brutal destruction of God's covenant people.[142] The word choice may be a play on the previous two verbs describing their actions as

---

[139] Bruce, "Habakkuk," 850. According to *HALOT*, 1197–1201, *rûaḥ* has a broad range of meanings, including "breeze, breath, wind, spirit, and Spirit." *Rûaḥ* can also mean "the mind or intellectual frame of mind"; for example, where the king "changes his mind" (e.g., KJV, NKJV). Robertson, *The Books of Nahum, Habakkuk, and Zephaniah*, 155, translates v. 11a this way: "Then his spirit changes, and he becomes angry and sins." In doing so, he emphasizes the shift from "mild-mannered mockery of fortifications" to the deadly serious business of "murderous mutilation." Roberts, *Nahum, Habakkuk, and Zephaniah*, 99, observes that *rûaḥ* occurs in conjunction with *'ābar* not only in Hab 1:11 but also in 1 Kgs 22:24: "Which way did the spirit (*rûaḥ*) of Yahweh pass (*'ābar*) from me to speak with you?" Based on this parallel passage, Roberts contends "it is best to take v. 11a not as a continuation of the description of the Babylonians but as a notice by the prophet that the revelation which brought him Yahweh's response to his lament ended at this point. The spirit departed" (p. 99).

[140] See 3.5, "The Neo-Babylonian Empire," in the Introduction.

[141] The term denotes a state of guilt, suffering for one's guilt by punishment, paying a penalty to atone for guilt, or pleading guilty by one's attitude (*HALOT*, 95). Eugene Carpenter and Michael A. Grisanti, "אָשַׁם," *NIDOTTE* 1:547, point out that in two-thirds of the OT occurrences, the nominative is a technical term referring to the guilt or reparation offering. The tense of *wə'āšēm* (lit., "and guilty") poses problems, where the *waw*-consecutive plus perfect verb follows the *waw*-consecutive plus imperfect verb. GKC §111a observes that "[a]s a rule the narrative is introduced by a perfect and then continued by means of imperfects with *wāw consecutive*." Thus, an action in progress (imperfect) normally reaches "a calm and settled conclusion" in the perfect (GKC §112a). In v. 11 we have the reverse. Goldingay and Scalise, *Minor Prophets II*, 59, describe the MT text of v. 11 as "jerky" in both grammar and train of thought.

[142] Carpenter and Grisanti, *NIDOTTE* 1:547.

"sweeping by" (Hb. *ḥālap*) and "passing on" (Hb. *ʿābar*)—both of
which when transitive convey a secondary meaning of overstepping or
transgressing.[143]

The root of the adversary's guilt is described in this emphatic
statement: "[T]heir strength is their god."[144] The Lord is the source
of all strength. When King Jehoshaphat faced foreign armies in vast
numbers, he confessed this reality: "LORD, God of our ancestors, are
you not the God who is in heaven, and do you not rule over all the
kingdoms of the nations? Power and might are in your hand, and no
one can stand against you" (2 Chr 20:6). David also recognized any
human wealth or strength was endowed by God. He said, "Yours,
LORD, is the greatness and the power and the glory and the splendor
and the majesty, for everything in the heavens and on earth belongs to
you. . . . Power and might are in your hand, and it is in your hand to
make great and to give strength to all" (1 Chr 29:11–12). The Babylonians arrogantly assumed their power stemmed from themselves as
a people,[145] as depicted by Nebuchadnezzar's arrogant boast leading
to his seven-year madness: "Is this not Babylon the Great that I have
built to be a royal residence by my vast power and for my majestic

---

[143] *HALOT*, 321, notes that *ḥālap* in Hab 1:11 means "to fly along, to pass over." Robert
Chisholm and Eugene Carpenter, "חָלַף" *NIDOTTE* 2:153, similarly list primary meanings for
ḥālap—"sweep through, pass through"—but they also include a secondary meaning, "violate."
As Chisholm and Carpenter point out, "In Isa 24:5 [*ḥālap*] is used of humankind's violating God's
statute (i.e., his passing over the boundary prescribed by God)." *HALOT*, 779, references both
meanings for *ʿābar*—"move through" and "overstep, contravene" Yahweh's commands—as does
Allan M. Harman, "עָבַר" *NIDOTTE* 3:313. Intriguingly, both Hb. terms—*ḥālap* and *ʿābar*—appear
as parallel synonyms in Isa 24:5. Although in Hab 1:11 the same two verbs are intransitive, there
may be a possibility that echoes of their secondary meanings come into play when the terms
occur in close proximity with *ʾāšam*. Floyd, *Minor Prophets Part 2*, 104, understands v. 11a to
mean "the Babylonians have 'violated' . . . Yahweh's divine commission, and in thus overstepping their assigned role they have 'transgressed.'"

[144] Bailey, "Habakkuk," 308.

[145] A few translations (KJV, JPS) suggest an alternate reading, where the Babylonians attribute their strength to their own god rather than to Yahweh. Shepherd, *A Commentary on the
Book of the Twelve*, 315, translates 1:11b this way: "*And this one whose strength is ascribed to
his god is guilty.*" (See also Shepherd, 315n.) If this reading is correct, the most likely god would
have been Marduk. By the latter half of the second millennium BC, Marduk had risen to the head
of the Babylonian pantheon and became the national god of Babylonia. Among the myriad gods
they worshiped, Marduk—the god of magic—was the deity most commonly invoked in incan-
tations. See H. W. F. Saggs, *The Babylonians: A Survey of the Ancient Civilisation of the Tigris-
Euphrates Valley* (London: The Folio Society, 1999), 266, 237.

glory?" (Dan 4:30). This attitude of "self-deification" laid bare the Babylonians' guilt before the Lord.[146]

1.4 HABAKKUK'S SECOND COMPLAINT (1:12–2:1)

Imagine Habakkuk's bewilderment following the description of events about to unfold in his day; the characterization of the Babylonian army borders on hyperbole.[147] The metaphorical language infuses the looming crisis—God's activity—with a sense of eschatological portent. God's announcement revealed the Babylonian invasion would originate with the Lord. Habakkuk was familiar with Babylonian brutality and self-interest. The Lord's actions were unexpected. Unable to stifle his dismay, the prophet voiced another round of questions to the Lord, describing his confusion.

1.4.1 Lord, You Are Holy (1:12–13a)

> [12] *Are you not from eternity,* Lord *my God?*
> *My Holy One, you will not die.*
> Lord, *you appointed them to execute judgment;*
> *my Rock, you destined them to punish us.*
> [13] *Your eyes are too pure to look on evil,*
> *and you cannot tolerate wrongdoing.*

1:12–13a Habakkuk expressed the heaviness of his heart in careful poetic form. Andersen observes the tone of this second prayer, which is twice as long as the first, is less strident and the poetic composition more disciplined.[148] The prayer includes several pivot patterns, including the names of God in v. 12a, the infinitives in v. 13, the two similes in v. 14, the two complements in v. 15a, and the nouns and adjectives in 16b.[149] The prophet opens and closes his prayer with questions introduced by the interrogative particle *ha*. Standing at the beginning of vv. 12 and 17, the particle acts as an inclusio, framing the second prayer. The opening interrogative *hălōʾ* (Eng. "Are you not?") often occurs in the Latter Prophets with God as the speaker, "chiding

---

[146] Floyd, *Minor Prophets Part 2*, 106.
[147] Fuhr and Yates, *The Message of the Twelve*, 228.
[148] Andersen, *Habakkuk*, 187, 171.
[149] Andersen, *Habakkuk*, 174, 185.

the hearer for overlooking an important fact."[150] Here, on the lips of Habakkuk, the rhetorical question amounts to a reproach of God himself. As Prior observes, there is a distinction "between bitter cynicism and believing confrontation: one is a denial that refuses to believe, the other is a belief that refuses to deny; one makes assertions and will not stay for an answer, the other makes assertions and will not move until there is an answer."[151] Habakkuk's anguished protests stemmed from a heart of faith.

Habakkuk's second prayer includes intimate terms characterizing his relationship with the Lord. This time he addressed the Lord by name—not just once, as he did in 1:2, but five times in v. 12 alone. The prophet chose names reaffirming the Lord's identity and clarifying his own relationship to him: "Yahweh" (2x), "my God," "my Holy One," "my Rock."[152] Habakkuk's use of these titles also functions as a polemic to the so-called "god" of the Babylonians mentioned at the end of the preceding verse: either the soldiers' own strength or a Babylonian deity (v. 11). Either way, theirs was a god of their own making. Habakkuk's God was wholly other than their god, who was no god at all.

Twice the prophet called on the "Lord"—Yahweh—the covenant name God revealed to Moses when he bound himself to his people. In response to Moses's query about his name, the Lord had replied: "I AM WHO I AM. This is what you are to say to the Israelites: I AM has sent me to you. . . . The LORD, the God of your ancestors, the God of Abraham, the God of Isaac, and the God of Jacob, has sent me to you. This is my name forever; this is how I am to be remembered in

---

[150] Andersen, *Habakkuk*, 175. For example, the construction occurs four times in Isa 40:21: "Do you not know? / Have you not heard? / Has it not been declared to you . . . ? / Have you not considered . . . ?" The particle assumes an affirmative answer and adds rhetorical emphasis to what is likely well known (BDB, 520).

[151] Prior, *The Message of Joel, Micah, and Habakkuk*, 222–23. Bruckner, *Jonah, Nahum, Habakkuk, Zephaniah*, 215, likewise observes a subtle distinction between faithful and unfaithful lament: "The faithful protest begins with an attitude that continues to address God ('God, how could you allow...?'). The unfaithful protest begins with the impersonal (and judging) abstraction ('How could God allow...?')."

[152] The CSB translation adds the first common singular suffix "my" to "Rock" (Hb. ṣûr). The term "my Rock" (Hb. ṣûrî) occurs in passages that have other parallels with Habakkuk: 2 Sam 22:3, 47 // Ps 18:2.46. References to the Lord as "my Rock" also occur in Pss 19:14; 62:2, 6; 92:15; 144:1. Some English translations render ṣûr as a vocative or direct address: "O Rock" (ESV, NASB, NKJV).

every generation" (Exod 3:14–15).[153] The name "Yahweh" communicates (1) the assurance of the Lord's presence with his people, and
(2) the declaration that the Lord is the only God who exists; "there
is no other" (Deut 4:39).[154] The mere mention of this name was a
reminder of God's promises to Israel's forefathers of Israel's faith. It
also placed Habakkuk, though generations removed, still squarely in
line with those who remembered and called on the name of Yahweh.

The prophet declared his personal allegiance to this God, referring
to him as "Yahweh, *my* God." In doing so, he echoed the prayers of
others who also faced desperate situations: David when pursued by
his enemies and when he faced the Lord's discipline (Pss 7:1; 38:15);
Jonah when he prayed from the belly of the fish (Jonah 2:6); Elijah
when he begged the Lord to restore life to the widow's dead son (1 Kgs
17:20); and Daniel when he confessed the sins of the Israelites (Dan
9:4). Habakkuk personalized the next title as well: "*My* Holy One."
Although "my God" occurs often in the OT, this is the only occurrence of "my Holy One." Only in Isa 43:15 does the name "Holy
One" occur with a pronominal suffix as it does here in Hab 1:12: "I
am the LORD, *your* Holy One, / the Creator of Israel, your King."[155]
A similar title, "the Holy One of Israel," surfaces repeatedly throughout the book of Isaiah.[156] At his commissioning, Isaiah's encounter
with the thrice-holy God whose glory fills the earth forever marked
his understanding of the Lord's identity (Isa 6). The holiness of God
had accentuated the sin of both Isaiah and his compatriots: they were
people of "unclean lips" (v. 5). The title, "the Holy One of Israel,"
ironically highlights the incredible grace of God who makes a way for
an unclean people to approach the One who by virtue of his holiness is
separate from human imperfections and impurities. Habakkuk appropriated this title and claimed the "Holy One" as his own. Habakkuk still experienced suffering and confusion about the ways of God

---

[153] The name Yahweh comes from the verb "to be" (Hb. *hāyâ*). Terence Fretheim, "Yahweh"
NIDOTTE 4:1293, records other possible translations for "I AM WHO I AM": "I will be what (who)
I will be"; "I will cause to be what I will cause to be"; "I will be who I am/I am who I will be."
Fretheim suggests that "the force of the name" is not simply God's existence or presence but
rather his faithfulness toward his people in all generations.

[154] Peter Toon, *Our Triune God: A Biblical Portrayal of the Trinity* (Wheaton: BridgePoint
Books, 1996), 87, makes this point.

[155] Italics added throughout this paragraph.

[156] Apart from the approximately thirty references in Isaiah, the title occurs a handful of
times in the OT (2 Kgs 19:22; Ps 78:41; Jer 50:29; 51:5; Ezek 39:7).

despite his relationship with him. As Job discovered before him, "[t]he old, easy assurances that peace, health, long life, and prosperity were tokens of divine approval have collapsed in the face of experience."[157] Still, the prophet clung to what he knew to be true of his Lord.

Perhaps the use of God's covenant, forever name "Yahweh" (see Exod 3:15), prompted the prophet's reflection on God's eternal, unchanging nature. Habakkuk highlighted this attribute of the Lord in the first two lines of Hab 1:12, which follow the pattern ABB'A', emphasizing God's name. The first line mentions the Lord is from eternity past;[158] the second looks toward eternity future. Psalm 90:2 expresses the same concept: "[F]rom eternity to eternity, you are God." Habakkuk expressed this attribute of God as a question: Are you not from before time?

A comparison of various English versions reveals that the CSB's "My Holy One, you will not die" stands in contrast to the majority. Most render the second part of this line as "*we* will not die."[159] These other versions translate the Hb. verb form *nāmût* (from Hb. *mōt*, "death") from the text of MT as first-person plural. The prophet declared by faith that God's judgment is redemptive; the covenant-honoring Lord would purify his people and spare a remnant.[160] As the result of God's promises, the nation of Judah would not die out.[161] If the subject is the line of Judah, then the first-person plural would be correct. However, this translation raises some problems. It ignores the parallelism of the two lines. In addition, the statement seems contextually awkward. Although Habakkuk could be reminding God of his promises to preserve his people, "we will not die" is a strong counter-assertion on the heels of God's announcement of sweeping judgment. In view of Hab 1:5–17, a more appropriate response might have been, "How can you let us die?" or even "Do not let us die!" Thomas suggests reading the phrase as an unmarked poetic interrogative where

---

[157] Bruce, "Habakkuk," 835.

[158] *HALOT*, 1070, notes that in Hab 1:12 *qedem* means "prehistoric times, primeval time." Harry F. Van Rooy, "קֶדֶם," *NIDOTTE* 3:896, observes that this Hb. noun can have a temporal meaning of "ancient" or "before time." See Deut 33:27; Prov 8:22–23; and Mic 5:2.

[159] The NIV 2011 makes the change from first person plural to second person: "LORD, are you not from everlasting? My God, my Holy One, you will never die." Moving "LORD" to the beginning of the verse, however, makes the original chiasm less obvious.

[160] Shepherd, *A Commentary on the Book of the Twelve*, 321, suggests, "The true remnant of the people of God who are righteous by faith will live indefinitely (Hab. 2:4b)."

[161] Achtemeier, *Nahum-Malachi*, 39–40.

the opening interrogative particle extends to the end of v. 12: "Will we not die?"[162] The transitory nature of humanity then stands in contrast to the eternal nature of God.

The CSB, however, follows a Jewish tradition described in the *BHS* textual apparatus as a *tiqqune sopherim*: a highly unusual scribal correction based on theological sensitivities.[163] Perhaps an early Jewish scribe shuddered at the mere mention of God's dying—even though the statement affirmed this was not possible: "[Y]ou will not die."[164] He may have chosen to emend the verb form from *tāmût* (Eng. "you will not die") to *nāmût* (Eng. "we will not die") in order to preserve God's honor. By reverting to the supposed original form of the verb, *tāmût* (Eng. "you will not die"), the CSB retains the original parallelism of the verse, where both lines extol the eternal nature of God.

Scholars remain divided over which was the original reading.[165] Either way, "Habakkuk is affirming that his life and identity are inextricably intertwined with the life and identity of the Lord. He has no existence apart from the Lord."[166] Neither Habakkuk nor this presumed scribe could have possibly imagined that according to the NT, "the Holy One of God" would indeed one day die for his people to gain eternal life.[167] Because the Holy One did die, we—who put our trust in him—will not die. This inconceivable sacrifice allows believers to stake their claim to holiness in their relationship with him, whom Habakkuk called "my Holy One."

In v. 12 Habakkuk recalls several of God's attributes. The mention of God's eternal nature appealed to his immutability. As an unchanging

---

[162] Thomas, *Habakkuk*, 91.

[163] This example is one of eighteen such corrections. Bruce, "Habakkuk," 853, argues that the correction must have occurred early enough that it was reproduced in the LXX (καὶ οὐ μὴ ἀποθάνωμεν; Eng. "we will not die"). Despite the strong attestation of traditional rabbinic sources that list Hab 1:12 as one of the *tiqqune sopherim*, there is no textual evidence for the emendation. Even so, Smith, *Micah-Malachi*, 103, claims "You shall not die" is "probably the best reading." On the other hand, after examining the possibilities, Carmel McCarthy, *Tiqqune Sopherim: And Other Theological Corrections in the Masoretic Text of the Old Testament* (Göttingen: Vandenhoeck und Ruprecht, 1981), 105–11, concludes that Hab 1:12 is a false correction. The "Commentary on the Critical Apparatus" in *BHQ*, 117, concurs.

[164] Peter demonstrated a similar inclination when Jesus informed his disciples that he would be killed and raised on the third day. The impetuous disciple attempted to rebuke him: "Oh no, Lord! This will never happen to you!" Jesus labeled such thinking a hindrance from Satan based not on "God's concerns but human concerns." See Matt 16:21–23.

[165] Haak, *Habakkuk*, 48.

[166] Prior, *The Message of Joel, Micah, and Habakkuk*, 220.

[167] Mark 1:24; Luke 4:34; John 6:69.

God, he would keep his covenant promises to his own people.[168] He is sovereign over all nations—even Babylon. As the righteous Judge, the Lord has the authority to execute judgment. Habakkuk reiterated the Lord's authoritative announcement: he appointed the Babylonians as his instrument of justice.[169] He established—"destined"—this pagan nation "to punish" his own people. Although no direct object is present in the text, the CSB provides the understood object of this punishment: "us"—the Judeans, for the wickedness cataloged in 1:2–4. The association of this infinitive with legal proceedings "to determine what is right" must have been especially galling for the prophet.[170] The Creator of the universe is free to move nations about like chess pieces to accomplish his sovereign will.

Dismayed, Habakkuk still relied on the relationship defined by the names of God. Referring to God as "Rock" (Hb. ṣûr) recalls many OT poetic passages where God is addressed as "my Rock" or "our Rock." Although other peoples in the ancient Near East also referred to their deities as a "rock,"[171] several OT passages specifically declare the uniqueness of the God of Israel: "But their 'rock' is not like our Rock, / as even our enemies concede" (Deut 32:31).[172] The epithet also appears in contexts with adjectives that describe this "Rock": "his work is perfect; / all his ways are just. / A faithful God, without bias, / he is righteous and true" (Deut 32:4). Other passages referring to "my Rock" figuratively attribute to God characteristics typical of rocks to describe the Lord: a refuge, a fortress, a shield, and a protector—Redeemer, Savior, and Father.[173] The connotations of the term evoked a God who shelters those who take refuge in him—which is ironic given his present context. A few OT passages warned that

---

[168] Num 23:19; 1 Sam 15:29; Isa 46:9–11; Ezek 24:14; Mal 3:6; 2 Tim 2:13; Titus 1:2; Heb 7:21; Jas 1:17.

[169] This is the fourth time the Hb. word mišpāṭ (Eng. "justice") appears in the text. The first two are part of Habakkuk's complaint that justice never emerged, and when it did, it came out "perverted" (1:4). The third occurs in 1:11, where the Lord observed that the Babylonians' sense of justice stemmed from themselves. Not surprisingly, the prophet chafed at the idea that the Lord would use the Babylonians to punish his own people.

[170] G. Liedke, "יכח," TLOT 2:542.

[171] Translating the term ṣûr as "mountain" rather than "rock," William F. Albright, *Yahweh and the Gods of Canaan: A Historical Analysis of Two Contrasting Faiths* (New York: Doubleday, 1968), 188–89, points out that in Syria and Anatolia, "mountain" was often a name for "god."

[172] See also Deut 32:37; 1 Sam 2:2; Pss 18:31; 62:2; Isa 31:9; 44:8.

[173] Pss 18:1–2; 91:4; 31:2–3; 71:3; 89:26. Bailey, "Habakkuk," 313, points out that the NT applies the same metaphor to Christ in 1 Cor 10:4 and 1 Pet 2:6–8.

the Israelites' actions would jeopardize this protective relationship: "[Israel] abandoned the God who made him, / and scorned the Rock of his salvation"; "You ignored the Rock who gave you birth"; "How could one pursue a thousand, / or two put ten thousand to flight, / unless their Rock had sold them, / unless the LORD had given them up?" (Deut 32:15, 18, 30; cf. Isa 17:10).[174] The prophet must have also realized that "the Rock" was not obligated to shelter a people who had abandoned their relationship to him.

The metaphor of a divine Rock surfaces in the NT as well. When Paul urged the Corinthians to withstand temptation, he pointed to the Israelites who rebelled against God despite his gracious provision for their needs. The apostle referenced the Lord's miraculous supply of abundant water from a rock (Hb. ṣûr) in the desert (Exod 17:6; Ps 105:41). Astoundingly, Paul identified this rock [Gk. petra] as "the preexistent Christ":[175] "the spiritual rock that followed them, and that rock was Christ" (1 Cor 10:4). Additional imagery describing Christ as Rock appears in Rom 9:33 and 1 Pet 2:8. Both NT passages quote Isa 8:13–14, which declares, "[T]he LORD of Armies . . . will be a sanctuary; / but for the two houses of Israel, / he will be . . . a rock [ṣûr] to trip over." Jesus is the reality previous sanctuaries merely foreshadowed; he is the true meeting place between God and humanity. This profound truth trips up those who trust in their own works; that is their destiny (1 Pet 2:8; cf. Hab 2:13). In contrast, those who trust in Jesus are not destined for shame; they will be "living stones," incorporated into the sanctuary that will one day fill the earth with glory (1 Pet 2:4–6; cf. Hab 2:14).

Verse 13 focuses on yet another of God's attributes—holiness. The first two lines express parallel ideas, and the underlying Hb. structure ABB'A' mirrors verse 12.[176] Using human characteristics to describe God (anthropomorphism), Habakkuk insisted the Lord's eyes are "pure"—morally and ethically clean—too clean to see evil. God's holiness cannot observe wrongdoing without responding. This is the same word pair, in the same order, Habakkuk used in 1:3: "Why do you force me to *look* at" evil? Why do you *observe* [lit.] wrongdoing?

---

[174] Note the frequency of "Rock" as a name for God in the Song of Moses—Deut 32 (5x) and in Ps 18 (5x // 2 Sam 22). Both passages appear to have influenced several verses in Habakkuk 3.

[175] BAGD, 809.

[176] The first line ends in an infinitive construct; the second line begins with an infinitive construct.

The Lord echoed the prophet in 1:5, using this same pair of words as commands—Look! Observe!—followed by a graphic summary of Babylonian wrongdoing. According to Habakkuk, the problem was not that the Lord *could not* look upon evil; rather, the Lord's character was such that he *should not be able* to observe evil without action.

The prophet's list of divine attributes served to reinforce God as holy, eternal, unchanging, and unique. He is the keeper of covenant promises, a just Judge of the wicked, and a shelter for the righteous. The Lord is too pure to tolerate evil. Habakkuk carefully set the stage for the questions that followed by recollecting God's names and divine attributes.

1.4.2   How Can You Use the Wicked? (1:13b)

> *[13] So why do you tolerate those who are treacherous?*
> *Why are you silent*
> *while one who is wicked swallows up*
> *one who is more righteous than himself?*

1:13b   Habakkuk's first question in v. 13 repeated his confusion from 1:3: "Why do you tolerate wrongdoing?" The prophet complained the Lord ignored injustices perpetrated by his own people. In v. 13, the object of God's seemingly disinterested observation was "those who are treacherous" (Hb. *bôgədîm*).[177] A survey of OT occurrences of the Hb. root reveals it sometimes refers to traitorous nations who betray their diplomatic commitments to others. Lamentations 1:2, for example, bemoans the treachery of Judah's neighbors: "All her friends have betrayed her; / they have become her enemies." Similarly, Isa 33:1 contains a warning for treacherous nations who had not yet experienced betrayal: their turn would come. Babylon, who had betrayed and destroyed Assyria, would herself be betrayed and destroyed by the Elamites and Medes (Isa 21:2). In OT usage the word also describes those who betrayed the marriage covenant (cf. Hos 5:7; 6:7; Mal 2:14–16), and by extension, both Israel and Judah, who were unfaithful to their exclusive covenant with the Lord (cf. Jer 3:20; 5:11; Isa 48:8).[178] Ironically, though Habakkuk pointed out the treachery of

---

[177] *HALOT*, 108.

[178] The LXX translates *bôgədîm* in 1:13 as καταφρονοῦντας (Eng. "despisers"). See the LXX translation of καταφρονηταί (Eng. "despisers" or "scoffers") in 1:5. See discussion on 1:5.

Babylon, he could not bear to see them as God's agent against Judah, who themselves were guilty of betraying God.

Habakkuk's second query in v. 13 echoed his dismay in 1:2: the Lord failed to answer his repeated pleas for help. If God had heard his cries, why did he not answer?[179] Habakkuk was not alone in his observation that the Lord sometimes seems silent. Several psalms, for instance, beseech the Lord not to remain silent (Pss 28:1; 35:22; 39:12; 109:1). Asaph likewise makes a threefold plaintive plea: "God, do not keep silent. / Do not be deaf, God; do not be quiet" (Ps 83:1). In answer to a similar question in Isa 64:12, the Lord responded his own people were themselves guilty of silence: "But you who abandon the Lord, / . . . I will destine you for the sword, / . . . because I called and you did not answer, / I spoke and you did not hear; / you did what was evil in my sight / and chose what I did not delight in" (Isa 65:11–12). For this reason, God declared he would no longer hold his peace: "I will not keep silent, but I will repay; / I will repay them fully / for your iniquities" (Isa 65:6–7). In 1:13, Habakkuk questioned God's silence in the face of escalating wickedness. In actuality, God *had* spoken in 1:5–11, but his revelation made things worse from the prophet's perspective. Not only did God seem to be silent in the view of the coming invasion; he was orchestrating that invasion.

The OT uses the imagery of "swallowing" in some instances to describe God's judgment against his enemies—both those outside of and within Israel (Exod 15:12; Num 16:32; Lam 2:16; Isa 49:19). According to Lamentations, regardless of the agent he used to destroy Judah, the Lord himself was behind it: "Without compassion the Lord has swallowed up / all the dwellings of Jacob. / In his wrath he has demolished / the fortified cities of Daughter Judah. / . . . The Lord is like an enemy; / he has swallowed up Israel. / He swallowed up all its palaces / and destroyed its fortified cities" (Lam 2:2, 5). Habakkuk's use of "swallowing" imagery in 1:13 recalls similar imagery in 1:8, where the Lord compared the Babylonian army to eagles swooping "to devour."

Habakkuk did not object to the Lord's right to judge but rather to his choice of agent, raising a contrast between the wicked and the righteous. In 1:4 the wicked were citizens of Judah who, because they had

---

[179] *HALOT*, 357, notes that the *qal* form means "to be deaf," and the *hiphil* form means "to keep, be silent." M. Delcor, "חרש," *TLOT* 2:477, observes that since there is a close relationship between deafness and speechlessness, the same Hb. root word, *ḥrš*, covers both conditions.

surrounded the righteous, the prophet considered ripe for punishment. Habakkuk acknowledged "the fact that God calls to account and punishes people for deterioration of their social relationships."[180] In 1:13, the wicked were the Babylonians, who were about to "swallow up" those more righteous than themselves.[181] Habakkuk presumed to declare those he formerly called "wicked" as "more righteous" than the wicked Babylonians. In doing so, he contradicted several OT passages challenging his claim (see Job 14:4; 15:14–16; Pss 14:1–3 // 53:1–3; Isa 64:6). Despite humanity's tendency to label some as "the good guys," none are truly righteous (Isa 64:6; Ps 14:1–3; Rom 3:10–11, 23).[182] Bruckner astutely observes, "Why must God use the 'less righteous' to chastise the 'less wicked'? It is because Yahweh has no righteous people remaining to do the work."[183] Habakkuk was aware of the Lord's use of the Assyrians to condemn the "ungodly" nation of northern Israel a century earlier (Amos 3:11–12; Isa 5:26; 10:5–6). In his own day, Zephaniah and later Jeremiah warned the same fate would befall Judah (Zeph 3:1–8; Jer 3:6–7; 25:9).

Habakkuk's questions articulate a perennial theological problem. From the prophet's perspective, God looked at evil, observed it, and still did nothing. The CSB translates this ongoing observation without action as God's "toleration" of wrongdoing. He sees evil but allows it to go unchecked. How can God sit in silence when bad things happen to good people and good things happen to bad people? If God has all the attributes Habakkuk listed in 1:12–13a, then why would he not intervene?

The same question almost always ranks among the top five reasons people give for rejecting Christianity: With all the evil and suffering in the world, how can God be good? Or possibly even exist? As the resiliency of the question shows, there is no simple answer to this complex and seemingly contradictory theological problem often called "theodicy." Apologetics typically differentiates between two ways of addressing the problem of evil and suffering: (1) intellectual

---

[180] Széles, *Wrath and Mercy*, 25.

[181] Shepherd, *A Commentary on the Book of the Twelve*, 321, agrees with the text critical apparatus of MT, which notes that the LXX and Syriac versions remove the comparative in 1:13b: "when the ungodly swallow the righteous."

[182] Other OT examples of comparing righteousness include Gen 38:26; 1 Sam 24:17; 1 Kgs 2:32.

[183] Bruckner, *Jonah, Nahum, Habakkuk, Zephaniah*, 217.

or (2) emotional.[184] Intellectual answers generally fall into two subcategories: logical or evidential. A logical defense might argue that a good God might have sufficient reason for allowing evil to occur—such as creating human beings with free will, capable of moral good, and therefore also capable of moral evil.[185] An evidential defense might provide a morally justified reason that a good God could allow evil, such as one of several theodicies: punishment, free will, natural consequences, natural law, or higher-order goods.[186] Where a particular instance of evil falls outside of these theodicies, the defender might fall back on "skeptical theism." It says, "We can't know God's reasons in all cases, but there is one."[187] Most of the time, however, the problem of evil emerges from an emotional, personal encounter with pain and suffering. In such circumstances, a detached intellectual or philosophical defense rings hollow and cold. A more appropriate response might be that the Lord stands with us in the face of evil and suffering. It requires "a turning of one's soul toward God . . . not to an answer, but to the Answerer."[188] God's ultimate answer to this problem is the sinless Son of God, who paid for our evil and suffering on the cross, who "will swallow up death forever" (Isa 25:8 NIV, ESV, NKJV).

In view of the encroaching invasion, God might have provided evidence that justified his reasons for his proposed actions. He could have explained—as he did in 2Kgs 24:2–4, 20—the attack was a just punishment for Judah's sins, a natural consequence of the nation's own violent actions. More importantly, the Lord would use it to accomplish the purification of his people through whom the Messiah would come. Understandably, the prophet was unprepared to accept

---

[184] Philip Whitehead, "Habakkuk and the Problem of Suffering: Theodicy Deferred," *Journal of Theological Interpretation* 10.1 (2016): 278–79, discusses these two approaches under the labels of "theoretical" and "practical." Since Habakkuk's struggle is personal and existential, a pastoral approach is preferable (p. 279). Whitehead observes, "[T]he book of Habakkuk may be read as reorienting the question toward the future, and thus allowing for a 'deferred' theodicy. On such a view, evil and suffering are not wholly inscrutable, but serve a divine purpose. However, since the purpose may not be known (or necessarily knowable) to the believer, the justice of God in doing so must be accepted by faith" (p. 280).

[185] Alvin Plantinga, *The Nature of Necessity* (Oxford: Clarendon Press, 1974), 166–67.

[186] Daniel Howard-Snyder, "God, Evil, and Suffering," in *Reason for the Hope Within*, ed. Michael J. Murray (Grand Rapids: Eerdmans, 1999), 86–101.

[187] Paul Gould, Travis Dickinson, and Keith Loftin, *Stand Firm: Apologetics and the Brilliance of the Gospel* (Nashville: B&H Academic, 2018), 153.

[188] Gould, Dickinson, and Loftin, *Stand Firm*, 161.

intellectual answers. Habakkuk was not a detached observer. The pain and suffering were personal, and they evoked an emotional response.

1.4.3   The Babylonians Are Voracious Idolaters (1:14–17)

¹⁴ You have made mankind
like the fish of the sea,
like marine creatures that have no ruler.
¹⁵ The Chaldeans pull them all up with a hook,
catch them in their dragnet,
and gather them in their fishing net;
that is why they are glad and rejoice.

1:14–15   The remainder of chap. 1 records an extended simile expressing Habakkuk's sense of helplessness before the invading army. First, he segues from his description of God in vv. 12–13 to a description of the Judeans in the face of their enemy: "You have made mankind / like the fish of the sea, / like marine creatures" (1:14).[189] These parallel similes distinguish between two different kinds of people. The Hb. noun *remeś* refers to a category of small "creeping" animals that swarm and multiply.[190] Though these creatures typically crawl on the ground, there is one other OT text besides Hab 1:14 where this same word refers to sea creatures (Ps 104:25). The related verb, *rāmaś* (Eng. "to crawl or swarm"), represented the category of all unclean foods forbidden to the Israelites in the dietary laws (Lev 11:44; Deut 14:9–10).[191] Thus the unclean aquatic "creatures" may have referred to the Gentiles and the clean "fish" to the Judeans.[192] The Babylonians gobbled up both indiscriminately.[193] The specific point of comparison

---

[189] The Hb. word for fish (*dāg*) likely comes from the verb meaning "to increase rapidly" (*dāgâ*). When the verb appears in Gen 48:16, it refers to the teeming number of Jacob's descendants. See "דָּג‚" *OTWSD*, 225.

[190] *HALOT*, 1246.

[191] Andrew E. Hill, "רָמַשׂ‚" *NIDOTTE* 3:1124–25.

[192] Richard Whitekettle, "Like a Fish and Shrimp out of Water: Identifying the *Dāg* and *Remeś* Animals of Habakkuk 1:14," *BBR* 24.4 (2014): 491–503. Whitekettle, pp. 502–3, observes that the distinction also plays into Habakkuk's ongoing theme regarding the righteous and the wicked.

[193] Jeremiah 51, a chapter with many parallels to Habakkuk, uses this same metaphor of devouring to describe how Nebuchadnezzar of Babylon "swallowed" the inhabitants of Jerusalem "like a sea monster; / he filled his belly with . . . delicacies" (Jer 51:34). Jeremiah, however, casts the Babylonian in the role of a brute creature of the sea rather than a fisherman.

appears in the second half of the verse: "[fish] have no ruler" (Hab 1:14).[194] An image of a school of fish comes to mind, where hundreds of fish swim in a crowded synchronized ballet, abruptly changing direction and at times reversing course completely. With no leader choreographing the whole, imperceptible movements of any one fish seem to affect the entire group. Swimming together works as a deterrent against marine predators, but it plays right into the hands of fishers seeking to bring in a large haul.

The prophet's observation carries a hint of blame, which he laid at the Lord's doorstep: "You made us this way!" Heath Thomas points out Habakkuk encases his complaint in "creation language" with clear echoes from Gen 1:26:[195]

> And God said, "Let us make man (ʾādām) in our image . . . and let them rule over the fish of the sea . . . and over every creeping thing . . ." (Gen 1:26 AT)

> And you have made man (ʾādām) like the fish of the sea, like creeping things that have no one ruling over him" (Hab 1:14 AT)

While underscoring God's role as Creator, Habakkuk contends God's commissioning of the Babylonians has turned the order of creation "topsy-turvy."[196] Instead of exercising dominion over these marine creatures as God originally intended, humanity had become like them, and the prophet felt the Lord was to blame.

Habakkuk's plaintive comparison reveals a wistful longing for a strong leader, especially as battle looms on the horizon. His longing is reminiscent of the Israelites who begged for a king so that they might be like the other nations (cf. 1 Sam 8:4–6). His metaphor reveals the prophet allowed his emotions to affect his theology. The prophet should have recognized that the true King of Israel was none other than the sovereign Lord (see 1 Sam 8:7). The Judeans were not like leaderless fish. God had made them image bearers tasked with ruling

---

[194] 1QpHab replaces lōʾ-mošēl (Eng. "over which is no ruler") with limšōl ("over which to rule"), thereby connecting Hab 1:14 to humanity's role of governance over all animal creatures (cf. Gen 1:26, 28). Under Babylonian domination, however, humanity lost this God-given role, and they themselves were reduced to the level of animals. See Brownlee, *The Midrash Pesher of Habakkuk*, 100.

[195] Thomas, *Habakkuk*, 93. Andersen, *Habakkuk*, 184, concurs: "[E]very word in Hab 1:14 is found in Genesis 1."

[196] Thomas, *Habakkuk*, 95.

over "the fish of the sea" (Gen 1:26). Whatever prompted the comparison in Habakkuk's mind, before the invincible Babylonians, Judah appeared as vulnerable as a skittish school of fish.[197]

The fishing metaphor was particularly apt since the original Chaldeans hailed from southern Mesopotamia, a marshy area filled with lagoons and lakes. The ancient shoreline of what is now the Persian Gulf extended inland, just south of the city of Ur. With fish being a significant part of their diet, fishing was an important occupation. Once the fish were caught, they were preserved by salting or drying.[198] A list of temple personnel for the estate of the goddess Bau of Lagash includes over one hundred fishermen, subdivided into specialties: "fresh-water fishers," "sea fishers," and "fishers in salt waters"—the latter group working in the tidal lagoons of the delta where the Tigris and Euphrates converged.[199]

Habakkuk observed the Babylonians used all means available to pull up, drag away, and gather their victims, including hooks, dragnets, and fishing nets.[200] The three methods demonstrate technological advances that effectively empty the waters of fish at all levels,[201] and figuratively, may even anticipate the three waves of deportations from

---

[197] Richard Whitekettle, "How the Sheep of Judah Became Fish: Habakkuk 1, 14 and the Davidic Monarchy," *Biblica* 96.2 (2015): 273–81, argues that Habakkuk's comparison of the Israelites to leaderless fish rather than to the stereotypical shepherd-led sheep indicates that 1:14 refers to the post-586–BC Babylonian appointment of Gedaliah as governor over the shambles of Judah. His argument thus implies a much later date for this passage than 1:5–11. There is nothing, however, in 1:14–17 that limits Habakkuk's analogy to the citizens of Judah. The fish/marine-creatures analogy actually describes the modus operandi of the Babylonians against "mankind" (v. 14) and the "nations" (v. 17) in general. The citizens of Judah are simply the next school of fish targeted by the Babylonians.

[198] Saggs, *The Babylonians*, 151–52.

[199] Saggs, *The Babylonians*, 134.

[200] Patterson, *Nahum, Habakkuk, Zephaniah*, 152, notes that although "precise differentiation" between the two types of nets is difficult, the LXX translates the first, *ḥerem*, as ἀμφίβληστρον ("casting net") and the second, *mikmeret*, as σαγήνη ("dragnet"). He also points out that Ezek 47:10 seems to relate *ḥerem* to throw-nets cast by fishermen from the shore; while Isa 19:8 indicates *mikmeret* refers to seines or dragnets used by fishermen in boats on the water (p. 153). These basic fishing implements have been in use since the Bronze Age with little changes to the long-lasting components until the last century. Exploration of a late Bronze Age shipwreck off the coast of Turkey, for example, has yielded fishhooks, netting tools, and lead sinkers for both net and line. Naturally, almost all organic fishing components—nets, lines, and floats—have not survived. See Ehud Galili, Avshalom Zemer, and Baruch Rosen, "Ancient Fishing Gear and Associated Artifacts from Underwater Explorations in Israel—a Comparative Study," *Archaeofauna* 22 (2013): 163.

[201] Thomas, *Habakkuk*, 94–95. The NT references all three of these same ancient fishing techniques: cast net (Matt 4:18), dragnets (Matt 13:47–50), and hooks (Matt 17:27).

Judah to Babylon.[202] Roughly 150 years earlier, the Lord used similar imagery to warn Samaria of a parallel fate: "The Lord GOD has sworn by his holiness: Look, the days are coming / when you will be taken away with hooks, / every last one of you with fishhooks" (Amos 4:2).[203] Closer to Habakkuk's day, the Lord declared the same destiny awaited the citizens of Jerusalem, who abandoned him for idols: "I am about to send for many fishermen . . . and they will fish for them . . . for my gaze takes in all their ways. They are not concealed from me, and their iniquity is not hidden from my sight" (Jer 16:16–17). Although Habakkuk had accused the Lord of tolerating evil, God himself had called for this judgment. Though some might manage to elude the Babylonians' hooks, none would escape their nets.

Oblivious that God was using them for his own purposes, the Babylonians were "glad" (Hb. śāmaḥ) and "rejoiced" (Hb. gîl) in the outcome of their own military might (cf. Hab 1:15). These two words often appear together to describe festivity in the OT, as in Ps 118:24: "This is the day that the LORD has made; / let's rejoice and be glad in it" (emphasis added). The Hb. word śāmaḥ does not refer to a sustained state of joy but a spontaneous, emotional outburst accompanied by shouts of jubilation, singing, clapping, and stomping of feet.[204] Such elation erupted at marriage festivals (Song 3:11), harvest (Isa 9:3), coronation (1 Kgs 1:40), victory (1 Sam 18:6), and religious holidays (Lev 23:39–40). Although all these occasions resulted in praising God for his good gifts, the expression "to be joyous before Yahweh" (Hb. śmḥ lipnê yhwh) is a stock phrase describing the celebration of religious festivals.[205] Deuteronomy, for example, frequently links "rejoicing before the Lord" to enjoying a festival meal in the presence of Yahweh (Deut 12:12, 18; 14:26; 16:11; 27:7). When God restores all things, this kind of gladness in his presence will be everlasting (Isa 35:10). The related

---

[202] (1) In 604 BC, Nebuchadnezzar extracted a handful of young noblemen to learn the language and literature of Babylon (2 Kgs 24:1; Dan 1:1–7). (2) In 597 BC, he again invaded Jerusalem, this time dragging away ten thousand soldiers and craftsmen, along with the king and his noblemen (2 Kgs 24:14–16). (3) In 586 BC, after a long siege, Nebuchadnezzar oversaw the destruction of Jerusalem and gathered up the rest of the city's inhabitants (2 Kgs 25:8–11). The Babylonians were determined to catch every last one of their enemies. But note v. 12.

[203] The prophecy anticipates the literal Assyrian practice of leading captives with ropes tied to fishhooks that pierce their cheeks. According to 2 Chr 33:11, Judah's wicked Manasseh experienced this brutal humiliation firsthand.

[204] E. Ruprecht, "שׂמח," TLOT 3:1273; HALOT, 1334–35.

[205] Ruprecht, TLOT 3:1275.

Hb. word *gîl* (Eng. "shout in exaltation, rejoice") occurs primarily in the Psalms and Prophets and has a cultic connection to rejoicing in the Lord because of his acts of salvation or deliverance.[206] Rarely does *gîl* refer to rejoicing in a profane context.[207] Similarly, there are only a few instances where *śāmaḥ* refers to the "malicious glee" of Israel's enemies rejoicing in triumph over her defeat (e.g., Ezek 25:6).[208] Here in Habakkuk, the Babylonians' great nautical haul of human victims resulted in a jubilation that bordered on religious fervor.

> [16] *That is why they sacrifice to their dragnet*
> *and burn incense to their fishing net,*
> *for by these things their portion is rich*
> *and their food plentiful.*
> [17] *Will they therefore empty their net*
> *and continually slaughter nations without mercy?*

1:16–17 While the Babylonians celebrated their triumph, they sought to assure its continuation by worshiping the objects that brought their success—the nautical implements symbolizing their weapons of war.[209] They therefore offered sacrifices and burned incense to the nets that garnered their riches. Considered an omen for divination,[210] smoke ascending from burning sacrifices and incense was believed to please, placate, or even feed their gods.[211] The worship they gave their nets was a reminder of the true worship Judah owed the Lord. He had prescribed offerings of sacrifices and incense as a requirement for proper worship of the one, true God (Lev 1–7; 16). The purpose of these temple sacrifices offered in Jerusalem differed from their pagan counterparts. They served to atone for the Israelites' sin, to cleanse from defilement, to remove guilt, to make restitution,

---

[206] *HALOT*, 189.

[207] C. Westermann, "גיל," *TLOT* 1:312–13.

[208] Ruprecht, *TLOT*, 3:1277.

[209] According to Herodotus, *The History*, 303, the Scythians would make annual sacrifices before all the district temples dedicated to Mars, the god of war. Worshipers placed an antique iron sword representing the god atop massive mounds of wood before sacrificing cattle, horses, and the blood of human prisoners of war. Herodotus explained, "[T]hey offer to these images more victims than to the other gods." There is no evidence that the Babylonians made similar sacrifices to their weaponry, but according to Habakkuk, they revered these things that supplied them with wealth and plunder.

[210] Joan Oates, *Babylon*, rev. ed. (London: Thames and Hudson, 1986), 178.

[211] Michael B. Hundley, "Divine Presence in Ancient Near Eastern Temples," *Religion Compass* 9.7 (2015): 209–10

to express thanksgiving, and to provide for fellowship with a holy God.[212] Tragically, by Habakkuk's day syncretism in Judah was widespread, and the so-called people of God regularly offered sacrifices and burned incense to the idols of the surrounding nations.[213] Through the prophet Jeremiah, the Lord warned these practices would result in disaster for Jerusalem and the temple. When it came, the false gods they worshiped would not deliver when called upon (Jer 11:12, 17; 18:15; 19:4). Ironically, the Lord's eventual judgment of Judah appeared—for a time—to shower Babylon with the spoils of war. The Babylonians wrongly attributed these to their own pagan powers.

Having originated in a land of flood-prone rivers, lagoons, marshes, and sea,[214] the Babylonian pantheon boasted several gods related to water. The threat of spring floods and a perennial struggle against the waters influenced Babylonian mythology, where the primeval beings were Tiamat (the Sea or Ocean) and Apsu (the Deep).[215] The Babylonian creation epic tells how the newcomer Marduk used a net to help subdue Tiamat before slaying the primordial goddess. He then took captive her helpers and smashed their weapons before ensnaring them in his net. When Tiamat was torn in two, the lower half of her corpse became the earth; the upper half became the waters in the heavens above.[216] Other gods associated with water were Ea—"[god of] the house (domain) of water" and Ninurta (god of the storm clouds

---

[212] Lev 3:1; 4:20; 6:5–7; 7:12; 16:30.

[213] According to *HALOT*, 261, the *qal* stem of the verb זָבַח (*zābaḥ*; "to slaughter/sacrifice") may denote sacrifices made to God or to pagan deities. A survey of the occurrences listed under the intensive *piel* stem, however, indicates that in the *piel*—as in Hab 1:16—it primarily refers to illegitimate sacrifices made on high places or to pagan gods—the only exception being the massive numbers of legitimate sacrifices offered by Solomon and Hezekiah (1 Kgs 8:5 // 2 Chr 5:6; 2 Chr 30:22). Similarly, *HALOT*, 1094, notes that the *hiphil* stem of קָטַר (*qāṭar*; "to cause to go up in smoke") may denote both true cultic sacrifices as well as pagan sacrifices. However, occurrences in the *piel* stem—including Hab 1:16—describe a sacrifice that is outside the official cult (the only exception being Amos 4:5). Baker, *Nahum, Habakkuk and Zephaniah*, 56, points out that when these two verbs—"sacrifice" and "offer incense"—occur together, they serve as "almost a fixed formula of condemnation" of pagan worship.

The Habakkuk Pesher (1QpHb) interpreted this verse considering the context of his day as fulfilled by the Kittim (Romans): "[I]ts prophetic meaning is that they / sacrifice to their standards and (that) their weapons of war are / their objects of veneration" (quoted from Brownlee, *The Midrash Pesher of Habakkuk*, 99).

[214] Oates, *Babylon*, 11.

[215] Saggs, *The Babylonians*, 139, 259.

[216] Wilfred G. Lambert, *Babylonian Creation Myths* (Winona Lake: Eisenbrauns, 2013), 91–95, provides a translation of the battle recorded in the Babylonian Epic of Creation, tablet IV, lines 93–146. For a discussion of the splitting of heaven and earth, see p. 169.

that drenched the mountains and flooded the rivers).[217] An ancient Sumerian poem (c. 2000 BC), entitled "House of the Fish," records a lyrical monologue by the goddess Nanše. As "mother of the fish," Nanše invites all kinds of fish to spend the night in the home she has built to keep them safe.[218] The poem may have been based on the idea that fishermen sometimes relied on "primitive magical spells . . . to charm fish into their nets."[219] In this instance, however, the Babylonians did not ascribe their triumph to any of these gods related to water. Instead, according to Habakkuk, they seem to have deified the nets that brought them success.

Echoing the imagery from vv. 8, 13, the Babylonians saw their vanquished enemies as abundant food. In the OT the Hb. word translated as "portion" typically refers to the division of an allotment of land (Josh 19:9), spoils of war (Gen 14:24), sacrifices (Exod 29:28), or food at a festival (2 Sam 6:19).[220] Here, all of these connotations may be in play, as the Babylonians' battles netted them both lands and plunder, causing them to rejoice over their allotment of "food" and to sacrifice to secure their ongoing prosperity. Habakkuk 1:16 closes with a brief pivot pattern that uses two Hb. synonyms for "fat" to describe the bounty their nets provide: lit., "fat (is) his share (of meal) and his food (is) fat."[221] Most recent English translations substitute synonyms more appealing to modern readers. In addition to the CSB's "rich" and "plentiful," others include words like "sumptuous" (NKJV); "luxury" (NIV; ESV); and "choicest" (NIV). According to the priestly instructions for sacrifices, "[a]ll fat belongs to the LORD" (Lev 3:16). Displaying a blasphemous disregard for this stipulation, Eli's sons had demanded the choicest of sacrificial meats for roasting rather than boiling—even before the fat was burned (1 Sam 2:15). Habakkuk 1:16 indicates that the Babylonians exhibited a similar craving for luxurious, fat "food."

---

[217] Saggs, *The Babylonians*, 258, 263. Ea was also known as Enki, lord of the subterranean region.

[218] M. Civil, "The Home of the Fish: A New Sumerian Literary Composition," *Iraq* 23 (1961): 154–75.

[219] Saggs, *The Babylonians*, 151.

[220] Furthermore, among the Israelites the Lord himself was to be the Levites' portion (Num 18:20), and the Lord's portion was to be his people (Deut 32:9) and the land of Judah (Zech 2:12).

[221] Specifically referencing Hab 1:16, Robert J. Way, "שָׁמֵן," *NIDOTTE* 4:172, translates *šāmēn ḥeleq* as "a fat share"; *HALOT*, 1567, "rich spoil"; 324, "share of meal"; and *maʾakāl barîʾāh*, *HALOT*, 540, as "food"; 156, "a fat meal."

The Babylonians' worship revealed all their previous large hauls of fish failed to satisfy an ever-increasing appetite for more. Paradoxically, they offered sacrifices of food to that which supplied them with food. They sought to please their fishing nets, so that they would continue to be full. Habakkuk underscored the ravenous motives behind their actions with the phrase *ʿal-kēn* (Eng. "therefore"; CSB: "that is why") in vv. 15–16.[222] Verse 17 begins with a third instance of the phrase, only this time an interrogative particle turns the sentence into an anguished question, essentially, Is that why they empty their net only to fill it again continually?

Alternate uses of the word "empty" may come into play in v. 17. Of the nineteen OT occurrences of the verb "empty" (Hb. *rîq*), ten refer to pouring contents out, such as oil or even blessings (Song 1:3; Mal 3:10), or to emptying out a container like a sack or vessel (Gen 42:35; Jer 48:11–12). The remaining nine instances, however, refer to "emptying a sword" as in drawing it from a scabbard. Of these, five times Ezekiel refers to the Lord himself "emptying a sword" against the citizens of Jerusalem (Ezek 5:2, 12; 12:14), Tyre (28:7), and Egypt (30:11). In all five instances, the agent God chose to draw the sword was the Babylonian army.[223] Ezekiel 30:11 contains "an interesting wordplay in that Nebuchadnezzar's armies will empty (רִיק) [Hb. *rîq*] their swords against Egypt, and then use them to 'fill (מָלֵא) [Hb. *mālāʾ*] the land with the slain.'"[224] Similar imagery appears in Habakkuk, where the Babylonian army emptied their net of its human contents; at the same time, the net was a metaphor for the sword they used to fill it.[225] This double connotation emphasized the Babylonians' greed.

In the second half of v. 17, Habakkuk abruptly dismisses the metaphor and brings reality back into sharp focus. His people were not

---

[222] The phrase *ʿal-kēn* (CSB: "that is why") also appears twice in Hab 1:4. The prophet appears to have filled his prayers with attempts to understand the reasons behind his circumstances. Habakkuk's "why?" questions drove him to provide his own answers.

[223] Ezekiel 12:13–14 also uses the imagery of a net capturing King Zedekiah and "a sword emptied" to pursue his troops: "But I will spread my net over him, and he will be caught in my snare. I will bring him to Babylon, the land of the Chaldeans, yet he will not see it, and he will die there. I will also scatter all the attendants who surround him and all his troops to every direction of the wind, and I will draw a sword to chase after them."

[224] Jerry Shepherd, "רִיק," *NIDOTTE* 3:1104.

[225] In v. 17 in both the Qumran Pesher (1QpHab) and the Naḥal Ḥever (8ḤevXII gr), the metaphor of emptying "his net" (Hb. *ḥermô*) is replaced with the related unsheathing "his sword" (*ḥarbô*). See Shepherd, *A Commentary on the Book of the Twelve*, 320, 322.

fish; the Babylonians were not fishermen.[226] They were bloodthirsty soldiers on a rampage, slaughtering nation after nation. In their quest to satisfy their growing hunger for more, they would spare no one.

Habakkuk's dialogue in chap. 1 is bursting with questions.[227] Just as his first and second prayers open with questions, so also his second prayer closes with one.[228] All three relate to time: "How long, LORD, must I call for help / and you do not listen?" (1:2): "Are you not from eternity, LORD my God?" (1:12); "Will they . . . continually slaughter nations without mercy?" (1:17). Interlaced throughout, the prophet's questions are even more pointed: "Why do you force me to look at injustice? / Why do you tolerate wrongdoing?" (1:3); "So why do you tolerate those who are treacherous? / Why are you silent / while one who is wicked swallows up / one who is more righteous than himself?" (1:13). The cumulative weight of all these questions begged for an answer. The distraught prophet was incapable of mounting a defense of God's goodness despite the evil surrounding him. Yet his concerns arose "not from a weak faith but a perplexed faith."[229] Habakkuk's assessment was correct; these perceive devil actions did not align with God's character. Still struggling to understand God's ways, Habakkuk boldly laid out his concerns before the only one who could possibly answer.

Habakkuk's questions are as relevant as today's headline news. Why doesn't God step in and stop all this? Martin Lloyd-Jones observes that we all want to prescribe the answers to our prayers. We want God to intervene and make things right. The Lord may need to chastise the nation or even the church, but then we want him to send a great revival.[230] Like Habakkuk, we would be shocked to hear that the Lord's prescription for his ultimate mission might call for sweeping destruction by forces we deem less righteous than ourselves. When we cannot comprehend the ways of God, we need to pour out our hearts

---

[226] Oates, *Babylon*, 196, observes that "[i]n Neo-Babylonian Uruk the word fisherman [having fallen into disuse] even came to have the connotation of a lawless person."

[227] As the CSB renders the Hebrew text, at least 25 percent of these two prayers are questions. Some other translations may interpret an even larger percentage of the text as questions.

[228] Although the interrogative ה, which introduces a question, is present in the MT, it is omitted from the Qumran commentary, as well as the LXX, Syriac, and Vulgate. See Bruce, "Habakkuk," 855.

[229] Robertson, *The Books of Nahum, Habakkuk, and Zephaniah*, 156.

[230] D. Martin Lloyd-Jones, *From Fear to Faith: Rejoicing in the Lord in Turbulent Times* (Downers Grove: InterVarsity, 2011), 14–15.

before his throne. Following Habakkuk's example, we need to focus on God's character, recall his attributes, and lash ourselves to the God who makes and keeps his promises—even when our prayers end in a question mark.

Habakkuk's extended metaphor suggests several NT correlations. The Gospels show God, incarnate in the Son, ruling over both sea and storm. But Jesus was not only master of wind and wave; he ruled over the fish of the sea (Luke 5:4–11). Instead of rejoicing over the miraculous economic windfall—so great that it threatened to sink two boats—Simon Peter recognized he was in the presence of the divine. The humbled fisherman pled, "Go away from me, because I'm a sinful man, Lord!" Jesus, however, redirected his thinking. God had not made humanity like the fish of the sea to be hauled in at the whims of their enemies. Rather, Jesus would make his disciples into fishers of humanity, rescuing others out of the sea: "Follow me," he told them, "and I will make you fish for people." The veteran fishermen "immediately" abandoned their nets and boats—their livelihood—and followed Jesus (Matt 4:19–20; John 21). The differences between God's intentions for humanity and the pagan worldview of the Babylonians present a stark contrast. Intriguingly, Jesus used the imagery of a dragnet to tell a parable about the judgment, when the wicked will be separated from the righteous (Matt 13:47–50). Even when we have unanswered questions, we can rest assured that the Lord will set things right in the end.

1.4.4   I Will Stand and Watch for the Lord's Reply (2:1)

> [1] I will stand at my guard post
> and station myself on the lookout tower.
> I will watch to see what he will say to me
> and what I should reply about my complaint.

2:1 Following the close of his second complaint, Habakkuk determined to wait for an answer. The English word order does not reflect the chiastic structure of the first two lines. In the Hebrew text, the order of the first line is reversed: "At my guard post I will stand." Thus "guard post" (Hb. *mišmeret*) and "lookout tower" (Hb. *māṣôr*) appear as bookends, emphasizing Habakkuk's willingness to wait.

The Hb. term *mišmarti*[231] ("my guard post") primarily occurs in the context of keeping the Lord's commands (Gen 26:5; Lev 18:30; 22:9) or protecting the Lord's sanctuary (Ezek 44:8, 16; 48:11). Habakkuk 2:1 closely parallels Isa 21:8: "Then the lookout reported, / "Lord, I stand on the watchtower all day, / and I stay at my post [*mišmereti*] all night."[232] The Hb. word *māṣôr* (CSB: "lookout tower"; NKJV: "rampart") can mean either a "fortified city" or a "stronghold."[233] Between these two military posts lie two verbs: "I will stand" and "I will station myself." In form, both are cohortative verbs, indicating an "emphatic statement of fixed determination."[234] Habakkuk patiently waited, determined not to move until the Lord answered.

The prophet figuratively described himself as a watchman manning the ramparts. Given the context of the preceding chapter, the reader might assume Habakkuk mounted the lookout tower, scanning the horizon for the approach of the Babylonians (cf. Nah 2:1). But instead of watching for a military opponent, the prophet awaited none other than the Lord of Armies himself.[235] God typically appointed prophets to serve as watchmen to deliver a word of warning to his people (e.g., Jer 6:17; Ezek 3:17; 33:7). In contrast, Habakkuk appointed himself as a watchman, waiting for God to respond to his complaint.[236] The syntactical function of the verb "to watch" conveys the intensity of his resolve: "I shall watch." The interplay of words describing "hearing" with terms of "seeing" echoes themes of seeing and hearing introduced in the opening superscription, where Habakkuk "saw" a "pronouncement" (1:1). Believing the Lord would answer, the prophet actively waited for the response that was sure to come.

The prophet expected the dialogue would continue beyond God's response. While he waited for the Lord's answer, he already anticipated formulating his own rejoinder: "[W]hat should I reply to my

---

[231] *HALOT*, 650, "observation post." From the verb *šāmar* meaning "to watch" or "to guard."

[232] Ironically, Isa 21:8 refers to a watchman scanning the horizon for news of the battle's outcome, when he receives word that "Babylon has fallen . . . the images of her gods have been shattered on the ground."

[233] *HALOT*, 623.

[234] GKC §108.

[235] The verb *yāṣab* ("to take a firm stand" or "to present oneself"; *HALOT*, 427) suits both contexts. Elmer A. Martens, "יצב," *NIDOTTE* 2:492, explains the two possibilities: (1) assuming a combative stance in a military face-off, and (2) presenting oneself formally before God in a cultic setting.

[236] The *hithpael* form of the verb יצב is reflexive: "I will station *myself*."

complaint."[237] The word Habakkuk used to describe his complaint is *tôkaḥat*, a Hb. noun deriving from the verb *yākaḥ*—often used in a context of judgment or punishment—meaning "to argue," "rebuke" or "reprove."[238] Often, the Lord rebuked his people, accusing them of breaking their covenant with him (e.g., Ps 50:21; Ezek 5:15; Mic 6:2). In v. 1 *tôkaḥat* means "reproachful complaint" or "objection."[239] Outside of Habakkuk, the only example of a person directing a *tôkaḥat* toward God is Job, who presented his case before God. In Job's context, *tôkaḥat* is translated by CSB as "argument" (Job 13:6; 23:4).

In Hab 2:1, who "reproves" whom? The strong sense of *tôkaḥat* seems to be an inappropriate response toward God by the prophet. A survey of English translations reveals they are equally divided. About half interpret *tôkaḥtî* as "my reproof," clarifying in their translations that the prophet expected God's response to be a reprimand: "when I am corrected/reproved." The other half translate it as "my complaint," as does the CSB. Even if Habakkuk expected a reproof, he did not receive one. In the dialogue that follows, the Lord did not rebuke the prophet for his sincere questions. Although Habakkuk did not presume to rebuke God, he sought an explanation consistent with God's character. Finally, the Lord answered him.

1.5 GOD'S SECOND RESPONSE (2:2–5)

Although the Lord responded to Habakkuk, his intended audience was much larger. The Lord answered the prophet with a message instructing him to record it for future generations. God's vision, revealed to Habakkuk, looked forward to the destruction and captivity of Judah. Furthermore, God's answer revealed the Lord clearly distinguishes between the wicked and the righteous and the final outcome of their lives.

---

[237] In the last line of 2:1, in place of "what I should reply about my complaint," the Syriac version reads: "what he will reply about my reproof." Andersen, *Habakkuk*, 194, suggests that Habakkuk did not plan to *respond* but rather to *repeat* the Lord's answer to his complaint to others.

[238] *HALOT*, 410.

[239] *HALOT*, 1698.

1.5.1 Write Down This Vision and Wait for It (2:2–3)

> 2 *The* LORD *answered me:*
> *Write down this vision;*
> *clearly inscribe it on tablets*
> *so one may easily read it.*
> 3 *For the vision is yet for the appointed time;*
> *it testifies about the end and will not lie.*
> *Though it delays, wait for it,*
> *since it will certainly come and not be late.*

2:2–3 Unlike Habakkuk's former complaint, God replied promptly. Habakkuk acknowledges, "The LORD answered me." This simple report belies the incredible nature of its content. Yahweh, the great "I AM," the Lord who condescended to covenant with his people, the God of Israel's forefathers—deigned to answer the heartfelt pleas of this prophet. Equally amazing, the Lord hears and responds to the cries of his children today.

Just as the Lord's first response used imperatives, so too does his second response. The Lord instructed Habakkuk to "[w]rite down this vision," followed by a command to "clearly inscribe it [God's answer] on tablets."[240] In the ancient Near East there were three basic kinds of tablets. The most durable were those cut from stone and engraved with an iron stylus.[241] Many such inscriptions—like those in Egypt—are still legible today, thousands of years after their composition. Although the OT contains approximately thirty references to stone tablets, all of them refer to the two tablets engraved with the Decalogue (e.g., Exod 31:18; Deut 10:1). In Mesopotamia, clay tablets were the preferred writing material for the wedge-shaped cuneiform script, the clay becoming hard when baked in the sun or oven.[242]

---

[240] Moses gave similar instructions to the Israelites to carry out once they had entered the land. They were to set up large stones, cover them with plaster, and *"[w]rite clearly* all the words of this law" (Deut 27:8; emphasis added). They were thus to make a plain, enduring record of God's covenant available for all to read.

[241] F. F. Bruce, *The Books and the Parchments: How We Got Our English Bible* (Old Tappan, NJ: Fleming H. Revell, 1985), 5. Job wished that his own words were "recorded on a scroll" or "inscribed in stone forever / by an iron stylus and lead!" (Job 19:24). They were indeed inscribed on some medium and still endure to the present day.

[242] André Lemaire, "Writing and Writing Materials," *ABD* 6:999.

The only OT mention of a clay tablet is in the Babylonian setting of Ezek 4:1.

The more probable candidate for Hab 2:2 was a wooden tablet[243] coated with wax, a writing medium used in Palestine, Syria, and Anatolia; later in Greece and Italy, and eventually throughout the Roman Empire. Several of these tablets would be hinged together to form diptychs or polyptychs, a practice well attested in eighth-century-BC Assyria and Northern Syria.[244] Because wax was easy to write on and allowed corrections, "[s]cribes used these tablets to write a first draft from dictation and could then copy the text carefully onto a sheet or roll of papyrus or leather."[245] A passage in Isaiah with parallels to Hab 2:2 reflects this two-step process: "Go now, write it on a tablet in their presence / and inscribe it on a scroll; / it will be for the future, / forever and ever" (Isa 30:8). Unfortunately, the writing materials commonly used by the Israelites—wooden tablets, papyrus, and parchment—all decayed easily in a humid climate. The enduring witness to Habakkuk's vision, however, depended not on the durability of the original materials but on the God who both gave the vision and oversaw the writing and preservation of its message.

Why was it so important that the inscription be clear? A comparison of two dozen English versions reveals two basic interpretations of the last line of 2:2.[246] (1) Most English versions interpret this line to mean that the reader is also a runner ("courier," ISV), who will

---

[243] Some of the other OT occurrences of the Hb. word translated "tablet" refer to wooden "planks" used in the construction of the bronze altar (Exod 27:8; 38:7) and ships (Ezek 27:5).

[244] Lemaire, *ABD* 6:1002–1003. Examples of diptychs and polyptychs crafted from wood or ivory have surfaced in excavations of eighth-century-BC Nimrud and Neo-Hittite reliefs dating to the same time. Common in the Hellenistic and Roman world, these hinged writing tablets became the probable precursors to the codex. Lemaire notes Luke 1:63 describes how Zechariah likely wrote his son's name on a wax writing tablet. Oates, *Babylon*, 113, provides an illustration of a reconstructed set of the earliest hinged writing boards.

It is fascinating to imagine how just such a triptych could have facilitated the painstaking parallelism of the three-paneled structure of Habakkuk. See 6.2.4: "Habakkuk as a Literary Triptych," in the Introduction.

[245] Lemaire, *ABD* 6:1002.

[246] A literal word-for-word translation reads this way: "in order that (the one) reading will run in it." The participle "(the one) reading" comes from the Hb. root *qr*ʾ, which means "to call" or "announce." When used with the preposition ב, *qārāʾ* means "to recite a book (scroll), to read in (from) a document"—sometimes with the connotation of reading aloud (*HALOT*, 1130). The NIV retains the root idea of proclamation, translating the nominative participle as "herald"; the NET renders it "the one who announces it." Most English translations, however, translate it as "reader."

"run" to pass on the message of the vision to others (NIV, ESV, NASB, KJV).[247] The inscription of the vision must be plain so the reader may understand it. (2) Others interpret the clause to mean that the reader might read the tablets "swiftly" (JPS 1985); "at a glance" (CEV, GNT); or "easily" (CSB, NET). The first two of these retain a sense of speed in reading; the last one conveys the idea of reading smoothly. Unlike the cuneiform and hieroglyphic systems of writing, the Hebrew alphabet consisted of only twenty-two letters—which even a child could theoretically master.[248] The number of literate people in Israel was higher than in these other nations.[249] Writing legibly—carefully inscribing the vision on tablets—ensured anyone capable of reading could read it aloud with ease, passing the message along to others. Even if the emphasis is on the ease of reading, the underlying intention is the vision's message be faithfully shared.

In the OT a "vision" (Hb. *ḥāzôn*) refers to a "word of revelation."[250] Since the Lord frequently gave visions through his prophets (see Hos 12:10), the word "vision" became a title for the prophetic work (e.g., 2 Chr 9:29; 32:32; Isa 1:1; Obad 1:1; Nah 1:1). A vision's content could be good news of an enduring kingdom (1 Chr 17:11–15) or sobering news of judgment (Ezek 7:13, 26). Despite the divine origin of legitimate visions, the Israelites often denied the truth of their messages (Ezek 12:22, 27), preferring instead the imaginative visions woven by false prophets (Jer 14:14; 23:16). The great majority of occurrences of the word "vision" are found in the texts of Ezekiel and Daniel. The Lord gave Daniel and King Nebuchadnezzar visions

---

[247] A herald who ran might bring devastating news of defeat (1 Sam 4:12–18), ambivalent tidings of victory over one's enemies (2 Sam 18:19–27), or good news of peace and salvation (Isa 52:7–8). In each of these passages, watchmen were anxiously waiting for runners with news. Jeremiah 23:21 describes false prophets the Lord did not speak to or send. Still, they "ran" with a message of their own invention. Robertson, *The Books of Nahum, Habakkuk, and Zephaniah*, 169, therefore equates "running (with a message)" to "prophesying." Haak, *Habakkuk*, 56, contends that "the message of judgment is to be so clear that the reader *will* run in terror." Thomas, *Habakkuk*, 108, observes that the Hb. reads: "[S]o that the one reading may run *into it*." He points out a similar construction in Prov 18:10: "[T]he name of Yahweh is a strong tower, and the righteous one will run *into it* . . . and find security." Thomas, contrary to Haak, concludes that the runner will find refuge in the vision's hopeful message (p. 109). All italics appear in the original.

[248] Lemaire, *ABD* 6:999–1000. Bruce, *The Books and the Parchments*, 23, observes that the timing of the alphabet's invention as concurrent with the writing of the first biblical texts points to God's providence.

[249] Lemaire, *ABD* 6:1005, observes, "Most paleo-Hebrew epigraphers agree that literacy was widespread in Judah toward the end of the 7th century B.C."

[250] *HALOT*, 301.

through dreams at night (Dan 2; 4; 7). Sometimes the content of a vision would be sealed because of the people's stubborn rebellion (Isa 29:11) or its reference to a distant future (Dan 8:26).

Habakkuk 2:3 provides only a few descriptive clues about the vision God gave the prophet. The fulfillment of the vision speaks regarding a future time, appointed by the sovereign Lord who controls history. Despite the prophet's insinuation God had failed to take action, the Lord had already initiated future events. The tablets provided advanced notice to the transgressors regarding future judgment. English translations are divided on how to translate the Hb. word *yāpēaḥ*, which could mean "breathes, blows [like a wind]" and thus "hastens" or "hurries" (ESV, NASB) or "to witness, testify [to the end]" (CSB). The word derives from one of two identical roots with different meanings.[251] A vision that "hurries" seems to be at odds with one that is delayed until the future. Those who translate the term as "speaks" (KJV, NIV), "testifies" (CSB), or "gives reliable testimony" (NET) understand the word (in the *hiphil* stem) as a "recounting" of a later event.[252]

The CSB and NET translations reflect research observing a correlation between *yāpēaḥ* and the Ugaritic word *ypḥ* ("witness"), which introduces the names of witnesses to legal economic contracts.[253] Almost half of the OT occurrences of *yāpēaḥ* contrast a false witness who "breathes lies" against the one who "breathes truth" (Prov 6:19; 12:17; 14:5, 25; 19:5, 9). Since the clause immediately following asserts the veracity of the vision, this appears to be a better translation than "hurries." The vision gives a truthful witness about the end.

Though the vision may seem to tarry, its fulfillment was still a long way off, requiring patient waiting with expectation—even when there was an underlying sense of urgency. The absolute certainty regarding the vision's fulfillment is conveyed by repetition for emphasis: Hb. *bōʾ yābōʾ*.[254] The CSB and most English versions capture the intensity of this repetition with an adverbial modifier—either "it will certainly come" or "it will come." Both convey God would follow through with his judgment of not only the Judeans but also, in their turn, the

---

[251] *HALOT*, 917.

[252] The meaning of the *hiphil* is causative: i.e., "cause to be made known." Cf. Joüon §54.d.

[253] Dennis Pardee, "YPH 'Witness' in Hebrew and Ugaritic," *VT* 28.2 (2013): 99–108.

[254] The phrase consists of an infinitive absolute before an imperfect verb. GKC §113n explains that this construction strengthens the verbal idea, emphasizing its certainty: it *will* come to pass.

Babylonians. Ultimately, the vision will not delay because God's timing is perfect. The believer's job is to trust God and wait faithfully.
The translators of the LXX used a feminine Gk. word for "vision"
(*horasis*) but retained the masculine pronoun *auton*: "wait for him!"
Andersen surmises they "seem to have taken v 3a as a description of
the vision, while v 3b talks about the activities of an unidentified person."[255] This is not as big a leap as it might first appear since several
verbs in v. 3 seem to personify the vision: it testifies (or breathes); it
appears to tarry (outside of Hab 2:3 spoken only of humans); it comes;
and it will not delay. In addition, Habakkuk's vision in chap. 3 also
describes the coming of the Divine Warrior to judge the wicked (Hab
3:3). Not only were they to wait *on* God; they were to wait *for* God.[256]

The vision testifies about "the end" (Hb. *qēṣ*).[257] The "end" spoken of in Hab 2:3 is admittedly ambiguous. The vision anticipates not
only the end of Judah but also the "day of distress" descending on the
invading Babylonians (Hab 3:16). It is unclear if "the end" foretold in
Habakkuk's vision is the total destruction prophesied by his contemporary Zephaniah: "The whole earth will be consumed / by the fire
of his jealousy, / for he will make a complete, / yes, a horrifying end
[Hb. *kālâ*] / of all the inhabitants of the earth" (Zeph 1:18). Still, the
chiastic center located in Hab 2:13–14 anticipates the eschatological
outcome of God's mission. The cataclysmic events of Habakkuk 3 also
raise the possibility the Divine Warrior's destruction of the "leader of

---

[255] Andersen, *Habakkuk*, 208. Andersen, 207–8, suggests that Yahweh is the subject of all
the verbs in v. 3.

[256] Robertson, *The Books of Nahum, Habakkuk, and Zephaniah*, 17–20, observes that the
messianic expectation of a Davidic king drops out of these three seventh-century prophetic
books. Following the depravities of Manasseh, these prophets no longer found hope in David's
descendants. Instead, "they could see none other than God himself fulfilling that role" (p. 18).
(Cf. Nah 1:2; Hab 3:3–7; Zeph 3:15.) Although the conventional concept of messianism returns
in the postexilic prophets, Robertson points out that "in the last hours before the Exile it is as
though the Lord interrupts the movement toward messiah to declare clearly that he alone can
be king in Israel" (p. 19). Like Nahum and Zephaniah, Habakkuk thus supplies "a vital contribu-
tion to the ongoing revelation of the God-man who would be Savior and king, even the Lord,
Jesus the Christ" (p. 20).

[257] This word can refer to the end of a season or period of time, such as days or years (Gen
8:6; Exod 12:41). In the context of the flood in Gen 6:13, God used it to describe cosmological
judgment: "I have decided to put an end to every creature." It can refer to the end of a person's
life (Ps 39:4) or the end of nations (Jer 51:13; Ezek 7:2–3, 6). The "end" may even signify the
eschaton, the end time, of human history (Dan 8:17, 19; 11:40; 12:4, 6). Although the eschatological end is usually described as an outpouring of wrath, it also coincides with the inauguration
of an eternal reign in a kingdom that knows no end (Isa 9:6–7).

the house of the wicked" looks beyond the Babylonian king to the final demise of the enemy of God's people.

In Peter's NT allusion to Hab 2:3, when scoffers ask, "Where is [Christ's] 'coming' that he promised?" (2 Pet 3:4), Peter exhorts believers not to grow weary in waiting:

> Dear friends, don't overlook this one fact: With the Lord one day is like a thousand years, and a thousand years like one day. The Lord does not delay his promise, as some understand delay, but is patient with you, not wanting any to perish but all to come to repentance. But the day of the Lord will come like a thief; on that day the heavens will pass away with a loud noise, the elements will burn and be dissolved, and the earth and the works on it will be disclosed. (2 Pet 3:8–10)

Peter understood Habakkuk's vision of the end anticipated a sweeping eschatological judgment of the earth. This time judgment would come with intense fire, and Christ's coming would inaugurate a new heaven and earth "where righteousness dwells" (2 Pet 3:13). The seeming delay of the Lord's coming has a purpose, and believers in both Testaments had to await the fulfillment of this vision with longing and long-suffering.

Since God instructed Habakkuk to record the vision, it should appear in this prophetic book by the same name, but where? There are several possibilities for the location of the vision: (1) the immediately following verse(s), 2:4–5; (2) the section of woes, 2:6–20; (3) the theophany in 3:3–15; (4) some combination of the above; or (5) the entire book of Habakkuk. Was the prophet to record on the tablets the words God spoke during his revelation? Or was he to record a description of something he saw? Once again, the themes of hearing and seeing surface as they did in the superscription of Hab 1:1: "The pronouncement that the prophet Habakkuk saw." This too is a clue affecting the revelation's content as we explore the above possibilities outlined in the chart below.

CONTENTS OF THE VISION: A SAMPLING OF SCHOLARLY OPINION					
HAB 2:4	2:4–5	2:6–20	3:3–15	2:6–20; 3:3–15	2:4–20; 3:3–19
Patterson (214) Smith (107)	Robertson (169) Prior (234) Heflin (89) Brownlee (324)[258]	Baker (59) Floyd (472) Amerding (510)	Shepherd (325) Bruce (859) Roberts (81)	Andersen: oracular 2:6–20 visionary 3:3–15	Wendland: dual/ compound Intro: 2:4–5; (1) 1: 2:6–20 (2) 2: 3:1–19

1. The vision as brief, summary statement (2:4, [5])

Verse 4 begins with the word "look/behold," similar to the first pronouncement beginning with commands to "look," "observe" (1:5) and "look/behold" (1:6). As noted in the discussion of 1:6, the word "behold" (Hb. *hinnê*) often introduces a prophetic announcement of judgment. The content of 2:4–5 is part of the Lord's second response to the prophet, the end of the first panel of discourse, and it serves to introduce the series of woes on the wicked. Despite Habakkuk's complaints, the Lord assured him that he sees the hearts and actions of all humanity and distinguishes between the wicked and the righteous.

2. The vision as the series of woes (2:6–20)

The middle panel of Habakkuk is God's verbal pronouncement of the certain destruction facing the Babylonians (and the wicked in general) as retribution for their wickedness. At the heart of this passage of woes, and at the heart of the book, is a glimpse of "the end." The chiastic pivot located in Hab 2:13–14 reveals the ultimate dual outcome of God's mission.

3. The vision as theophany (3:3–15)

Habakkuk 3, the third panel, presents a theophanic vision of this dramatic end in vv. 3–15. The Divine Warrior appears, striding the earth and sea with authority, striking the leader of the wicked a fatal blow, and delivering his people.

---

[258] See William H. Brownlee, "The Placarded Revelation of Habakkuk," *JBL* 82 (1963): 324.

4. *The vision as a combination of some or all of the above (see below).*

5. *The vision as the entire book (Habakkuk 1–3).*

Although the book is "written down," it is not imperative all three chapters constitute the vision. While peripheral to the actual revelation, these elements provide an essential framework for understanding the background and the transformation of the prophet who, in spite of his initial reaction to the first revelation in 1:5–13, becomes an exemplar of faith.

The above chart (p. 176) provides a brief scholarly overview of the vision's contents. A wide variety of opinions exist because the text does not specifically identify the vision. Factors in the discussion include the material for the tablets, the size of the lettering, the number of tablets, the intention for the tablets, and whether what was written on the tablets was the message of the vision or the vision itself.[259] In addition to those listed on the chart, Hassell Bullock suggests that the "vision" is 1:5–11 and 2:2–5.[260]

I believe a combination approach works best. The vision includes the announcement of the revelation (2:4–5), the verbal pronouncement of the woes (2:6–20), and the theophanic vision (3:3–15). My position falls between Andersen and Ernst Wendland, as they too recognize the multifaceted nature of the vision. Recognizing that 1:5–11 is also revelation is a reminder the entire book is a record of "the pronouncement (Hb. *maśśāʾ*) that the prophet Habakkuk *saw*."[261] Aside from Habakkuk's own words (1:2–4; 1:12–2:1; 3:2, 16–19), most of the book consists of divine revelation, whether recorded pronouncements or theophanic vision. There is no way of knowing conclusively whether the tablets recorded the essence of the vision, portions of the book, or the entirety of the prophetic book, which was later transferred carefully to a scroll.[262] Thankfully, the Lord has preserved the

---

[259] Several scholars point to the brevity of other written messages (Isa 8:1; 30:7–8) as indicative that Habakkuk's message should be similarly brief.

[260] Bullock, *An Introduction to the Old Testament Prophetic Books*, 215.

[261] Italics added. Although Hab 1:1 is the superscription for chaps. 1 and 2, what he *saw* includes the theophany of chap. 3 as well.

[262] The book of Revelation provides an interesting parallel of a prophetic revelation that is both seen and heard. In Rev 1:11, a loud voice commanded the prophet to "[w]rite on a scroll what you see and send it to the seven churches." Then John turned "to see whose voice it

enduring message of the entire book of Habakkuk for subsequent generations.

By the close of chap. 3, Habakkuk humbly resolved to wait, as the Lord had instructed, not only for the end of his own nation of Judah but also for the onset of the future "day of distress" by the invading Babylonians. The "end" of the Babylonians came and went, yet still we wait for *the* end hinted at in the vision. Since Habakkuk had a courageous faith that did not shrink back from asking God hard questions, he experienced not only the promise of God's justice but also God's presence. As a result of Habakkuk's obedience in recording the Lord's revelation, we—like the people of Habakkuk's day—have an enduring prophetic message that needs to be announced to others. The message speaks of the final end that is yet to come. We too must wait faithfully in the often-uncomfortable meantime, the "already pronounced not yet fulfilled" vision of the end.

1.5.2 The Wicked Will Perish, but the Righteous Will Live by Faith (2:4)

⁴ Look, *his ego is inflated;*
he is without integrity.
But the righteous one will live by his faith.

2:4 The Lord introduces the vision in v. 4 by pointing out the wicked: "Look" or "Behold!" This same Hb. interjection *hinnê* introduced the previous revelation in 1:6. In the earlier passage, God drew the attention of Habakkuk—and his audience—to the Babylonians, describing the military ferocity of the adversary in great detail (1:6–11). The prophet recoiled at the notion that God would judge his own people by means of those more wicked than themselves (1:13). Although the Lord did not specify whom Habakkuk was to behold in 2:4, the description that follows certainly fit both the Babylonians[263] and the wicked in general. The individual mentioned in 2:4 stands in

---

was that spoke to [him]" (Rev 1:12). Revelation includes a variety of audial and visual materials—visions, pronouncements, and even dictated letters—which form the vast majority of the book set within an explanatory framework.

[263] The first reference to the "Chaldeans" in 1:6 is plural, but most subsequent references in 1:6–11 are singular, even though most English versions retain the plural. In 2:4–6, the references to the wicked are singular as is the reference to "the righteous one" in 1:4.

contrast to "the righteous one," continuing the theme of the wicked versus the righteous first introduced in 1:4.

The text of Hab 2:4a is notoriously difficult for several reasons.[264] Although the first Hb. word *hinnê* ("behold" or "look") is clear, the second word, *ʿuppəlâ* (Eng. "to be impudent")[265] is a *hapax legomenon*—the only occurrence of this form in the OT. The related noun carries a connotation of "swelling."[266] In Num 14:44, the same verbal root (in the *hiphil* stem) describes how the Israelites rejected the report of the faithful spies, then "dared" (KJV: "presumed") to challenge their enemies without the direction or presence of the Lord. The CSB's translation in Hab 2:4 as "inflated" captures this idea of being swollen with arrogance. Another difficulty is the broad semantic range of the subject *nepeš*: "throat, neck, breath, living being, people, personality, life, soul."[267] Although most English versions translate this occurrence of *nepeš* as "soul," the CSB aptly describes the wicked this way: "[H]is *ego* is inflated." A second verb in 2:4 reveals more about the wicked: he is not "upright." The Hb. word *yāšār* includes a plain and a figurative meaning: an "upright" person can be standing up straight, or he can be morally "upright" in character.[268] The CSB translation captures both meanings well: "he is without integrity." King Nebuchadnezzar is a prime example of someone whose unbridled arrogance led to his shocking downfall (see Dan 4:29–33). The self-aggrandizement of the

---

[264] For in-depth discussion of these and other textual issues, see J. A. Emerton, "The Textual and Linguistic Problems of Habakkuk II. 4–5," *JTS* 28.1 (1977): 1–18; J. Gerald Janzen "Habakkuk 2:2–4 in the Light of Recent Philological Advances," *HTR* 73.1–2 (1980): 53–78; and James M. Scott, "A New Approach to Habakkuk II 4–5a," *VT* 35.3 (1985): 330–40.

[265] Although the verb appears to be third feminine singular *pual* perfect, *HALOT*, 860, notes that the text is uncertain; *BHS* proposes *ʿupal* (*pual* participle) or *ʿapāl*.

[266] *HALOT*, 860–61, indicates the noun *ʿōpel* has two possible meanings: (1) thickened tissue ("boils," Deut 28:27; "tumors," 1 Sam 5:6) and (2) "swellings" on the earth ("hill," Mic 4:8; "Ophel"—the land adjoining temple mount, 2 Chr 27:3). Scott, "A New Approach to Habakkuk II 4–5a," 330–40, argues that *ʿuppəlâ* is a place name referring to Ophel, the fortified acropolis in Jerusalem. Bullock, *An Introduction to the Old Testament Prophetic Books*, 217, speculates that the LXX rendering of v. 4 is based on a scribal error. He points to the interchange of letters between the Hb. word "puffed up" (Hb. *ʿuppəlâ*) and the LXX "shrink back" (Hb. *ʿulləpâ*).

[267] *HALOT*, 712–13. The feminine verb ending of *ʿuppəlâ* points to the feminine noun *nepeš* as its subject.

[268] *HALOT*, 449, notes that *yāšār* can mean "be straight" or "smooth"; figuratively, it may mean "right" or "pleasing"—as in Jer 18:4; cf. 1 Kgs 9:12. Sweeney, *The Twelve Prophets*, 472, renders the phrase as "not straight in him is his life." He thus translates v. 4, "Behold, he is arrogant, his life is not stable/secure, but the righteous shall live by their faith."

wicked precipitates his instability. He lacks the structural integrity to remain standing; eventually he will topple.

As J. A. Emerton observes, the reader expects the destiny of the wicked to be the antithesis of the righteous individual's. Without changing the consonantal text, Emerton suggests dividing the word ʿuppəlâ in two to read: ʿāp lōh: "he will fly away," i.e., "pass away, perish."[269] Michael Shepherd likewise suggests the Hb. term stands in contrast to the righteous one who lives: "[T]he one who is not upright . . . swells up and dies."[270] Although these proposals are conjectural, the outcome for the wicked is the opposite of the reward for the righteous. The person of faith/faithfulness will live, but the wicked, ultimately, will perish.

Habakkuk 2:4 closes with a brief mention of the righteous before returning to the subject of the wicked in 2:5. The clause almost appears to be an abrupt interruption—as if the Lord cannot continue to describe the wicked without briefly addressing the righteous. The vast majority of chap. 1 describes the wicked: 1:2–4; 6–11; 13–17; the theme resurfaces in 2:4–5 and continues throughout the rest of chap. 2. How were righteous people like the prophet supposed to live in a world overrun by those who were not upright? They were, and are, to live by faith.

The frequently quoted last line of Hab 2:4 is only three words in the Hebrew text, but each term is theologically rich. The first of these terms is the nominative form of the Hb. root ṣdq ("to prove someone upright"). The form of ṣādaq used here (ṣaddîq) denotes the nuance of "equitable actions, right actions, loyalty, honesty, and justice," describing those who persevere in faith despite adversity.[271] Throughout the OT text, the Scriptures testify that God himself is righteous (Deut 32:4; Ps 112:4; Zeph 3:5). Humanity, created in his image,

---

[269] Emerton, "The Textual and Linguistic Problems of Habakkuk II. 4–5," 17.

[270] Shepherd, *A Commentary on the Book of the Twelve*, 326–27. Explaining such an unusual verb choice, Shepherd observes, "The root עפל ("swell") features transposition or metathesis (הפך) of the first two root letters of the key word פעל ("work") in Habakkuk 1:5 and 3:2. This is a common technique for associating passages with one another in biblical composition, inner biblical exegesis, and in rabbinic exegesis." Habakkuk 2:4 thus contrasts "those who lack faith and those who have faith in the future work of God (i.e., Hab. 3:3–15) in Christ" (p. 326). Shepherd notes other examples of transposition: ערף and פרע in Exod 32:9b, 25a; and בער and עבר in Num 11:1 and Ps 78:21, and directs the reader to Wilhelm Bacher, *Die exegetische Terminiologie der jüdischen Traditionsliteratur* (Hildesheim: Georg Olms, 1965), 44.

[271] *HALOT*, 1003–5.

should therefore reflect this attribute of his character (Gen 1:26–27). In fact, the great majority of OT occurrences of the word "righteous" refer to people whose actions demonstrate their righteousness. The righteous one follows the law, cares for the poor, and benefits the community through generosity; he speaks wisdom and takes refuge in the Lord (Prov 29:16; Ps 37:26, 30, 40). The OT frequently contrasts the righteous with the wicked, not only their deeds but also their destinies (e.g., Prov 10:25, 30). Psalm 37:37–38 states this succinctly: "Watch the blameless and observe the upright, / for the person of peace will have a future. / But transgressors will all be eliminated; / the future of the wicked will be destroyed." This distinction between the righteous and the wicked demonstrates that the Lord's own judgments are righteous (Gen 18:25; Mal 3:13–18). Job therefore chafed when he suffered as a righteous man while the wicked lived a life of ease (Job 12:4). Habakkuk, too, lamented that the wicked prospered at the expense of the righteous (Hab 1:4, 13). The Lord's response in Hab 2:4–5 shows despite appearances, he distinguishes between these two groups, as their eventual outcomes will reveal.

However, the OT Scriptures clearly state that none are righteous on their own: "[A]ll our righteous acts are like a polluted garment" (Isa 64:6; cp. Pss 14:3; 53:1–3). The same was true even for the patriarch Abram. Nevertheless, when God told him his descendants would be as numerous as the stars in the desert sky, "Abram believed the LORD, and he credited it to him as righteousness" (Gen 15:6). That same declaration of righteousness would one day express itself in history through the only one of Abram's (that is, Abraham's) descendants who was truly righteous. Of Jesus, God said, "[M]y righteous (Hb. *ṣaddîq*) servant will justify (Hb. *yaṣdîq*) many / and he will carry their iniquities" (Isa 53:11). Abraham became the forefather not only of the Israelites but of all who put their faith in the Lord who declares them righteous (cf. Rom 4:11). Palmer Robertson thus sees "a deliberate echo of Gen 15:6" in Hab 2:4b.[272]

The second Hb. phrase "*be'ĕmûnātô*" ("by his faith") consists of a combination of the Hb. preposition *bet* with a noun derived from the Hb. verbal root "*'āman*," meaning "reliable, faithful, enduring,

---

[272] Robertson, *The Books of Nahum, Habakkuk, and Zephaniah*, 178. Cf. S. Lewis Johnson, Jr., "The Gospel That Paul Preached," *BSac* (1971): 340.

and believable."[273] The prefixed preposition is causal.[274] The upright subject's faith (Hb. ʾemûnâ, "trustworthiness, faithfulness") will result in his life. Many of the OT occurrences of this word refer to the faithfulness of God (e.g., Deut 32:4; Lam 3:23; Ps 89:1–2, 5, 8, 24, 33, 49). When the word refers to people, it is translated as "faithful" (Prov 28:20), or "faithfully" (2 Chr 31:12, 15, 18) but also as "loyalty," "trusted (positions)," "integrity," "honesty" (1 Sam 26:23; 1 Chr 9:22; 2 Chr 19:9; Isa 59:4). Tragically, several of the references to people point out that God searches for faithfulness among humans but cannot find it (Jer 5:1–3; 7–28; 9:3; cf. Isa 59:4). Some English versions translate ʾemûnâ in Hab 2:4 as "faithfulness" (NIV, NET); others render it as "honestly" (CEB); "stedfastness" (YLT); or "fidelity" (JPS, 1985[275]). The large majority, however, use the word "faith"—even though the Hebrew language has no equivalent noun form that represents the verb "believe."[276] Our familiarity with this clause likely stems not from its original context in Habakkuk but from Paul's quotation of it in the NT: **"The righteous will live by faith"** (Rom 1:17; Gal 3:11; cf. Heb 10:38; see the discussion below). Do these NT quotations overly influence the translation of ʾemûnâ in Hab 2:4b as "faith" rather than "faithfulness"?

What did the Lord intend when he first revealed to the prophet "the righteous shall live by his faith(fulness)"? From the prophet's initial perspective (Hab 1:4, 13), the identity of the righteous was defined in terms of faithfulness: those who keep the covenantal statutes of the Lord and walk in his ways. In Psalm 18—from which the prophet quotes v. 33 in Hab 3:19—the psalmist observed, "The LORD rewarded me / according to my righteousness; / he repaid me / according to the cleanness of my hands" (Ps 18:20; cf. 24). No doubt Habakkuk expected a similar reward for his own uprightness, but this only added to his confusion when he measured his faithfulness next to the faithlessness of the wicked around him who seemed to prosper. From God's perspective, none are righteous apart from his gracious gift that declares them righteous. God's judgment against Judah was simply the next step in his unswerving mission to accomplish the goal

---

[273] *HALOT*, 63.

[274] *IBHS* §11.2.5e.

[275] The JPS 1917 translation reads this way: "But the righteous shall live by his faith."

[276] James Barr, *The Semantics of Biblical Language* (London: Oxford University Press, 1961), 173.

of declaring his people righteous. The struggling nation teetered on the brink of assimilation into the wickedness of the surrounding peoples. The destruction of Jerusalem was a severe mercy intended to purify and preserve a remnant through whom would come the only one who truly deserved the name, "the Righteous One" (Acts 3:14; cf. 7:52; 22:14).[277] Habakkuk 2:4 marks the shift to a definition of the righteous in terms of faith rather than faithfulness.[278]

By the end of chap. 3, it becomes clear that even in this OT prophetic book, salvation comes by grace through faith rather than solely by faithfulness. Ray Clendenen helpfully enumerates the reasons ʾemûnâ in Hab 2:4 means "faith": (1) it fits the context of the vision in vv. 2–3; (2) it was likely the meaning in 1QpHab; (3) the NT writers who quote Hab 2:4b interpreted it as "faith"; (4) it was the "natural choice" for the word "faith" if Habakkuk was alluding to Gen 15:6; and (5) the rest of the book calls for "faith," a quality the prophet exhibits in its concluding verses.[279] Habakkuk's right standing before God required faith in God. The coming invasion did not mean Habakkuk himself had not been faithful.[280] But as his world disintegrated

---

[277] Peter's sermon in Acts 3 reverberates with the words of Hab 2:4: "You denied the . . . *Righteous* One. . . . You killed the source of *life*, whom God raised from the dead. . . . By *faith* in his name, his name has made this man strong, whom you see and know" (Acts 3:14–16; emphasis added). Peter recognized that as "the Righteous One," Jesus is the source of life. Faith in his name could grant not only physical healing but also eternal life.

[278] Andersen, *Habakkuk*, 215, also notes this shift in the definition of a righteous person, from one characterized by "morality" in chap. 1 to one who "trust[s] in the dependability of God's announced plan" in 2:4. But the faith is not in the vision per se but in God. Ultimately, faith rests in the "Coming One" whom the vision anticipates. Shepherd, *A Commentary on the Book of the Twelve*, 328, observes, "Given the eschatological context set by Habakkuk 2:2–3, the message of Habakkuk 2:4b is that a person who is declared to be in righteous standing with God by means of his or her faith in the future work of God (i.e., Hab. 3:3–15) in Christ (i.e., the unidentified anointed one in Hab. 3:13; cf., Heb. 10:37) will live."

[279] E. Ray Clendenen, "Salvation by Faith or by Faithfulness in the Book of Habakkuk," *BBR* 24.4 (2014): 505–13.

[280] R. David Moseman, "Habakkuk's Dialogue with Faithful Yahweh: A Transforming Experience," *PRSt* 44.2 (2017): 270, offers an interesting perspective on the prophet. He suggests that God anticipated Habakkuk's failure to believe the astounding pronouncement of 1:6–11: "[Y]ou [plural] will not believe (Hb. ʾmn) when you hear about it" (1:5). Since "the righteous one will live by his faith (Hb. ʾmwnh)" (2:4), Moseman, 270, asserts, "Habakkuk cannot necessarily be numbered among the righteous (though he certainly perceives himself that way in vv. 12–17)." Moseman contends that "[the prophet] must rethink his earlier statement in 1:12 where he says, "We shall not die,'" (p. 269). Not only does 2:4 serve as a personal corrective for the prophet, but so does the final woe. Moseman contends that although Habakkuk "[did] not physically fashion idols," he had fashioned a "mental image of Yahweh" that did not square with the identity of the sovereign Lord (p. 271). Moseman therefore concludes that the book traces the transformation

around him, the prophet would have to exercise faith as he waited for the vision to come to pass. His faithfulness flowed from a heart that believed God and staked his trust in him, even if he struggled initially with God's silence. Over the course of the book, the prophet moved from a simplistic faith to a mature faith, forged by the experience of God's presence in the midst of troubles. Habakkuk's profound expression of faith in the closing verses of the book demonstrates faith and faithfulness are as closely intertwined in the OT as in the NT. Faith and faithfulness, in fact, are two sides of the same coin; they are inseparable, but the imprint struck first is faith.

The clause closes with the declaration that the righteous one "will live" (Hb. *yiḥyeh*) as the result of his trust in God. From the beginning, Scripture contrasts life with death. The first occurrence surfaces in the garden of Eden even before the fall. Life was a gift in the context of a loving relationship with the Creator, but it came with a warning: the rejection of God and his word would result in death. After the fall, the Lord repeatedly emphasized the connection between life and obedience: "You are to keep my statues and ordinances and carefully observe them, so that you may live securely in the land" (Lev 25:18; cf. Deut 4:1, 40; 5:16, 33; 8:1; 11:9; 25:15; 30:16). Obedience was not simply keeping a list of rules, as the language of Deut 30:15–20 reveals:

See, today I have set before you life and prosperity, death and adversity. For I am commanding you today to love the LORD your God, to walk in his ways, and to keep his commands, statutes, and ordinances, so that you may live and multiply, and the LORD your God may bless you in the land you are entering to possess. But if your heart turns away and you do not listen and you are led astray to bow in worship to other gods and serve them, I tell you today that you will certainly perish and will not prolong your days in the land you are entering to possess across the Jordan. I call heaven and earth as witnesses against you today that I have set before you life and death, blessing and curse. Choose life so that you and

---

of Habakkuk's faith (p. 274). I agree that Habakkuk's encounter with the Lord transformed his faith. My understanding, however, is not that Habakkuk came to faith but rather that, through his encounter with the Lord, Habakkuk moved from a confused, immature faith to a much deeper, richer faith. Christian sanctification is likewise an ongoing process that continually reshapes our understanding of God and ourselves. As our experience with the Lord deepens, so our trust in him grows.

your descendants may live, love the LORD your God, obey him, and remain faithful to him. For *he is your life*, and he will prolong your days as you live in the land the LORD swore to give to your ancestors Abraham, Isaac, and Jacob.

As the added italics emphasize, the Lord himself is our life. A biblical understanding of "life" is much more than physical breath and a heartbeat; "life" is flourishing in right relationship to God. Gerleman suggests the Hebrew description of recovering from illness as "coming to life" (e.g., Num 21:8; 2 Kgs 20:7) lends support to this understanding that "'life' in the OT does not mean simply being alive, but having complete, fulfilled life."[281] The obedience God requires of his people stems from a love relationship grounded in a faith that results in faithfulness.

That relationship, springing from faith and faithfully maintained, is a choice to live. In Ezekiel 18, the Lord carefully outlines individual responsibility in a series of scenarios resulting in life or death. Verses 5–9 describe the actions of a righteous man: he does not worship idols; he is sexually pure; he does not rob or oppress but rather gives to the poor and seeks justice. Ezekiel 18:9 echoes all three root words found in Hab 2:4b (emphasis added): "He follows my statues and keeps my ordinances, acting *faithfully*. Such a person is *righteous*; he will certainly *live*." The chapter ends in v. 32 with this admonishment: "So repent and live!"[282] God graciously extends the offer of forgiveness and acquittal to anyone who chooses to repent, believe, and live.

What does the verb behind "he will live" mean in Hab 2:4b? Several possibilities exist: the word could indicate: (1) an exhortation of how to live in this life, (2) an extension of this life, or (3) the intimation of eternal life. If the verse describes the conduct of God's people, then the righteous are to live by faith—trusting God and remaining faithful.[283] The verse encourages the righteous of Habakkuk's generation

---

[281] G. Gerleman, "חיה," *TLOT* 1:413. See John 10:10. The MT of Num 21:8 lit. reads "each one his life" and 2 Kgs 20:7 "and lived."

[282] God had previously extended a similar choice for life to the Israelites in the account of the bronze snake in Numbers 21. When the people complained they had no bread or water, but only "wretched food," the Lord sent poisonous snakes among them. When they recognized their sin, the Lord provided a bronze snake mounted on a pole. Healing required faith expressed through action: look and live. Jesus, in John 3:14–15, explained that this event foreshadowed his coming crucifixion: "Just as Moses lifted up the snake in the wilderness, so the Son of Man must be lifted up, so that everyone who believes in him may have eternal life."

[283] Debbie Hunn, "Habakkuk 2.4 in Its Context: How Far Off Was Paul?" *JSOT* 34.2 (2009):

to remain true through the horrific days fast approaching. Whether they lived or died, their faith(fulness) demonstrated their right standing with God. Most of the contemporary audience would probably not live to see the judgment of the Babylonians proclaimed in the woes of chap. 2. If God waited until death to distinguish the righteous from the wicked, what would it matter if this life was all there was? The very thing disturbing the prophet was the apparent lack of distinction between the righteous and the wicked in this life. The righteous were not flourishing, and the wicked were not toppling.

It is also possible the idea "he will live" affirms that the Lord would extend the length of days of the righteous in this life: the righteous, those who have faith and remain faithful, will live long on the earth. The verse provides assurance that God would preserve the physical lives of the righteous. Upon reflection, this too seems unsatisfying. Habakkuk already complained the Lord failed to preserve the righteous from the violence of the wicked Judeans (vv. 1:2–4), and many more would die at the hands of the wicked Babylonians during the protracted siege and destruction of Jerusalem, predicted in 1:5–11. The few remaining upright citizens who survived would face a degrading forced march into exile following the destruction of a smoldering Jerusalem. Only a precious few from Habakkuk's day might actually live to see God's justice meted out to the Babylonians in 539 BC and the subsequent return from exile. An extension of this sort of life could hardly approximate the Hebrew understanding of life in its fullness.

Finally, the concept "he will live" in Hab 2:4b might suggest eternal life: those who are righteous by faith will live after death. Though the concept of life after death was not fully formed in the OT, it was not completely foreign and develops from progressive revelation. As the tree of life in the center of Eden indicates, God's intention for humanity has always been eternal life—in contrast to Mesopotamian cosmologies, in which deities created humans to be mortal.[284] The author of Ecclesiastes bemoans the hopelessness of Sheol and observes God has "put eternity" in the hearts of human beings (Eccl 3:11; 9:4–6). Some of the psalms hint of everlasting life (Pss 21:4; 133:3) or

---

229–30, observes that such a reading is unlikely. Of the 279 OT occurrences of *hāyâ* (Eng. "to live") outside of Hab 2:4, "there are no examples where it means 'to behave' or 'to conduct life in a given manner.'" Hunn, 231, argues that since the people were to wait for the vision because they would see it fulfilled, "the life they would live must be resurrection life."

[284] Elmer B. Smick, "חָיָה," *TWOT* 1:280.

redemption from Sheol (Pss 16:10–11; 49:9, 15; 73:23–28; cf. Job 19:25–27). Isaiah likewise envisions a future where death is no more, and those held in its grip will rise from the dust (Isa 25:7–8; 26:19). Daniel 12:1–3 clarifies that some will awaken to eternal life; others, however, to eternal contempt. Even in Habakkuk there are faint traces of this eschatological future in the chiastic center of 2:13–14, in the actions of the Divine Warrior in 3:3–15; and perhaps even in Habakkuk's conclusion that the Lord would enable him to tread the "heights" (3:19). The possibility that Hab 2:4 points to eternal life becomes even more convincing when we remember it is the Lord and not the prophet who declares "the righteous will live by faith."[285]

EXCURSUS 1: The New Testament Use of Habakkuk 2:4

Two NT writers recognized the significance of Hab 2:4b as they appropriated it under the inspiration of the Spirit. The clause appears in three different NT passages. The following chart highlights some of the different textual traditions.[286]

Hab 2:4 MT	"But the righteous by his faith/faithfulness shall live." (Hb. *wəṣaddîq beʾĕmûnātô yiḥyeh*)
Hab 2:4 LXX	"But the righteous shall live by my faithfulness" [or "by faith in me"]. (Gk. *ho de dikaios ek pisteōs mou zēsetai*)
Rom 1:17; Gal 3:11	"But the righteous by faith shall live." (Gk. *ho de dikaios ek pisteōs zēsetai*)
Heb 10:38	"But my righteous one by faith shall live." (Gk. *ho de dikaios mou ek pisteōs zēsetai*)

The primary differences involve the use of various pronouns. The MT references the individual ("*his* faith/faithfulness"), whereas the LXX attributes the faithfulness to God ("*my* faithfulness"). Paul drops the pronouns altogether, and in Hebrews the pronoun "my" modifies "the righteous." All three of the NT quotations "emphasize the importance of personal faith."[287]

---

[285] As previously discussed (1:5), Jesus may well have alluded to Hab 1:5–6 in reference to his own astounding work of raising to life those who believe (cf. John 5:20–21, 24).

[286] This chart was adapted from Thomas R. Schreiner, *Romans*, BECNT, 2nd ed. (Grand Rapids: Baker Academic, 2018), 80.

[287] Schreiner, *Romans*, 80. Although Hab 2:4 is missing from the DSS text, the Qumran commentator on Habakkuk applied the verse to his own context. He wrote, "[T]his concerns all those who observe the Law in the House of Judah, whom God will deliver from the House of Judgement because of their suffering and because of their faith in the Teacher of Righteousness" (1QpHab8.1–3). Richard N. Longenecker, *The Epistle to the Romans*, NIGTC (Grand Rapids: Eerdmans, 2016), 183, explains that in contrast to Paul, the Qumran commentator(s) interpreted

The first NT quotation of Hab 2:4 occurs in Romans 1. When Paul desired to stress in his letter the connection between righteousness and faith, he naturally turned to Hab 2:4. It is unclear by his omission of pronouns whether he drew from the MT or the LXX.[288] Paul linked Hab 2:4 to the heart of the gospel, quoting from it as he penned the theme for Romans:

> For I am not ashamed of the gospel, because it is the power of God for salvation to everyone who believes, first to the Jew, and also to the Greek.[289] For in it the righteousness of God is revealed from faith to faith, just as it is written: **"The righteous will live by faith."** (Rom 1:16–17; emphasis in original)

Paul quoted Hab 2:4 as support for his emphasis on the crucial importance of faith for salvation: "from faith to faith." Throughout Romans Paul repeatedly underscored that "righteousness is by faith (3:22, 28, 30; 4:3, 5, 9, 11, 13, 20–22; 5:1; 9:30; 10:4, 5, 10)."[290] The main interpretations of "the righteousness of God" in v. 17 include (1) "God's being in the right," (2) "his action of making people right before him," and (3) "the resultant status of those made right."[291] Although greatly debated, these three are not mutually exclusive, and many scholars hold varying combinations of these three views.[292] The phrase also appears twice in Rom 3:21–26, where Paul revisits his earlier thesis statement from chap. 1:

Hab 2:4 "as exhorting a strict observance of the Mosaic law and an absolute fidelity to the sect's founding teacher."

[288] C. H. Dodd, *According to the Scriptures* (London: Nisbet, 1952), 51, suggests that Paul's quotation may have come from an early Christian usage of Hab 2:4 as a *testimonium*—a declaration drawn from various translations.

[289] Hunn, "Habakkuk 2.4 in Its Context," 233–34, argues that since the taunt of 2:6–20 is sung by those from all nations and peoples speaking "righteous words against sin, against idolatry, and for the Lord," these Gentiles are included among those righteous by faith who live in the eschaton. Hunn concludes that Paul's application of Hab 2:4 to Gentiles fits within its original application. Even aside from Hunn's argument based on the identity of the singers of the taunt song, the promise of Hab 2:14 also includes representatives from every people in every place.

[290] Schreiner, *Romans*, 79.

[291] Douglas Moo, *The Epistle to the Romans*, NICNT (Grand Rapids: Eerdmans, 1996), 72.

[292] Moo, *The Epistle to the Romans*, 72. Moo, for example, combines elements of activity and status, defining "the righteousness of God" as "*the act by which God brings people into right relationship with himself*" (74; italics in original). Schreiner, *Romans*, 66–77, argues that the phrase is primarily a forensic term referring to believers' "not guilty" status. Both Moo, 74, and Schreiner, 72, agree that this status is a declaration of acquittal rather than a moral transformation. Longenecker—who sees Paul's emphasis as attributive and communicative (p. 176)—maintains that regarding righteousness, Paul always joined forensic and ethical categories. (See Longenecker, *The Epistle to the Romans*, 174–75.)

But now, apart from the law, **the righteousness of God** has been revealed, attested by the Law and the Prophets. **The righteousness of God** is through faith in Jesus Christ to all who believe, since there is no distinction. For all have sinned and fall short of the glory of God; they are justified freely by his grace through the redemption that is in Christ Jesus. God presented him as the mercy seat by his blood, through faith, to demonstrate his righteousness, because in his restraint God passed over the sins previously committed. God presented him to demonstrate his righteousness at the present time, so that he would be just and justify the one who has faith in Jesus. (Rom 3:21–26; emphasis added).

The righteousness of God, attested to by the Law and Prophets, has now been revealed as a gift from God, received by faith. Although the prophet Habakkuk could not have imagined it, God's plan from the beginning has been to declare believers righteous based on the atoning sacrifice of his righteous Son. That status, just as in the OT, depends on faith, not works, so that all glory belongs to God. Paul therefore appeals to the example of Abraham to illustrate this concept: **"Abraham believed God, and it was credited to him for righteousness"** (Rom 4:3; cf. Gen 15:6). The righteousness received by faith results in eternal life (Rom 5:18; 8:10).[293] God's purpose for this great gift of salvation is ultimately for the glory of his name[294]—which correlates with God's mission stated in Hab 2:14.

A second place Hab 2:4 appears in the NT is Galatians 3. Paul's Jewish contemporaries had typically viewed Abraham's obedience, especially regarding his offering of Isaac, as keeping the law.[295] Incensed by the Judaizers who were leading his readers astray with a false gospel based on works, Paul asked the "foolish Galatians" a series of questions. His final question contained the right answer: all they had received in Christ came not by doing "the works of the law" but "by believing what [they] heard—just like Abraham who **believed God, and it was credited to him for righteousness**" (Gal 3:2, 6; cf. Gen 15:6). Paul assured the Galatians the true gospel of Jesus is rooted in the OT, proclaimed "ahead of time" to none other than Abraham himself, to whom God had promised, **"All the nations will be blessed through you"** (Gal 3:8; cf. Gen 12:3). The blessing of Abraham had come to the Galatians by faith in Abraham's ultimate descendant—Jesus Christ. As in Romans, Paul similarly pairs the example of Abraham's faith with a recitation of Hab 2:4 to show that justification comes by faith rather than works: "Now it is clear that no one is justified before God by the law, because **the righteous will live by faith"** (Gal 3:11). Paul had already expounded on the

---

[293] Moo, *The Epistle to the Romans*, 78.
[294] Schreiner, *Romans*, 76.
[295] Douglas Moo, *Galatians*, BECNT (Grand Rapids: Baker Academic, 2013), 188.

quality of that life in Gal 2:20 (emphasis added): "I have been crucified with Christ, and I no longer live, but Christ lives in me. The life I now live in the body, I *live by faith* in the Son of God, who loved me and gave himself for me." Right standing with God results in an entirely new life now, and this life extends into eternity.

Two questions arise out of Paul's quotation of Hab 2:4 in Romans and Galatians. First, where does the phrase "by faith" go? Does it modify "righteous" ("the *righteous by faith* will live") or "live" ("the righteous will *live by faith*")? Most English translations connect the phrase to the verb "live"—as in Gal 2:20. Others reflect Paul's strong tendency to connect "by faith" to righteousness language (RSV, NASB).[296] Still others maintain that the phrase modifies both words: "righteous by faith" and "live by faith."[297] Thomas Schreiner maintains that the distinction between the two is not that clear. Since Paul often used the verb "live" in an eschatological sense, "'to be righteous by faith' and 'to live by faith' are alternate ways of communicating the same reality."[298] Those who have been declared righteous by faith will live by faith.

The second question is whether Paul's use of Hab 2:4 gave an entirely new meaning to "the righteous will live by faith." As Douglas Moo points out, Paul used the clause to show how "to attain right standing with God and so live eternally."[299] Some argue this purpose is different from the original context of Hab 2:4, which served to encourage the Judeans to remain faithful through the coming tribulation—even when God seemed distant. Although he agrees these are dissimilar, Moo counsels that we should not magnify the differences.[300] Likewise, Schreiner asserts because the primary call of Hab 2:4 is trust rather than faithfulness. Although the two are closely related, "Paul reads Habakkuk in both its historical and canonical context and doesn't distort its message."[301] As discussed above, the Lord may have intended to communicate the outcome of Habakkuk's faith was right standing with God, a relationship enduring long after the inhabitants of Jerusalem returned to dust. Paul's usage, stated much more clearly from a Christian perspective, may not deviate from the original context in Habakkuk. Both passages emphasize the importance of personal faith and

---

[296] Moo, *Galatians*, 206, lists several interpreters who argue for this position, including F. F. Bruce, *The Epistle to the Galatians*, NIGTC (Grand Rapids: Eerdmans, 1982), 161; and Leon Morris, *Galatians: Paul's Charter of Christian Freedom* (Downers Grove: InterVarsity, 1996), 104.

[297] J. D. G. Dunn, *The Epistle to the Galatians* (Peabody, MA: Hendrickson, 1993), 174.

[298] Schreiner, *Romans*, 82.

[299] Moo, *The Epistle to the Romans*, 77.

[300] Moo, *The Epistle to the Romans*, 78.

[301] Schreiner, *Romans*, 81. Moo, *Galatians*, 207, likewise concludes, "Paul's application of Hab. 2:4 is . . . a legitimate reappropriation of a key prophetic witness to the priority of faith in relating to God."

trusting in God. And even if the prophet was not fully able to comprehend it, the Lord declared although this faith would not confer immunity from suffering in this life, it would result in something far better: an enduring relationship with God.

The third NT quotation of Hab 2:4b occurs in Hebrews. According to Heb 9:28, Christ came the first time "to bear the sins of many"; the second time, he will come to "bring salvation to those who are waiting for him." Hebrews 10 continues the theme of Christ's coming (10:5–9) and exhorts readers to "draw near with a true heart in full assurance of faith . . . since he who promised is faithful" (10:22–23). After a stern warning (10:26–31), the writer of Hebrews admonished his readers to remember their own earlier example of faithfulness under persecution, including the joyful acceptance of the plunder of their possessions (10:34). The parallels between these believers and Habakkuk led the author to turn to the prophetic message of Habakkuk. Hebrews 10 closes by encouraging readers to persevere through the coming tribulations so they might receive God's promises recorded in the OT:

> For yet in **a very little while,**[302]
>   **the Coming One will come and not delay.**
> **But my righteous one will live by faith;**
>   **and if he draws back,**
>   **I have no pleasure in him** (Heb 10:37–38; emphasis in original).

The citation is a conflation of Isa 26:20–21 and Hab 2:3–4. Isaiah 26 opens with the Song of Judah, describing a strong city, which has salvation for walls and ramparts and open gates for the righteous to enter (Isa 26:1–2). In contrast, the Lord destroys the "inaccessible city" where the wicked have hidden themselves "in lofty places" (Isa 26:5–6). Isaiah then contrasted the wicked who die (Isa 26:14) with the righteous: "Your dead will live; their bodies will rise. / Awake and sing, you who dwell in the dust!" (Isa 26:19). The prophet also warned the faithful:

> Hide for a little while until the wrath has passed.
> For look, the Lord is coming from his place
>   to punish the inhabitants of the earth for their iniquity. (Isa 26:20–21)

The similarities in context between Isaiah 26 and Hab 2:3–4 likely contributed to the writer's appeal to both passages in Hebrews. Both anticipate the Lord's judgment against the wicked, which the righteous must await with patience. Though Isaiah expresses it more clearly, Hab 2:4 also suggests the reward of the righteous will be life beyond death. The larger context

---

[302] The Gk. text reflects the LXX: *Mikron hoson hoson* (Eng. "a very little while").

for both calls for faith(fulness). The Isaiah passage also underscores ultimately, the righteous wait for the Lord himself: "Yes, LORD, we wait for you";
"the LORD is coming" (Isa 26:8, 21). In Hab 2:3 the approaching future vision
morphed into "the Coming One" in Heb 10:37. In order to heighten the
messianic expectation, the writer of Hebrews added the definite particle to
the participle "coming." As in the LXX, he also shifted the subject from the
vision in Hab 2:3a to a person, "an expected deliverer": "If he is late, wait
for him" (Hab 2:3 LXX).[303] The LXX translators had already understood the
vision announced the coming of Yahweh. As discussed above, Peter drew
from the language of Hab 2:3 to answer the question of scoffers: "Where
is [Christ's] 'coming' that he promised?" (2 Pet 3:4). Peter, like the writer of
Hebrews, understood that Habakkuk's vision of the end pointed ultimately
to the second coming of Christ.

The second half of Heb 10:38 in English is almost unrecognizable as Hab
2:4a because the writer of Hebrews quoted the verse from the LXX and
reversed the order of the two independent clauses in Hab 2:4 to fit his purposes.[304] The Greek OT renders *ʿāpal* (Eng. "to swell")—an obscure Hb. word
occurring only once in the OT—as *hupostello* (Eng. "draws back") rather
than "inflated" (CSB) or "puffed up" (ESV). Additionally, the LXX uses an
alternate meaning for the Hb. word *yāšār*, translating it as "pleasing" rather
than "integrity" (CSB) or "upright" (ESV).[305] A comparison of the different
possibilities may be helpful here:

Hab 2:4 CSB	Look, his ego is inflated; / he is without integrity./ But the righteous one will live by his faith.
Hab 2:4 ESV	Behold, his soul is puffed up; it is not upright within him, but the righteous shall live by his faith.
Hab 2:4 LXX (AT)	If he draws back, my soul takes no pleasure in him, But the righteous by my faithfulness [or "by faith in me"] will live.
Heb 10:38 CSB	**But my righteous one will live by faith; and if he draws back, /I have no pleasure in him.**

---

[303] F. F. Bruce, *The Epistle to the Hebrews*, NICNT (Grand Rapids: Eerdmans, 1990), 273–74.
Bruce notes that John the Baptist sent his disciples to inquire about Jesus's identity in terms of
this same messianic title: "'Are you the Coming One, or are we to expect someone else?' (Matt.
11:3 // Luke 7:19)." Jesus's reply in Matt 11:4–6 // Luke 7:22–23 implied an affirmative answer.

[304] Bruce, *The Epistle to the Hebrews*, 274, observes that the inversion makes "my righteous
one" (i.e., "the Christian believer") the subject of both clauses in Heb 10:38, which fits the context of encouraging believers to remain faithful and not draw back. The chiasm formed between
Heb 10:38–39 emphasized the author's expectation that both he and his readers would live by
faith and be saved.

[305] A person can be pleasing to another (e.g., "the right one" in Judg 14:3, 7) or to the Lord
(Jer 27:5); a matter can be pleasing (1 Sam 18:20, 26; 2 Sam 17:4) or not (1 Kgs 9:12).

The LXX translation perfectly fit the purposes of the author of Hebrews, who desired to encourage believers whose faith was flagging in the face of ongoing persecution.[306] He was confident they would not draw back and be destroyed. He encouraged them to cling to the promise tucked away in Hab 2:3–4; they would be saved by faith.

The OT quotations found in Heb 10:37–38 serve as an introduction for the "Hall of Faith" following in Hebrews 11. There the writer compiled a long list of examples of OT believers whose faithful actions demonstrated their faith in the Lord. The phrase "by faith" introduces each of these with the regularity of a metronome. Hebrews 11:6 explains: "Now without faith it is impossible to please God, since the one who draws near to him must believe that he exists and that he rewards those who seek him." The chapter showcases the faith of Abraham, who believed God's promises and placed his trust in the God who spoke them. His obedient actions demonstrated his faith. He left his homeland—ironically, Chaldea—to follow the Lord to the land of promise. He obeyed to the brink of sacrificing his beloved son, believing God would raise him from the dead (Heb 11:19). Like all the examples in Hebrews 11, Abraham died without having received God's promises. Some of the faithful even suffered horrific mistreatment, including torture that ended in death (Heb 11:35–38). Faith, however, allowed them to see beyond their current tribulations to a heavenly homeland, a city "whose architect and builder is God" (Heb 11:10). The writer of Hebrews may have drawn this image of a city from the one described in Isaiah 26:1, since he already quoted from this same chapter in Heb 10:37.

In essence, the faith of the Hebrew believers addressed in this NT letter differed little from the faith of these OT examples. The author of Hebrews used the faith(fulness) of these OT believers to encourage those with faith in Christ to remain faithful. He referred to Hab 2:3–4 to introduce his subject—verses containing the Lord's promise of a reward for faith realized in a life yet to come. Such a reward bolstered Habakkuk's own faith and, like his NT counterparts, encouraged him to trust the Lord and remain faithful. Hebrews 11:39–40 explains that although God "approved" of these OT examples through their faith, they did not yet "receive what was promised" since something better was coming. Jesus indeed came. "[T]he pioneer and perfecter of our faith" endured the cross to make this promise possible at his second coming (Heb 12:2). A biblical theological examination of faith

---

[306] Roberts, *Nahum, Habakkuk, and Zephaniah*, 106–7 argues that the MT, properly understood, contrasts two responses to the vision. He suggests emending ʿuppĕlah (Eng. "swollen") to ʿlp, yʿp, or ʿyp, roots that all imply "exhaustion, weariness, or fainting away." The first line of v. 4a would describe "one who faints or loses heart in the presence of the vision"; the second line, one who trusts in the reliability of the vision and the God who gave it (p. 113).

positions Jesus squarely in the center of the canon and God's ultimate purposes for his people in both Testaments.

The rising tide of evil of Habakkuk's day threatened to overwhelm the prophet. Flung into the midst of the growing flood, this three-word Hb. clause—translated as "the righteous one will live by his faith"—was a three-stranded lifeline. New Testament writers grasped the significance of the last clause in Hab 2:4 and claimed it for their own.[307] Augustine believed the vision promised in Hab 2:2–4 referred to the advent of Christ.[308] When Martin Luther struggled with the realization that he could never be good enough to merit God's favor, he meditated on this statement quoted in Rom 1:16–17 until it opened the door for his salvation and ultimately sparked the Reformation. Luther described that glorious moment: "Then I grasped the truth that the justice of God is that righteousness whereby, through grace and sheer mercy, he justifies us by faith. Thereupon I felt myself to be reborn and to have gone through open doors into paradise. . . . This passage of Paul became to me a gateway to heaven."[309] On November 11, 1883, Charles Haddon Spurgeon commemorated the four hundredth anniversary of Luther's birth by preaching from Hab 2:4, calling it the "[golden] key of truth by which Luther unlocked the dungeons of the human mind, and set bondaged hearts at liberty." He also said, "'The just shall live by his faith,' produced the Reformation. Out of this one line, as from the opening of one of the Apocalyptic seals, came forth all that sounding of gospel trumpets, and all that singing of gospel songs, which made in the world a sound like the noise of many waters."[310] This key doctrine of the gospel shaped much of Spurgeon's ministry as well. When we ponder the immeasurable impact of these three Hebrew words across the pages of Christian history, it is no wonder the Lord instructed Habakkuk to record the vision carefully.

For today's generation, Hab 2:4 still proves to be a lifeline for believers. When the wickedness of the world presses in, we need its reminder. God sees and distinguishes between the wicked and the righteous by faith.

---

[307] In the Talmud, Rav Simlai observed that Habakkuk reduced the 613 precepts of the Torah down to one principle: "[T]he righteous shall live by their faith." Calling Hab 2:4b "the quintessence of mitzvot [commands]," Shimon Bakon, "Habakkuk: From Perplexity to Faith," *JBQ* 39.1 (2011): 28, notes, "It is the interpretation of the term *emunah* that caused the division of Judaism and Christianity. In the Jewish Interpretation, *emunah* stands for steadfastness and loyalty to God and the mitzvot. . . . By an ironic twist, Paul made it into faith without the encumbrance of mitzvot that leads to salvation."

[308] Augustine, *City of God,* 31 (*NPNF* 1:377–78).

[309] Martin Luther, "Preface to Latin Writings," in *Luther's Works*, vol. 34 (St. Louis: Concordia), 337.

[310] Charles Haddon Spurgeon, "A Luther Sermon at the Tabernacle," in *Metropolitan Tabernacle Pulpit*, vol. 29. The Spurgeon Center. Online: https://www.spurgeon.org/resource-library/sermons/a-luther-sermon-at-the-tabernacle#flipbook, accessed October 1, 2023.

These two ways of life result in two different outcomes. Whether this present life turns out to be long or short, though it may be filled with undeserved suffering, God declares there is hope for eternal life for all who trust in him. May the Lord strengthen our faith so we may be found faithful on the day of his coming.

1.5.3   The Wicked Are Never Satisfied (2:5)

[5] *Moreover, wine betrays;*
an arrogant man is never at rest.
He enlarges his appetite like Sheol,
and like Death he is never satisfied.
He gathers all the nations to himself;
he collects all the peoples for himself.

2:5 The description of the wicked resumes from v. 4. The desire for wine[311] only contributes to the demise of the wicked. Wine was a common beverage (Gen 14:18) and represented one of the covenant blessings the Lord promised the Israelites when they entered the land: if they were obedient, he would give them "grain, new wine, and fresh oil" along with flocks and herds (Deut 7:13). Wine comprised part of the daily sacrifice the Lord required from the Israelites (Exod 29:40–41) and represented a portion of the tithe the Israelites enjoyed as they feasted in the Lord's presence (Deut 14:23). But Scripture also reveals wine can lead to sin in a fallen world: for example, consider Noah's drunkenness (Gen 9:20–27), Lot's daughters' deception (Gen 19:30–38), and the disturbing imagery of Hab 2:15–16. Although wine can make the heart glad (Ps 104:15), it is also a mocker that makes fools of those who abuse it (Prov 20:1); it impoverishes those who love it (Prov 21:17). Habakkuk 2:5 personifies the evils of excessive wine, making it a traitor. The inebriated are unable to walk a straight line or remain upright, so they, like the wicked, will topple.

---

[311] Although the MT, Targum, and Vulgate support a reading of "wine," 1QpHab substitutes "wealth" for "wine"—a variant explained by the close similarity between Hb. letters ׳ and ׳. Shepherd, *A Commentary on the Book of the Twelve*, 332–33 (like Wellhausen, 1893), speculates that the original word may have been "woe": "Woe, a proud man deals treacherously." The chiastic structure of the central panel and the careful parallel symmetry of panel I:D and panel III:D′ argue against this proposal of a sixth woe.

The warning of Hab 2:5a also foreshadowed the end of the Babylonian empire (539 BC). Daniel 5 describes how a drunken Belshazzar sought to entertain a thousand of his noblemen at a great feast. Under the influence of wine, the ruler sent for silver and gold goblets from the temple in Jerusalem, which Nebuchadnezzar had seized as trophies of his conquest. While the wine flowed freely to and from the sacred vessels, the crowd drank and "praised their gods made of gold and silver, bronze, iron, wood, and stone" (Dan 5:4). Suddenly, a disembodied hand appeared, frightening the arrogant ruler and etching his fate on the wall. Daniel supplied the interpretation: Babylon had come to an end. The prophecy was immediately fulfilled as "[t]hat very night Belshazzar the king of the [Babylonians] was killed," and the formerly awe-inspiring kingdom of Babylonia was divided between the Medes and the Persians (Dan 5:30).

The wicked person's ego enlarged and so too his appetite and desires. An "arrogant" (Hb. *yāhir*, lit. "presumptuous, proud") man is therefore never at rest.[312] The only other OT occurrence of this Hb. word (Prov 21:24) occurs alongside the adjectives "proud" and "mocker." The haughty one looks down on others and exalts himself rather than the Lord. He attributes his successes to his own hands, so he is always maneuvering for more. He cannot settle down and find contentment. *Yinweh* ("abide") is the only OT occurrence of the Hb. verb *nāwâ*, meaning to rest as in "to reach an objective" i.e., one's destination.[313] The noun form of this word "abode, dwelling" relates to pastureland or home—and by extension—the dwelling place of God (Exod 15:13; 2 Sam 15:25).[314] Because the Lord himself is the heart's true dwelling place, the proud cannot make their way home—neither can they find contentment elsewhere.

Habakkuk 2:5 compares the ever-increasing appetite of the arrogant to Sheol and Death. The comparison works extremely well. As

---

[312] *HALOT*, 397.

[313] *HALOT*, 678. Emerton, "The Textual and Linguistic Problems of Habakkuk II. 4–5," 6, suggests the wicked "will not reach his goal," or "will not be successful." Such a reading would align with the LXX περάνῃ (Eng. "achieve" or "finish"). Wendland, "'The Righteous Live by Their Faith' in a Holy God," 597, points out that *yinweh* ("he will [not] rest/abide") rhymes with *yiḥyeh* ("he will live") in 2:4: "the phonological similarity perhaps highlighting the semantic antithesis between this focal pair of finite verbs." Wendland concludes, "The former 'will live' before the LORD 'by his faith/steadfast trust,' but the latter will not 'abide/endure.'" The destinies of the righteous and the wicked are starkly different.

[314] Gerald H. Wilson, "נָוֶה," *NIDOTTE* 3:54–55.

seen in 2:4a, *nepeš* has a broad range of meanings, including "appetite" and—closely related—"throat." Both v. 5 and Isa 5:14 depict
Sheol as ravenous, always enlarging its appetite/throat for more.[315]
The verb "enlarge" (Hb. *rāḥab*) can refer to opening one's mouth wide
to receive food to satisfy one's appetite. The Lord admonished Israel
to look to him for sustenance rather than to a foreign god: "I am
the LORD your God, / who brought you up from the land of Egypt. /
Open your mouth wide, and I will fill it" (Ps 81:10). The same word
also refers to the increase of Israelite territory by extending her borders (Exod 34:24; Deut 19:8). In contrast, the wicked person—like the
Babylonian in chap. 1—does not look to God for sustenance; instead,
his enlarged appetite consumes more territory. This kind of voracity
is comparable only to Sheol and Death, which are personified in v. 5
as living things.[316] Perhaps because burial involved "opening up" the
ground, several OT passages depict Sheol as "swallowing" her inhabitants. Although the ground literally opened and swallowed the trou-
blemakers in Num 16:30–33, in other places the metaphor figuratively
describes death (Ps 141:7; Prov 1:12). As the place of the dead, Sheol
is continually expanding its borders to make room for new occupants.
Like Death, Sheol is "never satisfied" (see Prov 27:20; 30:15).

The graphic imagery of Hab 2:5 resembles that found in Isa
5:13–15:

> Therefore my people will go into exile
> because they lack knowledge;
> her dignitaries are starving,

---

[315] *HALOT*, 712, lists this occurrence in v. 5 along with Isa 5:14, under the meaning "throat."
In Isa 5:14, CSB translates *nepeš* as "throat."

[316] *HALOT*, 1369, defines *šə'ōl* as "wasteland, void, underworld"—a substantive that never
occurs with an article since it evolved into a proper name. Theodore J. Lewis, "Dead, Abode
of the," *ABD* 2:103–4 observes that because Sheol and Death are frequently personified, there
is "fluidity between Sheol/Death as a person and a locality." Sheol and the grave are naturally
closely connected. Some scholars contend that Sheol is the abode of all who die, wicked and
righteous alike. Others argue that Sheol is the destiny of the wicked only, since the usual way of
referring to natural death is being "gathered to his people" (e.g., Gen 25:8), a phrase that never
occurs in conjunction with Sheol. Although Jacob fretted about going down to Sheol in grief
should harm come to Benjamin (Gen 42:38; 44:27–31), when Jacob died, he described his imminent death as being "gathered to [his] people" (Gen 49:29, cf. v. 33). R. Rosenberg, "The Concept
of Biblical Sheol within the Context of ANE Belief," (Ph.D. Thesis, Harvard University, 1980), 178–
252, suggests that Sheol may therefore be associated with premature or "evil death," in contrast
to natural death. Regardless, most OT references to Sheol indicate the final abode of the wicked.

and her masses are parched with thirst.
Therefore Sheol enlarges its throat
and opens wide its enormous jaws,
and down go Zion's dignitaries, her masses,
her crowds, and those who celebrate in her!
Humanity is brought low, each person is humbled,
and haughty eyes are humbled.

Both passages refer to the proud who never find satisfaction because they look to sources other than God to fill them. Not only are the wicked greedy like Sheol/Death, but in the end, death is their ultimate destination. The mention of Sheol in v. 5 heightens the contrast to the preceding verse where "the righteous one will live by his faith." Habakkuk asked the Lord in 1:13, "Why are you silent / while one who is wicked swallows up / one who is more righteous than himself?" The Lord gave Habakkuk a definitive answer in 2:4–5. Although Babylon and her king would devour the righteous for a season (cf. Jer 50:7, 17; 51:34, 44), Sheol ironically swallows the wicked "swallower." The Babylonian oppressor would die because he had "swallow[ed] more nations than he [could] chew."[317] The ultimate irony awaits the moment when Death itself will be swallowed up by life (Isa 25:7–8). God indeed distinguishes between the wicked and the righteous. The one perishes in Sheol; the other he rewards with eternal life.

The end of v. 5 concludes this section with "a final bicolon in strict formal and semantic parallelism," bringing the first panel of the literary triptych to a close.[318] The arrogant man continually scans the horizon with the aim of gathering "all the nations" (cf. Hab 1:9, 15). He selfishly amasses "all the peoples" as if they were grain or riches. Nebuchadnezzar enacted this imagery as he marched across the ancient Near East, besieging cities, gathering up survivors and plunder alike, hoarding everything for his kingdom. Caught in his clutches,

---

[317] Sweeney, *The Twelve Prophets*, 473.

[318] Wendland, "The Righteous Live by Their Faith," 597. The final two lines in v. 5 display both syntactical and semantic parallelism; the only difference between them is the substitution of semantic/lexical equivalents: "he gathers" = "he collects"; "all the nations" = "all the peoples." Because the two lines exhibit proximity, similarity of surface structure, and multiple linguistic equivalences, they are easily processed and have a greater effect. (See Berlin, *The Dynamics of Biblical Parallelism*, 130–41.) The heightened emphasis of this parallelism suggests that the bicolon serves a structural purpose, indicating the conclusion of the first panel. The significance of this formal parallelism is that it helps solve the ongoing debate about which verse begins the section of woes.

Jerusalem would soon be left in smoldering ruins, her survivors plodding toward exile in Babylon; the treasures of her temple and palace proudly displayed before pagan gods (2 Kgs 24:10–25:21). The first panel of the literary triptych ends with the final image of a violent man bloated with greed, seated at a bountiful table of food and drink, ravenously reaching to devour everything in sight.

The powerful picture of an arrogant, greedy person as ravenous as death is just as apt in our day. Nebuchadnezzar's lust for all the nations and all the peoples reverberates in today's cravings for all the riches, all the food, all the fun. The indicators of insatiable appetites are perhaps clearer now than ever before. A glass of wine per meal yields to binge drinking, recreational drug use, and life-altering addictions. Desire for entertainment leads to hours of fruitless searching on all manner of devices—from tiny watches to massive ultra-high-definition televisions, and a longing for stories that resonate prompts binge watching an entire year's series over one weekend. Dissatisfaction with sex in marriage morphs into multiple partners, same-sex partners, and even sex with virtual partners available via screens 24-7. Even good gifts from God, like family time and outdoor recreation, are still poor substitutes for God. Only he is big enough to satisfy us. Evidence of a deep-seated, desperate dissatisfaction in our culture reveals a God-sized hunger and thirst only God can assuage. When the wicked seek to satisfy insatiable appetites with tasteless substitutes, they themselves become fodder for an equally insatiable Sheol.

Each generation needs to hear that their cravings point to a deeper hunger and thirst that nothing can fill but the gospel of the one who is himself both Living Water and Bread of Life. As Jesus explained, "No one who comes to [him] will ever be hungry, and no one who believes in [him] will ever be thirsty again. . . . [E]veryone who sees the Son and believes in him will have eternal life, and [Jesus] will raise him up on the last day" (John 6:35, 40b). This message must be shared with the same urgency as that of Habakkuk's day when the prophet placed his faith in the Lord's promise of deliverance. Despite all appearances to the contrary, the wicked will perish, but those righteous by faith will live.

2 GOD PRONOUNCES JUDGMENT ON THE WICKED (2:6–20)

2.1 Woe 1 (2:6–8)
    2.1.1   Woe to the plunderer! (2:6)
    2.1.2   His victims will wake up and plunder him. (2:7)
    2.1.3   Refrain: The reason for judgment (2:8)

2.2 Woe 2 (2:9–11)
    2.2.1   Woe to the one who profits at others' expense! (2:9)
    2.2.2   He has planned shame for his house. (2:10)
    2.2.3   His ill-gotten gains will testify against him. (2:11)

2.3 Woe 3 (2:12–14)
    2.3.1   Woe to the one who builds with bloodshed! (2:12)
    2.3.2   The peoples labor only to fuel the fire. (2:13)
    2.3.3   The earth will be filled with knowledge of the Lord's glory. (2:14)

2.4 Woe 4 (2:15–17)
    2.4.1   Woe to the predator who exploits his neighbors' drunkenness! (2:15)
    2.4.2   He will drink the cup of the Lord's wrath. (2:16)
    2.4.3   Refrain: The reason for judgment (2:17)

2.5 Woe 5 (2:18–20)
    2.5.1   What use is a god made by human hands? (2:18)
    2.5.2   Woe to the one who worships a lifeless idol! (2:19)
    2.5.3   The Lord in his holy temple silences the whole earth. (2:20)

2   GOD PRONOUNCES JUDGMENT ON THE WICKED (2:6–20)

The second panel—and centerpiece—of Habakkuk's literary triptych focuses on 2:6–20, which serves as the verbal pronouncement of the vision announced in 2:2.[1] The framework of this oracle consists of a series of five woes. Even though the woes may be placed on the lips of others, the entire section is still part of the Lord's second answer to Habakkuk, begun in 2:2. In chap. 1 the prophet questioned the Lord's plan to use the Babylonians: "Why are you silent / while one who is wicked swallows up / one who is more righteous than himself? . . . Will they therefore empty their net / and continually slaughter nations without mercy?" (vv. 13, 17). The Lord's answer was emphatic. Judgment was inevitable, even for the Babylonians. God saw their deeds and knew the hidden motives of their hearts. In 2:6–20, he exposed their wickedness with vivid imagery.

The Hb. word *hôy*, mentioned repeatedly throughout chap. 2, is an interjection most versions translate as "Woe!" (thirty-five of forty-eight times).[2] Besides the exception in Kings, OT occurrences of *hôy* appear in the Prophets, where it functions as "a grievous threatening cry."[3] The concentration of five woes in Habakkuk ranks second only to Isaiah, which contains a total of fifteen woes. Sometimes the woes targeted individuals by name (e.g., Jehoiakim; Jer 22:13) or a group (false shepherds, Jer 23:1; false prophets, Ezek 13:3), but most often the woes primarily addressed cities or nations, including Israel and Judah. The only other series of woes in the OT—besides the five spoken against Babylon in Habakkuk 2—is a set of six woes pronounced against Judah (Isa 5:8, 11, 18, 20, 21, 22). Isaiah's list of woes enumerated Judah's sins as (1) accumulating houses and fields; (2) obsession with beer and wine; (3) dragging sin with "cords of deceit"; (4) calling "evil good and good evil"; (5) considering themselves wise; and (6) drinking excessively and committing social

---

[1] The chiastic structure of this middle panel draws the focus of the entire literary triptych to the chiastic center found in 2:12–14. For a discussion of the structure of Habakkuk, see 6.2.4: "Habakkuk as a Literary Triptych."

[2] CSB translates the remaining dozen or so occurrences as "Alas!" or "Listen!" or "Oh!" and "Ah!" (e.g., Zech 2:6–7; 1 Kgs 13:30). Robertson, *The Books of Nahum, Habakkuk, and Zephaniah*, 186, translates *hôy* as "Ha!" Roberts, *Nahum, Habakkuk, and Zephaniah*, 114, describes *hôy* as "a vocative particle normally followed by direct address." He therefore translates it as "Hey, you" (112–13). A second Hb. interjection (*'ôy*) that is also translated as "woe" occurs twenty-four times in the OT.

[3] *HALOT*, 242.

injustices for bribes. These transgressions of Judah parallel those committed by the Babylonians.[4]

Who was the intended recipient of Habakkuk's series of woes? According to 2:6, the woes refer to the arrogant man in 2:4–5, who greedily gathered "all the nations" and "all the peoples for himself." These same descriptors recur in later verses: "[Y]ou have plundered many nations" (v. 8), "wiping out many peoples" (v. 10). Other clues include "your uncircumcision" (v. 16) and idolatry (vv. 18–19). The woes condemned the Babylonians, represented by the masculine singular reference to either the king or the army as a single unit as in chap. 1.[5] The first, second, and fourth woes begin by addressing the individual in third-person singular (e.g., "Woe to him who amasses what is not his," v. 6) before switching to second-person singular ("[Y]ou will become spoil for them," v. 7). This technique is reminiscent of the opening sermon in Amos 1–2, which had listeners affirming the judgment of others before the prophet turned and accused his audience of Israelites. Although the woes in Habakkuk targeted the Babylonians, they also applied to anyone guilty of similar sins. The offenses parallel those of Jehoiakim of Judah, though his transgressions were on a smaller scale (Jer 22:13–17). The absence of a subject allows the Lord to target the guilty. The woe oracles condemn the sins of an aggressive empire, but they are framed as proverbs addressing the sins of an individual.[6] The deeds of the wicked still carry within themselves the seeds of their own destruction. They, too, will one day face judgment.

2.1   WOE 1 (2:6–8)

2.1.1   Woe to the Plunderer! (2:6)

6 *Won't all of these take up a taunt against him,*
with mockery and riddles about him?

---

[4] Woes are not limited to the OT. In the NT Jesus pronounced a series of seven woes in Matthew 23 and six woes in Luke 11. Both series targeted the religious leaders of Jesus's day, who were guilty of hypocrisy. See also Matt 11:21; 18:7; Luke 6:25; 10:13; Jude 1:11; Rev 8:13; 11:14; 18:10, 16.

[5] For discussion of Hb. countables and collectives, see *IBHS* §7.2.1. Floyd, *Minor Prophets Part 2*, 137, notes that this "indirectly accusatory speech" is appropriate for denouncing a "doomed but still powerful conqueror."

[6] The transgressions are expressed as participles denoting continual, ongoing action. See *IBHS* §37.1d.

> *They will say:*
> *"Woe to him who amasses what is not his—*
> *how much longer?—*
> *and loads himself with goods taken in pledge."*

2:6 The second panel opens with a question, a fitting response to Habakkuk's questions in the previous chapter: "Won't all of these take up a taunt against him?"[7] The Hb. noun *kōl*, "all," refers to the closing bicolon in the first panel, where the arrogant man collected "all the nations" and "all the peoples." The Hb. phrase *kullām*, "all of these" in v. 6, is placed in the emphatic position after the demonstrative pronoun it qualifies, translating as, "Won't these—all of them."[8] Every one of his victims will have a voice in the adversary's judgment.

The victims would not simply accuse him; they would deride him with "a taunt," "mockery," and "riddles." The first of these (Hb. *māšāl*) is sometimes translated as "poem" (Num 23:7) or "proverb" (1 Kgs 4:32).[9] Even as a proverb, however, the term can reflect a negative idea, appearing in conjunction with Hb. *šənînâ* "sharp word, taunt" as in 1 Kgs 9:7: "Israel will become an object of scorn and ridicule among all the peoples." Isaiah 14:4 uses the same phrase, "lift up a taunt," to express a "song of contempt" against the same oppressor—the king of Babylon.[10] The ridicule also involves "mockery" (Hb. *məlîṣâ*) and "riddles" (Hb. *ḥîdâ*)—like the one composed by Samson (Judg 14:14) or the challenging questions posed by the queen of Sheba to Solomon (1 Kgs 10:1). Though difficult to imagine, the once-mighty Babylonian oppressor would topple to the amusement of his emboldened victims.

The Lord placed his pronouncement of woe on the lips of the formerly oppressed peoples. Many scholars include the entire series of woes in the taunt song (vv. 6–20). Clearly, the plundered pronounce the first woe (vv. 6b-8), and possibly even the second (vv. 9–11).[11] The

---

[7] Bailey, "Habakkuk," 333, observes that the negative rhetorical question—posed by the word "Won't" in 2:6 and 2:7—functions as an emphatic assertion: "Of course they will!"

[8] *HALOT,* 474.

[9] *HALOT,* 648, notes that *māšāl* is "a saying of different types and genres."

[10] The formal taunt song is a prophetic subgenre. See 6.1.1: "Habakkuk's Use of Prophetic Subgenres" in the Introduction.

[11] The quotation could conclude as early as the end of v. 6 or v. 7 since the latter ends with "them" rather than "us." Ward, "Habakkuk," 15, argues that only the couplet found in 6b is pronounced by the oppressed nations.

remaining woes, however, sound strange coming from the nations since they speak of the futility of the peoples and the eschatological glory of the "LORD of Armies" (vv. 13–14); they warn of the cup of wrath in "the LORD's right hand" (v. 16); and they mock idolaters and silence the whole earth before "the LORD . . . in his holy temple" (vv. 18–20). Debbie Hunn points to this peculiarity as evidence these people have come to know Yahweh. She argues, "They include Gentiles because they are from among all peoples and all nations (2:5)," and because they express faith in God, they are included in the righteous of 2:4b.[12] Perhaps some did come to believe in the Lord; it seems unlikely, however, that any such conversion would have been comprehensive enough to include "all of these" "nations" and "peoples" (vv. 5–6), who taunt their former oppressor. Perhaps placing the entire taunt song in the mouths of the nations was symbolic of those Gentiles who will together be included among those who fill the earth "with the knowledge of the LORD's glory" (2:14). It seems more probable the Lord introduced the woes which were then elaborated on by the oppressed in v. 6b. The Lord then finished pronouncing the woes through his prophet. The ambiguity may be intentional. It allows the Lord to confront each one who hears the woes, as if he were addressing them personally[13]—regardless of his or her nationality or even generation.

The first woe condemns the one "who amasses what is not his" (v. 6). The word "amasses" translates the (*hiphil*) participle form of the Hb. verb *rābâ*, as causative: "to cause to multiply or increase [for oneself]."[14] The same form appears in Exod 16:17–18, describing those Israelites who unsuccessfully tried to gather more manna than they needed. Jesus warned about this human tendency in his parable of the rich fool, where the farmer dreamed of building bigger barns to store his grain and goods, yet he died before morning (Luke 12:13–21). The hoarder in Hab 2:6 was an even bigger fool, however, because he dared to accumulate what was "not his" (Hb. *lōʾ-lô*). This pair of homonyms occurred previously in Hab 1:6, where the Babylonian perpetrators seized territories that were not theirs. The words draw attention to the audacity of stockpiling territories, nations, and even peoples that belong to another.

---

[12] Hunn, "Habakkuk 2.4b in Its Context," 233–34.

[13] Floyd, *Minor Prophets Part 2*, 118–20.

[14] *IBHS* §27.1d; *HALOT*, 1176–77.

Even as the victims pronounced "Woe!" toward the one causing their oppression, they were unable to hold back their suffering.
Interrupting the description of their oppressor, a cry of lament erupts
mid-sentence: "[H]ow much longer?" Their lament echoes the first
words that broke forth from Habakkuk's own lips in 1:2: "How
long?" These injustices were so great they begged to be resolved. The
answer is implied: "Not much longer." Judgment was coming; the
tables would turn.

A second (*hiphil*) participle from the Hb. root "*kābôd*" meaning "to make heavy," or to "honor or glory," describes the arrogant
man as one loading "himself with goods taken in pledge" (2:6).[15] The
wealthy man's excess in 2:6 came at the expense of the poor. Although
the Lord had forbidden usury among his people, others in the ancient
Near East had no such scruples. In the Old Babylonian period, common
interest rates on loans had been 33 percent on barley and 20 percent
on silver. Loans were common in Babylon in all periods.[16] Economic
inequalities led to social injustices. Small landholders and sharecrop-
pers often took the brunt of natural disasters like floods, famine, or
blight, causing them to borrow at interest from the wealthy. As debts
mounted, the wealthy could foreclose on a loan at a time when the
debtor was unable to pay and then collect the collateral—an animal or
goods or even land—that far exceeded the amount owed.[17] Although
Hammurabi sought to curb some of these economic abuses, they flour-
ished again in Nebuchadnezzar's day, especially in the wake of war.
The extortionist of v. 6 was nothing more than a robber, albeit on a
grander scale. He would fall under the cumulative weight of pledges
he collected dishonestly.

2.1.2   His Victims Will Wake Up and Plunder Him (2:7–8a)

> [7] *Won't your creditors suddenly arise,*
> *and those who disturb you wake up?*
> *Then you will become spoil for them.*
> [8] *Since you have plundered many nations,*
> *all the peoples who remain will plunder you—*

---

[15] *IBHS* §27.1d; *HALOT*, 456.
[16] Saggs, *The Babylonians*, 226–27.
[17] Saggs, *The Babylonians*, 39, 161.

2:7–8a The plunderer and his victims would experience a huge role reversal. The riches he amassed to multiply his own glory would ironically become a burdensome debt he himself would have to pay. His victims would recognize because he had taken what was rightfully theirs, *he* was indebted to *them*. Used seldomly in the OT, the Hb. word for "creditors" comes from the verb *nāšak*, which has two meanings: (1) the denominative form "to bite" (e.g., the snake bites in Num 21:6, 8, 9) or (2) "to loan with interest" (Deut 23:19–20).[18] The occurrence in v. 7 is possibly a wordplay alluding to both meanings in a way that recalls the English metaphor of a "loan shark." As a harsh creditor, he had bitten his victims; they, in turn, would bite him back. This imagery also draws on the devouring motif so prominent in Habakkuk. Without notice, his creditors would suddenly call in his loan and make him pay.

Framing v. 7a as a two-pronged question—"Won't your creditors suddenly arise, / and those who disturb you wake up?"—forced the arrogant man to recognize his victims, the wrongs he perpetrated against them, and the appropriateness of the verdict he would face. Though he had cowed them into submission with violence, they would no longer suffer his abuse. They would suddenly arise and revolt against their oppressor. His victims would "wake up" to the injustice of their oppression. The word translated here as "disturb" (Hb. *zûaʿ* lit. "to tremble, be startled") represents a rare participial form denoting intensive action caused by an outside agent.[19] It was the oppressor's turn to tremble. In this sudden and terrifying reversal, the predator would become the prey.

A sense of retributive justice is reflected in this reversal. The Lord already had turned the northern kingdom of Israel over to robbers and plunderers because his people refused to walk in his ways (Isa 42:22, 24). Likewise, because of King Manasseh's sin, he warned Judah would "become plunder and spoil to all their enemies" (2 Kgs 21:14; cf. Zeph 1:13). Though the ruler of Babylon boasted in his military victories over "all the nations" and "all the peoples," he failed to see

---

[18] *HALOT*, 729.

[19] *HALOT*, 267. The NIV and ESV translations bring out this connotation: "[They] will make you tremble." The term is a *pilpel* participle, which GKC §55f observes "commonly expresses rapidly repeated movement, which [is indicated] by a repetition of the sound." (See *IBHS* §21.2.3a.) *HALOT*, 276, observes that this *pilpel* participle (similar to the Hb. *piel* form) may be a play on words: "those who bark at you." The verb may be related to or derived from the Hb. root *zûah*, meaning to "get agitated or excited."

he was merely an instrument in the Lord's hands to purify a remnant. In spite of the enormous guilt and innumerable sins of his people, the Lord would restore Israel and Judah and judge their enemies. He declared, "Nevertheless, all who devoured you will be devoured. . . . Those who plunder you will be plundered" (Jer 30:16).[20] Jeremiah's wording is reminiscent of Habakkuk 2. God assured the prophets that he would call the Babylonians to account for their own oppressive actions. As a fitting punishment, the one who "plundered many nations," would be plundered by "all the peoples" who survived his rampage. In the ancient Near East, the "spoils" of war referred not only to material goods but also to people. The plunderer would himself become plunder.

Though Habakkuk may not have lived to see this woe fulfilled, the tide of economic prosperity for the Babylonians began to turn less than three decades after Jerusalem fell. Although the nation experienced a flood of wealth under Nebuchadnezzar, he spent it on massive construction projects exalting his own glory rather than building the economy. The flow of imperial resources acquired through conquest began to recede. As other nations gained control of strategic trade routes, inflation soared in Babylon, with prices doubling between 560 and 540 BC.[21] When Cyrus the Great arrived at the ornate city gates in 539 BC, the once great and mighty Babylonian Empire simply fell into his lap.

2.1.3   Refrain: The Reason for Judgment (2:8b)

[8b] *because of human bloodshed*
    and violence against lands, cities,
    and all who live in them.

2:8b   The first woe summarizes the Babylonians' crimes, highlighting the reason for their judgment. They were guilty of brutality on a global scale. The plural form of the word for "blood" signifies the Babylonians had shed much blood—specifically, "blood[s] of humans" (Hb. *middəmê ādām*).[22] The phrase reminds readers of Gen-

---

[20] Zephaniah warns that on the last day the Lord himself will "rise up for plunder" when he gathers the nations to pour out his wrath on them (3:8).

[21] Saggs, *The Babylonians*, 224.

[22] The Hb. word for "blood" is inherently plural; see *HALOT*, 223–25.

esis 4, the first time human blood was shed when Cain murdered his
brother Abel. The Lord confronted Cain and exclaimed, "Your brother's blood [lit. "the voice of the blood of your brother"] cries out to me
from the ground (Hb. 'ădāmâ)!" (Gen 4:10). Habakkuk 2:8b serves
as a reminder that the Lord will not let blood stain the earth without
consequence (see Gen 9:5–6). Just as Habakkuk cried out to the Lord
about violence in 1:2, bloodshed cries out to the Lord for redress.

The Babylonians, like their predecessors, had little regard for life.
The Stele of the Vultures (ca. 2500 BC), the world's most ancient historical document yet discovered, records how a ruler of the ancient
city-state of Lagash exacted from his god a promise that "the heaps
of enemy corpses would be so vast as to touch the base of heaven."[23]
Although this feat proved impossible, the annals of Assyrian King Sennacherib describe the graphic carnage of a seventh-century-BC battlefield: "Assyrian chargers wading through the blood; the plain littered
with mutilated bodies of the slain, hacked to bits for the sake of their
rings and bracelets or for mere bloodlust; terrified horses plunging
madly across the battlefield dragging chariots of the dead."[24] The Babylonians, survivors of this defeat, learned their battle methods from
their conquerors before turning and practicing them in their own
imperial quest.

But Judah herself was not innocent of bloodlust or violence. The
author of Kings records, "Manasseh also shed so much innocent
blood that he filled Jerusalem with it from one end to another" (2 Kgs
21:16). Jeremiah condemned Jerusalem for her own sin: "This city
must be punished. / There is nothing but oppression within her. / As
a well gushes out its water, / so she pours out her evil. / Violence and
destruction resound in her" (Jer 6:6–7). Ezekiel likewise enumerated
Israel's sins before pronouncing the Lord's judgment:

> [T]he land is filled with crimes of bloodshed,
> and the city is filled with violence.
> So I will bring the most evil of nations
> to take possession of their houses. . . .
> I will deal with them according to their own conduct,

---

[23] Saggs, *The Babylonians*, 36.
[24] Saggs, *The Babylonians*, 103. Oates, *Babylon*, 27, provides an illustrated detail of one of
the stele's fragments—located in the Louvre—depicting a phalanx of soldiers brutally marching
over enemy corpses.

and I will judge them by their own standards.

Then they will know that I am the LORD. (Ezek 7:23–24, 27; cf. 22:2–6)

Habakkuk witnessed these same transgressions in Judah. Of the five occurrences of "violence" in Habakkuk, the first two describe Judah (1:2, 3); the latter three, the Babylonians (1:9; 2:8, 17). The Lord is no respecter of persons (see Rom 2:11). He would allow the Babylonians to turn his people's hearts back to him, but then the Babylonians would face judgment for their own oppressive brutality.[25]

Habakkuk 2:8b forms a refrain, repeated verbatim in v. 17: "because of human bloodshed [dəmê] / and violence against lands [ʾereṣ], cities [qiryâ], / and all who live in them." The repetition frames the middle three woes, alerting the reader to the chiastic structure of this central panel, since repetition often occurs at the beginning, middle, and end of a chiasm. The third woe (vv. 12–14), which is in the middle, contains three of these same words found in the refrain: bloodshed [dāmîm], town [qiryâ], and earth [ʾereṣ].[26]

The refrain focuses on the violence in stages. With a wide perspective, the first Hb. word ʾereṣ can refer both to the earth as a whole and to land(s). Although the ESV translates the word as "earth," almost all other English translations render it as "land(s)." The Babylonians aggressively swept across the face of the earth, seizing others' territories and dwelling places as their own (see 1:6).[27] The focus of the second term narrows, describing their violence against a single city—the buildings and homes within its walls. Finally, the perspective narrows further, centering on "all" the city's inhabitants. This is the fifth occurrence of the word "all" in this chapter (2:5 [2x], 6, 8 [2x]). Each one of these occurrences emphasizes the totality of Babylon's victims. This progression of lenses confronts the oppressor with both the global scale of his crimes and the faces of all his victims.

---

[25] Patterson, *Nahum, Habakkuk, Zephaniah*, 184, observes that the Babylonians had to learn the lesson of every divinely appointed agent: "When carrying out God's will is twisted to selfish advantage, the executor of divine justice must himself be judged."

[26] The three words are the same in Hb.; the only difference is that "bloodshed" is a plural absolute in v. 12 and a plural construct in vv. 8, 17. See 6.2.4.1: "Chiastic Features in the Central Panel." *IBHS* §6.3.2c notes that "[n]on-animate feminine nouns may designate a collective"; therefore, qiryâ, ("city/town"; singular, feminine) may function in a collective sense, representing the violence against many cities.

[27] Ironically, the Lord had previously given others' lands and homes to the Israelites (Deut 6:10–11; Josh 24:13).

2.2 WOE 2 (2:9–11)

2.2.1 Woe to the One Who Profits at Others' Expense! (2:9)

⁹ *Woe to him who dishonestly makes*
wealth for his house
to place his nest on high,
to escape the grasp of disaster!

2:9 The second woe moves from the victims' dwelling places
(2:8) to the house of the oppressor. This pronouncement of woe targeted the "one who gains unjust gains" (Hb. *bōṣēaʿ beṣaʿ*). The verb
form followed by the accusative from the same root, often called a
cognate accusative, denotes emphasis.[28] The verb means "to cut off or
sever the thread of life," carrying the connotation of violently stripping others of those possessions necessary for survival.[29] Other prophets from the final days of Judah used this same alliterative construction
(the verbal form plus the related accusative form) to condemn those
"making profit dishonestly" (Jer 6:13 // 8:10; Ezek 22:27). Ironically,
Jeremiah and Ezekiel were not rebuking the Babylonians for this practice but rather the Israelites, including everyone from prophet to priest:
"They have oppressed the poor and needy and unlawfully exploited
the resident alien" (Ezek 22:29). But even if everyone else was doing
it, the wealth gained by such unjust actions was evil and carried the
hefty price tag of judgment. Even Judah's king was not above the
law, as Jeremiah brought similar charges against him: "Woe for the
one who builds his palace / through unrighteousness, / his upstairs
rooms through injustice, / who makes his neighbor serve without pay
/ and will not give him his wages" (Jer 22:13). As the result of Judah's
wickedness, the Lord would summon the Babylonians to refine them
(Jer 6:22–30), eventually consuming them with "the fire of [his] fury"
(Ezek 22:31). Habakkuk records that in time the Babylonians would
also face similar judgment for the same transgression.

---

[28] This construction is a cognate accusative since both the verb and object are derived from
the same root. See *IBHS* §10.2.1f.

[29] *HALOT*, 147–48. John N. Oswalt, "בָּצַע," *TWOT* 1:122, notes "rip-off" is an English parallel,
as is "a racketeer who takes his 'cut' from the profits."

This woe exposes one of the motives behind the plundering: to build a house that would be unassailable. The extortionist aimed to spend the wealth he had acquired from destroying others' homes to build his own. Since the word for house (Hb. *bayit*) can refer to any dwelling place from a humble tent to a temple to a royal palace, he envisioned something on a grand scale. His gains would afford him an impressive structure. Since the oppressor perceived his actions would invite vengeance, he desired to build securely "on high" (Hb. *bam-mārôm*) because such a setting could be more easily defended, like the nest of a soaring bird.[30] Those who bring unspeakable suffering on others think it prudent to station themselves high beyond the reach of the hand of retribution.[31]

Situated on the plains of Mesopotamia, Nebuchadnezzar could not build on the heights; he expended great efforts to make Babylon impregnable. The king's own inscription describes how he used riches from his conquests to transform his father's palace into his home:

> I built very high in its tower a large chamber with bitumen and burned brick for my royal dwelling place, and joined it to my father's palace. . . . I firmly laid its foundation in the bowels of the earth, and I raised high its turrets like a mountain. . . . Mighty cedar trees from the snow-capped mountains, ashuhu trees with broad trunks, and cypress trees, (with) costly stones I laid in rows for its roofing. . . . I surrounded its turrets with a cornice of ugnu-stone and threw around it mountain-high a strong wall of bitumen and burnt bricks. On the sides of the wall of Babylon I built a large wall out of large blocks of stone, such as are found on the lofty mountains, and like a mountain I raised on high its battlements. I

---

[30] Bruce, "Habakkuk," 867, points out that the Kenites (Num 24:21) and the Edomites (Jer 49:16; Obad 3–4) had built their "nests" on what they thought were unassailable cliffs. Even so, they could not evade the Lord. Adolf Hitler's Eagle's Nest comes to mind, being perched on a mountain summit high above Berchtesgaden. The conference center, with granite walls and beamed ceilings, was a marvel of engineering, accessible only through miles of tunnels, bunkers, and an elevator hewn in the middle of the mountain. Though Hitler made less than twenty visits to the Eagle's Nest, he spent much time below at Berghof, his mountainside residence where he hatched evil schemes to invade Russia, Poland, and France.

[31] In Hab 2:9 the CSB translates the Hb. word *kap* (Eng. "palm [of hand]") as "grasp." Manfred Dreytza, "כַּף," *NIDOTTE* 2:678, notes that the metaphorical usage of *kap* suggests "the actual exercise of power" or someone's "grip," while a metaphorical usage of *yād*, the more common Hb. word for "hand," communicates an "abstract concept of power."

built that house for the astonished gaze (of all people), and for the spectacle of the whole world I filled it with splendor.[32]

Nebuchadnezzar's words brim with boasting: when he lacked a mountain for his luxurious palace, he simply constructed his own.

There is also another, even more sinister motive behind the desire to build above everyone else. "On high" often describes the dwelling place of God himself: "For the High and Exalted One / . . . says this, 'I live in a high and holy place, / and with the oppressed and lowly of spirit, / to revive [them]" (Isa 57:15; cf. Jer 25:30). In essence, Nebuchadnezzar desired to set himself in the place of God. The taunt song of Isa 14:4–21 mocks this kind of audacious aspiration: "I will ascend to the heavens; / I will set up my throne / above the stars of God. . . . / I will ascend above the highest clouds; / I will make myself like the Most High" (Isa 14:13–14). Though the Lord has compassion for the oppressed and lowly, he cannot abide the proud and haughty. No matter how seemingly impregnable a structure, no one can hide beyond the reach of the Most High God.

2.2.2 He Has Planned Shame for His House (2:10)

> [10] *You have planned shame for your house*
> *by wiping out many peoples*
> *and sinning against your own self.*

2:10 The oppressor unwittingly devised plans that would bring disgrace on his household. Nebuchadnezzar fortified the city's defenses with massive inner and outer walls, which included the gate of Ishtar, and its inscription which boasted of his personal involvement in the project. Similarly, the king was the architect behind his own demise, having offered counsel regarding the construction of his own house. Here the meaning of "house" shifts from "dwelling place" to "dynastic household" or even "realm." Since he was king, his evil designs ensnared all who lived under his rule. Intending to plan for security, he instead set a course for destruction.

The ancient Near East embraced an honor-shame culture, so the pronouncement of shame (Hb. *bōšet*) was a horrifying prospect.

---

[32] "East India House Inscription of Nebuchadrezzar," *Assyrian and Babylonian Literature: Translations into English*, trans. C. D. Gray (New York: Appleton, 1901), 141–42.

Nebuchadnezzar's careful designs for personal glory would result in his everlasting shame. The kingdom he carved out would be synonymous with ultimate evil rebellion against God. Revelation 18:2 records her collapse: "Babylon the Great has fallen! / She has become a home for demons, / a haunt for every unclean spirit, / a haunt for every unclean bird, / and a haunt for every unclean and despicable beast." The name of Babylon would be repeated throughout the ages, but regarding her infamy rather than her fame.

The Babylonian king devised plans to establish world dominion. His military strategies allowed him to enfold nation after nation into his empire, annihilating "many peoples." He "cut them off" (Hb. root $q\ṣh$, lit. "to put an end to"[33]), scraping them from their land as if scraping plaster to rid a wall of mold (cf. Lev 14:41). Nebuchadnezzar's disregard for his victims prompted him to lay siege to Jerusalem three times (604, 597, 588 BC) before removing Judah's inhabitants from their homeland. As the Lord prophesied through Ezekiel, a third of the population would die under siege, a third would die in battle, and a third would be scattered to the winds in exile. Only by the mercy of God would a remnant be spared to return to the land (cf. Ezek 5:1–3).

The strategies Nebuchadnezzar used to destroy many nations would cause his own empire to unravel. Isaiah records the Lord's response to the king's brutality and arrogance: "I will rise up against them . . . and I will cut off from Babylon her reputation, remnant, offspring, and posterity. . . . I will sweep her away with the broom of destruction" (Isa 14:22–23). In Hab 2:10 the word translated "sinning" is the participial form of the Hb. verb $\ḥ\ā\ṭ\ā\ʾ$, which means "to miss the mark," or "to commit a sin so as to incur guilt."[34] The most frequently used word for sin in the OT, $\ḥ\ā\ṭ\ā\ʾ$ disqualifies because it inflicts injury to relationship[35]—against God (Gen 39:9), others (Gen 42:22), or even oneself (Prov 20:2). Nebuchadnezzar had egregiously erred against God and humanity, but v. 10 highlights the third category: "sinning against your own self [Hb. $nepeš$]"; (sinning "against your soul," NKJV; "forfeiting your life," NIV).[36] The Babylonian

---

[33] *HALOT*, 1120.

[34] *HALOT*, 305.

[35] R. Knierim, "חטא," *TLOT* 1:410.

[36] See the discussion of 2:4 for the broad semantic range of *nepeš*. The NIV translation reflects the 1QpHab variant וחוטי with the proposed meaning of $\ḥ\ûṭê$ i.e., "the threads [of

king's sin invoked the wrath of God against himself and his people. He had not only demolished lands, cities, and their inhabitants, then; he also had ensured his own destruction. As others have pointed out, we don't break God's commands; we break ourselves on them. Ultimately, sin against others is also sin against oneself.

2.2.3 His Ill-Gotten Gains Will Testify against Him (2:11)

> [11] For the stones will cry out from the wall,
>   and the rafters will answer them
>   from the woodwork.

2:11   There is no safe place to hide from God's justice. The beautifully constructed house introduced in v. 9 bore witness not only to the oppressor's great wealth but also to the evil way he had amassed it. The thick stone walls erected to shield him from disaster would call for his destruction. The heavy-beamed ceiling raised to shelter him from vengeance would expose his location. Found only here in the OT, the Hb. word *kāpîs* (Eng. "rafter") sounds like the Hb. word *kap* ("palm"). The powerful hand of retribution the king intended to evade now loomed just over his head. Like the saying, "If these walls could talk," these personified walls verbally testify as "witnesses" to Nebuchadnezzar's crimes.[37] The stones cry out just as the prophet did in Hab 1:2, and the rafters call out in response. The antiphonal accusation continued to resound until justice was done. There is a sense of irony in the retributive justice demonstrated here. The oppressor built a sturdy house as his defense, yet the walls and woodwork testify against him.

The book of Daniel provides a glimpse into the king's thoughts. As the Babylonian surveyed the city of Babylon from his palace rooftop, he exclaimed, "Is this not Babylon the Great that I have built to

---

life]." *HALOT*, 296, notes the possible parallel with Prov 20:2, where the one provoking the king "endangers himself." It is also possible to read the participle not as reflexive, but rather as a construct phrase where the genitive-governing participle indicates a repeated, enduring state: "your ongoing sinning." See *IBHS* §37.3e.

[37] This is not the only instance where inanimate objects find a voice. Abel's blood likewise cried out from the ground for justice (Gen 4:10). More often, however, all of creation bursts forth in praise: e.g., heaven, earth, seas, mountains, fields, and trees of the forest (Pss 69:34; 96:11–12; Isa 44:23; 55:12; Hab 3:10). See also Luke 19:40, where if the disciples were silent, the stones of Jerusalem would cry out praises.

be a royal residence by my vast power and for my majestic glory?" (Dan 4:30). A voice from heaven immediately declared his kingdom would be stripped from him while he endured seven years of madness. Nebuchadnezzar's pride kept him from heeding the Lord's warning through a dream given the previous year. Overnight, the mighty king was reduced to the level of a cow eating grass, and his unkempt appearance resembled that of the bird whose high nest he had coveted. Only after seven years was he willing to acknowledge the rightful King of the World: "[T]he Most High is ruler / over human kingdoms. / He gives them to anyone he wants" (Dan 4:25). Although Nebuchadnezzar's account of the story sounds repentant, Isa 14:4, 15 implies that the "king of Babylon" would "be brought down to Sheol / into the deepest regions of the Pit." This once powerful king, who caused the earth to tremble in terror, would experience a precipitous fall from great heights to even greater depths. Although the final outcome to Nebuchadnezzar's story rests with the Lord, his life stands as a warning to others who would try to usurp the place of God.

Jesus issued a similar caution in Mark 8:36 (ESV): "For what does it profit a man to gain the whole world and forfeit his soul?" He could have pointed to Nebuchadnezzar as an example, but he was addressing an informal group of disciples and a crowd of commoners. Nevertheless, his words still apply today to those who dream of carving out economic or political empires, who aspire to own a penthouse apartment or to achieve the corner office—if they arrive there dishonestly at the expense of others. His warning gives pause not just to the wealthy, however, but to all who struggle to scale life's ladder by climbing over the backs of others only to discover too late they have propped the ladder against the wrong wall.

2.3 WOE 3 (2:12–14)

The third woe rests in the middle of the central panel of the literary triptych, making it the center of the entire book of Habakkuk.[38] If there is a chiastic structure in this middle panel, the third woe should provide evidence of a pivot. The chiasm embodies a shift in worldview continuing throughout the rest of the book of Habakkuk.

---

[38] A Hb. word count shows Hab 2:12 begins after 309 of 613 words in the *BHS*.

2.3.1   Woe to the One Who Builds with Bloodshed! (2:12)

¹² Woe to him who builds a city with bloodshed
and founds a town with injustice!

2:12   Verse 12 shifts from a house that testifies against its wicked inhabitant to an entire city built by oppression. The couplet, an example of synonymous parallelism, describes the same thing in different ways; it condemns the one building a city with bloodshed and establishing a town with injustice. These two lines introduce the central woe statement using two terms found in the refrains that frame the woe oracles: "bloodshed" and "city."[39] The refrains (2:8b, 17b) relate the violent destruction of a city by the bloodshed of its inhabitants. The contrast in verse 12 describes the construction of a city built out of that bloodshed and injustice.

The construction of houses, palaces, temples, and altars occurs throughout the OT. The psalmist declares that ultimately it is the Lord who (re)builds Zion, the walls of Jerusalem, and the cities of Judah (Pss 102:16; 51:18; 69:35). Psalm 127:1 affirms that "[u]nless the LORD builds a house, / its builders labor over it in vain; / unless the LORD watches over a city, / the watchman stays alert in vain." How utterly futile to attempt to build a city with blood!

The Babylonians were not the only nation attempting to do so. A century before Habakkuk, the prophet Micah leveled these same charges against the rulers of Israel: "who build Zion with bloodshed / and Jerusalem with injustice" (Mic 3:10). The crimes called for judgment: "Zion will be plowed like a field, / Jerusalem will become ruins, / and the temple's mountain / will be a high thicket" (Mic 3:12). In Habakkuk's day, Jeremiah pronounced woe on Jehoiakim of Judah for "build[ing] his palace . . . through injustice" and "shedding innocent blood" (Jer 22:13, 17). Ezekiel likewise warned Jerusalem, calling her "the city of blood": "A city that sheds blood within her walls so that her time of judgment has come" (Ezek 22:2–3). Though the Lord would hand Jerusalem over to Nebuchadnezzar, eventually the Babylonians would face judgment for similar crimes. Ezekiel's pronouncement against the Babylonians uses language reminiscent of

---

[39] The CSB translates *qiryâ* in vv. 8 and 17 as "cities," and here in v. 12, as "town." The word translated as "city" in v. 12 is the synonym, *ʿîr*.

Habakkuk's third woe: "Woe to the city of bloodshed! / I myself will make the pile of kindling large" (Ezek 24:9).

Since human life is sacred, the Israelites considered blood to be sacred because it is so closely identified with life (Gen 9:6). Biblical legislation allotted the blood (and fat) of animals to God alone (Lev 3:16–17).[40] In contrast to the practice of surrounding societies, the consumption of blood was prohibited by law in Israel in Lev 17:14 and Deut 12:23. The close association between blood and life also explains the careful prescriptions for animal sacrifice and the power of blood for purification: "For the life of a creature is in the blood, and I have appointed it to you to make atonement on the altar for your lives, since it is the lifeblood that makes atonement" (Lev 17:11). By substitution, the animal's death conveyed life to the repentant sinner. The willful shedding of human blood was particularly egregious because humanity bears the image of God (Gen 9:6). The stain of human blood defiled the ground, and it called—literally—for the judgment of the one who spilt the blood (Gen 4:10; Num 35:33). Even the blood of a wild animal considered clean was to be drained and then covered with dirt so that it would not pollute the earth (Lev 17:13). Cities of refuge shielded those guilty of manslaughter, so the loss of human life did not escalate through revenge killings. Murder, however, was a capital offense so that the land could be purged of "the guilt from shedding innocent blood" (Deut 19:13). Blood made for a strange building material, as did injustice. A city built on this kind of foundation was doomed from the start.

2.3.2 The Peoples Labor Only to Fuel the Fire (2:13)

> [13] *Is it not from the* LORD *of Armies*
> *that the peoples labor only to fuel the fire*
> *and countries exhaust themselves for nothing?*

2:13 Like the first and final woes, this middle woe contains a rhetorical question, formed by the prefixed interrogative *he* to the negative adverb *lōʾ* (Eng. "no/not"): "Is it not?" The question presumes an affirmative answer: "Yes, it is." The text of Habakkuk is interspersed with sixteen negative statements or questions: (Hab 1:2 [2x], 4, 5,

---

[40] S. David Sperling, "Blood," *ABD*, 761.

6, 12 [2x], 13, 14, 17; 2:3 [2x]; 4, 6 [2x], 7). These negatives often appear on the lips of the prophet as he voices his confusion to the Lord,[41] or when the Lord answers with his own negative responses.[42] After the seventeenth instance—"Is it not from the LORD of Armies" (v. 13)—the negative particle does not occur again until the end of chap. 3.[43] What accounts for the sudden absence of negative particles and the reversal in the prophet's outlook in 3:17? A clue to the answer to both questions lies in the chiastic center found in this third woe.

Although not readily apparent, the phrase "Is it not" is followed by the Hb. interjection *hinneh*—an emphatic particle that introduces "a new, unsuspected moment"[44] or a fact that is the basis for the command or statement that follows.[45] The term is typically rendered by visual commands—"behold!" or "look!"—but the particle does not signify a reference to vision as much as "a new situation of perception."[46] The interjection functions as a bridge indicating a logical connection—temporal, causal, conditional, or purposive—between clauses, and translators indicate those connections with adverbs or conjunctions, or they leave the particle untranslated—as the CSB does here.[47] Elsewhere in Habakkuk, the CSB renders three other instances of this word at significant junctures as "Look!" (1:6; 2:4; 2:19). Though the NIV also leaves *hinneh* untranslated in v. 13, most English translations retain the word, rendering it as "behold" (ESV, KJV, NKJV, RSV, JPS) or "indeed" (NASB). Since the proposed center of the chiasm occurs between vv. 13 and 14, the presence of *hinneh* makes perfect sense at this critical juncture. It is only natural to draw attention to the chiastic center with an introductory "Behold!" or "Look!" This is especially true since what follows are (1) an announcement of judgment (v. 13)

---

[41] "Why do you not listen; why do you not save? . . . Justice does not prevail. . . . Are you not from everlasting? You will not die! . . . You cannot tolerate wrong. . . . You made us like fish, not men. . . . Will the Babylonians not show mercy?"

[42] The Lord answers with his own negative responses: "If you heard, you would not believe. . . . The Babylonian gathers what is not his. . . . The vision will not prove false; it will not delay. . . . His ego is not upright. . . . Will not all these taunt the one amassing what is not his? Will they not suddenly rise up against him?"

[43] In the first thirty verses of Habakkuk, the negative particle occurs seventeen times; the prophet does not resume use of the negative particle until 3:17, where it occurs twice.

[44] *HALOT*, 252.

[45] *IBHS* §40.2.1c.

[46] *IBHS* §40n4; §40.2.1c.

[47] *IBHS* §40.2.1c. The CSB likewise does not translate *hinneh* when the same rhetorical question construction—*hălōʾ hinneh*—occurs in 2 Chr 25:26.

and (2) a prophetic glimpse of God's eschatological mission fulfilled (v. 14).[48] The prophet accused God of inactivity and indifference to evil, but vv. 13–14 emphatically declare the Lord will accomplish his purposes. Translating the interjection as "Behold!" underscores the central theological point of the book of Habakkuk.

Verse 13 calls God "the LORD of Armies" (Hb. *yhwh ṣəbāʾôt*), often translated, "the LORD of Hosts" (ESV, KJV, NKJV). Occurring 285 times in the Hebrew Bible, the noun *ṣəbāʾôt* is "the most frequently used divine epithet in the OT."[49] The related Hb. verb *ṣbʾ* means "to go to war" (Num 31:42) or "to be on duty" at the tabernacle (Exod 38:8; Num 4:23); the noun *ṣābāʾ* can indicate military service or troops—both singular (Num 2:8) and plural (Exod 6:26). From the concept of military service developed meanings of cultic service (Num 4:3) and compulsory labor (Isa 40:2). The "host of heaven" refers to both the celestial bodies (sun, moon, and especially stars; Deut 4:19; Neh 9:6) and the Lord's heavenly entourage (1 Kgs 22:19).[50]

The origins and significance of the title are debated. The most obvious interpretation—*the troops of Israel*—is expressed in the appositive located in 1 Sam 17:45: "the name of the LORD of Armies, the God of the ranks of Israel."[51] Some scholars advanced the theory that "the LORD of Armies" is *a cultic title* based on its initial appearance in the birth narrative of the prophet Samuel (1 Sam 1:3) and its close association with the ark at Shiloh: "the ark of the covenant of the LORD of Armies, who is enthroned between the cherubim" (1 Sam 4:4).[52] Joyce Baldwin, for example, observes the title was originally connected "with worship rather than with battles"; thus, the army hosts are *angelic beings* or possibly even *the stars*.[53] Jared Hood contends

---

[48] D. Vetter, "הִנֵּה," *TLOT* 1:381, observes that *hinnêh* sometimes introduces an announcement of judgment, or it may precede a report of a prophetic vision.

[49] H. J. Zobel, "צְבָאוֹת *ṣᵉbāʾôṯ*," *TDOT* 12:216, 232.

[50] *HALOT*, 994–96.

[51] *HALOT*, 996.

[52] Frank Moore Cross Jr., "Yahweh and the God of the Patriarchs," *HTR* 55 (1962): 256, has suggested that *yhwh ṣəbāʾôt* was originally an ancient cultic epithet for the Canaanite god ʾEl: "He who creates the (heavenly) armies." See also Theodore Mullen Jr., *The Divine Council in Canaanite and Early Hebrew Literature*, HSM 24 (Chico: Scholars Press, 1980), 187.

[53] Joyce G. Baldwin, *Haggai, Zechariah, Malachi*, TOTC 24 (London: Tyndale, 1972), 44–45. Zobel, *TDOT*, 12:222, calls the cultic association the "present consensus." Jared Hood, "Yhwh Tsevaot in Samuel: God of the Davidic Age," *JETS* 62.3 (2019): 499, labels the cultic study a "diachronic contextual history" that traces the name from its cultic origins at Shiloh to a broader significance in the Latter Prophets.

recent study of ancient Near Eastern parallels has erroneously fueled the understanding that the hosts concern angelic beings or the Lord's heavenly council.[54] Exploring the occurrences of the word "hosts" and the parallel term "the God of Israel," Hood concludes that "[t]he title, Yhwh Tsevaot, . . . is thoroughly rooted in the pre-Samuel canon," and it "refers to the deity of the federated tribal armies of Israel."[55] Hood also proposes a synchronic contextual theory which views "the LORD of Armies" as "a marker of social transition."[56] He maintains that "Yhwh Tsevaot is a *programmatic title*"—a "Davidic, monarchical, covenantal name" with "epochal significance"—just "as El Shaddai is to Genesis and Yhwh is to Exodus."[57] Finally, some scholars interpret the title as an *intensive abstract plural* and translate the title as "the LORD Almighty" (NIV).[58]

A brief survey of the occurrences of the divine title provides insight into the militaristic significance of "the LORD of Armies." When the Israelites struggled to overcome the Philistines, the wicked sons of Eli carried the ark into combat believing they could manipulate both "the LORD of Armies" and the outcome of the battle. Although the ark was captured, the Lord single-handedly conquered Dagon, the lifeless idol of the Philistines (1 Sam 4–5). When David boldly challenged Goliath, he did so "in the name of the LORD of Armies, the God of the ranks of Israel" (1 Sam 17:45). The Lord referred to himself by this title when he promised David a forever kingdom: "[T]he LORD of Armies says: '. . . I have been with you wherever you have gone, and I have destroyed all your enemies before you'" (2 Sam 7:8–9). Several psalms

---

[54] Jared Hood, "Yhwh Tsevaot before Samuel: Canonical Foundations for a Davidic Title," *RTR* 81 (2022): 2.

[55] Hood, "Yhwh Tsevaot before Samuel," 32.

[56] Hood, "Yhwh Tsevaot in Samuel," 502. Plotting the occurrences of the title within the metanarrative of 1 and 2 Samuel, Hood, p. 513, maintains that the initial clusters of occurrences in 1 Sam 1:1–2:11 and 2 Samuel 5–7 form "an *inclusio* of David expectation and realization."

[57] Hood, "Yhwh Tsevaot in Samuel," 513. Other scholars who link the divine title to installation of the Davidic dynasty include John Paton Ross, "Jahweh S̩ǝḇāʾôt in Samuel and Psalms," *VT* 17.1 (1967): 82–83; Bruce K. Waltke, *An Old Testament Theology: An Exegetical, Canonical, and Thematic Approach* (Grand Rapids: Zondervan, 2007), 398. Waltke renders the divine title "*I AM of Hosts.*"

[58] *HALOT*, 996. *IBHS* §7.4.3b notes that most honorific plurals in the Bible reference the God of Israel: e.g., Elohim, Adonai, and "Holy One" (kǝḏōšîm).

praise "the LORD of Armies." He is "mighty in battle" and "the King of glory" (Ps 24:8, 10). He "brings devastation on the earth," and he is "exalted among the nations" (Ps 46:8, 10–11). This divine title is a favorite of the prophets Isaiah (62x) and Jeremiah (82x), frequently appearing in the postexilic prophetic writings as well.[59] Not only does "the LORD of Armies" fight on behalf of his people, and against them when they are wayward, but he will also be victorious in the last battle when he is established as King over all the earth forever (Zech 14:3, 16; cf. Isa 13).

Even OT narratives in which the divine title does not occur clearly reveal the command of the Lord of Armies extends far beyond mere earthly militia. Scripture is full of stories of the unusual military tactics of the God who is "*yhwh ṣəbāʾôt.*"[60] If the Lord of Armies had launched a mission, then no king, army, nation, or spiritual forces of darkness could ever stand against it.

The single occurrence of the title in the center of Habakkuk suggests multiple meanings are in view. Panel I describes how the Lord of Armies summons pagan Babylonian troops to discipline his rebellious people (1:5–11, 14–17). Panel III pictures the wide array of military forces marshaled by the Divine Warrior/King of creation: plague, pestilence, bolts of lightning, sun, and moon (3:3–15). The Babylonian army may have scoffed at Judah, but "the leader of the house of the wicked" would be conquered by the Lord of Armies, who is sovereign over all the earth (v. 13). Panel II, the declaration of woes, details "God's just judgment and the debate with idolatry" often associated with the formula.[61] The chiastic center (2:12–14) also hints at the eschatological goal of the Lord of Armies: the knowledge of his glory inundating the entire world—just as his glory descended on the tabernacle and temple in ages past.[62] The divine epithet appears in a cultic context (cf. 2:20). The name, "the LORD of Armies," (v. 13) is

---

[59] *HALOT*, 996.

[60] The sea split before Hebrew slaves fleeing for their freedom. Fortress walls fell without a fight. Sun and moon stood still as hailstones flung from above struck down enemy forces. Stars fought from the heavens, and overflowing rivers rendered enemy chariots useless. Three hundred men armed with pitchers, and torches overcame an army that outnumbered them four hundred to one. Unseen horses and chariots of fire outnumbered enemy troops, and an angel of the Lord struck down 185,000 warriors overnight; see Exod 14:1–15:21; Josh 5:13–6:21; 10:8–15; Judg 5:20–21; 7:1–25; 2 Kgs 6:8–23; 19:32–36.

[61] Zobel, *TDOT*, 12:228.

[62] See the discussion of 2:14 below.

particularly suited to embody prophetic, cultic, royal, and military—both earthly and supernatural—connections all at the same time.

The final two lines of v. 13 reveal what comes "from the LORD of Armies." Using synonymous parallelism, they describe the futility of human activity apart from the Lord: "[T]he peoples labor only to fuel the fire / and countries exhaust themselves for nothing." The subjects of these two clauses may refer to Israel or to other nations. The two verbs, "labor" (Hb. *yāgaʿ*, "to work or grow weary from work"), and "exhaust themselves" (Hb. *yāʿēp*) describe excessive fatigue and fainting.[63] In contrast, "the everlasting God, / the Creator of the whole earth / . . . never becomes faint or weary" (Isa 40:28).[64] On occasion, God expressed his weariness of the Israelites' sin (Isa 43:24; Mal 2:17). If that was true for his own people, it would be even more so for the Babylonians.

All the Babylonians' labor of battle and building was in vain. They had expended energy, resources, and blood in a futile bid to have it all, but it would never be enough to satisfy. Ironically, v. 13 concludes with the idiomatic expression "enough for, only enough for," rendering the prefixed preposition (Hb. *b-*) on the substantive "enough, sufficiency" (Hb. *dê*) as "only enough for fire" and "only enough for nothing."[65] An examination of the figurative uses of the term "fire" in the OT (Hb. *ʾēš*) reveals the term frequently describes physical manifestations of God's presence (Gen 15:17; Exod 3:2; 13:21; Ezek 1:13, 27). The Lord's divine anger is described as "a consuming fire," and God's presence on the earth is preceded by "[d]evouring fire" (Deut 4:24; Ps 50:3). God's wrath is often expressed as a fire that burns against his enemies—accounting for about half of the occurrences.[66] Although fire falling from heaven sometimes consumed pleasing sacrifices (Lev 9:24;

---

[63] OT occurrences of these verbs show people grew weary from labor in the fields (Isa 62:8). They also tired from battle, as did David's elite warrior who fought so hard "his hand . . . stuck to his sword" (2 Sam 23:10). God had given the Israelites land and cities for which they did not labor, but still they toiled to make themselves rich (Josh 24:13; Prov 23:4). When they grew "weary of" the Lord (Isa 43:22), they labored at sorcery and exhausted themselves making idols in order to worship a "block of wood" (Isa 47:12; 44:12, 19). See *HALOT*, 386, 421.

[64] These same two verbs are paired together three times in Isa 40:28–31. Even though youths may grow faint and weary, the Lord strengthens those who trust in him so that they will not become weary or faint.

[65] *HALOT*, 219.

[66] The remaining occurrences are divided between physical references to fire and figurative usages that compare fire to fighting, anger, wickedness, gossip, adultery, or love.

1 Kgs 18:38), it more often consumed sinners (Lev 10:2; Num 11:1, 3; 2 Kgs 1:10, 12, 14). The prophets warned of God's punishment by fire—on both Jerusalem and her enemies alike, including Assyria and Babylon (Isa 29:6; Nah 3:13; Jer 50:32).

The final word of the verse, "nothing" (Hb. *rîq*), is rendered elsewhere in the book as "empty" (Hab 1:17). The nuance of the term, meaning "to pour out, or leave empty" conveys effort expended "in vain" or accomplishing little of value.[67] The Babylonians' efforts were ineffective.

The same two lines appear in Jer 51:58b, where the terms "fire" and "nothing" reverse places.[68] The first half of v. 58 includes more specific details: "This is what the LORD of Armies says: / 'Babylon's thick walls will be totally demolished, / and her high gates set ablaze.'" Part of Nebuchadnezzar's extensive building projects, two massive parallel walls encompassed the entire city of Babylon. The outer wall was twelve feet thick; the inner, twenty-one feet thick. The inside wall boasted a total of nine gates, including the main entrance, the elaborately decorated Ishtar Gate. Almost forty feet tall, this double entryway with cedar doors towered over all who entered the city, filling them with awe.[69] Although the city must have seemed impregnable, its gates would swing open wide for Cyrus of Persia, after his defeat of the Babylonian army at Opis in 539 BC. Overnight, the legacy Nebuchadnezzar labored so hard to build was left to another.

The words of Jeremiah conclude with what may be a modified quotation of Hab 2:13.[70] The similar lines conclude his prophecy against Babylon (50:1–51:58), which he recorded on a scroll, with instructions for it to be delivered to the doomed city. As soon as these words were read aloud, the messenger was to tie a stone to the scroll and cast it into the middle of the Euphrates River, with this pronouncement:

[67] *HALOT*, 1227–28.

[68] See also Jer 12:13.

[69] The Ishtar Gate still awes onlookers today. Excavated and restored, the smaller of the double gates is on display in the Museum of Pergamum in Berlin, Germany.

[70] Some scholars argue that Habakkuk may have borrowed the lines from Jeremiah, but it is just as likely that Jeremiah quoted the earlier seventh-century prophet since Jer 51:58 occurs at the end of Jeremiah's "words" (cf. Jer 51:64). Jeremiah commanded Seraiah to take the scroll to Babylon when the quartermaster accompanied King Zedekiah "in the fourth year of Zedekiah's reign," or approximately 593 BC (Jer 51:59). Robertson, *The Books of Nahum, Habakkuk, Zephaniah*, 196, concurs. Bailey, "Habakkuk," 339, and Andersen, *Habakkuk*, 245, believe both prophets quoted a popular proverb. Shepherd, *A Commentary on the Book of the Twelve*, 333, suggests the Jeremiah verse was added to Habakkuk by a composer of the Twelve.

"In the same way, Babylon will sink and never rise again because of the disaster I am bringing on her. They will grow weary" (Jer 51:64). The final word recorded from Jeremiah was Babylon would grow "weary." The last chapter of Jeremiah narrates the horrifying details of Nebuchadnezzar's two-year siege and fiery destruction of Jerusalem. Just as the Lord used the Babylonians to punish his people for their sin, Babylon would one day pay for her savagery against the nations, including Judah.

Those seeking a historical record signaling the end of Babylon come up a bit disappointed. Nebuchadnezzar died in 562 BC after a forty-three-year reign. His kingdom began to unravel in the hands of his less competent descendants; but when Persian king, Cyrus the Great, conquered Babylon in 539 BC, there was no siege, no famine, no flames, no widespread destruction. The Babylonians lost patience with the decade-long absence of Nabonidus, the last Neo-Babylonian king, and his representative, Belshazzar.[71] When the Persians entered the city—likely through water channels—the citizens of Babylon hailed Cyrus as a liberator rather than a conqueror.[72] Two decades later in 522 BC, Babylonian claimants to the throne revolted under Darius I, who was forced to recapture the city. The ancient historian Herodotus recounted that Darius impaled three thousand leading Babylonians as punishment, but Edwin Yamauchi casts doubt on Herodotus's further assertion that Darius destroyed the city's walls and gates at that same time.[73] When Babylon revolted twice more under Xerxes I—in 484 and 482–81 BC—the Persian king dealt a harsh blow, destroying Babylon's fortifications and some of its temples. Subsequently, the city lost its independent status.[74] After Alexander the Great defeated Darius III, he occupied Babylon in 331 BC, only to return in 323 BC, when he suddenly became ill and died. Over the next few centuries, the once glorious city faded into oblivion. By mid-second century AD, Babylon was abandoned. In comparison to Jeremiah's powerful prophecies

---

[71] Edwin M. Yamauchi, *Persia and the Bible* (Grand Rapids: Baker Books, 1996), 86, notes that the Daniel 5 account of Belshazzar's sacrilegious feast on the night the Persians captured the city corresponds to a festival on the eve of the invasion as recorded in the historic accounts of Herodotus (1.191) and Xenophon (Cyropedia 7.5.15).

[72] Yamauchi, *Persia and the Bible*, 87.

[73] Yamauchi, *Persia and the Bible*, 173, reasons that (1) such a measure was unnecessary, (2) Darius continued to use Babylon, and (3) Herodotus described an intact city when he visited "less than a century later."

[74] Yamauchi, *Persia and the Bible*, 193–94.

against Babylon (chaps. 50–51) echoing the woes of Habakkuk 2, Babylon's slow demise seems anticlimactic.

But there are indicators Hab 2:13 looks beyond a mere historical fulfillment of these prophecies to an eschatological fulfillment. First, the two lines refer to a more general audience than the Babylonians: both "peoples" and "countries" are plural. Though Babylon had become a multicultural city, this warning was not limited to the one country of Babylonia. Unlike the Jeremiah quotation, in the immediate context of Hab 2:13 there is no specific mention of Babylon.

Second, the NT uses the ancient city of Babylon as a metaphor for Rome (e.g., 1 Pet 5:13). Similarities between the two cities make for an apt comparison. Both ancient cities were centers of idolatry and commerce; both had vast armies equal to their expansive ambitions to carve out world empires. In NT symbolism, however, Babylon also represents more than just the city of Rome. Revelation calls Babylon a "mystery" and names her: "BABYLON THE GREAT, THE MOTHER OF PROSTITUTES AND OF THE DETESTABLE THINGS OF THE EARTH" (Rev 17:5). Although she seduces kings and peoples of the earth with her sexual immorality, lust for blood, excessive luxuries, and promise of wealth, they will turn against her and destroy her as part of God's plan (Rev 17:15–17). This proud city will drink "a double portion" of the cup of God's wrath (Rev 18:6). Babylon "will be burned up with fire"; "Her smoke ascends forever and ever!" (Rev 18:8; 19:3). While kings, merchants, and sailors mourn her loss, crying, "Woe, woe, the great city!" (Rev 18:10, 16, 19), all the saints of heaven will rejoice over her sudden collapse (Rev 18:20). Babylon thus becomes an eschatological symbol of all human rebellion against God. The proud excesses of the ancient historical city influenced this identification. Perhaps another factor was the number of prophecies against ancient Babylon yet to be completely fulfilled.

Third, Jeremiah instructed Seraiah to throw a stone attached to his scroll—with its concluding quotation from Hab 2:13—into the Euphrates River as an enacted parable: "Then say, 'In the same way, Babylon will sink and never rise again'" (Jer 51:63–64). This prophecy finds its ultimate fulfillment in Rev 18:21: "Then a mighty angel picked up a stone like a large millstone and threw it into the sea, saying, 'In this way, Babylon the great city / will be thrown down violently / and never be found again.'" At some point, the world and all its wickedness, personified as the ancient city of Babylon, will come to an end. There will be an ultimate day of judgment when everything will be put right.

Fourth, fire is often used to describe the final eschatological judgment, in both the OT and the NT. For example, Zephaniah—another seventh-century-BC prophet—warns,

> Their silver and their gold
> will be unable to rescue them
> on the day of the LORD's wrath.
> The whole earth will be consumed
> by the fire of his jealousy,
> for he will make a complete,
> yes, a horrifying end
> of all the inhabitants of the earth (Zeph 1:18)[75]

Jesus likewise spoke of the final judgment in terms of the wicked being cast into a "blazing furnace"—"the eternal fire prepared for the devil and his angels" (Matt 13:41–42; 25:41; cf. 3:12). The NT further describes that last day:

> By the same word, the present heavens and earth are stored up for fire, being kept for the day of judgment and destruction of the ungodly. . . . Because of that day, the heavens will be dissolved with fire and the elements will melt with heat. But based on his promise, we wait for new heavens and a new earth, where righteousness dwells (2 Pet 3:7, 12–13).

Scripture makes clear that at the final judgment, not just the works of the wicked will be fuel for the fire but also the wicked themselves (2 Thess 1:7b–10; Rev 20:11–15).

Finally, the context of the verse immediately following Hab 2:13 opens up the possibility this verse has an eschatological dimension as well. As Robertson succinctly states, "Only when the problem of the wicked is resolved will the glory of God fill the earth."[76] Habakkuk 2:14 not only displays eschatological imagery; it also clearly depicts the consummation of the mission of God since the beginning of the world. The verses on either side of the chiastic hinge look to the end of time as the final answer to the prophet's questions.

---

[75] See also Isa 66:15–16, 24; Zech 12:6; Mal 4:1.
[76] Robertson, *The Books of Nahum, Habakkuk, and Zephaniah*, 198.

Just as in Habakkuk's day, our culture is filled with frenetic activity as people try to make headway. Toilsome labor is always exhausting but especially so when the laborer discovers it is futile and only ends in emptiness. Judgment has never been a popular message, in Habakkuk's day or in ours. But it is a necessary message, perhaps now more than ever. As much as we want to push past v. 13 to get to v. 14, we cannot. Habakkuk 2:13 is a crucial part of the chiastic structure. The consummation of God's mission in Hab 2:14 cannot occur without the ultimate judgment hinted at in v. 13. Wickedness must be dealt with before the restoration commences. Thankfully, the hope-filled message of v. 14 immediately follows the promise of judgment in v. 13.

2.3.3   The Earth Will Be Filled with Knowledge of the Lord's Glory (2:14)

[14] For the earth will be filled
with the knowledge of the LORD's *glory,*
as the water covers the sea.

2:14   The beginning of Hab 2:14 marks the pivot point of the chiastic structure found in Hab 2:6–20.[77] First impressions suggest the verse appears to be out of place, puzzling some readers. Scholars describe the unexpected nature of v. 14 in positive terms, such as Richard Fuhr and Gary Yates's "hymnic interlude."[78] Lim describes the sudden shift in mood as an intentional "vent" for the emotional buildup in the first three woes, a "temporary relief" before bracing for the final two.[79] Others take a more neutral tone. Donald Gowan observes "the third woe" appears "to get off the subject somewhat, as compared to others."[80]

Some scholars concluded the quotations in 2:13–14 are simply glosses, editorial insertions from Jer 51:58 and Isa 11:9. Shepherd attributes vv. 13–14 to the work of the "composer of the Twelve."[81]

---

[77] See 6.2.4.1 and the "Proposed Concentric Literary Triptych" chart.

[78] Fuhr and Yates, *The Message of the Twelve*, 233. The authors apply the same label to Hab 2:20.

[79] Lim, "Rhetorical Analysis of the Book of Habakkuk," 29.

[80] Donald E. Gowan, *The Triumph of Faith in Habakkuk* (Atlanta: John Knox, 1976), 54–55.

[81] Shepherd, *A Commentary on the Book of the Twelve*, 332. Shepherd bases this assertion on the assumption that said composer consistently inserts Jeremiah citations elsewhere in the Twelve (p. 332).

His solution leads him to propose significant changes to the structural outline of the woe oracles, including the addition of a new first woe, the reduction of v. 12 to a refrain, and the relegation of vv. 13–14 to "an authorial insertion of citations."[82] Andersen raises the possibility 2:14 does not even belong in woe three: "Verse 14 has no obvious connection with the rest of this 'woe oracle'; thus it is hard to think why anyone would have put it in at this point."[83] Like Shepherd, Andersen's solution is an alternative "structural design," where 2:14 becomes a refrain following woe three (2:12–13).[84] His alteration leads him to locate the "climax of the entire set and the key theological statement of the whole" in the monocolon: "Isn't this—Behold!—from Yahweh Sebaoth?"[85] Still others are a bit less charitable. Roberts is convinced that 2:13 is a late gloss and calls 2:14 "just a partial and somewhat garbled quotation of Isa 11:9." He concludes both glosses "miss the point" of the woe oracles; his solution is to "bracket out" confusing secondary glosses.[86] Finally, Ward dismissed 2:14 as a late scribal addition without "any particular bearing on the subject . . . merely a pious reflection thrown in at hazard."[87] The failure to recognize the overall structure of Habakkuk builds on the chiastic structure of this central panel loses the heart of God's message through the prophet Habakkuk and results in reducing the theological centerpiece to a refrain or secondary gloss or, worse yet, rejects it altogether.

This problematic turbulence is exactly what the reader should expect to find at the center of an extended chiasmus. According to Craig Blomberg, the first of several criteria for macro-chiasm is a problem that conventional structures fail to resolve.[88] The abrupt change of thought in the middle of the woe poses just such a problem solved by understanding the nature of chiasm. The evidence also aligns with Lund's observation that chiasmus introduces "an antithetic

---

[82] Shepherd's outline consists of "five woe oracles (Hab 2:5–6a, 6b–8a, 9–11, 15–17a, 18–20), three refrains (Hab 2:8b, 12, 17b), and one authorial insertion of citations (Hab 2:13–14)." See Shepherd, *A Commentary on the Book of the Twelve*, 332.

[83] Andersen, *Habakkuk*, 242.

[84] Andersen, *Habakkuk*, 18.

[85] Andersen, *Habakkuk*, 227.

[86] Roberts, *Nahum, Habakkuk, and Zephaniah*, 123–24.

[87] Ward, "Habakkuk," 17. Ward's rejection of 2:14 is not that out of all the woes (Hab 2:6–20), he considers only the first woe (2:6–8a) as genuine.

[88] Blomberg, "The Structure of 2 Corinthians," 5.

idea" before resuming the original train of thought.[89] Verse 13 speaks
of end-time judgment, whereas v. 14 describes end-time restoration.
Verse 13 warns that all the effort of wicked humanity will end in emptiness. In contrast, v. 14 pictures the earth filled to overflowing with
the glory of God. Verse 14 is by no means a random verse inserted as
an afterthought but rather a careful and intentional contrast to the
preceding verse.

Other clues in Hab 2:14 point to chiasm as well. A chiastic center
will often repeat words mirrored in outer parallel frame passages. In
v. 14, a third echo surfaces from the refrains found in Hab 2:8b and 17b.
Just as v. 12 echoes Hb. words from the refrain *dāmîm* [bloodshed]
and *qiryâ* [town], v. 14 repeats the Hb. word *'ereṣ* (Eng. "land(s)" or
"earth").[90] Key words from other places in Habakkuk also surface
in v. 14, including "earth" (1:6; 2:20; 3:3, 6, 9, 12), as well as "sea"
(1:14; 3:8, 15), "water," (3:10, 15), and "glory" (16 [*kābôd*, 2x]).

According to Lund, divine names and quotations also gravitate to
the central position of a chiasm.[91] This is true in Habakkuk, where
the verses on either side of the chiastic hinge refer to God by the names
"the LORD of Armies" (v. 13) and "LORD" (v. 14). In addition, v. 14
may be a quotation of Isa 11:9.[92] The original Isaiah context is significant because it has several parallels to the context of Hab 2:14. In
Isaiah, the verse follows chap. 10, which pronounces woes on Assyria
and her king, whom the Lord had used as a rod to chastise Israel. The
fiery judgment against Assyria contains some semantic parallels to the
pronouncement in Hab 2:13:

> Therefore the Lord GOD of Armies . . .
> will kindle a burning fire
> under its [Assyria's] glory.
> Israel's Light will become a fire,
> and its Holy One a flame.
> In one day it will burn and consume Assyria's thorns and thistles.
> (Isa 10:16–17)

---

[89] Lund, *Chiasmus in the New Testament*, 41.
[90] The ESV translates *'ereṣ* as "earth" in all three verses (2:8, 14, 17).
[91] Lund, *Chiasmus in the New Testament*, 41.
[92] Some will argue that the similarity stems from formulaic phrasing rather than quotation.
Besides Isa 11:9, other verses that contain similar echoes include Num 14:21; Ps 72:19; and Isa
6:3. Even so, Hab 2:14 and Isa 11:9 both contain the unique feature of the sea being filled with
water.

After God's judgment of Israel, Isaiah prophesies, a future Davidic king will arise "from the stump of Jesse," and "[t]he Spirit of the LORD will rest on him" (Isa 11:1–2). This messianic passage shows him ruling over an ideal kingdom, so peaceful that domestic and wild animals will dwell in harmony (11:6–9a). In its immediate context in Isaiah, the original passage is clearly eschatological. The verse that follows it declares on that same day the Gentiles will seek this King in his glory. The parallel verses appear in italics below:

> They will neither harm nor destroy
> on all my holy mountain,
> *for the earth will be filled with the knowledge of the LORD*
> *as the waters cover the sea.*
> In that day the Root of Jesse will stand as a banner for the peoples; the nations will rally to him, and his resting place will be glorious. (Isa 11:9–10; NIV; emphasis added)

> *For the earth will be filled with the knowledge* of the glory
> of the LORD
> *as the waters cover the sea* (Hab 2:14 NIV; emphasis added).[93]

In its original location, the passage surrounding Isa 11:9b concludes with a song of praise for the day when the Messiah will gather the remnant of Israel and Judah from the nations (Isa 12):

> Give thanks to the Lord; proclaim his name!
> Make his works known among the peoples.
> Declare that his name is exalted.
> Sing to the LORD, for he has done glorious things.
> Let this be known throughout the earth. (Isa 12:4–5)

If the prophet quotes Isa 11:9, then Habakkuk retains the eschatological sense found in the original context as well as the global scope of the knowledge of the Lord and his glorious actions on that day. Even though Habakkuk slightly modifies Isa 11:9 by adding "of his glory," even the original context speaks of the glory of "the resting place" of the Root of Jesse (Isa 11:9).

---

[93] The Hb. verbal parallels between the two verses are a bit clearer in the English NIV translation.

The language of "filling" and "glory" plays a significant role in the unfolding mission of God in the OT. Several other OT verses besides Hab 2:14 speak of the Lord's glory filling the earth.[94] Just as God's presence fills the heavens and earth, so his glory extends to the farthest reaches of the cosmos. A biblical worldview recognizes the extensive or general presence of God as expressed by the Lord in Jer 23:24: "Do I not fill the heavens and the earth?" The focus of Scripture, however, is more on the intensive or special presence of God in relationship to humanity. Genesis 1:28, arguably the "first 'Great Commission,'"[95] records God's blessing the first human couple and commanding them to "fill the earth" with worshipers who rightly reflect the image of God. His intention was that the whole earth would be both his dwelling place and a sanctuary filled with the knowledge of his glory. As a result of the fall, however, humanity was shut out from the unmediated glory of God, and "the earth was filled with wickedness" instead.[96]

God's missional purpose shifted to a rescue mission, the means of which was the same as its goal: the presence of God dwelling in the midst of his people. After he delivered the Israelites out of Egypt, they gathered at Mount Sinai, where the Lord's glory "settled" (Hb. *šākan*; "tabernacled") on the mountaintop, "like a consuming fire" (Exod 24:16–17). The Lord then condescended to dwell among his people, "and the glory of the LORD filled the tabernacle" (Exod 40:34–35). The same thing occurred at the dedication of the temple centuries later: "[T]he glory of the LORD filled the temple" (1 Kgs 8:11). In Habakkuk's generation, because God's people continually failed to acknowledge and glorify God, the Lord gave Ezekiel a vision of God's glory departing from the temple and Jerusalem (Ezek 8–11), making way for Nebuchadnezzar's troops. Though the Babylonians would destroy both city and temple, Ezekiel envisioned God's glory returning to a final sanctuary: "[T]he glory of the LORD filled the temple. . . . He said to me: 'Son of man, this is the place of my throne . . . , where I will dwell among the Israelites forever'" (Ezek 43:5–7).

Although Habakkuk could not have anticipated it, the NT shows the unique, full, and particular presence of God found only in Jesus.[97]

---

[94] Num 14:21; Ps 72:19; Isa 6:3; 11:9; see also Ps 57:11; Hab 3:3.
[95] Beale, *The Temple and the Church's Mission*, 117.
[96] Gen 6:11, 13; see also Lev 19:29; 2 Kgs 21:16.
[97] James Leo Garrett, *Systematic Theology: Biblical, Historical, and Evangelical*, vol. 1 (Grand Rapids: Eerdmans, 1990), 201–2.

John declares, "The Word became flesh and dwelt [lit. "tabernacled"] among us. We observed his glory, the glory as the one and only Son from the Father, full of grace and truth" (John 1:14).[98] Jesus is the reality the tabernacle and temple foreshadowed. Ultimately, the meeting place of God and humanity is not a place but a person (cf. John 2:19–22). As the Lamb of God who takes away the sin of the world, Jesus made a way for God to make his home in the hearts of his redeemed people (John 14:16, 23). At Pentecost God's presence descended on believers, filling the place with wind and the people with the Holy Spirit (Acts 2:2–4). The church is now the temple of God, filled with his presence and power so that they might expand the knowledge of the Lord's glory globally as they fulfill his commission to make disciples of all nations.[99] The NT culminates in a restored creation where God will dwell in the midst of his redeemed people forever. God's holy-of-holies presence will fill the New Jerusalem, the bride of the Lamb, with his glory (Rev 21:2–3, 10). Just as the glory of God radiated briefly in previous earthly sanctuaries, the Lord will fill this final temple-less sanctuary with the unfading glory of his presence, and the perfected people of God will reflect his glory forever (Rev 21:22–23).

Several other OT passages besides Isa 11:9 and Hab 2:14 refer to the "knowledge of the LORD" reaching the corners of the globe. The Lord multiplied his wonders in the land of Egypt, "to make [his] name known on the whole earth" (Exod 9:16; cf. 11:9; 14:4). By the time the Israelite spies reached Jericho, knowledge of the Lord and his exploits had preceded them (Josh 2:9–11). In his dedicatory prayer for the new temple, Solomon anticipated that "all peoples of the earth will know [God's] name" (1 Kgs 8:43). Later, Hezekiah prayed for deliverance from Assyria "so that all the kingdoms of the earth may know that [the] LORD [is] God—[he] alone" (Isa 37:20). By Habakkuk's generation, when the rebellious Israelites failed to display God's glory, the Lord declared he would display his own glory through judging and restoring his people (Ezek 39:21). Then both Israel and the nations would know he alone is God (Ezek 39:28). As news of God's mighty acts of judgment and deliverance encompassed the earth, all peoples would come to acknowledge the God of Israel (Ezek 38:23).

---

[98] See also Luke 9:28–35; 2 Pet 1:16–18.
[99] Matt 28:19; 1 Cor 3:16; 6:19–20; 2 Cor 6:16; Eph 2:18–22; 1 Pet 2:4–5.

This would be the outcome of Babylon's destruction of Jerusalem and her subsequent demise as well.

The Lord told the prophet Jeremiah that a day is coming when God will write his teaching on the hearts of his people: "No longer will one teach his neighbor or his brother, saying, 'Know the LORD,' for they will all know me, from the least to the greatest of them" (Jer 31:33–34). In this eschatological context, "knowledge of the LORD" assumes the concept of intimate knowledge and love of the Lord. Jesus, in his high-priestly prayer, equated this kind of knowledge of "the only true God" and his Son with eternal life (John 17:3). Knowledge implies knowers. There must be people in every place who not only know of the Lord but whose hearts are filled with "the light of the knowledge of God's glory in the face of Jesus Christ" (2 Cor 4:6).

Although Habakkuk's addition of "glory" to Isa 11:9 appears to be a slight alteration, it has profound theological implications. The word expands the concept of God's filling earthly sanctuaries with his glory to his filling the entire cosmos with his presence. Habakkuk 2:14 capsulizes the mission of God since the dawn of creation: the whole earth will become a future sanctuary filled with worshipers who know and experience the glory of the Lord present in every inch of the new creation. To describe the extensive reach of the worship of God's glorious presence, Hab 2:14 borrows Isaiah's poetic imagery: "as the water covers the sea." The metaphor communicates a fullness so excessive that it almost becomes a non sequitur. As N. T. Wright notes, the water not only fills the sea; it is the sea: "It looks as though God intends to flood the universe with himself, as though the universe, the entire cosmos, was designed as a receptacle for his love."[100] In the past, when the glory of God filled the historical sanctuaries of Israel, work came to a standstill and the priests could not even enter. In contrast, in the new heaven and earth, all creation will be awash in God's Shekinah glory: all the people will be priests; every object, holy; and every activity, swimming in an ocean of God's unmediated presence.[101]

---

[100] N. T. Wright, *Surprised by Hope: Rethinking Heaven, the Resurrection, and the Mission of the Church* (New York: HarperOne, 2008), 102.

[101] See Zech 14:20–21. The word *Shekinah* is derived from the Hb. verb *šākan*, meaning "to settle for a certain period of time," or "to reside" (*HALOT*, 1498). Although the verb applies to humans and animals, it also describes God, whose mission is to dwell among his people (Exod 25:8; 29:45; Ezek 43:7). Just as "[t]he glory of the LORD settled [*škn*] on Mount Sinai" (Exod 24:16), the cloud of his presence "rested" (*škn*) on the tabernacle, filling it with glory, as it did later at the dedication of the temple (Exod 40:34–35; 1 Kgs 8:10–11). Henry Donaghy, "Holy Scripture:

Revelation 19:6–7 offers a glimpse of the praise that will bubble up in those waters: "[T]he voice of a vast multitude, like the sound of cascading waters, . . . 'Hallelujah, because our Lord God, the Almighty, reigns! / Let us be glad, rejoice, and give him glory.'"

The hope conveyed by Hab 2:14 along with the abrupt shift in thought between Hab 2:13 and 2:14 would have signaled to Habakkuk's readers these verses comprise the theological centerpiece of his book.[102] The content of these verses meets Blomberg's criteria: the chiasm should carry theological weight worthy of climactic significance.[103]

Today's readers—possibly influenced by NT quotations—tend to view Hab 2:4 as the focal point of Habakkuk. As significant as this verse is, it must not overshadow Habakkuk's centerpiece located in 2:13–14. The two passages are related. In some sense, Hab 2:4 is an answer to the prophet's questions on the level of individuals. God sees the actions of humanity and makes a distinction between the just and the unjust: the wicked will perish, and the righteous will live. Habakkuk 2:13–14 follows that trajectory to its ultimate end. The chiasm provides the answer to the prophet's questions on a cosmological level. One day the Lord of Armies will end all rebellion and put everything right. This beautiful glimpse of the restoration provides a tantalizing hint of what that life will look like. The answer is not just that the Babylonians will get their due or that the righteous will live long in this broken world. The answer is that God will fulfill his mission. All of the new creation will be a holy sanctuary filled with the knowledge of his glory, a home he plans to share with the people he has redeemed for himself.

2.4 WOE 4 (2:15–17)

As expected in a chiastic structure, following the theological apex in woe three, the text immediately reverts to pronouncements of judgment against the Babylonians in woes four and five. The jarring effect

---

God with Us," *Worship* 31 (1957): 277, explains that first-century Targum writers (interpreting the Hb. Scriptures in Aramaic) developed the term as a periphrasis—an indirect way of maintaining reverence when speaking about God's dwelling among his people. Donaghy defines the term "Shekinah" as "a special presence, a localization, so to speak, of [God's] power in a given time and in a given place."

[102] Thomson, *Chiasmus in the Pauline Letters*, 28, calls the chiastic center "the interpretive key" to the text.

[103] Blomberg, "The Structure of 2 Corinthians," 7.

highlights the contrast between the descriptions of breathtaking beauty in v. 14 and stomach-turning depravity in v. 15. It underscores the world's need for judgment and total restoration.

2.4.1 Woe to the Predator Who Exploits His Neighbors' Drunkenness! (2:15)

> ¹⁵ Woe to him who gives his neighbors drink,
>   pouring out your wrath
>   and even making them drunk,
>   in order to look at their nakedness!

2:15 The fourth woe parallels the second woe. The setting of both scenes is the house of an individual. While the owner in the second woe intended to build a safe haven to escape danger, the owner in the fourth woe uses his house as a trap to exploit his neighbors. An indication of the extent of his treachery, the Hb. word (*rēʿēhû*) translated "neighbors" can also be translated as "friends."[104] The Lord specifically commanded the Israelites to protect the rights of their neighbors, not bearing false witness against another or coveting a neighbor's belongings (Exod 20:16–17). The Israelite community was instructed to "love [one's] neighbor as [one's] self" (Lev 19:18). In Habakkuk's day, the Israelites failed to obey these commands. The targets of Isaiah's woes pronounced against Judah included those "who linger into the evening, / inflamed by wine" and those who are "champions at pouring beer" (Isa 5:11, 22). The alcohol bolstered their oppression of the vulnerable (Isa 5:23). Although Habakkuk's fourth woe takes aim at the depraved actions of the Babylonians, his audience recognized some of these transgressions in their own midst.

Verse 15 describes the host's evil intentions; he did not simply offer a drink out of hospitality. The rendering of the Hb. phrase translated in CSB as "pouring out your wrath" is difficult. The verb *sāpaḥ* translated as "pouring out" is rare; in the *Qal* stem, the term lit. means "join to, associate," which seems to make no sense in the text. In addition, the noun "wrath" (Hb. *ḥămātəkā*) could derive from the root *ḥēmâ* ("heat, poison") or the root *ḥēmet* ("wine bottle, skin").[105] A survey

---

[104] *HALOT*, 1264.

[105] *HALOT*, 326; 331. In addition, Barthélemy, 5:359, notes a wordplay since the word for "wrath, fury" can also mean "your wine which inflames."

of English versions shows some other translations for this phrase: "[p]ressing *him* to your bottle" (NKJV); "pouring it from the wineskin" (NIV); and "mix in your venom" (NASB). If we retain the meaning of the verb as "pour out," the text would translate either as "pouring out your anger," or "pouring out your cup," neither of which fits well with the verb *šaqâ*, "to give to drink." If we read with the emendation in *BHS* (cup, bowl) and retain the meaning of the object as "anger" or "fury," the line would be rendered "from the cup of your anger," a contextually better reading which reflects a play on words in expression, since the word can mean both "wrath" and "inflaming wine."[106] The figurative language describes the "host," who intentionally plied his guests with drink until they became intoxicated or "full" of his wrath. He pushed his guests to drunkenness so that he might "look at their nakedness," exploiting their vulnerability to enhance his own perverted pleasure.[107] No doubt his predatory intentions went beyond mere observation. Scripture records other examples of exploitation fueled by drunken parties in homes of the wealthy and powerful in Babylon and Persia (Dan 5; Esth 1).[108]

The imagery in the fourth woe serves as a metaphor for exploitation on a national/international level. Babylon exposed and exploited the vulnerability of the neighboring nations. For example, when Hezekiah received the Babylonian delegation aimed at forging an alliance against Assyria, he made the costly mistake of showing off every single object in his treasury(2 Kgs 20:12–19). The Babylonians later betrayed any sense of trust when they returned and Nebuchadnezzar stripped the treasuries of Judah bare, hauling away even the gold, silver, and bronze articles used in the temple (2 Kgs 25:13–16).

Although the metaphor applies on an international level, a literal reading of the Habakkuk text still strongly condemns the depraved drunkenness and sexual exploitation described in the imagery of 2:15.

---

[106] Dominique Barthelemy, *Preliminary and Interim Report on the Hebrew Old Testament Text Project*, vol. 5 (New York: United Bible Society, 1980), 359.

[107] In Gen 9:20–24, Noah's nakedness signified his shame and disgrace.

[108] Ancient historian Curtius Rufus Quintus describes Babylon in the days of Alexander the Great in similar terms: "[T]he Babylonians in particular are lavishly devoted to wine and the concomitants of drunkenness. The women who take part in these feasts are in the beginning modestly attired, then they take off their outer garments one by one and gradually disgrace their modesty." In *History of Alexander* (Book 5.1.38), trans. John C. Rolfe (Cambridge, MA: Harvard University Press, 1946), 341. Notably, Quintus neglected to mention any responsibility on the part of the hosts.

The metaphor implies the rape and sexual assault typically following in the wake of war—humiliation that captives have often endured at the hands of their conquerors.[109] Tragically, this woe appears to be as contemporary as today's headline news. As painful as it is to stumble across a text like this in the Bible, it is at least some comfort to know that the Lord takes note of this twisted behavior; he is appalled, and he will administer justice.

2.4.2 He Will Drink the Cup of the Lord's Wrath (2:16)

> [16] *You will be filled with disgrace instead of glory.*
> *You also—drink, and expose your uncircumcision!*
> *The cup in the* LORD'*s right hand*
> *will come around to you,*
> *and utter disgrace will cover your glory.*

2:16 Parallel to the second woe, the premeditated plans of the perpetrator ironically result in his shame. The phrasing of v. 14—"[T]he earth will be filled / with . . . glory"—contrasts ironically with the expression of v. 16: "You will be filled with disgrace instead of glory." The distinction between the two verses defines the outcome clearly. Since the fall, people have twisted God's command to "multiply [and] fill the earth" with image bearers who reflect his glory (Gen 1:28). Seeking their own glory instead of God's, fallen humanity has repeatedly filled the earth with wickedness and their own souls with shame. The Hb. word translated "filled" (*śābaʿtā*) can mean "to eat or drink one's fill" or "to be satisfied, satiated."[110] The one with an insatiable appetite for lust will finally get his fill of disgrace. The root of the term "disgrace" (Hb. *qālôn*) signifies "to treat contemptuously," thus leading to "shame" or "ignominy."[111] The prophet Hosea warned Israel that God is the one who disciplines sinners, and they

---

[109] See Sweeney, *The Twelve Prophets*, 479.

[110] *HALOT*, 1303. God's promises to fill the Israelites with good things often came with a warning against forgetting him (Deut 6:11; 8:10–11) because he recognized that once his people were satisfied, their proclivity was to "turn to other gods" (Deut 31:20). When the Israelites abandoned God, they would eat but no longer be filled (Hos 4:10; Mic 6:14); like Death, they would never find satisfaction (Hab 2:5). Instead, God would cause them to find their fill of troubles, scorn and contempt, bitter herbs and gall (Pss 88:3; 123:4; Lam 3:15 NIV). The Lord alone can satisfy the heart's deepest desire (Ps 17:15).

[111] *HALOT*, 1101.

have only themselves to blame: "The more they multiplied, / the more they sinned against me. / I will change their honor [glory] into disgrace" (Hos 4:7). The entire fourth chapter of Hosea describes both the spiritual and physical adultery among the Israelites. It concludes, "When their drinking is over, / they turn to promiscuity. / Israel's leaders fervently love disgrace" (Hos 4:18). Although the fourth woe primarily addresses the Babylonians, tragically, it also highlights some of Judah's sins as well.

Retributive justice follows in the form of two strong imperatives: "You also—drink, and expose your uncircumcision!" (Hab 2:16). In this verse, however, the repetition of the subject is emphatic: "You also, (you) drink!" Those victims exploited by the adversary who caused them to "drink wrath" will witness the shame of the enemy, who will be forced to drink God's wrath. The same may be true for the second command: "[E]xpose your uncircumcision!"[112] The uncovering figuratively identifies the foreign nation and signifies the humiliation of the Babylonians through God's judgment.

Other OT prophetic books declare God's judgment on nations using similarly graphic language. Nahum, for example, warned the personified Nineveh: "[God] will lift your skirts over your face / and display your nakedness to nations, / your shame to kingdoms" (Nah 3:5; see Babylon's fate described in Isa 47:3). Although the word choice "uncircumcised" indicates the woe addresses the Babylonians, both Jeremiah and Ezekiel used similar exposure imagery to warn Jerusalem of the consequences of her spiritual promiscuity as well (Jer 13:26; Ezek 23:29). The description of the Lord's punishment in an Ezekiel passage combines the imagery of exposing nakedness with drinking "a cup of devastation and desolation"; Jerusalem would "be filled with drunkenness and grief" (Ezek 23:33). Judah's sin and punishment thus parallels the sin and punishment of Babylon as described in Habakkuk's fourth woe.

Some scholars maintain there is evidence for metathesis in this verb.[113] The two middle consonants may have been transposed, so that the text would no longer read "expose your uncircumcision" (Hb.

---

[112] The *niphal* stem of the Hb. verb ʿāral "to be uncircumcised" lit. means "to show the foreskin," and probably should be translated as a tolerative "[allow] your foreskin to be revealed." See *HALOT*, 885. GKC §51.c; *IBHS* §51c.

[113] Leslie C. Allen, "עָרֵל," *NIDOTTE* 3:534; Ronald B. Allen, "עָרֵל," *TWOT* 2:696.

hēʿārēl), but rather "stagger" (Hb. *hērāʿēl*).[114] The NRSV, for example, follows this line of reasoning, translating the imperatives as "Drink, you yourself, and stagger!" (cf. JPS 1988). Though this emendation fits well in the context of drunkenness, it no longer addresses the depraved motivation behind the drinking. The graphic nature of "exposure" language is disturbing even if it is "merely" symbolic; however, it precisely captures the spirit of the law of *lex talionis*, where the punishment fits the crime both in kind and degree (cf. Exod 21:23–27). Those who have exploited others will likewise face the shame of exposure.

The punishment comes in the form of "[t]he cup in the LORD's right hand." Of the approximately thirty OT occurrences of this word for "cup," a third of them refer to a physical vessel for drinking, and the remaining two-thirds are used metaphorically. Although the OT contains a few instances where "cup" can be a blessing (Pss 16:5; 23:5; 116:13), the metaphor usually refers to "the cup of wrath," through which the Lord administers justice.[115] Isaiah refers to it as "the cup of his fury" and "the cup that causes staggering" (Isa 51:17, 22). The Lord commanded Jeremiah to make all the nations drink from a cup "the wine of wrath from [God's] hand" (Jer 25:15). Jerusalem was first on the prophet's list of twenty-two places/people groups who would drink this cup. The last on the list was "king of Sheshak"—i.e., Babylon (Jer 25:26).[116] The instructions accompanying the cup were stern: "Drink, get drunk, and vomit. Fall down and never get up again, as a result of the sword I am sending among you" (Jer 25:27).[117] The Lord's cup of fury would pass along to every nation on the list; in the end, Babylon's turn to drink would come. When it did, "utter disgrace" would cover her glory.[118] Ironically, the one who had uncovered others would ultimately be draped in shame.

---

[114] *BHS* notes that several ancient versions support this reading, including 1QpHab, Greek LXX, Syriac, and Vulgate.

[115] "For there is a cup in the LORD's hand, / full of wine blended with spices, and he pours from it. / All the wicked of the earth will drink, / draining it to the dregs" (Ps 75:8).

[116] Both "Sheshack" and "Babylon" appear in parallel clauses in Jer 51:41. The title "Sheshack" is likely a cipher for Babylon, formed by substituting letters in reverse order in the alphabet. The second letter in the Hb. alphabet (b), for example, would become the second to last letter (š). See *CSB Study Bible* notes on Jer 25:26.

[117] If a nation dared refuse, the Lord commanded, "You must drink! For I am already bringing disaster on the city that bears my name, so how could you possibly go unpunished?" (Jer 25:28–29).

[118] *HALOT*, 1099, notes the Hb. word *qīqālôn*, lit. "dung, excrement" (Eng. "utter disgrace") appears only once in the OT. According to the "Commentary on the Critical Apparatus," in *BHQ*,

The metaphor of the cup appears in the NT as well. The passages in Revelation depicting Babylon as a symbol of all human rebellion against God describe the once-great city in terms reminiscent of Hab 2:16: "She made all the nations drink the wine of her sexual immorality, which brings wrath" (Rev 14:8). Babylon, in turn, would be forced to drink "the cup filled with the wine of [God's] fierce anger" (Rev 16:19). "[D]runk with the blood of the saints," Babylon held "a golden cup . . . filled with everything detestable" (Rev 17:4, 6). Because she enticed others to sin, Babylon would receive a double portion of the cup of God's wrath: "They will make her desolate and naked, devour her flesh, and burn her up with fire" (Rev 17:16; 18:6). These verses in Revelation reveal the ultimate fulfillment of Habakkuk's fourth woe is eschatological. These scenes of final judgment make the agony of Jesus in the garden of Gethsemane even more shocking. Although he prayed that the cup might pass from him, Jesus submitted to the will of the Father.[119] The sinless Son of God took the cup of wrath from the Father's hand and drank down every last drop. His substitutionary sacrifice on the cross for the sin of the world filled the cup of salvation with his own blood. This was the symbolism behind the new covenant cup he offered his disciples at the Last Supper, promising that one day he would drink it again with them in the kingdom of God.[120] Because Jesus drained the cup of God's wrath on humanity's behalf, the cup of God's future wrath will pass by those who place their trust in Jesus.

2.4.3   Refrain: The Reason for Judgment (2:17)

> [17] *For your violence against Lebanon*
> *will overwhelm you;*
> *the destruction of animals will terrify you*
> *because of your human bloodshed and violence*
> *against lands, cities, and all who live in them.*

121, it is "most probably an intensified variant" of *qālôn* (Eng. "disgrace") in the first line of v. 16. Robertson, *The Books of Nahum, Habakkuk, and Zephaniah*, 204, suggests that the first syllable of *qîqālôn* "may be an abbreviation of *qîʾ*, meaning 'to spew, to vomit.'" He therefore translates *qîqālôn* as "putrid shame."

[119] Matt 26:39; Mark 14:36; Luke 22:42.

[120] For a description of the cup at the Last Supper, see Matt 26:27; Mark 14:23; Luke 22:20. For a description of the cup in remembrance of the Lord's Supper, see 1 Cor 10:16, 21; 11:25–28.

2:17 Verse 17 reveals the extent of the Babylonians' violence against creation: nothing was exempt from their wrath. Plants, animals, humans, and even the earth itself all experienced Babylonian brutality firsthand. The "violence against Lebanon" likely refers to Nebuchadnezzar's reckless deforestation of the majestic cedars of Lebanon.[121] Prized for their great height, upwards of 130 feet, the cedars provided the massive beams needed for construction of ancient palaces and temples for centuries, including those built in Solomon's day.[122] Letters to Tiglath-pileser III indicate by 740 BC the Assyrians established control of the mountain of cedar forests and the wood supply. The Assyrians taxed Tyre and Sidon from the profits of the cedar trade and forbade them from trading with the Philistines and Egyptians.[123] In Isa 37:24, the Lord mocked Sennacherib's proud boast:

> With my many chariots
> I have gone up to the heights of the mountains,
> to the far recesses of Lebanon.
> I cut down its tallest cedars,
> its choice cypress trees.
> I came to its distant heights,
> its densest forest.

With poetic irony, the Lord determined to cut down Sennacherib and his army, as one would fell the lofty trees of Lebanon "with an ax" (10:33–34).

According to Hab 2:17, the Babylonians must have continued the Assyrian practice of exploiting this natural resource. Nebuchadnezzar's own inscriptions refer to his use of cedars in roofing the temples of Babylon: "I selected the best of my cedar trees, which I had brought from Mount Lebanon, the snow-capped forest, for the roofing of E-kua, the shrine of his lordship."[124] In a taunt song similar to the one

---

[121] Baker, *Nahum, Habakkuk, and Zephaniah*, 61, refers to the Babylonians "denuding lands of their tree covering." The metaphor echoes the theme that plays out in the fourth woe.

[122] See 1 Kgs 5–7.

[123] Henry W. F. Saggs, ed. *The Nimrud Letters, 1952*, Cuneiform Texts from Nimrud V (Trowbridge: British School of Archaeology in Iraq, 2001), 155–57. For a critical edition of the letters, see Mikko Luukko, *The Correspondence of Tiglath-pileser III and Sargon II from Calah/Nimrud.* State Archives of Assyria 19 (Helsinki: Neo-Assyrian Text Corpus Project, 2012).

[124] "East India House Inscription," 137.

cited above, Isaiah recorded all nature would rejoice at the demise of
the king of Babylon:

> The whole earth is calm and at rest;
> people shout with a ringing cry.
> Even the cypresses and the cedars of Lebanon
> rejoice over you:
> "Since you have been laid low,
> no lumberjack has come against us." (Isa 14:7–8)

The rafters referred to in Habakkuk's second woe may have come
from these same cedar forests. Just as these wooden beams cry out
against the house's wicked occupant, the stand of trees they originated
from would sing at the death of the ruler of Babylon.

The Babylonians were guilty of violence not only against the forests of Lebanon, but also against the creatures inhabiting them. The
builder who felled the majestic cedars to secure his own nest destroyed
the habitat of birds and forest creatures alike. Psalm 104 makes clear
that all plant and animal life ultimately belong to the Lord:

> The trees of the LORD flourish,
> the cedars of Lebanon that he planted.
> There the birds make their nests;
> storks make their homes in the pine trees.
> The high mountains are for the wild goats;
> the cliffs are a refuge for hyraxes. . . .
> The young lions roar for their prey
> and seek their food from God. . . .
> [T]he earth is full of [his] creatures. (Ps 104:16–18, 21, 24)

The Lord shows concern for creatures as part of his creation. He cov-
enants with them (Gen 9:10; Hos 2:18) and shows them mercy (Gen
8:1; Jonah 4:11); he hears their cries of distress and feeds them (Job
38:41; Ps 147:9).[125] God observes when even a single sparrow "falls to
the ground" (Matt 10:29). Deforestation results in soil erosion, loss of
animal habitat, and loss of entire species. Because most trees depend
on animal dispersal for regeneration, the initial damage to the cedar
forests was cyclical and ongoing.

---

[125] N. Kiuchi, "בְּהֵמָה," *NIDOTTE* 1:603.

Habakkuk 2:17a makes clear that Nebuchadnezzar and his army would be culpable for the violence perpetrated against plant and animal life. Their violence would "cover" them (Hb. *kāsâ*; CSB: "overwhelm"), just as the water "covers" (Hb. *kāsâ*) the sea in v. 14. The devastation they wrought on animals would be meted out to them; they in turn would be terrified. The artistic reliefs that lined the walls of Ashurbanipal's palace in Nineveh capture such terror precisely as they record the Assyrian king's penchant for lion hunting.[126] Although the sculptures (ca. 645–635 BC) predate Habakkuk by a few decades, they depict animal cruelty as a sport among Mesopotamian kings.[127] Ironically, after Babylon's demise, only desert creatures—owls, wild goats, hyenas, and jackals—would make their homes in the ruins of her strongholds and luxurious palaces (Isa 13:21–22).

Babylon's violence against the forests of Lebanon and its inhabitants pales in comparison to modern humanity's capacity for exploitation. In World War I the British Army decimated entire stands of these majestic trees for railroad fuel. Although Lebanon proudly displays the symbol of a cedar tree on her flag, by 1997 less than 6 percent of the land was protected forest—of any kind.[128] Thankfully, in 1998, UNESCO named the cedar forests in the Arz Mountains of Lebanon a protected World Heritage Site. Since then, efforts at reforestation across the country have brought the percentage of forests in Lebanon to over 13 percent.[129] Habakkuk 2:17 clearly warns the Lord cares

[126] For photos and descriptions of these ancient reliefs on display in the Middle East collection of the British Museum, see Osama S. M. Amin, "Assyrian Lion-Hunting at the British Museum," *Ancient History Et Cetera* (March 15, 2016). Online: https://etc.ancient.eu/photos/assyrian-lion-hunting-british-museum.

[127] Scene after scene portrays Ashurbanipal in his chariot, on horseback, and on foot, slaying these magnificent creatures with arrows, spears, and even a sword in face-to-face combat. Closer inspection reveals that the hunts were staged: an attendant releases lions from a cage into an arena formed by soldiers armed with shields and spears to assist the king and to keep the lions from escaping. Even though no similar artistic record exists from Babylon, this bloody and violent sport had been a source of entertainment for Mesopotamian royalty for centuries. Julian Reade, *Assyrian Sculpture* (London: British Museum Press, 2013), 39, notes Ashurnasirpal II (883–859 BC) boasted his hunting trophies included not only lions (370) but also wild oxen (257) and elephants (30).

[128] Rania Masri, "The Cedars of Lebanon: Significance, Awareness and Management of the Cedrus libani in Lebanon." A paper presented at Massachusetts Institute of Technology, Nov. 9, 1995.

[129] The Forest and Landscape Restoration Mechanism in Lebanon has a goal to increase that percentage to 20 percent. See Food and Agriculture Organization of the United Nations. Online: http://www.fao.org/in-action/forest-landscape-restoration-mechanism/our-work/countries/lebanon/en, accessed October 1, 2023.

for all his creation, including plant and animal life. Humanity must rediscover our God-given responsibility of governing and caring for all creation (see Gen 1:26). The whole earth belongs to the Lord and will play an important role as the global arena of his worship (Hab 2:14; 3:3).[130]

Habakkuk 2:17 concludes with the same refrain first recorded in v. 8 and echoed in the chiastic center found in vv. 13–14.[131] This repetition underscores the reason behind Babylon's judgment. As tragic as the Babylonian crimes were against trees and animals, their gross disregard for human life was even more horrifying. According to Gen 9:6, the Lord would demand an accounting for the rivers of blood shed: "Whoever sheds human blood, / by humans his blood will be shed, / for God made humans in his image." Isaiah warned of this same outcome in his pronouncement against Babylon:

> Like wandering gazelles
> and like sheep without a shepherd,
> each one will turn to his own people,
> each one will flee to his own land.
> Whoever is found will be stabbed,
> and whoever is caught will die by the sword. (Isa 13:14–15)

The Lord would ensure that justice would be served. Since Babylon had slain their enemies like animals, they too would be hunted down and slain in divine retribution.

2.5 WOE 5 (2:18–20)

The fifth woe begins not with a pronouncement of woe but rather a rhetorical question. This seeming deviation from the pattern of the previous woes led many scholars to see a structural problem in the fifth woe. Some attempted to solve the problem by reversing the order of vv. 18 and 19.[132] Roberts contends, as a transition, v. 18 stands "awk-

---

[130] For a discussion on the significance of creation care as part of holistic mission, see Christopher J. H. Wright, "Mission and God's Earth," in *The Mission of God: Unlocking the Bible's Grand Narrative* (Downers Grove: Intervarsity, 2006), 397–420.

[131] See discussion of Hab 2:8b.

[132] For example, the footnote for Hab 2:18 in the JPS 1988 translation suggests, "This verse would read well after v. 19."

ward and unparalleled"; this "misplaced gloss" should follow v. 19.[133] Ward argues it is a "prosaic" outbreak such "as a scribe might have hastily jotted in the margin." His solution is drastic: "[V]. 18 must be expunged."[134] Others suggest the reversal is an intentional rhetorical device that heightens tension[135] or provides "variety and climax."[136] Understanding the series of woes in Hab 2:6–20 as a chiasm helps the reader recognize this last woe follows the same structural pattern as the first, as might be expected in a chiasm.[137] The two refrains (vv. 8b and 17b) bracket the inner three woes from the outer woes. Outside the refrains, the structural order is the same: (1) a question; (2) a pronouncement of woe; (3) a second question; and (4) and a statement of *lex talionis* (retributive justice).[138]

Although the subject of this last woe seems to be a departure from the aforementioned crimes against humanity, their wicked actions stemmed from the root of idolatry.

2.5.1   What Use Is a God Made by Human Hands? (2:18)

> [18] *What use is a carved idol*
> *after its craftsman carves it?*
> *It is only a cast image, a teacher of lies.*
> *For the one who crafts its shape trusts in it*
> *and makes worthless idols that cannot speak.*

2:18   The first question in this final woe presumes a negative answer: What use is an idol? None! The Hb. term *hôʿîl* rendered "use" in CSB lit. means "to profit, value, or benefit," which better conveys the meaning of the verb.[139] Although the term describes illegal gains, valueless works, deceitful words, and false prophets,[140] one third of

---

[133] Roberts, *Nahum, Habakkuk, and Zephaniah*, 126.

[134] Ward, "Habakkuk," 18.

[135] Eaton, *Obadiah, Nahum, Habakkuk, Zephaniah*, 105.

[136] Robertson, *The Books of Nahum, Habakkuk, and Zephaniah*, 207.

[137] Ko, *Theodicy in Habakkuk*, 79–80, briefly mentions that the deviation from the "woe first" pattern is evidence of a chiastic structure in the woe oracles. For some reason, however, Ko narrows the woe oracle section to 2:6b-19, eliminating the "outer edges" (the first rhetorical question in 2:6a and the statement of retributive justice in 2:20). Unfortunately, Ko never discusses the theological significance of the chiastic structure.

[138] See Introduction, 6.2.4.1: "Chiastic Features in the Central Panel."

[139] *HALOT*, 420.

[140] See Prov 10:2; Isa 57:12; Jer 7:8; 23:32.

the occurrences refer to idols that have no value or benefit.[141] As Isa 44:9 points out, idol makers become like the objects they worship: "All who make idols are nothing, / and what they treasure benefits no one." Worse by far, idols prove to be poor substitutes for God himself: "[M]y people have exchanged their Glory for useless idols" (Jer 2:11).

Verse 18 emphasizes the concerted work that went into crafting an idol. The word "idol" (Hb. *pesel*) comes from the verb "to hew" or "to carve" (Hb. *pāsal*).[142] The English equivalent for this cognate accusative might be "he carved a carving."[143] Three times this verse uses derivations from the Hb. root *yṣr*[144]: the worker "forming" the molten image is "forming his form upon it,"[145] with the intention "to make" an idol. This repetition emphasizes the human activity involved in manufacturing a handmade "god," but it produces a poor English translation. The CSB wording captures the intensity of the effort: the craftsman carves, casts, crafts, shapes, and makes the object of his worship. Isaiah 44:9–20 similarly mocks idol makers and the work of their hands, describing their toilsome labor in painstaking detail. The ironworker heats coals, hammers metal, and shapes it (v. 12a). He hungers, thirsts, and grows faint (v. 12b). The woodworker cuts down a tree, measures, outlines, shapes, and chisels (vv. 13–14). Bowing down in worship before this "block of wood," he is blind to the irony that he used the same log to bake his bread, roast his meat, and warm his hands (v. 19). Likewise, Isa 40:19–20 refers to the handiwork of the smelter who casts a molten image and the metalworker who plates an idol with gold or silver. Even a poor man searches for wood that will not rot and a skilled craftsman so his idol might not topple. Regardless of the skill, quality of materials, or energy invested, the result is the same. The idol maker is only human; the work of his hands, absolutely worthless.

---

[141] See 1 Sam 12:21; Isa 44:9–10; Jer 2:8, 11; 16:19; Hab 2:18.

[142] *HALOT*, 949.

[143] GKC §117p.

[144] This is the same root word used in Gen 2:7, when God made man in his image/likeness: "Then the LORD God formed the man out of the dust from the ground and breathed the breath of life into his nostrils, and the man became a living being." Ironically, idol makers attempted to make images of gods in their own likeness. Not surprisingly, there is "no breath" in the result (Hab 2:19). This verb *yāṣar* illustrates the distinction between God and his human creation. Humans form pottery vessels (e.g., Jer 19:1) and graven images (e.g., Exod 32:4). God, on the other hand, forms "all things," including light, earth, mountains, and even humanity for his own glory (Jer 10:16; Isa 45:7; 45:18; Amos 4:13; Isa 43:7).

[145] The *BHS* apparatus suggests the repetition of this phrase is due to dittography.

The fifth woe dismisses a graven image as "a teacher of lies."[146] The Hb. word rendered "teacher, teaching" (2x in vv. 18–19) comes from the root *yārâ* (and the familiar noun form *tôrâ*), referring specifically to "instruction in cultic or technical matters."[147] The same term *môreh* ("teacher") elsewhere applies to God; since the Lord is the "master teacher," people should look to him for instruction (cf. Isa 30:20; Job 36:22).[148] The Hb. root *šqr* (Eng. "deceive") has a semantic word field that "underscores both the basic meaning 'breach of faith' and the 'aggressive' character of the action." Accusing the idol of being "a teacher of lies" may well be an evaluation of "the soothsaying and magic associated with idolatry as useless nonsense."[149] Furthermore, the idol deceives because it is based on a lie: both it and the god it represents are "human constructs."[150] A skilled artisan would carve a piece of wood into "a human form, / like a beautiful person" (Isa 44:13). People then bowed before such things, declaring, "You are our gods!" (Isa 42:17). Worse still, the people put their trust in the work of their own hands. They pled, "Tell us the coming events, / then we will know that you are gods. / Indeed, do something good or bad, / then we will be in awe when we see it" (Isa 41:23). In desperation they cried, "Save me, for you are my god" (Isa 44:17). In the end, any idol's human form was a pretense; its claim to deity, preposterous. Though the human likeness had ears, it could not hear; though it had lips, it could not speak. The same is true of the so-called gods they represented. Since they are nothing, the promises they offer are empty, and the hopes they raise are vain.[151] The one who places his trust in an idol will be sorely disappointed.[152]

---

[146] Boadt, *Jeremiah 26–52, Habakkuk, Zephaniah, Nahum*, 187, observes that as teachers of lies, the idols "offer the exact opposite of the vision of Habakkuk announced in 2:3, a word that will not lie."

[147] *HALOT*, 437, 1711.

[148] *HALOT*, 560,

[149] M. F. Klopfenstein, "שקר," *TLOT* 3L1401–2. *HALOT*, 1649, defines it as "a lying oracle."

[150] Wright, *The Mission of God*, 152. Wright, 142–48, categorizes OT references to idols in three ways: as physical objects in creation (e.g., Deut 4:15–19, including humans, animals, and heavenly bodies); demons (mentioned only in Deut 32:16–17; Ps 106:35–38; cf. 1 Cor 10:20); or, especially, "the work of human hands" (e.g., 2 Kgs 19:17–19). The description of idols in Habakkuk's fifth woe falls in this final category.

[151] Hermann J. Austell, "שֶׁקֶר," *TWOT* 2:956.

[152] In addition to worthless idols, *HALOT*, 120, notes that people also mistakenly trust (Hb. *bāṭaḥ*) in "fortified walls" (Deut 28:52); "oppression and deceit" (Isa 30:12); "horses," "chariots," and "horsemen" (Isa 31:1). In contrast, only the Lord proves worthy of our trust (Pss 31:6; 86:2; Isa 12:2).

Countering the claims of some scholars, Wright explains the Israelites were not naïve in their understanding of the idolatrous practices of their religiously sophisticated neighbors like Babylon. They knew the Babylonians did not believe the idols were gods but rather represented deities who were "invisibly somewhere else 'up there.'"[153] Still, the prophets ridiculed them as man-made objects. For example, the portrayal of Babylon's gods in Isa 46:1–7, which Wright calls a "cartoon," mocks Bel and Nebo for crouching down from above in fear that the idols depicting them would fall off the oxcarts carrying them.[154] Such idols, hoisted on the shoulders of those who crafted them, could not possibly answer their supplicants' calls for help. In stark contrast, the God of Israel created his worshipers, and he promised, "I will carry you . . . and rescue you" (46:4). Wright observes most of the OT mockery of idols as "the work of human hands" targets national or state gods in particular.[155] Although the images embodied the "pride, greed, and aggression" of a powerful empire, these gods were not even as powerful as the hands that made them.[156] Prophets like Isaiah and Habakkuk boldly exposed the idols and the gods they depicted as frauds.

Habakkuk 2:18 closes with a play on words that does not transfer easily into English. The line uses a pair of words that rhyme in Hebrew: ʾĕlîlîm ʾilləmîm (CSB "idols that cannot speak"). In the singular, the Hb. word ʾĕlîlîm means "worthless," but the plural form usually refers to idols that are worthless. They are "nothings" or "nobodies."[157] The vocalization of the word for *idol* closely sounds like the Hb. word for

---

[153] Wright, *The Mission of God*, 150.

[154] Wright, *The Mission of God*, 150. Bel, or "Lord," is a reference to Marduk, the head of the Babylonian pantheon. Nabu (Nebo in the OT) was considered to be the son of Marduk. (Theophoric names like Nebuchadnezzar II and Belshazzar contain echoes of the names of these pagan deities.) Isaiah may have had in mind the historical humiliation of these so-called gods and their idols. Centuries earlier, Assyrian king Tukulti-ninurta I (1244–1208 BC) invaded Babylon and carted off the statue of Marduk to his own capital, Ashur. After a time, Babylonia regained independence, only to fall to the invading Elamites in 1157 BC. The statue of Marduk was hauled off yet again, this time to Elam, where it remained until the resurgence of Babylon during the reign of Nebuchadnezzar I (1124–1103 BC). See Saggs, *The Babylonians*, 78–81. According to Herodotus (1.183 in Yamauchi, *Persia and the Bible*, 194), when Xerxes crushed a Babylonian revolt in 481 BC, he carried off a gold statue of Marduk that weighed eight hundred talents and stood eighteen feet tall.

[155] Isaiah 40–45 contains a collection of "'idol parody' poems." Other examples include Isa 48:5; Jer 10:1–16; and, of course, Hab 2:18–19. See Judith M. Hadley, "פֶּסֶל," *NIDOTTE* 3:643.

[156] Wright, *The Mission of God*, 153.

[157] Judith M. Hadley, "אֱלִיל," *NIDOTTE* 1:405.

God/gods, *'ĕlōhîm*. The Hb. adjective *'illəmîm* describes these idols as "mute," or "dumb." Derived from a term that means "to bind," the word means "to be silent" or "dumbfounded."[158] The lips of idols are closed tight. They cannot utter a sound. An awkward attempt to retain the rhyme in English might be "wordless worthlessness." The playful repetition of sounds underscores the irony of "gods" or idols that cannot even speak.

Historically, God's chosen people struggled with idolatry. When the Israelites of Elijah's day called on Baal, the power contest on Carmel exposed the hollowness of their misplaced trust (1 Kgs 18:29). Judah likewise fell for the deception of graven images, polluting the land "with the carcasses of their abhorrent and detestable idols" (Jer 16:18). By Habakkuk's day, God was therefore ready to send his rebellious people into exile in Babylonia, where they would get their fill of idols, "worship[ing] other gods both day and night" (Jer 16:13).

Idolatry and sorcery were deeply engrained in Babylon. Nebuchadnezzar's feverish building included dozens of temples dedicated to various gods, including three devoted to the national god Marduk. Because the Babylonian worldview inextricably wove together religion and state, the Babylonians considered their king to be the link between pantheon and people.[159] Stories in Daniel reflect the empire's devotion to idolatry.[160] The Babylonians worshiped "gods made of silver and gold, bronze, iron, wood, and stone, which do not see or hear or understand" (Dan 5:23). Daniel 2 recounts how the Lord revealed the future to Nebuchadnezzar in a dream of a colossal statue representing successive empires in descending order of value—from the gold head symbolizing Babylon down to the feet of iron mixed with clay. A stone representing the kingdom of God struck and shattered the statue into bits that blew away like chaff, while the stone grew into a great mountain that filled the entire earth (Dan 2:35). Daniel 3 describes

---

[158] *HALOT*, 57.

[159] Saggs, "The Religious Role of the King" in *The Babylonians*, 283–308.

[160] The Apocrypha also contains a tale in which Daniel mocked the idol Bel as "but clay within, and brass without, and did never eat or drink any thing [sic]" (v. 7). The Persian king, Cyrus, pointed out that since the copious offerings of flour, wine, and sheep disappeared day after day, Bel must be alive to consume them. To prove otherwise, Daniel had ashes scattered on the floor before sealing off the room to the idol. The next morning the food was gone, but a myriad of footprints revealed who ate it. The priests and their families had entered through a secret door and eaten it all as was their custom. In response, Cyrus allowed Daniel to destroy the idol and his temple. See Bel and the Dragon 1:1–22.

how Nebuchadnezzar later erected his own colossus—ninety feet tall, covered in gold—and commanded everyone on pain of death to worship the massive idol. The day was coming when Babylon and all her gods would be punished (Jer 51:47, 52), and the glory of God's future kingdom would indeed fill the entire earth (Hab 2:14).

2.5.2   Woe to the One Who Worships a Lifeless Idol! (2:19)

> ¹⁹ Woe to him who says to wood: Wake up!
> or to mute stone: Come alive!
> Can it teach?
> Look! It may be plated with gold and silver,
> yet there is no breath in it at all.

2:19   As expected in a chiasm, there are several parallels between the first woe and this verse in the fifth woe. Just as in the first woe, the opening question is followed by the actual pronouncement of woe. There are also semantic parallels to the speechless victims in the first woe, who find their voice. They "arise" and "wake up" (2:7) in order to speak out against their oppressor (2:6). Here in the last woe, the supplicant pleads with his mute idols to "[w]ake up!" and "[a]rise!"[161] The idol, however, remains speechless. The first woe is pronounced on those who violently snuffed out human life to load themselves down with "goods" and "spoils" from many nations. The final woe is pronounced on those who have encased lifeless wood and stones with "gold and silver," begging them in vain to "[c]ome alive!" The provenance of these precious metals was likely the spoils described in the first woe. The irony is palpable, especially if it is the survivors of the first woe who pronounce this final woe against those who robbed them of their valuables only to wrap them round wood and stone.[162]

Verse 19 is pregnant with parody. The idolaters spoke to their handiwork, which could not even answer. Calling the idols "wood" (Hb. ʿēṣ) and "stone" (Hb. ʾeben) emphasized these were merely inanimate

---

[161] Victor P. Hamilton, "קיץ," *NIDOTTE* 3:915, notes several similar uses for the two Hb. verbs, even though "awake" קיץ (qîṣ) occurs only in the *hiphil* or causative stem (2:19), whereas the related word "awake" יָקַץ (yāqaṣ) appears only in the *qal* stem (2:7).

[162] The word "plated" (overlaid with metal) is a secondary meaning of the root תפש (tpś), whereas the primary meaning is "to lay hold of, seize" ("תָּפַשׂ," *HALOT* 81–1780:4). Its appearance in the final woe may be a double entendre, an intentional echo of the first woe.

objects.[163] These Hb. words echo the "woodwork" and "stones" of the second woe, which ironically were granted a voice, as they cried out continually against the wicked builder of the house (2:11).[164] The idolaters' pleas to a block of wood—"Wake up!"—evoke Elijah's ridicule of the priests of Baal on Mount Carmel. When the Canaanite god failed to answer their cries, he taunted, "Shout loudly, for he's a god! Maybe he's thinking it over; maybe he has wandered away; or maybe he's on the road. Perhaps he's sleeping and will wake up!" (1 Kgs 18:27). In response, the false prophets shouted and cut themselves "until blood gushed over them" (v. 28). Despite their frenzied activity, however, the result was resounding silence: "[N]o sound; no one answered, no one paid attention" (v. 29). Likewise, here in Hab 2:19, the Babylonian supplicants implore a "mute stone" (lit. "stone of silence")[165]: "Come alive!" Like "awaken," this second imperative (Hb. *ʿûr*; CSB "come to life") is sometimes translated as "be awake" or "stir."[166] In the same semantic field as "arise" (Hb. *qûm*) in 2:7, the word has the connotation of rousing to activity. God is often the subject of the verb, raising nations to do his bidding—whether to come in judgment or in deliverance of Israel (e.g., 1 Chr 5:26; Jer 51:1). Several psalms include prayers imploring the Lord to rise up and help his people (e.g., Ps 59:4). Some address God with both of these words spoken to idols: "Rise up, LORD, in your anger. . . . [A]wake for me" (Ps 7:6; cf. Pss 35:23; 44:23). There is a significant difference, however; these prayers to the living God for help are based on the precedent of his gracious activity in the past (e.g., Isa 51:9–10). Furthermore, Ps 121:3–4 clearly teaches that "the Protector of Israel does not slumber or sleep." In contrast, the idol worshipers described in Hab 2:19 beg in vain for the idol to come to life.

---

[163] In times of apostasy the Israelites were guilty of similar actions: "[T]he house of Israel has been put to shame. / They, their kings, their officials, / their priests, and their prophets / say to a tree, 'You are my father' / and to a stone, 'You gave birth to me'" (Jer 2:26–27). In contrast to such idolaters who foolishly worshiped a rock as their god, Habakkuk worshiped God as his "Rock." See Hab 1:12; Deut 32:31.

[164] Because the word *ʿēṣ* also means "tree," it recalls the Babylonians' deforestation of Lebanon (2:17). The wood for the idol may have originated from these prized cedar trees. To understand how the repetition of "wood" and "stone" plays out in a concentric chiastic reading, see the discussion of the "rhetorical helix" in 6.2.4.1: "Chiastic Features in the Central Panel."

[165] Paul may be alluding to Hab 2:18–19 when addressing the Corinthian church in 1 Cor 12:2: "You know that when you were pagans, you used to be enticed and led astray by mute idols."

[166] *HALOT*, 802.

The actions described in v. 19 are not far removed from religious practice in Mesopotamia. Although the Babylonians recognized their idols were not actually gods, they performed an "opening the mouth" ceremony inviting a particular god to dwell in the idol depicting it. This elaborate ritual involved transporting a newly fabricated statue to the bank of a river and repeatedly washing its mouth with holy water over the course of a night. The next morning, after the sacrifice of a ram, the idol would become "a sentient thing." A priest would utter an incantation while touching the eyes of the image with a magical twig from a tamarisk tree. He would then lead the "live" statue—and the supposed deity who now indwelt it—back to the temple, where it would be seated on a throne. At significant festivals the adorned image would make public appearances, carried about by priests who intently watched for any sign of movement by the statue.[167]

The living God of Israel is diametrically opposed to that of a graven image. He "formed" the first human and breathed into him "the breath of life" so that he "became a living being" (Gen 2:7). He forbade any attempt to craft an image representing him, whom not even the highest heavens can contain (Exod 20:4; 1 Kgs 8:27). He watches over his children as an eagle who "stirs up" (Hb. *ʿûr*) its nest; he leads his people "with no help from a foreign god" (Deut 32:11–12). He comforts his people; he helps them; he delivers them. The Lord alone is the master teacher. Job rightly concludes, "Look, God shows himself exalted by his power. / Who is a teacher like him?" (Job 36:22). In contrast, the speaker in Hab 2:19 regards an impotent idol and asks pointedly, "Can it teach? / Look! It may be plated with gold and silver, / yet there is no breath in it at all." No amount of silver and gold overlay could cover up the naked truth.[168] In spite of the Babylonians' practices of divination, spells, and sorceries[169], their idols could not possibly teach because they—and the gods they represented—were not even alive.

The phrase "there is no breath in it at all" has interesting parallels. Jeremiah 10:14 similarly declares that "cast images are a lie; / there is no breath in them." A more literal translation of Hab 2:19 reads,

---

[167] Saggs, *The Babylonians*, 282.

[168] God would uncover the shame of the Babylonians in the judgment pronounced in the fourth woe. Here, in the fifth woe, the Babylonians ironically try to cover their false gods with "glory."

[169] See Isa 47:12–13.

"[T]here is no breath at all [with]in its midst." The common Hb. word *rûaḥ* or "breath" can mean "wind" or "spirit." Other OT passages likewise combine the words *rûaḥ* (Eng. "spirit") and *bəqereb* (Eng. "in the midst" or "within").[170] The same Lord who created the heavens and the earth "formed the *spirit* of man *within* him" (Zech 12:1).[171] When David repented of his sin, he asked God to "renew a steadfast *spirit within* [him]" (Ps 51:10). In Ezekiel, God promised he would exchange the remnant's heart of stone for a heart of flesh: "I will . . . put a new *spirit within* you; . . . [and] I will place my *Spirit within* you" (Ezek 36:26–27; cf. Isa 63:11). The NT deepens this understanding of the Holy Spirit taking up residence in the midst of his people (cf. Rom 8:23; 1 Cor 6:19). This language points to the goal of God's mission since the beginning: "I . . . will set my sanctuary among them forever. My dwelling place will be with them; I will be their God, and they will be my people" (Ezek 37:26–27). Idolatry, by its nature, short-circuits this plan. God will not put his Spirit in an idolater bowing before a stone that has no spirit within it. Tragically, the wicked idolater will become like the object he worships: he will not live.

Should we congratulate ourselves that our hands do not produce idols, our hearts do nevertheless. As John Calvin pointed out, "[M]an's nature, so to speak, is a perpetual factory of idols."[172] Our culture's pervasive consumerism and individualism has led us to think we can assemble our own eclectic spirituality from an array of religious beliefs. These designer deities often end up resembling their makers, producing "a God who is familiar, safe, accommodating, but also very small."[173] The end result is not so different from the hand-hewn idols of Hab 2:19. Cloaking even ideas in "precious metals" to convey glory and value still fails to cover up the facts: they are lifeless and unworthy substitutes for the living God. To discern today's idols, Wright suggests examining the deeper longings of the human heart:

> Having alienated ourselves from the living God our Creator, we have a tendency to worship whatever makes us tremble with awe as we feel our tiny insignificance in comparison with the great

---

[170] Leonard J. Coppes, "קֶרֶב," *TWOT* 813.

[171] Italics have been added to the verses in this paragraph.

[172] John Calvin, *Calvin: Institutes of the Christian Religion*, ed. John T McNeill, trans. Ford Lewis Battle, vol. 1, Library of Christian Classics 20 (Philadelphia: Westminster, 1960), 108.

[173] David F. Wells, *The Courage to Be Protestant: Truth-lovers, Marketers, and Emergents in the Postmodern World* (Grand Rapids: Eerdmans, 2008), 120.

magnitudes that surround us. We seek to placate and ward off whatever makes us vulnerable and afraid. We then counter our fears by investing inordinate and idolatrous trust in whatever we think will give us the ultimate security we crave. And we struggle to manipulate and persuade whatever we believe will provide all our basic needs and enable us to prosper on the planet.[174]

The only corrective for deep-rooted idolatry, in Habakkuk's day and in our own, is to anchor our awe and fear in the one true, living God and to trust in him alone for our security and provision.

2.5.3   The Lord in His Holy Temple Silences the Whole Earth (2:20)

> [20] *But the* LORD *is in his holy temple;*
> *let the whole earth*
> *be silent in his presence.*

2:20   Verse 20 closes out the middle panel with a vision of the only God worthy of worship. The magnitude of the contrast to the preceding verses is out of proportion to the tiny size of the single-letter Hb. conjunctive prefix—*waw* (ו)—that introduces it. The English equivalent in this instance, "but," functions syntactically to show contrast.[175] Though small, this prefix signals a massive shift. Unlike the dead wood or "stone of silence" worshiped in v. 19, the "LORD is." He is alive; he is the everlasting "I AM." The covenant name of God is a reminder not only that he exists but also that he reveals himself by name and binds himself to his people—forever. This God is not confined to an earthbound shrine; he is in his "holy temple." Though the phrase "holy temple" can refer to the temple in Jerusalem (e.g., Pss 5:7; 65:4; 79:1), describing the temple as "holy" may imply a location other than the Jerusalem temple, which at this time was itself defiled by syncretistic idolatry (cf. Ezek 8:5–18). The closest OT parallel to Hab 2:20 suggests the setting is none other than the heavenly temple: "The LORD is in his holy temple; / the LORD—his throne is in heaven" (Ps 11:4).[176] The psalm asserts that from this lofty vantage point, the

---

[174] Wright, *The Mission of God*, 171.

[175] *IBHS* §8.3b.

[176] The Hb. word for "temple" (*hêkāl*) can also refer to the "palace" of a king. It is a reminder that the Lord is the sovereign King of the universe he created.

Lord carefully examines everyone. He sees both the wicked and the righteous and differentiates between them, a theme that resonated with Habakkuk's heart.[177]

Unlike gods represented by sticks and stones, the Lord is not dependent on his supplicants to rouse him or to open his mouth. Psalm 18—Habakkuk likely quotes from v. 33 in 3:19—celebrates the Lord's response to the righteous man's plea for help as he answered from his temple: "The LORD thundered from heaven; / the Most High made his voice heard" (Ps 18:6, 13). Similarly, Jer 25:30–31 declares that from his "holy dwelling" on high, the Lord "roars," "makes his voice heard," and "calls out with a shout." The subject of this "tumult [that] reaches to the ends of the earth" is the "judgment [of] all humanity."

Habakkuk 2:20 demonstrates irony, as the Lord silences those who worship mute idols. His command encompasses the "whole earth." Other OT passages also record the Lord's directives to silence idolaters. Isaiah 41:1 contains a similar imperative: "Be silent (Hb. root ḥāraš) before me, coasts and islands!" The prophet Micah writes that the Lord in "his holy temple" commands all the inhabitants of the earth: "Listen, all you peoples; / pay attention, earth and everyone in it. . . . Look, the LORD is leaving his place, / and coming down to trample / the heights of the earth" (Mic 1:2–3). The reason behind this imperative is the Lord's intention to destroy Israel along with "[a]ll her carved images" and "all her idols" (Mic 1:7). When Nebuchadnezzar ordered "people of every nation and language" to bow down and worship the ninety-foot gold statue, the Daniel account carefully lists the accompanying instruments four different times (Dan 3:4–5, 7, 10, 15). Jeremiah prophesied such noise would one day cease: "The LORD will destroy Babylon; / he will silence her noisy din" (Jer 51:55 NIV; "loud noise," NASB; "mighty voice," CSB).

The sovereign Lord shushes the entire world with just one syllable. In Hab 2:20, the word translated "be silent" is actually the Hb. interjection has!, which sounds like its onomatopoeic counterpart in English: "Hush!" Six other passages where the same interjection appears call for silence before an important person (Moses, a king, the Lord) or a weighty event (the reading of the Law, disastrous

---

[177] Psalm 11:6–7 declares that the Lord will "rain burning coals . . . on the wicked," but "[t]he upright will see his face."

judgment).[178] The same command for silence before the Lord appears in two other Minor Prophets.[179] In Zeph 1:4–7, the Lord rebukes the residents of Judah and Jerusalem who worship a long list of false gods: "Be silent [*has!*] in the presence of the Lord GOD, / for the day of the LORD is near" (Zeph 1:7). After Judah's judgment and exile, the Lord comforts Zion with the promise he is coming to dwell among his people and the nations who will become his people: "Let all humanity be silent [*has!*] before the LORD, for from his holy dwelling he has roused himself" (Zech 2:13).[180] In contrast to mute, lifeless idols, the living God commands silence as he comes from his heavenly dwelling place to take possession of his land and to plunder Babylon and others for their wanton destruction of Judah (see Zech 2:7–9).

The Lord will not allow any nation—his own included—to fill his temple with praise directed toward false gods. Since "the LORD is in his holy temple" and "the whole earth" stands "in his presence," the geographic scope of the Lord's heavenly temple appears to encompass the entire world (Hab 2:20). The context of Zech 2:7–13 affirms this same understanding. The Lord, who hushes "all people" from "his holy dwelling" intends to reside among his people—a people that includes both the restored remnant *and* the "[m]any nations [who] will join themselves to the LORD on that day and become [his] people" (vv. 10–11). This language evokes the eschaton as well as the essence of God's mission from the beginning. The Lord intends to extend his sanctuary presence from Jerusalem to the ends of the earth. Just as God filled previous earthly sanctuaries with his glory, his final goal is to fill the entire earth with his glory. Habakkuk 2:14 already anticipates the accomplishment of this mission: "[T]he earth will be filled / with the knowledge of the LORD's glory, / as the water covers the sea."

Verse 20 is a fitting conclusion for this central panel (2:6–20) of the literary triptych. On the outer perimeters of the chiasm, the first and fifth woes reflect the same global setting as the middle woe. The first woe is a cacophony of speech, as "all of these" taunt, mock, riddle, and accuse their oppressors (2:6). The "all of these" refers to

---

[178] See Num 13:30; Judg 3:19; Zeph 1:7; Zech 2:13 in relation to persons; and Neh 8:11; Amos 6:10 in relation to events. John N. Oswalt, "הָס," *NIDOTTE* 1:1024.

[179] Mark Boda, "A Deafening Call to Silence," 193–217, maintains that these three verses—Hab 2:20; Zeph 1:7; Zech 2:13—constitute a unified "Call to Silence." See "Themes Shared by Habakkuk and the Twelve" in the Introduction.

[180] Zechariah uses the same Hb. word for "roused" (*ʿûr*) as that found in Hab 2:19, where an idol worshiper vainly admonishes the silent stone to "rouse" himself (CSB: "Come alive!").

"all the nations" and "all the peoples" of 2:5. The fifth woe resounds with the desperate cries of idolaters trying to stir to life the objects of their affection (2:19). The Lord silences not only these fakes and those who worship them, but also "all the earth" (2:20).[181] The Lord must address both the universal injury of sin and the universal guilt of sin. These two parallel subsections point the spotlight back on the chiastic center in Hab 2:13–14, which is the ultimate answer to the prophet's questions. God will bring the wicked to justice, and he will make all things right—if not fully in the present, then in the future.

The final verse in chap. 2 also serves as the conclusion for the entirety of Habakkuk's oracle beginning in 1:1. Like the central panel, the first panel (1:1–2:5) reverberates with noise: the prophet's plaintive prayers throughout are interrupted by the scoffing derision of the Babylonian soldiers (1:10); the rejoicing of the fishermen over a human haul (1:15); and the arrogant boasts of the wicked, fueled by wine (2:5). The Lord of heaven and earth silences them all—including the confused questions of the prophet. In 1:13 Habakkuk had brazenly accused God of remaining silent and doing nothing in the face of wickedness. In response, Hab 2:20 issues a majestic "call to silence" as a prelude to the Lord's powerful activity that follows in the final panel. As Lloyd-Jones observes, Hab 2:20 urges Christians to be silent as well:

> There must be no querying, no questioning, no uncertainty about the goodness and the holiness and the power of God. Do not complainingly ask, "Why does God allow this?" or "Why does God do that?" Consider the Word of the Lord to His prophet. Look up to God. Look at the ultimate and the absolute. Then let us put our hands upon our mouths that are so ready to speak foolishly. . . . Let us silently humble ourselves and bow down before Him and worship Him.[182]

Awed silence and worship are appropriate responses for every generation in the presence of the one and only holy God.

When the world seems to be coming apart at the seams, v. 20 offers the only reassurance possible. God is still on his throne; he is still

---

[181] In John's apocalyptic vision, the host of heaven observe a half hour's silence after the Lamb opens the seventh seal (Rev 8:1).

[182] Lloyd-Jones, *From Fear to Faith*, 54.

in control. Just as in Habakkuk's day, the sins of the world—materialism, aggression, violence, perversion—press in and threaten to overwhelm us. The functional gods of our culture prove just as unresponsive, unable to give guidance, let alone save. We need the reminder of Habakkuk: "Don't just look at the woes. Lift your eyes a little higher and see God."[183] He calls us to quiet our hearts in worship before the King of kings. Nothing, not even the most powerful army on earth, can thwart his mission. The Lord of Armies will bring the wicked to justice, and he will fill the earth with the knowledge of his glory as the water covers the sea.

---

[183] Warren W. Wiersbe, *From Worry to Worship: Studies in Habakkuk* (Lincoln: Back to the Bible, 1983), 54.

3 HABAKKUK'S PRAYER (3:1–19)

Although the OT contains several ancient hymns appearing outside of the Psalter, Habakkuk 3 stands apart from typical inset poetry occurring in either a narrative or poetic context. This is the only poetic/prophetic passage clearly marked as a psalm by multiple genre labels

261

and liturgical instructions.[1] The superscription in v. 1 identifies it as a prayer of a prophet and adds this enigmatic notation: "According to *Shigionoth*." The equally inscrutable liturgical instruction "*Selah*"—elsewhere found only in the book of Psalms—occurs in vv. 3, 9, and 13. Habakkuk 3 differs from other psalms with the additional subscription in v. 19: "For the choir director: on stringed instruments." All these markings identify Hab 3:1–19 as a psalm intended for worship. Habakkuk's psalm was later extracted from its context and appended to the LXX Psalter in the "Odes," a collection of inset hymns from the OT.[2]

This chapter reveals close parallels between the final panel of the literary triptych and the first. The theodicy that catalyzed the first panel's questions finds resolution in the final panel's theophany.[3] These

---

[1] James W. Watts, "Psalmody in Prophecy: Habakkuk 3 in Context," in *Forming Prophetic Literature: Essays on Isaiah and the Twelve in Honor of John D. W. Watts*, ed. James W. Watts and Paul R. House, JSOTSup 235 (Sheffield: Sheffield Academic, 1996), 212.

[2] Watts, "Psalmody in Prophecy," 218. The superscription and subscription of the Habakkuk psalm do not appear in the "Odes."

[3] "Theophany" means an "appearance" or "manifestation" of God. Frank Moore Cross, *Canaanite Myth and Hebrew Epic: Essays in the History of Religion in Israel* (Cambridge: Harvard University Press, 1973), 147–94, argues that the OT drew on the language and imagery of Canaanite theophany to describe Yahweh's appearances. Cross discerns two basic patterns or genres of Canaanite theophany, which may be mixed: (1) armed with thunderbolt arrows the Divine Warrior marches into battle or rides his cloud-chariot, the cosmos collapsing before him; (2) the Divine Warrior ascends to his temple mount, newly acquired in battle. Cross observes that hymnic descriptions, like the Song of Habakkuk (3:3–15), typically follow the first pattern, exemplified in the parting of the Red Sea (Exodus 15).

Claus Westermann, *Praise and Lament in the Psalms* (Atlanta: John Knox, 1981), 96, notes that although the Hebrew Bible used the schema of other ancient religions, the language describes historical occurrences where the Lord arrives to deliver his people and destroy his enemies. Westermann, in *Praise and Lament*, 93–101, and in *Elements of Old Testament Theology* (Atlanta: John Knox, 1982), 25–26, discusses the differences between "theophany" and "epiphany" (essentially Cross's pattern 1). I summarize his distinctions in this chart:

	EPIPHANY: GOD ACTS	THEOPHANY: GOD SPEAKS
APPEARANCE	God appears from afar.	God appears to communicate.
MODEL PASSAGE	Red Sea (Exod 15)	Mount Sinai (Exod 19, 34)
OTHER PASSAGES	Deut 33; Judg 5:4–5; Isa 30:27–33; Mic 1:3–4; **Hab 3**; Ps 18:7–15; Nah 1:3–6	Gen 28:10–22; Exod 3; 1 Kgs 19; Isa 6; Ezek 1–2
GOAL	God's wrathful intervention—to save his people, to judge his foes	1. God reveals himself, or 2. God calls/commissions a prophet

counterparts offer intentional contrasts which raise the possibility the prophet was drawn to theophanic and cosmic imagery and terminology reminiscent of ancient OT hymns. Habakkuk adopted their archaic language and imagery which was perfectly suited to theophany. Whether he composed the lines himself or adapted them from an existing ancient hymn, they are essential to the message of the book, and it would stand incomplete without them.

	EPIPHANY: GOD ACTS	THEOPHANY: GOD SPEAKS
ACCOMPANYING COSMIC PHENOMENA	Mountains/hills quake; Meteorological activity: Clouds pour rain; lightning; thunder	*One* mountain quakes; Volcanic activity: Fire, smoke, and cloud obscure
PLACE/TIME	Event in history: Whenever/wherever his people are in distress	Cultic features: Specific sacred space; specific day; God speaks to an individual mediator.

The distinctions between "epiphany" and "theophany," however, are not always so neat. If Exodus 15 is the model passage for epiphany, its broader context records God not only acts but also speaks (Exod 14:15–18). Additionally, the chart indicates Westermann's further subdivision of theophany according to two distinct goals: (1) revelation or (2) call/commission. Since the differences between these two "theophany" categories are at least as distinct as the differences between Westermann's labels of "epiphany" and "theophany," the argument could be made for at least a third category, if not more.

Samuel Terrien, *The Elusive Presence: Toward a New Biblical Theology* (San Francisco: Harper & Row, 1978), 68–69, uses the following terms: "epiphany" for visitations in the patriarchal era; "theophany" for manifestations at Sinai; "vision" for the period of the prophets (chap. 5); "mystical quest" for psalmists' encounters (pp. 304–20), and "the final epiphany" for the day of the Lord (chap. 8).

In their investigation of the literary nature of theophany in the Hebrew Scripture, N. F. Schmidt and P. J. Nel, "Theophany as Type-Scene in the Hebrew Bible," *Journal for Semitics* 11.2 (2002): 256–81 argue for distinguishing between theophany and epiphany. In his own exploration of theophany as type-scene, George W. Savran, *Encountering the Divine: Theophany in Biblical Narrative*, JSOTSup 420 (New York: T&T Clark, 2005), 6, does not follow Westermann's terminology. Instead, he limits his discussion of theophany to OT narrative: "[A]lthough the rich tradition of poetic descriptions of theophany has much to contribute to the biblical understanding of such appearances of the divine, it will serve only as background . . . since these texts lack the narrative framework which describes the reception of theophany." Savran's parameters thus eliminate the same passages that fall under Westermann's "epiphany" label. Savran, p. 241n, considers Habakkuk 3 a "poetic theophany" that "lacks the component of interaction with the divine." One could counter that vv. 16–19 describe "the reception of theophany" and that Habakkuk as a whole demonstrates "interaction with the divine."

Although the exploration of distinctions may be helpful when comparing theophanic passages, the attempt to categorize God's varied appearances remains elusive. For this reason, this commentary follows the traditional convention of referring to the Lord's appearance in Hab 3:3–15 as "theophany" rather than "epiphany."

The details of this psalm suggest Habakkuk's familiarity with the ancient hymns of Israel (e.g., Exod 15; Deut 32–33; Judg 5; Pss 18; 68; 77). The global temple setting of the immediately preceding verse (2:20) compelled the prophet to meditate on and sing of God's great works in the past as he contemplated with trepidation the work God was about to do (1:6). The Lord may have even used these ancient songs to usher Habakkuk into the theophanic vision described in vv. 3–15. James Watts makes the astute observation that "the introspective perspective of psalmody" has the unique ability to convey "the interior experience of the prophetic vision."[4] Habakkuk's emphasis on the liturgical nature of his psalm expresses an invitation for other worshipers to join in singing the same hymn as a way of actualizing that same transformative experience.[5]

3.1   SUPERSCRIPTION (3:1)

[1] *A prayer of the prophet Habakkuk. According to* Shigionoth.

3:1   This final panel (III) of the literary triptych provides a contrast to the first panel (I) on the other side of the chiasm located at the center of the woe oracles (II).[6] These corresponding sections of the two outer panels of Habakkuk demonstrate parallels as well. The final panel of Habakkuk's literary triptych opens with a superscription in 3:1, similar to that found in 1:1. Whereas the first superscription functions as a title for the entire book, the second serves as a title for all of chap. 3. Significantly, "[t]he pronouncement that the prophet Habakkuk saw" (1:1) moved him to prayer and praise (3:1). Like the first superscription, 3:1 identifies Habakkuk as "the prophet" (Hb. *nābîʾ*), recalling his role as one who communicates God's message to his people.[7]

Verse 1 refers to the poem as Habakkuk's "prayer." This word for prayer (Hb. *təpillâ*) first occurs when David addressed the Lord before the ark in Jerusalem in response to the announcement of his covenant

---

[4] Watts, "Psalmody in Prophecy," 217.
[5] Watts, "Psalmody in Prophecy," 222. Similarly, Floyd, *Minor Prophets Part 2*, 89, calls Habakkuk 3 a "ritual dramatization" that invites readers to relive the prophet's experience vicariously.
[6] See 6.2.4: "Habakkuk as a Literary Triptych," in the Introduction.
[7] See the discussion of *nābîʾ* in 1:1.

(2 Sam 7:27). Solomon utters it several times at the dedication of the temple when he entreated the Lord to hear the prayers of his people—and even those of the foreigners who hear of the Lord's great name and "pray toward this temple" (1 Kgs 8:42; cf. 8:22–53 // 2 Chr 6:14–42).[8] When Hezekiah led the people in a time of renewal and Passover celebration, "God heard them, and their prayer came into his holy dwelling place in heaven" (2 Chr 30:27). The vast majority of the occurrences in Psalms are prayers asking the Lord to acknowledge the psalmist's prayer (e.g., Pss 4:1; 55:1; 61:1).[9] Half of these include specific directions "for the choir director," as does this psalm in Habakkuk (3:19). The close associations of this kind of liturgical prayer with the temple—both on earth and in heaven—suggest such a prayer appropriately follows the "call to silence" from the heavenly temple in Hab 2:20.

The title indicates Habakkuk's prayer was incorporated into public worship. The appearance of his name in the title of a psalm—"A prayer of . . . Habakkuk"—places the prophet in a group including Moses (Ps 90:1), David (Pss 17:1; 72:20; 86:1), and the "suffering person who is weak" (Ps 102:1).[10] These individual supplications have long been folded into corporate prayer and worship. Although the entire chapter is labeled a "prayer," several commentators relegate the prayer to v. 2, since this is the only verse containing a petition. It is important to remember, however, that prayer involves not only petition but also meditating in the Lord's presence and communing with him. Roberts believes the vision described in Hab 3:3–15 is the Lord's final response to the prophet—the promised vision of 2:2–3.[11] Habakkuk's response follows in 3:16–19.

Although the meaning is unclear, the phrase "According to *Shigionoth*" is a musical term.[12] Unfortunately, the rarity of this noun contributes to its obscurity. The related noun likewise occurs only

---

[8] The Lord heard and answered the prayer (Hb. *taphillâ*) of King Manasseh in shackles in Babylon (2 Chr 33:12–13) and of Nehemiah in Susa (Neh 1:4–7). The Lord even heard Jonah's prayer directed toward the heavenly temple from the belly of the fish (Jonah 2:7).

[9] Though most of the *taphillâ* references implore the Lord to listen, some specifically indicate that God rebuffs the hollow entreaties of the wicked (e.g., Prov 15:8, 29; 28:9; Isa 1:15; Jer 7:16; 11:14; Lam 3:8, 44).

[10] *HALOT*, 1777.

[11] Roberts, *Nahum, Habakkuk, and Zephaniah*, 149.

[12] A similar musical term appearing in other superscriptions may refer to a type of stringed instrument: "according to *Sheminith*" (1 Chr 15:21; Pss 6:1; 12:1).

once, in the superscription of Ps 7:1: "A Shiggaion of David, which he sang to the LORD." Thematic parallels between Psalm 7 and Habakkuk 3 include the Divine Warrior vindicating the righteous and demonstrating his wrath against the wicked, and the violence of the evil one "com[ing] down on his own head" (Ps 7:16).[13] Working from the assumption the term may derive from the Hb. verb *šāgâ*, meaning to "go astray, err, stagger," Andrew Hill suggests it is a psalm with "a sporadic rhythm or frenzied cadence" or "a peculiar lament form characterized by wandering thought and language."[14] The significance of the term remains a mystery.

3.2 HABAKKUK'S HUMBLE PETITION (3:2)

3.2.1   I Have Heard and Stand in Awe of Your Deeds (3:2a)

> [2] LORD, *I have heard the report about you;*
> LORD, *I stand in awe of your deeds.*

3:2a   The prayer opens with Habakkuk's response to all the Lord had said in 2:2–20. Twice the prophet addressed the Lord by his covenant name "Yahweh." The mention of the name echoes Hab 2:20, which declared, "The LORD [Yahweh] is in his holy temple; / let the whole earth / be silent in his presence." The prophet, however, was not silent. Instead, his response was a prayer, respectfully spoken.

Habakkuk appears to have progressed significantly from his opening prayer in Hab 1:2–4 (section I:A). There the prophet asked three questions, one after the other voicing his despair over God's apparent silence. The first of these questions introduced "hearing" as a central theme of the book: "How long . . . must I call for help / and you do not listen?" (1:2). Though the prophet initially assumed the Lord did not hear his previous cries, by the beginning of chap. 3 (III:A'), Habakkuk acknowledged he had heard the Lord's response to his pleas. The first line of his prayer in 3:2 recalls this same theme with just two Hb. words: "I have heard the hearing of you" (*šāmaᶜtî šimᵃkā*). The prophet's fondness for cognate accusatives, typical of poetry, does not

---

[13] The psalmist implores the living Lord to "[r]ise up" and "awake" on behalf of his servant—semantic parallels to the cry of the supplicant before his impotent idol in Hab 2:19.

[14] Andrew Hill, "שָׁגָה," *NIDOTTE* 4:44. Perhaps the English word "reel" would be a rough parallel, in that it can mean both "to stagger" and the lively music of a folk dance.

always translate well in English.[15] Habakkuk intended to emphasize the word "hear." When a similar phrase occurs in other OT passages referring to people, translators typically render it as "They will hear the report/news about you" (e.g., Deut 2:25; Nah 3:19). When the same phrase refers to a report about God, it is translated as "have heard of your fame" (Num 14:15). In these other OT passages, the radius of the report is global: "[T]he nations . . . have heard" (Num 14:15); "[T]he peoples everywhere under heaven . . . will hear" (Deut 2:25); and [A]ll who hear" (Nah 3:19).

What exactly did Habakkuk hear in Hab 3:2? The translations are varied: "I have heard the report about you" (CSB, NASB; "the report of you" ESV); "I have heard of your fame" (NIV); and "I have heard Your speech" (NKJV). In 3:3–15, the "report" may refer to the Lord's historical reputation established by his mighty saving acts in the past. The following verses describe the Lord in ways that parallel past events, like the exodus. Perhaps the prophet meditated on the Lord's famous deeds for previous generations as he called out for the Lord to renew them "in these years." On the other hand, Habakkuk appears to be referring to a specific report he had just heard, one he was not aware of in his initial prayers in chap. 1. The content of the report is found in the Lord's second response to the prophet in 2:2–20, and may center on the vision in 2:4: The wicked will perish; "the righteous one will live by his faith." More probably, the report consisted of the woes, which spelled out God's judgment on the Babylonians (2:6–20). The chiasm indicates the cosmological implications of the report extend over the entire earth "as the water covers the sea" (2:14).

Parallelism in the Side Panels I:A and III:A′		
	I: A (1:2–4)	**III: A′ (3:2)**
Setting	Prophet in prayer	Prophet in prayer
Actions	He accuses the Lord of not listening.	He's heard the report about the Lord.
	Why won't the Lord do something?	He stands in awe of the Lord's deeds.
	He asks three questions.	He makes three petitions.
Complaint	"The wicked restrict the righteous; . . . justice comes out perverted."	
Shift		"In wrath, remember mercy."

---

[15] When both verb and object are derived from the same root, the object is called a cognate accusative (*IBHS* §10.2.1f).

The prophet reversed his position regarding the Lord's work. His prayers in section I:A (1:2–4) in the first panel questioned the Lord's inactivity since he seemed to tolerate the evil deeds of the wicked. In section III:A′ (3:2) of the final panel, the Lord's deeds caused the prophet to "stand in awe."[16] The word behind this phrase is the common Hb. word for fear (yārēʾ), often translated as "I feared" or "I was afraid." Although one can fear people or circumstances (1 Sam 15:24; Exod 14:10), the majority of biblical occurrences regard God as the object of fear (Exod 14:31; Deut 6:2; Josh 24:14).[17] Occasionally fear is associated with terror of God's wrath or judgment, but primarily fear of the Lord is associated with worship.[18] When "hearing" and "fearing" are paired together in Deuteronomy, as they are here, they indicate "what was heard was heeded (13:11; 17:13; 19:20)."[19] Hearing the accounts of God's mighty deeds often resulted in worship (1 Sam 12:18, 24). "Your deeds" in Hab 3:2 echoes the memorable phrase found in 1:5, where God explained he was "doing a deed" or "working a work" (Hb. pōʿal pōʿēl). The Lord's work described in 1:6–11 elicited terror of a fierce human foe. The pronouncement of woes, however, engendered a reverent fear of divine judgment. Habakkuk would have heard those woes through the structural chiasm, which emphasized judgment (2:13) and restoration (2:14) as the work of God: "Is it not from the LORD of Armies?" In the first panel Habakkuk had mistakenly thought the Lord was doing nothing; by the final panel he stood in awe of a God actively involved in the affairs of humanity.

3.2.2   Revive Your Work; in Wrath, Remember Mercy (3:2b)

> [2b] *Revive your work in these years;*
> *make it known in these years.*
> *In your wrath remember mercy!*

---

[16] *BHS* notes the proposed reading of (וְ)רָאִיתִי (Eng. "I have seen [your work]") for יָרֵאתִי (Eng. "I feared") based on the LXX.

[17] *TDOT* 6:296; *HALOT*, 433. H.-P. Stähli, "ירא," *TLOT* 2:573, observes that fear has a religious aspect when it occurs in the context of (1) the sanctuary (Lev 19:3, 26:2; 2 Sam 6:9), (2) theophanic encounters with God (Exod 20:18, 20; Deut 5:5), and (3) the Lord's powerful activity in history (as here in Hab 3:2 and also in Isa 25:3; 41:5; Jer 10:7; Zech 9:5).

[18] M. V. Van Pelt and W. C. Kaiser Jr., "יָרֵא," *NIDOTTE* 2:521–22.

[19] Van Pelt and Kaiser, *NIDOTTE* 2:522.

3:2b   Habakkuk's three anxious questions in I:A (1:2–4) shift to three humble requests in III:A' (3:2). These requests in the second part of v. 2 reveal a change was underway in the prophet. In I:A (1:2–4) he demanded justice while teetering on the edge of accusing God of injustice. In III:A' (3:2), however, he acquiesced to the Lord's administration of justice. In the first panel God informed Habakkuk he was doing an astounding work in raising up the Babylonians to punish his wayward people. The prophet immediately questioned the propriety of such actions. Through the series of woes in the middle panel, the Lord reassured the prophet: he is a God of justice; he will not allow sin to go unpunished. In the third panel, the prophet petitions God to "revive" his work in his generation.[20] The intensive (*piel*) stem of this verb conveys the idea of letting something live or bringing back to life.[21] Following the description of the idolater vainly attempting to bring the work of his hands to life, the petition is ironic. It echoes Hab 2:4, which declares those who are righteous by faith will live.[22] The work of the Father/Son mentioned in John 5 was raising the righteous to life and the wicked to condemnation.[23] The chiastic center in Hab 2:13–14 already hinted at God's work of judgment and restoration. The prophet's second request in 3:2 asked God to revive his work in order to reveal his sovereignty, a request aligning with the promise of 2:14 that the earth will be filled to overflowing with the knowledge of God's glory. Habakkuk became the answer—at least in part—to his

---

[20] The object of the verb "revive" is not specified, but its masculine singular suffix matches the masculine singular noun "work." Although "work" is not repeated, it is understood to be the object of subsequent verbs, "revive" and "make known." Robertson, *The Books of Nahum, Habakkuk, and Zephaniah*, 217–18, identifies the pronoun "make him/it live" as a reference not to "work"
  but rather as a plea for the Lord to preserve the life of the one who trusts in him: "make him live . . . make (him) understand."

[21] G. Gerleman, "חיה," *TLOT* 1:414. *HALOT* notes that in Hab 3:2, the *piel* form may mean "to realize something."

[22] Shepherd, *A Commentary on the Book of the Twelve*, 326, observes that the unusual choice of the verb "to swell" (Hb. ʿpl) in Hab 2:4 may be an intentional transposition of letters that point to the "work" (Hb. pʿl) in Hab 1:5 and 3:2. He concludes that Hab 2:4 uses it to show that those who lack faith will "swell and die," whereas "those who have faith in the future work of God" will "live," or "revive, return to life" (*HALOT*, 309). See the discussion of Hab 2:4. Robertson, *The Books of Nahum, Habakkuk, and Zephaniah*, 217–18, discerns yet another echo of 2:4. Translating "revive it" as "make him live," Robertson believes Habakkuk's plea is "a deliberate reflection on the vision for the eschaton which he had received earlier" in 2:4: "The proud will not stand; but the just—he shall *live*!" (Italics in original.)

[23] See the discussion of Hab 1:5 regarding the possibilities of Jesus's allusion to Hab 1:5 in John 5.

own prayer. By recording and clearly inscribing the vision on tablets so others might easily read them, Habakkuk helped reveal God's work.

Habakkuk introduced the first two requests with the phrase "in the midst of the years" (ESV, NASB, NKJV).[24] This phrase recalls a similar temporal phrase from Hab 1:5, where the Lord told Habakkuk, "I am doing something *in your days*."[25] In the first panel the prophet objected to God's using a wicked nation to punish Judah during his lifetime, but in the third panel he implored God to renew his work and make it known in his generation. The shift from "in your day" to "in these years" may be influenced by the Lord's instruction in 2:3 to wait for the vision even if it seems to tarry. In the Hebrew text of 3:2, the placement of this phrase at the beginning of consecutive clauses emphasizes the immediacy of God's activity. The same phrase can also refer to the inner parts of a person[26]—as it did in 2:19, which declared the work of human hands had no breath "in the midst of it." The recurrence of this prepositional phrase a few verses later intentionally highlights the contrast between the lifeless idol and the powerful God whose "revived" activity instills awe.

Habakkuk's third request in 3:2 acknowledges the Lord's anger. The word translated "wrath" comes from the Hb. root *rāgaz*, which conveys "trembling or restlessness" or expresses emotional upheaval caused by anger, fear, anxiety, or even excitement.[27] Although other Hb. words describe anger (*'ānap*) or rage (*zā'ap*), the focus here is on the depth of the emotion: *shaking* with anger.[28] Habakkuk did

---

[24] Because the Hb. phrase "in the midst of years" is unusual, it has sparked speculation and debate about its meaning. For example, Sweeney, *The Twelve Prophets*, 481, suggests that it "refers to the manifestation of YHWH's actions in the temporal framework of human history. Such an appeal would call upon the Deity, the infinite master of all creation whose heavenly dwelling exists outside of the finite of time, to enter into the finite human realm to intervene on behalf of the oppressed people of Israel." In time, that is just what the second person of the Trinity did. Prior, *The Message of Joel, Micah, and Habakkuk*, 263, however, suggests that "[t]his striking phrase . . . probably has an eschatological thrust, denoting the interval between the present time and the end (2:3) appointed by God." Although for Habakkuk the interim period may seem long and God may seem absent, the Lord is at work bringing about all things to fulfill his desired mission.

[25] Italics added.

[26] *HALOT*, 1135–36.

[27] *HALOT*, 1182–83; M. V. Van Pelt and W. C. Kaiser Jr., "רָגַז," *NIDOTTE* 3:1042. Hiebert, *God of My Victory*, 14, prefers a translation of "in turmoil" rather than "in wrath."

[28] Van Pelt and Kaiser, *NIDOTTE* 3:1043 cite Dan 3:13 as an example. There Nebuchadnezzar shook with furious rage. Significantly, the Hb. root *rgz* appears four times in Habakkuk 3. The nominative form in v. 2 describes the Lord's fury about to be expressed in the impending

not question the Lord's right to be angry. The prophet himself listed numerous reasons for righteous anger against Judah in 1:2–4, and the Babylonian threats in vv. 1:6–11 and 13–17 begged for redress. Although the woes in 2:6–20 focused on the Babylonians, the Lord had charged the Judeans with similar sins. Injustices and idolatry cannot go on unchecked before a holy and just God.

Habakkuk beseeched the Lord to temper his wrath with compassion. The Hb. verb *rāḥam* means "to love, to have compassion for, or to take pity on someone."[29] The noun form, which reflects the notion of parental affection, lit. means "womb," and "speaks of the anxious solicitation of parents toward their children."[30] "Compassionate" is first on the list of attributes the Lord uses to describe himself to Moses after his judgment provoked by the golden calf (Exod 34:6–7). The word seems to encompass the whole list of attributes summarizing God's character, including his *ḥesed* ("covenant love, loyalty"). Old Testament occurrences of this word almost always refer to God's compassion for his people *after* he has disciplined them (e.g., Deut 13:17; Isa 54:8; Jer 12:15). Notable exceptions compare the Lord to a human parent who has compassion for his/her children (Ps 103:13; Isa 49:15). Occasionally, the Lord declares he will *not* have mercy on unrepentant evildoers or on idolaters (Isa 9:17; 27:11; Jer 13:14). He engaged foreign armies who showed no mercy for their foes as agents of his wrath—e.g., Babylon versus Judah (Jer 6:23; 21:7; 50:42) and the Medes versus Babylon (Isa 13:18). The Lord remembers humans are but dust, so he demonstrates his compassion by removing their sins completely when they repent (Ps 103:12–14; Isa 43:25; Jer 50:20; Mic 7:19). When there is no repentance, the Lord disciplines his people so they will remember and return to him.

Habakkuk 3:2 is a significant verse to meditate on today. Our culture seems to have latched onto the truth "God is love" with such fervency that many refuse to acknowledge the holiness which governs his attributes, including justice (1 John 4:16). The result resembles a

---

judgment; the verb form in v. 7 describes the reaction of the nomadic residents in the path of God's arrival, and in v. 16 it twice articulates the anguish of the prophet who trembled in response to witnessing said judgment.

[29] *HALOT*, 1217.

[30] Széles, *Wrath and Mercy*, 46. Széles observes that wrath and mercy are "anthropomorphic and anthropopathic pictures [that] bring the Being of God all the closer to us. . . . Habakkuk's God is the mighty Lord who directs history, the gentle, loving Father of his people." Both attributes deserve recognition.

god made by human hands rather than the Creator and Sustainer of the universe. Thankfully, God is merciful, but he is also holy and just. He will not allow evil to go on unchecked forever. Ultimately, this work will require his stepping into human history as the Divine Warrior. We would do well to join the prophet in praying that God renew his work in these years and that he would temper his righteous wrath with mercy.

3.3 THE DIVINE WARRIOR ARRIVES (3:3–7)

Habakkuk 3:3–7 is the first of two sections describing the prophet's theophanic encounter with the Lord. A theophany is an appearance of God. Vern Poythress defines it as "a manifestation of divine presence accompanied by an extraordinary display *mediating* that presence."[31] God often uses his creation as "media through which he manifests himself as the Creator."[32] These phenomena include thunderstorm, cloud, glory (or light), human form, warrior, chariot, fire, and royal court—all of which appear in the theophany recorded in Hab 3:3–15, except for the last two.[33] Each of these forms communicates various aspects of God's character, and they often overlap—as they do in Habakkuk—demonstrating the singularity and incomprehensibility of God.[34] The Lord graciously reveals himself, but he is far greater than humanity can apprehend. These OT appearances of God, especially those in human form, anticipate the ultimate and permanent theophany of God: the incarnation of Jesus Christ.[35]

As the prophet's response in Hab 3:16 reveals, the theophany described in 3:3–15 was no mere recitation of God's activity from the distant past. Thomas provides a beautiful illustration of Habakkuk's experience in chap. 3:

> It is as if the prophet is looking at a vast painting of the exodus experience that hangs in the gallery of Israel's faith. Surveying the various

---

[31] Vern S. Poythress, *Theophany: A Biblical Theology of God's Appearing* (Wheaton: Crossway, 2018), 30. Italics in original.

[32] Poythress, *Theophany*, 33.

[33] Poythress, *Theophany*, 107. Even these exceptions may arguably appear elsewhere in Habakkuk: in the mention of fire in Hab 2:13 (as paired with glory in 2:14) and in the court/temple setting of Hab 2:20.

[34] Poythress, *Theophany*, 109.

[35] Poythress, *Theophany*, 108.

details of the masterpiece, the prophet surprisingly . . . *steps into* the painting and walks alongside Yahweh as he marches through the desert to deliver. As he walks with the Lord, Habakkuk wonders at the majesty and power of God. He is overwhelmed by Yahweh's move to save his people, to save his anointed (v. 13). . . . From his new perspective, [Habakkuk] can see his place in a whole new way, encouraged by the power and compassion of Yahweh at his side.[36]

This theophanic experience allowed Habakkuk to step "out of the painting and [settle] back into his place"; "Yahweh's march down to save [had] become part of Habakkuk's reality in the present."[37] The imagery found in 3:3–15 draws on traditional metaphorical language describing the Divine Warrior, recollecting OT psalms of the past.

Habakkuk 3:3–15 resembles multiple OT poetic passages celebrating God's intervention in the affairs of humanity. Scholars have long noted similarities between this psalm and the songs of old, including Exod 15; Deut 32–33; Josh 10; Judg 5, Ps 18 // 2 Sam 22; Pss 68; 77; and Nahum 1. The middle sections of Habakkuk 3 echo these passages, depicting God as a Warrior-King who marched through the desert to judge and to save. As the history of Israel unfolded, the Lord used pestilence and plague, rivers and sea, as well as storms and lightning as weapons against his enemies.[38] These OT passages often include declarations of the Lord's incomparability. Although this prophetic psalm does not contain an explicit claim to the Lord's preeminence, Hab 2:20 calls the whole world to silence in his presence, and 3:3 illustrates the global extent of his rule.

> ³ *God comes from Teman,*
> *the Holy One from Mount Paran.*
>
>   *Selah*
>
> *His splendor covers the heavens,*
> *and the earth is full of his praise.*

---

[36] Thomas, *Habakkuk*, 149.

[37] Thomas, *Habakkuk*, 149. Thomas, p. 150, adds that "memory provides the opportunity for the believer to *actively emplace* one's present situation *in light of* God's work in the past." Italics here and in the Thomas quotation above are original.

[38] Tremper Longman III and Daniel G. Reid, *God Is a Warrior*, Studies in Old Testament Biblical Theology (Grand Rapids: Zondervan, 1995) 42, calls the broader creation God's "ally" in battle; the elements of nature serve as his weapons.

3:3 This section of the third panel of the literary triptych (III:B′, Hab 3:3–7) describes the arrival of the Divine Warrior, who stands in sharp contrast to the Babylonian army described in the parallel section of the first panel (I:B, Hab 1:5–11).[39] ʾĔlôâ, the singular form of the traditional name for God (Hb. ʾĕlōhîm) occurring in v. 3, also appears in two ancient biblical poems demonstrating close affinities with Hab 3: Deut 32:15, 17 and Ps 18:31. The same title for God appears in the parallel section in the first panel, where the Babylonian soldiers considered their military strength to be their god—ʾĕlôâ (Hab 1:11).

Robertson points out the seventh-century-BC prophets had become disillusioned with the royal descendants of David. Although the nation still needed a king/messiah/savior, they no longer looked to a human throne for deliverance. Instead, "they could see none other than God himself fulfilling that role."[40] In v. 3 the Lord arrived to fulfill the functions of the king. The opening line, "God comes," is startling.[41] These simple words imply God's imminent intervention, an answer to Habakkuk's prayers in the first panel. The prophet complained God failed to answer his prayers; he ignored the injustices among his people, and he tolerated—even orchestrated—the wickedness of the Babylonians against his own. The Lord eventually responded to Habakkuk's pleas verbally, but in 3:3, the

---

[39] For a thorough treatment of the Divine Warrior motif in the Bible, see Longman and Reid, *God Is a Warrior*. For a discussion of Divine Warrior as metaphor, see Marc Brettler, "Images of YHWH the Warrior in Psalms," *Semeia* 61 (1993): 135–65.

[40] Robertson, *The Books of Nahum, Habakkuk, and Zephaniah*, 18.

[41] See Deut 33:2; Pss 50:3; 96:13; 98:9; Isa 40:10; Zech 14:5; Mal 3:1. Savran, *Encountering the Divine*, 5–6, observes that even though the Bible often portrays God with human attributes, "theophany narratives reveal to the reader something of the shock and surprise of the encounter with the divine. In these texts the individual is jolted sharply out of his or her normal existence in the face of something which he does not fully grasp at first, but which ultimately induces a sense of self-awareness (and awareness of the Other) which is nothing short of transformative." Although Habakkuk 3 is poetic theophany rather than narrative, the prophet experiences the same level of shock and resulting transformation. CSB translates *yābôʾ* (*qal* imperfect 3ms) not as future ("he will come") but rather as present tense: "he comes." GKC §107a notes that the imperfect may be represented as "certainly imminent." As Habakkuk reflected on God's intervention in the past, he announced God's imminent arrival in the present and glimpsed his future coming at the eschaton.

anthropomorphic language describes God's intervention. God not only saw the wicked and the righteous; he intervened by stepping down into human history by punishing the Babylonians. The personification of the vision in Hab 2:3 already hinted at the coming of the Lord.[42] The Lord, who was "in his holy temple" at the end of chap. 2, demonstrated his divine claim over all the earth as his sanctuary as well.

The outer limits of this stanza are marked by an inclusio consisting of two pairs of geographic place names (3:3, 7). The first line announces the Lord's arrival from a southern region or city called "Teman."[43] Teman first appears in a genealogy in Genesis, as the proper name of Esau's oldest grandson, a chief of the clan (36:11, 15). Teman's name was eventually attached to a city or region belonging to the Edomites, who lived in the mountains of Seir, southeast of the Dead Sea. Almost every time the OT mentions "Teman," it is in the context of God's judgment for Edom's cruelty to Judah: "[T]hey will fall by the sword from Teman to Dedan" (Ezek 25:13); "I will send fire against Teman, / and it will consume the citadels of Bozrah" (Amos 1:12); "Teman, your warriors will be terrified / . . . [they] will be destroyed by slaughter" (Obad 1:9); "At the sound of [Edom and Teman's] fall the earth will quake" (Jer 49:20–21). Clearly, if the Lord was coming from Teman, he had gone there for the purpose of judgment. Teman serves as an example of God's wrath punishing a people for their cruelty against Judah.

The second place name in Hab 3:3 is Mount Paran. The OT mentions the Wilderness of Paran several times: it was, for example, the dwelling place of Ishmael (Gen 21:21) and the location of Kadesh-barnea, the staging ground for the twelve spies who scouted Canaan (Num 13:3, 26). Besides Hab 3:3, the only other reference to Mount Paran is in Moses's farewell blessing on the Israelites. Moses began with these words:

> The LORD came from Sinai
> and appeared to them from Seir;
> he shone on them from Mount Paran
> and came with ten thousand holy ones,

---

[42] See the discussion of the LXX version of Hab 2:3.

[43] The OT contains almost two dozen references where the Hb. word *tēmān* means the compass direction "south" (e.g., Exod 26:18; Isa 43:6). See *HALOT*, 1725.

with lightning from his right hand for them.
³ Indeed he loves the people.
All your holy ones are in your hand,
and they assemble at your feet. (Deut 33:2–3)

Moses's description recalls the physical manifestation of the Lord as his glory settled over Mount Sinai before all the Israelites.[44] Deuteronomy 33:2 describes the host of angels who are set apart as "holy ones." The same phrase recurs in 33:3: "holy ones," whom the Lord loves (cf. 7:6; 14:2; 26:19: 28:9).[45] The Lord's movements in Hab 3:3 trace this same desert route out of Sinai the Israelites traveled while following the pillar of cloud on their journey to the promised land (Num 10:12; 12:16; 13:3, 26).[46] The focus in Hab 3:3 is not on the "holy ones"—angelic or human—but rather on the one who is himself

---

[44] Shmuel Ahituv, "The Sinai Theophany in the Psalm of Habakkuk," in *Birkat Shalom: Studies in the Bible, Ancient Near Eastern Literature, and Postbiblical Judaism Presented to Shalom M. Paul on the Occasion of His Seventieth Birthday* (Winona Lake: Eisenbrauns, 2008), 227, specifically identifies Mount Paran as Mount Sinai. Theodore Hiebert, "Theophany in the OT," *ABD* 6:505–11, explains the suitability of a mountain for theophany in that it physically links heaven and earth: "the point at which contact is made between the divine and human."

The ancient Canaanites understood the mountain as center of the cosmos and the location of divine theophany. For example, Cross, *Canaanite Myth and Hebrew Epic*, 147–48, quotes a Canaanite text where "Ba'al sits enthroned, (his) mountain like a dais, . . . / In the midst of his mount, Divine Ṣapon, / On the mount of (his) victory." The storm-god, it was thought, would march out from his temple-palace to conquer his enemies and return in victory (pp. 164–65). Similarly, the chief Canaanite deity, El, dwelt on a high, fertile mountain where he held court over his assembled divine council (p. 179). Cross, p. 165, points out that "[t]he revelation at Sinai . . . presumes a tradition in which Yahweh's cosmic mount and ancient sanctuary were in the southern mountains." Commenting on the parallels between the OT and ancient Near Eastern archaeology and texts that "portray ancient temples as microcosms of heavenly temples or of the universe," Beale, *The Temple and the Church's Mission*, 51, observes that the similarities may have been an intentional "protest statement" by Israel or possibly the pagan counterparts were "garbled, shadowy representations about the being of the biblical God and of his design for his dwelling place." Not surprisingly, the ancient Hebrew poets used language and imagery from the surrounding culture but divested them of their pagan religious significance (e.g., Ps 68:15–17; Isa 30:27–30; Mic 1:3–4).

Hiebert, "Theophany in the OT," 507, observes that from the time of David, Mount Zion supplanted Sinai as "the most prominent place of self-disclosure." Description of poetic theophanies—like the Song of Habakkuk—often recalled the Lord's earlier appearances.

[45] *HALOT*, 1067, suggests that Deut 33:3b may refer either to holy people or to heavenly beings. Presumably, 33:2 may as well.

[46] Though it does not mention Mount Paran, Deborah's song (Judg 5:4–5) celebrates this same march from Sinai across Seir, as does Ps 68:7–8. The psalmist adds that "God's chariots are tens of thousands, / thousands and thousands; / the LORD is among them in the sanctuary / as he was at Sinai" (Ps 68:17).

holy. Habakkuk already addressed the Lord by this divine title—"My Holy One"—in the first panel (Hab 1:12).[47]

The word "*Selah*" signals a break at the midway point of Hab 3:3.[48] The term may come from the Hb. verb *sālal*, meaning to "build up [the highway]" (e.g., Isa 57:14 [2x]); "lift up a song" (Ps 68:4 ESV); or "exalt" (Prov 4:8). *Selah* occurs seventy times in the Psalms and three times in Habakkuk 3.[49] Although the meaning is unclear, it may have served as a musical interlude encouraging singers—and readers—to pause and meditate on the words. A silent pause was especially appropriate in light of the Lord's call for silence from his holy temple (Hab 2:20). The announcement of God's coming in 3:3 is reason enough to be still and meditate.

There are clear contrasts between the first panel and this final panel. The Babylonian army would arrive from the north, whereas God would come from the south. The motivation of the arrogant Babylonians was to enrich and exalt themselves. The Lord's motivation in coming was twofold as well. The mention of Teman signals that he was coming to pour out his wrath on the wicked; Mount Paran recalls the Holy One coming in glory to bless his people, his holy ones whom he loves. These twin purposes also surface at the theological center located in Hab 2:13–14: judgment and restoration. The eternal perspective of the chiasm surfaces again in the following clause in chap. 3.

The final clause in Hab 3:3 articulates the mission of God since the dawn of creation: "His splendor covers the heavens / and the earth is full of his praise." This verse resembles 2:14, which describes God's mission as the earth overflowing with "the knowledge of the Lord's glory."[50] The words "heavens" and "earth" form a merism, a figure of speech in which two parts—often extremes—together represent the whole.[51] Just as God's splendor fills every place in heaven and on earth,

---

[47] See the discussion of this divine title in Hab 1:12.

[48] *Selah* occurs midway through 3:9 and follows 3:13 as well.

[49] *HALOT*, 756. Other possible meanings include a change of voice or repeat from the beginning.

[50] See the discussion of the mission of God regarding Hab 2:14. See also Num 14:21; Ps 72:19; Isa 6:3; 11:9.

[51] Matthew 28:18 contains the same merism, whereby Jesus underscores that the Father had given him *all* authority—"in heaven and on earth." Jože Krašovec, "Merísm—Polar Expression in Biblical Hebrew," *Biblica* (1983): 231–39, offers many other biblical examples of merism, including Job 21:33 ("behind him . . . before him") and Jer 36:30 ("exposed to the heat of the day and the frost of night").

so should his praises. Panel 1 implies that the Babylonians prided themselves on subjugating land (Hab 1:6–11) and sea (1:14–17), another merism. Panel 3 shows their temporary rule over land and sea pales in comparison to the King who forever reigns over heaven and earth. The whole earth, having been silenced before the Lord in his heavenly temple, now erupts in adoration of the One whose presence fills all things.

Verse 3:3 implies this heavenly temple will be extended to the earth and her inhabitants: "His splendor covers (Hb. root *ksh*) the heavens, / and the earth is full (Hb. root *ml²*) of his praise." Roughly half of the two dozen OT occurrences of "splendor" refer to God.[52] Shmuel Ahituv calls it "the atmosphere around a deity or a king."[53] When the Lord is in view, the word "splendor" (Hb. *hôd*) is almost always paired with its synonym, "majesty" (Hb. *hādār*; Pss 96:6; 104:1; 111:3; Job 40:10).[54] The term "praise" (Hb. *təhillâ*) derives from the familiar verb (Hb. *hālal*) meaning "praise" or to cry "Alleluia!"[55] The call to worship in Psalm 148 exemplifies the extensive reach of God's praise. It charges all in the heavens (angels, heavenly armies, sun, moon, and stars) and all on earth (sea creatures, weather, mountains, animals, and peoples of all ages) to worship: "Let them praise the name of the LORD / . . . ; His majesty covers heaven and earth" (Ps 148:13). This verse mirrors the merism and wording of Hab 3:3. Since the splendor of God fills the heavens and earth, so should the reach of his praises.

The evidence for a universal temple in Hab 3:3 goes beyond the praises which one would expect to find in a temple setting. The two verbs "cover" and "fill" frequently appear in worship settings in the OT. (See the chart below.) Additionally, Andersen believes "[t]he verbs in v 3b are in chiasmus with the same verbs in 2:14."[56]

---

[52] The remaining occurrences describe the authority or majesty of a king, a man's vitality, or a horse.

[53] Ahituv, "The Sinai Theophany in the Psalm of Habakkuk," 228.

[54] *HALOT*, 241, defines it as "weight, power, splendour, majesty." Although several English translations render the word in Hab 3:3 as "splendor" (e.g., CSB, ESV, NASB), others translate it as "glory" (e.g., NIV, RSV, NKJV, KJV), as it certainly falls in the same semantic domain.

[55] *HALOT*, 1692; 249. As might be expected, over half of the occurrences of the word "praises" appear in Psalms. The term "hallelujah" comes from the combination of the Hb. imperative "praise" and the shortened name of Yahweh often found in poetry: "Ya," meaning "Praise Yahweh."

[56] Andersen, *Habakkuk*, 294, observes this chiasmus is an important link between the two major sections of the book in his structure. I would argue that it points to the theological centerpiece of the book in my structure.

OT WORSHIP SETTINGS					
OT PASSAGE	LOCATION	GLORY	CLOUD	COVER	FILL
Exod 24:15–16	Mount Sinai	x	x	x	
Exod 40:34	tabernacle	x	x	x	x
Num 9:15	tabernacle		x	x	
1 Kgs 8:10–11	temple	x	x		x
Isa 4:5	Mount Zion	x	x	(canopy)	
Ezek 43:5	Temple court in Jerusalem	x			x
Hab 2:14	earth	x		x	x
Hab 3:3	heavens/earth	(splendor)		x	x

After the dedication of Solomon's temple, the trajectory of worship slowly expands from the sanctuary as a structure in a specific locale[57] to a wall-less sanctuary that fills both heaven and earth.[58] This eventuality is the essence of God's mission and hints at the eschatological setting of the psalm in chap. 3.

3.3.2   He Strides across the Earth with Power (3:4–6)

4 *His brilliance is like light;*
   rays are flashing from his hand.

HAB 2:14	HAB 3:3
For the earth **will be filled** with the knowledge of the Lord's glory	His splendor **covers** the heavens,
as the waters **cover** the sea.	and the earth **is full** of his praise.

[57] Robertson, *The Books of Nahum, Habakkuk, and Zephaniah*, 224, observes that these previous manifestations on a smaller scale anticipate "the great final epiphany of the glory of God, when the Son of Man shall come in the clouds, accompanied by lightning shining from the East to the West (Matt 24:27)."

[58] The NT depicts Jesus as the true meeting place between God and humanity, the reality that earthly sanctuaries merely foreshadowed (see John 1:14; 2:19–21). The account of the Transfiguration "on a high mountain" (Matt 17:1) includes several of these same details: the "glory" of Christ and the "cloud" that "overshadowed" or covered him (Luke 9:32, 34). With the outpouring of the Spirit at Pentecost, believers were incorporated into the temple that has Christ as its foundation and cornerstone. Revelation describes the people of God as the New Jerusalem, "coming down out of heaven from God, arrayed with God's glory. . . . [T]he Lord God the Almighty and the Lamb are its temple" (Rev 21:10–11, 22). Ultimately, "God's dwelling [tabernacle] is with humanity, and he will live with them" (Rev 21:3).

This is where his power is hidden.
⁵ *Plague goes before him,*
and pestilence follows in his steps.
⁶ *He stands and shakes the earth;*
he looks and startles the nations.
The age-old mountains break apart;
the ancient hills sink down.
His pathways are ancient.

3:4   Verse 4 relates God's figurative appearance in a variety of ways, including light, human form, and Divine Warrior. The context of Habakkuk 3 suggests the Divine Warrior comes to judge the Babylonians who so cruelly asserted their dominion in their quest for a global empire. Ultimately, Habakkuk 3 anticipates the end of the age, when the Lord will establish his dominion over the whole earth.

Like v. 3, v. 4 describes the appearance of the Divine Warrior in language recalling God's glory displayed in the sanctuaries of Israel's past. Various English versions render the Hb. word *nōgah* (Eng. "gleam, bright light")[59] as "brilliance" (CSB), "splendor" (NIV), "radiance" (NASB), or "brightness" (ESV, NKJV). Although the OT uses this word to describe the lights of the cosmos, over half of the occurrences appear in the context of theophanic visions, including Isa 4:5 (above). The word *nōgah* occurs repeatedly in Ezekiel's vision of God "in the land of the Chaldeans" (Ezek 1:3). "Brightness" describes the cloud, the fire surrounding the living creatures, the one seated on the throne, and the brilliant light all around this human-like figure (Ezek 1:4, 13, 27, 28); it also describes Ezekiel's vision of the radiant cloud of God's glory departing the Jerusalem temple preceding the destruction of the city and temple by Nebuchadnezzar's armies (Ezek 10:4). Although the Lord abandoned the temple, he would return as a Divine Warrior (Isa 59:16–17), and his glory would shine over Zion so that nations and kings would be drawn to her "shining brightness" (Isa 60:3).

Habakkuk 3:4 compares the Lord's radiance to "light." Since God is the source of everything, the only metaphors available for God originate from him. God created light and the heavenly luminaries for humanity. Many OT occurrences of "light" contrast it to "darkness"

---

[59] *HALOT*, 667.

(e.g., Isa 60:1–2); and in several instances, light describes God's presence in "covenantal relationships" (Pss 4:6; 27:1; 44:3; 89:15).[60] Light is a "divine quality" [61]—as the NT clearly affirms (1 John 1:5; 1 Tim 6:16). The prophecies at Jesus's birth describe him as the source of light and glory for Gentiles and Jews alike (Luke 1:78–79; 2:30–32). Jesus boldly claimed to be "the light of the world" (John 8:12). At the Transfiguration, Jesus's face and clothes shone "dazzling white" with the glory of God, or as the NIV renders it, "as bright as a flash of lightning" (Luke 9:29). As the "lamp" of the New Jerusalem, his own brilliance will eliminate the need for sun and moon (Rev 21:23).

Verse 4 observes that "rays" of light (lit. "horns") flashed from the hand of the Divine Warrior. Figurative language in the Bible often uses "horns" as a symbol of power and strength. Deuteronomy 33:17, for example, compares the strength of Joseph's sons to "the horns of a wild ox." Often, however, God's strength is in view: "The LORD is . . . the horn of my salvation" (e.g., Ps 18:2 // 2 Sam 22:3). The mention of bright light in Hab 3:4, contextually determined "horns," translates as "rays," likely a reference to bolts of lightning.[62] Other biblical passages link the power of lightning to the Lord. He creates, stores, and sends lightning throughout the earth (Job 36:30–32; 37:3; Pss 97:4; 135:7; Jer 10:13), dispensing its bolts like arrows (Pss 18:14, 144:6; Zech 9:14). Lightning served as a theophanic sign of his presence at Sinai (Exod 19:16; 20:18). Other ancient Near Eastern cultures reflect this same imagery. A relief discovered at Ugarit depicts Baal as raising a club aloft in one hand while holding a lightning-bolt staff in the other, and Akkadian literature portrays Hadad, "the Flooder," carrying a bolt of lightning. [63]

---

[60] Martin J. Selman, "אוֹר," *NIDOTTE* 1:322.

[61] Selman, *NIDOTTE* 1:322.

[62] The same root occurs in Exod 34:29, which describes how Moses's face shone because he had been in the presence of God. The mistranslation of this word as "horns" in the Latin Vulgate led Michelangelo to include a pair of horns on the head of his sculpture of Moses holding the Ten Commandments (See *HALOT*, 1144). David Toshio Tsumura, "Janus Parallelism in Hab. III 4," in *VT* 54/1 (Jan 2004): 126, observes that v. 4 may be an example of Janus parallelism, where both connotations of the word—light and strength—are in play in the same sentence: "The brightness shall be as the light; / he has *rays/horns* from his hand, / where his *power* is hidden" (emphasis added).

[63] Yitzhak Avishur, *Studies in Hebrew and Ugaritic Psalms* (Jerusalem: Magnes Press Hebrew University, 1994), 160–61.

Lightning was the greatest expression of raw natural power experienced by humans in the ancient Near East.[64] Since a human hand wields a weapon, the "hand" became a symbol of power and rule. The Lord often delivered his people from the "hand" of a human king (e.g., 2 Kgs 19:19 NIV); but at other times, a nation would fall under the oppression of God's own hand (e.g., 1 Sam 5:6, 11). The phrase "this is where" in Hab 3:4 is emphatic. Looking back to God's hand in the previous line, it underscores the divine source of this power.[65]

Verse 4 describes God's power as concealed in a "hiding place" (Hb. *ḥebyôn*). This noun appears once in the OT and derives from a verb that means "to hide" from an enemy or from disaster (Josh 2:16; Isa 26:20).[66] The reason for the concealment is obvious and may stem from the metaphor itself. Just as dark clouds hide the source of lightning, the Lord's presence is not readily perceived until he displays his powerful works.[67] The hiddenness of power in v. 4 signifies the Lord is

---

[64] A single lightning bolt generates between 100 million and 1 billion volts and contains billions of watts—power that still evokes awe today. The average lightning bolt generates the equivalent of 186 horsepower-hours. Since the average bolt lasts only one microsecond, the number of horses required to produce an equivalent amount of energy for that miniscule increment of time is a staggering 670 billion.

[65] Most OT references to "strength" show this attribute belongs to God and to those who receive it from him. About half of the OT occurrences of this word for "strength" (Hb. *ʿōz*) refer to the Lord's might (e.g., Ps 29:1). The other half are evenly divided between references to those who derive their strength from the Lord (e.g., Ps 29:11) and descriptions of the strength of humans and their strongholds (e.g., Lev 26:19–20).

[66] *HALOT*, 285.

[67] P. Jensen, "חֶבְיוֹן," *NIDOTTE* 2:6, observes that the "hiding" may "suggest that even the splendor of the theophany was a gracious veiling of God's being (cf. Judg 13:22; Job 26:14). Or it may allude to the paradoxical phenomena that both revealed and concealed God's glory, such as the dark cloud that allowed someone to look at the sun but also obscured it (. . . cf. Ps 18:12)."

Exploring the Hebraic theology of presence, Terrien, *The Elusive Presence*, 83, traces "the paradox of presence in absence." Throughout the OT, appearances of God are always accompanied by "hiddenness." In the theophanic visitations to the patriarchs, the Lord "showed himself," but only through visible signs of his presence: a smoking firepot/flaming torch (Gen 15); three unexpected guests at Mamre (Gen 18); a stairway-to-heaven dream (Gen 28); and a midnight wrestling match with an unknown assailant (Gen 32). The distinctive hidden quality of divine manifestation continued in later theophanies as well: an angel speaking from a flame-engulfed bush (Exod 3); battle directives from a fire-cloud pillar (Exod 14); a storm-and-smoke-enveloped mountain in total darkness (Exod 19–20); a glory-cloud-engulfed tabernacle and temple (Exod 40; 1 Kgs 8). Terrien, p. 259, observes that even the blinding light of Ezekiel's vision was just "as effective a mask of the Deity as darkness." Not surprisingly, the "psalmody of presence"—including Habakkuk 3—"mirrors both the uniqueness and the universality of the Hebraic theology of presence" (p. 278). Like other prophet-poets, Habakkuk recalled the celebrated theophanies of the past yet recognized that God's transcendent-yet-hidden presence erases the strictures of sacred time and space (2:14, 20; 3:3, 18–19).

"slow to anger," and he does not flaunt his "weaponry." He does not hesitate to administer judgment according to his divine will. Lightning hidden up one's sleeve is obviously figurative language, but it is potent. God is the source of all light. When he chooses, he easily harnesses and unleashes its power to achieve his ends.

3:5 Verse 5 personifies the forces that accompanied the Divine Warrior: "Plague goes before him, / and pestilence follows in his steps." The presence of these two terms, personified as part of the Divine Warrior's processional retinue, reinforce the ancient origins of the poem. The first word, "plague" (Hb. *deber*), appears approximately fifty times in the OT. Though the reader is familiar with the ten plagues brought on Egypt by "the LORD's hand" (Exod 9:3), only a handful of the OT occurrences of *deber* concern other nations: Egypt (Exod 5:3; 9:3; Ps 78:50), Sidon (Ezek 28:23), Gog (Ezek 38:22), and nations in general, including Israel (Jer 27:8; 28:8). Two other events come to mind—(1) the outbreak of "tumors" among the Philistines who had captured the ark (1 Sam 5:6–12), and (2) the Assyrians who came to besiege Jerusalem in Hezekiah's day but turned back when the angel of the Lord killed 185,000 soldiers overnight (2 Kgs 19:35–36). Although these two incidents do not use the word *deber*, they certainly bear the hallmarks of a plague.[68] In fact, the vast majority of occurrences of *deber* concern plagues directed at Israel.[69] Of those, only twice does the Lord state in a positive way that he would deliver from the plague "[t]he one who . . . dwells in the shadow of the Almighty" (Ps 91:1, cf. 3, 5–7). The remaining references are warnings the Lord would send plagues against Israel or Judah. The warning became formulaic by the time of Jeremiah and Ezekiel: "I am about to send sword, famine, and plague against them" (e.g., Jer 24:10). Habakkuk 3:5 stands out as unique in its personification of "plague."

---

[68] The Philistines' offering of gold objects in the shape of tumors and mice "that [were] destroying the land" (1 Sam 6:5) suggests the possibility of a rodent-born contagion like the bubonic plague. The Greek historian Herodotus, *The History*, 192–93, tells a similar story in which Sennacherib's forces, on their way to Egypt, were overrun by field mice gnawing on their bows, quivers, and shields. The correlation of disease and rodents again points to an epidemic like the plague.

[69] When the Israelites refused to enter the land of promise, for example, the Lord threatened to wipe them out "with a plague" before Moses dissuaded him (Num 14:12). Other times, however, the Lord did not relent, and great numbers of Israelites died in plagues (e.g., 14,700 in Num 16:49; 24,000 in Num 25:8–9; and 70,000 in 2 Sam 24:15). These two passages in Numbers refer to "plague" using the Hb. word *maggēpâ*; the Samuel passage uses both synonyms: *maggēpâ* and *deber*.

The Divine Warrior's rearguard was just as fierce as his vanguard. The second Hb. word, *rešep*, is translated here as "pestilence" (CSB, NIV). Other versions render this word as "plague" (ESV, NASB), "fever" (NKJV), and "burning coals" (KJV).[70] One of the symptoms of the plague is a burning fever, so in Hab 3:5, the two words function as synonyms, just as "plague" and "pestilence" may in English (see Deut 32:24). The same Hb. word *yēṣēʾ* that appears twice in Hab 1:4—"justice never *emerges*" and "justice *comes out* perverted"—is translated in 3:5 as "*follows* in his steps" (lit. "*goes forth*" as in procession.).[71] Although God is Spirit, other OT passages also use poetic language referring to God's "feet" to indicate his heavenly origin. For example, "[b]eneath his feet" is sky-blue pavement (Exod 24:10); "total darkness" (Ps 18:9 // 2 Sam 22:10) or clouds like dust (Nah 1:3). The Lord's feet will also stand on the earth to fight the nations (Zech 14:4) and to dwell among his people forever (Ezek 43:7). The anthropomorphic imagery of Hab 3:5 counters the prophet's previous complaints. Not only does God see the injustices of the wicked; he figuratively steps down into a broken world. When he does, righteous judgment naturally follows.

Plague and pestilence have not been limited to the pages of the Bible. Since biblical times history has recorded wave after wave of pandemics with staggering death tolls. The following chart offers a brief listing of pandemics with the greatest death tolls up to the present day.

---

[70] *HALOT*, 1297, notes that most of the other occurrences of *rešep* include some sense of burning: "flaming arrows" (Ps 76:3); "lightning bolts" (Ps 78:48); and "fiery flames" (Songs 8:6, 2x). Job 5:7 translates it as "trouble" and compares it to sparks. Its use in Deut 32:24 is similar to Hab 3:5: "They will be weak from hunger, / ravaged by pestilence (Hb. *rešep*) and bitter plague (Hb. *qeteb*, Eng. "destruction")—another Hb. synonym paired with plague and/or pestilence.

[71] Italics added. Albright, *Yahweh and the Gods of Canaan*, 139, notes that Ugaritic literature identifies a Canaanite god by the name of Resheph, "He who burns." This deity was equated with Nergal—a Babylonian god of the underworld, pestilence, death, and destruction. (See Avishur, *Studies in Hebrew and Ugaritic Psalms*, 164–65.) Since this discovery, some scholars have suggested that Resheph and Deber were angels that accompanied the Lord. There is no evidence, however, of a god named Deber in the Ugarit pantheon (Albright, 186). The pagan god who "burns" is not the ready equivalent of an angel. Perhaps it is better to consider these references as literary device. The stealthy advance of the plague seems particularly suited for personification.

NAME OF PLAGUE	DATE	DEATH TOLL
Antonine Plague	165–180 AD	5 million
Plague of Justinian*	541–542 AD	30–50 million
Black Death*	1347–1351	200 million
New World Smallpox	1520	56 million
17th-Century Great Plagues*	1600	3 million
Third Plague*	1855	12 million
Spanish Flu	1918–1919	40–50 million
HIV Aids	1981-present	25–35 million
COVID-19	2019-present	7 million+

The thought of God as a source of plague is alarming—especially in light of a planet still reeling from the COVID-19 pandemic.[72] Many history books dismiss the "primitive" beliefs of ancient cultures attributing the advent of pestilence to the displeasure of God/gods. Although we do not presume to attribute particular outbreaks of disease to the wrath of God, we cannot discount the biblical accounts that do. God used plague and pestilence in the past; and, according to prophecies, he will again in the future (Zech 14:12–15; Rev 15:1). The biblical paradigm of a plague of judgment indicates the Lord typically warns of its coming and exercises precise control over its scope, duration, and purpose so "[they] will know there is no one like [him] on the whole earth" (Exod 9:14). When an epidemic threatens on our horizon, it is reassuring to know that God is still in control and sovereign. Plague and pestilence are subject to him; they follow in his steps, according to his directions and purposes.[73] He will not fail to

---

[72] The above pandemics marked by asterisks have been identified as the bubonic plague, which is caused by the *Yersinia pestis* bacteria—a contagion that typically spreads from infected rodents to fleas to humans. The symptoms of this deadly disease are terrifying: fever, chills, muscle aches, pneumonia, blackened skin, bleeding from mucous membranes, and swollen, painful lymph nodes (called buboes). Approximately seven people a year are diagnosed with the bubonic plague, which is still endemic in the western United States. The mortality rate of the plague decreases from 90 percent when left untreated to 10 percent when diagnosed and treated with antibiotics. Centers for Disease Control and Prevention Statistics, October 20, 2022.

[73] The advent of two plagues in the early history of the church (Antonine Plague, 165 AD; Cyprian Plague, 251 AD) contributed greatly to the spread of Christianity in the Roman Empire. In contrast to the pagan response of panic and abandonment, the early Christians nursed the sick, regardless of whether they were Christian. Two-thirds of those who were cared for survived, and the Christlike actions of the early church gained respect as well as converts. See Rodney Stark, *Discovering God* (New York: HarperOne, 2007), 319–20.

accomplish his mission to vanquish all evil and to establish justice and restoration on the earth.

3:6   The anthropomorphic imagery of Hab 3:5 carries over into v. 6 where the Lord "stands" (Hb. *ʿāmad*)[74] and "looks" (Hb. *rāʾâ*). The posture of standing indicates judgment. The same verb "to stand" or "take one's stand"appeared in 2:1, where the prophet determinedly resolved to take his "stand" on the lookout tower and "watch" (Hb. *ṣāpâ*) for God's answer to his complaint. The contrast between the two scenes is vivid; the first panel indicates the prophet took his stand and waited for God's response, and in the final panel God stood and the whole earth quaked in response. Several OT passages record earthquakes often accompanied physical manifestations of God's presence.[75] An apparent difficulty arises over the meaning of the Hb. verb form *wayəmōded* as reflected in 3:6 of CSB ("shakes"). The lexical information behind the word suggests it comes from the verb *mādad*, lit. "measures, assesses."[76] Alternatively, the term could translate the Hb. root *mwd*, meaning "move, shudder."[77] Either fits the context. Verses 6–7 indicate the Lord "measures, assesses" the earth, based not only on the parallelism with "looks" (Hb. *rāʾâ*) but also by virtue of the verb stem (*poel*), which functions as factitive: "takes measure" of the earth.[78] In either scenario, the Divine Warrior stands in preparation for judgment, and the whole earth trembles in fear under his scrutiny. God, who instructed Habakkuk to "look at the nations" and be amazed (1:5), now "looks and startles the nations." The word translated "startles" (Hb. *nātar*) occurs in Job 37:1 to describe Job's heart that "leaps" from his chest when the Lord's voice thunders in a theophany. The nations had been oblivious to the Lord's presence, busy

---

[74] Elmer A. Martens, "עָמַד," *NIDOTTE* 3:430, notes that—as in Habakkuk 3—other descriptions of theophany not only report that God comes but also that he stands. He also observes that "[i]n the eschatological battle God will appear and plant his feet (עָמַד) on the Mount of Olives (Zech 14:4)." Avishur, *Studies in Hebrew and Ugaritic Psalms*, 166, points out the similarity between the Lord's standing in Hab 3:6 and Isa 3:13–15, where the Lord "stands to judge the people." Ironically, the Lord's charge against Israel's leaders—oppressing the poor—is not unlike Habakkuk's complaint in 1:2–4. Notably, when God stands, he brings judgment.

[75] See, for example, Exod 19:18; Judg 5:5; Ps 68:7–8; Isa 64:1, 3.

[76] *HALOT*, 552.

[77] *HALOT*, 555. Some, such as C. F. Keil, suggest an emendation of *mdd* to *mwt* "to totter, shake." Such a proposal is unwarranted since either word fits the context.

[78] Allen P. Ross, *Introducing Biblical Hebrew* (Grand Rapids: Baker, 2001), 196; GKC §152c notes that the *poʿel* stem "takes the place of the ordinary causative *piʿel* stem expressing an aim or endeavor to perform a hostile action."

establishing their own dominions. They were startled as they suddenly became aware the King of kings stood in their midst.

The earth itself shook violently in response to the Divine Warrior's arrival. Two parallel lines capture the reactions of the mountains and hills, which were "shattered" (Hb. *pāṣaṣ*)[79] and "sunk down" (Hb. *šāḥaḥ*; lit. "to bow in submission").[80] The verb translated "sink down" usually describes humans who bow down in humility or are brought low in subjugation. The two adjectives—"age-old" (Hb. *ʿad*; "everlasting") and "ancient" (Hb. *ʿôlām*; lit. "eternal, forever")—underscore the antiquity of the topographical features. These descriptors frequently appear as synonyms describing God, his reign, his attributes, and his praises, which extend beyond time.[81] Habakkuk 3:3 already mentioned two mountain peaks, Teman and Mount Paran, but perhaps the entire mountain chains situated east and west of the Jordan Rift are in view in 3:6. Centuries before Habakkuk, the patriarchs hiked the ridge routes forming the backbone of the Israelite homeland. Countless caravans and armies wound their way along the International Coastal Highway beneath the shadows of the Western Mountains (1,500 to 4,000 feet elevation) west of the Jordan Valley.[82] In the presence of the Divine Warrior, these seemingly eternal mountains crumbled into dust, and the foothills bowed low at his feet. Other Hebrew poets adopted similar ancient Near Eastern imagery to capture the response of mountains in theophanies: they quaked and trembled; they melted like wax in the presence of their Creator (Ps 97:5; Mic 1:4; Nah 1:5).

The Hb. adjective *ʿôlām* (Eng. "forever, ancient") describes both the hills and the Lord's pathways. The longevity of the hills evaporates in view of God's eternal nature. Psalm 90:2 puts the comparison in perspective: "Before the mountains were born, / before you gave birth to the earth and the world, / from eternity to eternity, you are God." Because the Lord is eternal, his ways are far more ancient than the mountains and hills on which he stood.

---

[79] The CSB reads "breaks apart." Biblical Hebrew poetry often uses "fancy" forms. The *hithpoʿel* form of the root "*pṣṣ*" occurs only once and functions to show intensity; other uses of the word occur in rare minor stem forms. See *HALOT*, 954.

[80] *HALOT*, 1458.

[81] *HALOT*, 786; 798.

[82] Likewise, the King's Highway skirted the edges of the mountains that rose (up to 5,000 feet in Edom) from the Eastern Plateau in the Transjordan.

The word translated as "pathways" (Hb. *hălīkâ*) derives from the Hb. verb *hālak*, meaning "to go" or "walk." In Nah 2:5, the noun describes the military "advance" of the Assyrians. Psalm 68, which also celebrates the arrival of the Divine Warrior, describes the "procession" of the King as he enters the sanctuary (Ps 68:24 [2x]). Both passages shed light on the context of Hab 3:6. God is the Divine Warrior who terrifies the wicked and delivers the righteous, but he is also the King who intends to dwell in the midst of his people in his global sanctuary. A related form of this verb (Hb. *mithallek*) appears in Gen 3:8, describing God's custom of "walking back and forth" with Adam and Eve in Eden.[83] Similar related forms occur in tabernacle settings as well (Lev 26:12; Deut 23:14; 2 Sam 7:6–7). Not only does the Divine Warrior march across the earth to establish his dominion; he does so to reclaim the whole earth as his rightful sanctuary (cf. Hab 2:14; 3:3). Habakkuk 3 contributes to the concept of a "pedestrian" God who walks ancient pathways amid his people. Other OT passages speak of ancient paths, understanding the term figuratively to describe behavior. The Lord directed his people to seek the "ancient" or eternal paths (Hb. *ʿôlām nətîbôt*), those that are "good" and provide "rest" (Jer 6:16). Tragically, God's people had veered off these ancient trails in their pursuit of idols (Jer 18:15). The wicked had their own well-worn paths (Hb. *ʾorah ʿôlām*)[84] that led to destruction (Job 22:15).[85] As Habakkuk pointed out, the Lord's pathways are eternal (Hab 3:6) and he himself is "from eternity" (1:12). Isaiah 40:3–5 anticipates the leveling of mountains and hills to "make a straight highway for our God in the desert," and all humanity will see "the glory of the LORD" appear along this path as he comes to rescue and redeem his people.[86]

3.3.3 The Inhabitants of the Nations Tremble (3:7)

> [7] *I see the tents of Cushan in distress;*
> *the tent curtains of the land of Midian tremble.*

---

[83] *IBHS* §26.1.2b notes that the *hithpael* stem indicates iterative (repeated) action.

[84] These three synonyms can all be translated as "path(s)": *hălīkâ*, *nətîbôt*, and *ʾorah*.

[85] The *BHS* apparatus suggests that the last line of 3:6—"His pathways are ancient"—may be a gloss.

[86] All four Gospels record John the Baptist's use of this Isaiah passage to refer to the repentance required in anticipation of the coming of Christ and his kingdom (see Matt 3:3; Mark 1:3; Luke 3:4; John 1:23).

3:7 An inclusio closes this section of the third panel with a pair of proper names paralleling the mountains mentioned by name in v. 3. "Cushan" and "Midian" may refer to either geographical locations or ethnic groupings. The OT makes several references to Midian elsewhere, beginning with the name of one of Abraham's sons (through Keturah), who settled in "the East" (Gen 25:1–6). By Moses's day, the homeland of the Midianites was located east of the Gulf of Aqaba, but their nomadic wanderings took them far afield. Although Moses married a Midianite, the group's treachery turned them into enemies of the Israelites.[87] The sole biblical reference to Cushan in Hab 3:7 seems to indicate a similarly nomadic people located in roughly the same region. Cushan may even be another name for the Midianites or one of its subgroups.[88]

"Tents" and "curtains" refer to the dwelling places of these nomadic peoples and, by extension, their residents.[89] These words are examples of synecdoche, where the part (tents and tent curtains) stands for the whole (the nation). Outside of the references to the tabernacle, "tents" and "curtains" appear as synonyms in parallel lines of poetry. Isaiah 54:2, for example, uses the pair to illustrate Israel's restoration: "Enlarge the site of your tent, / and let your tent curtains be stretched out." In Jeremiah, their imagery depicts destruction: "Disaster after disaster is reported / because the whole land is destroyed. / Suddenly my tents are destroyed, / my tent curtains, in a moment" (4:20; cf. 10:20; 49:29). Habakkuk 3:7 also takes place in a judgment setting. The tents are "in distress"—affliction resulting from their iniquity. The curtains "tremble" (Hb. *rāgaz*) in fear of the coming judgment. Not only were the tents trembling; the residents behind the tent flaps

---

[87] Exod 2:21; Num 25:16–18; Judg 6:2–3.

[88] David W. Baker, "Cushan," *ABD* 1:1220. Genesis 2:13 notes that the Gihon River flowed through "the entire land of Cush," south of Egypt. The Table of Nations in Gen 10 records that Cush was Ham's oldest son, whose kingdom included Babylon and Assyria (Gen 10:6–12). Baker, p. 1219, suggests that Cush may thus be the ancestor of either the Kassites, "who ruled Babylon until the 12th century B.C. . . . or of the *Kash*, who conquered Babylon in the 18th century B.C." Both locations seem an unlikely match for Cushan. Judges 3:8–10 narrates the first of several cycles of oppression by foreign nations and deliverance by judges. In this instance, the oppressor is King Cushan-rishathaim of Aram (*nahărayim*). Scholarly attempts to unearth links to Edom within this title fall short, so the king and his location remain obscure. See Baker, *ABD* 1:1220. Any connection to Cushan in Hab 3:7 is simply speculative.

[89] According to Anthony Tomasino, "אֹהֶל," *NIDOTTE* 1:297, the connection between tent and tent dweller is so close that the two words are virtual synonyms.

were terror stricken as well. If even mountains and hills quake before
the coming of the Lord, how much more so do humans?

The Divine Warrior in this portion of the third panel (III:B′, 3:3–7)
offers a clear contrast to the Babylonian army in the first panel (I:B,
1:6–11).

Parallelism in the Side Panels I:B and III:B′		
	I: B (1:5–11)	**III: B′ (3:3–7)**
Setting	"earth's open spaces"	"the heavens, and the earth"
Actors	The Babylonian soldiers	The Divine Warrior
Attendants	Horses—like wild animals	Plague and pestilence
Actions	They "come from distant lands."	ʾĔlôâ comes from southern mountains.
	They march across the earth.	He stands and shakes the earth.
	Look at the nations; be astounded.	He looks and startles the nations.
	They build siege ramps.	Age-old mountains crumble; hills sink.
	They sweep by like the wind and pass.	His pathways are ancient.
	Their strength is their god (ʾĕlôâ).	His power is hidden in his hand.
	They are guilty.	He is the Holy One.
Complaint	All of them come to do violence, to seize territories not their own.	
Shift		"His splendor covers the heavens, and the earth is full of his praise."

The Babylonians marched from the north, intent on seizing the
dwelling places of other nations (1:6). The Lord strode from the south
to reclaim land rightfully belonging to him, causing the earth and
dwelling places alike to tremble before him (3:6–7). The soldiers who
mocked earthly kings (1:10) would face the wrath of the divine King
who ruled the world (3:3). The marauding army's reliance on their
own strength as god (ʾĕlôâ) (1:11) would melt away before the God
(ʾĕlôâ) whose praises fill the earth (3:3). No human army could match
the one who comes in brilliant splendor with a fistful of lightning bolts
(3:4). The Babylonians' horses resembled swift leopards, fierce wolves,
and swooping eagles (1:8). Charging from distant lands, their cavalry
swept through like the wind (1:11). These intimidating forces must
have evoked dread in the nations who cowered before them. But the

power of warhorses paled in comparison to the supernatural power of the Divine Warrior. Mighty warriors bent on violence (1:9) would be felled by plague and pestilence—invisible and indefensible foes (3:5). Steely faces set with determination (1:9) would be startled with a mere glance (3:6). The Babylonian army marched through open spaces to heap up siege ramps from the dust (1:6, 10). In contrast, the Lord simply stood, and the mountains and hills that belonged to him bowed low, opening the way before him (3:6). Human warriors might pass through "like the wind" (1:11), but the pathways of the Divine Warrior are eternal (3:6).

The supernatural tactics described in 3:3–7 expose the frailty and weaknesses of any human army opposing the Lord. It is a comfort to realize no foe can compare to God. The imagery of theophany is sobering, engendering two kinds of responses. The announcement of God's arrival can sound an alarm that strikes terror in the heart of the evildoer, or it can evoke a grateful whispered prayer: "Thank God!" The difference is based on the spiritual condition of the hearer.

3.4   THE DIVINE WARRIOR FIGHTS (3:8–15)

The second part of the theophanic description depicts the Divine Warrior as ruler of the waters, sea, and sky. This section of the third panel (III:C′, Hab 3:8–15) contrasts the parallel section of the first panel (I:C, Hab 1:12–17). Both of these sections begin with a series of questions the prophet posed to the Lord.

3.4.1   The Lord Rides Victorious over the Sea (3:8)

> ⁸ *Are you angry at the rivers, Lord?*
> *Is your wrath against the rivers?*
> *Or is your fury against the sea*
> *when you ride on your horses,*
> *your victorious chariot?*

3:8 The rhetorical questions in 3:8 counter the complaints Habakkuk raised in 1:13. In the first panel, Habakkuk questioned the Lord's toleration of the treacherous and his silence while the wicked swallowed up the righteous (v. 13). This parallel section in chap. 3 contains three questions asking whether the Divine Warrior's anger was directed at the waters. All three rhetorical questions presume a negative answer. The Lord is not angry at the rivers; the obvious object of his wrath is the wicked.[90] The poem demonstrates emphatically that in his time God will bring about justice and deliverance.

Verse 8 uses three words to describe the Lord's anger. The first, a Hb. verb (*ḥārâ*), denotes intensive anger meaning "to burn"; it refers both to humans (Gen 4:6) and to God (Exod 4:14). When combined with the Hb. noun *'ap* ("nose, wrath, anger"), it means "to be kindled."[91] The verb can also appear alone as it does here.[92] The second Hb. term *'ap*—translated "wrath"—describes human anger but more frequently characterizes divine anger.[93] By extension, the same noun also applies to the emotion of anger—somewhat like the modern emoticon of a face where puffs of smoke fume from the nose. Although the OT often uses this word to describe human anger, it refers more frequently to divine anger. The third term, (Hb. *'ebrâ*) translated "rage," denotes "outbursts of anger."[94] Old Testament occurrences of the word refer to the fury of individuals (Gen 49:7) and nations (Isa 14:6). More often, the term characterizes the Lord's anger (Ps 90:11) and the day of his wrath (Isa 13:9; Zeph 1:18). Ezekiel repeatedly connects it to "the fire of [God's] fury" (Ezek 21:31; 22:21, 31). Habakkuk 3:8 exhibits an unusual structure: a series of three parallel lines followed by a fourth line elaborating on the first three. The triplet builds to a crescendo to emphasize the depth of God's wrath against all that is evil. He will not let it go on unpunished forever.

We find it difficult to extricate anger from sin (see Eph 4:26). As James admonished his readers, "Everyone should be quick to listen, slow to speak, and slow to anger, for human anger does not accomplish God's righteousness" (Jas 1:19–20). His use of the phrase "slow to anger" alludes to the Lord's description of himself in Exod

---

[90] Aron Pinker, "Problems and Solutions of Habakkuk 3:8," *JBQ* 31/1 (2003): 7, suggests that *neharim* ("rivers") could be read as *neharayim* ("two rivers"), "a code-name for Babylon, which was located between the two rivers Tigris and Euphrates." Similarly, *yam* ("sea") could be a reference to the Euphrates delta region referenced in Jer 51:36, 42.

[91] *HALOT*, 351. See Gen 44:18, Exod 4:14.

[92] Similar metaphors occur in English, influenced by the universal physiological effects of anger. Thermal infrared imaging reveals that the emotion of anger triggers an increase in body temperature that emanates from an accelerated heart rate in the chest and moves upward to flushed cheeks and outward to sweaty palms and fingertips. English allows for both as well: "His anger burned white-hot" or "He was fired up!"

[93] *HALOT*, 77.

[94] *HALOT*, 782.

34:6–7. God's character is weighted toward love, grace, and compassion. However, though he is "slow to anger," "he will not leave the guilty unpunished." Paul addresses the human argument directly: "Is God unrighteous to inflict wrath? Absolutely not! Otherwise, how will God judge the world?" (Rom 3:5–6). Paul's defense of God's character lays any blame at the feet of those who do evil:

> [D]o you despise the riches of his kindness, restraint, and patience, not recognizing that God's kindness is intended to lead you to repentance? Because of your hardened and unrepentant heart you are storing up wrath for yourself in the day of wrath, when God's righteous judgment is revealed. (Rom 2:4–5)

Furthermore, Paul points out the depth of God's sacrificial love: Through Christ's blood God declares believers righteous, saving them from his wrath (Rom 5:8–9). In contrast to human anger, God's wrath is purposeful and controlled. His perfect righteousness demands the proper administration of justice. As Zephaniah observes, "The righteous LORD . . . does no wrong. / He applies his justice morning by morning; / he does not fail" (Zeph 3:5). Although this prophet records a terrifying description of the Lord's wrath (Zeph 1:14–18), the book also describes its glorious outcome:

> Be glad and celebrate with all your heart,
> Daughter Jerusalem!
> The LORD has removed your punishment;
> he has turned back your enemy.
> The King of Israel, the LORD, is among you;
> you need no longer fear harm. . . .
> The LORD your God is among you,
> a warrior who saves.
> He will rejoice over you with gladness. (Zeph 3:14–17)

The purpose of God's wrath is to eliminate evil. Christians need not be embarrassed by it or try to explain it away. We need to recognize that there is a time for righteous anger and to rejoice that God always does what is right. When justice finally prevails, it is by no means a tragedy but rather a victory.

The three references to bodies of water in Hab 3:8 recall other OT passages where God displayed his power in settings involving water. Foremost among them is the miraculous deliverance of the exodus, where the Red Sea parted for the Israelites but drowned the Egyptian pharaoh and his army. Exodus 15 celebrates this victory of the Divine Warrior, who directed his anger toward his wicked adversaries:

> You unleashed your burning wrath;
> it consumed them like stubble.
> The water heaped up at the blast from your nostrils;
> the currents stood firm like a dam. . . .
> The enemy said:
> "I will pursue, I will overtake . . .
> my hand will destroy them."
> But you blew with your breath,
> and the sea covered them.
> They sank like lead
> in the mighty waters. (Exod 15:7–10)

Later the Lord performed a similar miracle when the Jordan River parted before the Israelites as they crossed into the promised land. Although the book of Joshua does not frame the Jordan crossing in terms of the Divine Warrior's anger, the presence of the commander of the Lord's army before the battle of Jericho clearly indicates the conquest belonged to him (Josh 5:13–15). Joshua 4:23–24 spells out the purpose of the river crossing: "[S]o that all the peoples of the earth [might] know that the LORD's hand is strong." In the period of the judges, the Divine Warrior demonstrated his sovereignty over the waters as he marshalled a rainstorm, and the Kishon River swept away the wicked Canaanite forces (Judg 5:4, 21). Deborah's song celebrated these "righteous acts of the LORD" (Judg 5:11). Still other OT passages recount theophanic appearances with similar water imagery as well (e.g., Pss 18:15; 77:16–20; Nah 1:4). God did not rage at deified rivers or sea; instead, he used the waters to accomplish his sovereign purposes.

Since the discovery of Old-Canaanite literature from Ugarit in 1931, scholars suggested the bodies of water in Hab 3:8 represent pagan deities in Canaanite mythology.[95] The JPS 1988 translation of

---

[95] Albright, "The Psalm of Habakkuk," 2, contends that U. Cassuto "showed convincingly that Habakkuk iii. contains reminiscences of the conflict between Yahweh and the primordial." Albright, *Yahweh and the Gods of Canaan*, 95, mentions a late Babylonian tablet that narrates the story of a deity who took his own sister, River, as his wife before killing his father (Lahar) and mother (Nether) Sea. However, he labels W. A. Irwin's hypothesis of a Babylonian influence

Hab 3:8, for example, reflects this line of thinking. In place of the JPS 1917 version "rivers" (Hb. *nəhārîm*) and "sea" (Hb. *yām*), the 1988 version transliterates these Hb. words, treating them as proper nouns that allude to ancient Near Eastern mythologies: "Are You wroth, O LORD, with Neharim? / Is Your anger against Neharim, / Your rage against Yam?" The Canaanite pantheon conflated these two in a cosmogonic myth, where Baal destroyed a monster of chaos called "(his) Majesty, the Sea" and "Judge River."[96] Baal was a storm god, and his consort, Asherah, was known in Ugaritic as "The Lady Who Treads on the Sea (Dragon)."[97] Chisholm lists three possibilities for parallels between the Lord's "mighty deeds" recorded in Israel's early literary history and "the mythological description of Baal's exploits": (1) the parallels are evidence of "a demythologizing phase in Israel's religious evolution"; (2) they demonstrate either "literary borrowing" or "a common Semitic literary milieu"; or (3) they reveal that OT writers "utilized the mythological motifs for polemical purposes."[98] Chisholm believes it is the latter: The OT record of the Lord's exploits in "Baal-like" terms serve as "proof of Yahweh's incomparability and kingship . . . and validated His right to demand Israel's exclusive loyalty and worship."[99] By Habakkuk's day, any supposed parallel imagery in chap. 3 may also simply stem from literary metaphors that describe the normal military practices of human kings in the ancient Near East.[100]

The last two lines of v. 8 present the Lord riding a horse-drawn "chariot"—presumably over the surface of the waters. Since the same image recurs in v. 15, these two verses form an inclusio bracketing this second half of the theophany. The first chariots mentioned in the OT belonged to Pharaoh (Exod 15:4), followed by the Canaanites' (Josh 11:6). The vast majority of OT occurrences refer to chariots belonging

---

in Habakkuk 3 "remote" and "wholly unsuccessful" (Albright, "The Psalm of Habakkuk," 3). See William A. Irwin, "The Mythological Background of Habakkuk 3." *JNES* 15.1 (1956): 47–50.

[96] Albright, *Yahweh and the Gods of Canaan*, 125.

[97] Albright, *Yahweh and the Gods of Canaan*, 121. Albright considers the suggestion plausible "that Yam was the sea-dragon rather than the literal sea."

[98] Robert B. Chisholm Jr., "The Polemic against Baalism in Israel's Early History and Literature," *BSac* 150 (July-September 1994), 268. See also A. H. W. Curtis, "The 'Subjugation of the Waters' Motif in the Psalms: Imagery or Polemic?" *JSS* 23 (1978): 245–56.

[99] Chisholm, "The Polemic against Baalism in Israel's Early History and Literature," 276.

[100] See David Toshio Tsumura, "Ugaritic Poetry and Habakkuk 3," *TynBul* 40 (1988): 33. Andersen, *Habakkuk*, 351, provides a brief outline of the debate and concludes, "Habakkuk 3 does not correspond closely to any other text that we now have. Its nearest congeners are within the Hebrew Bible itself."

to Israel. As Isa 2:7b observes, "[T]heir land is full of horses, / and there is no limit to their chariots." Tragically, the nation often relied on the strength of these numbers rather than on their God (Ps 20:7). God's figurative chariots were innumerable: "tens of thousands, / thousands and thousands" (Ps 68:17). Various passages describe God as riding on the heavens, the clouds, and cherubim.[101] When visible, his mounts and vehicles glowed with fire (2 Kgs 2:11; 6:17). Although this imagery may be poetic, it serves to emphasize the omnipotence and omnipresence of the Lord of Hosts and the spiritual forces he commands.

The last line of Hab 3:8 is a construct phrase, where the Hb. word *yəšûʿâ* (Eng. "salvation" or "victory") indicates what kind of "chariot" the Lord rides.[102] The Hb. root (*yāšaʿ* "to save") primarily refers to the Lord's action on behalf of his people.[103] Against a similar setting of God's deliverance at the Red Sea, Israel sang, "The LORD is my strength and my song; / he has become my salvation" (Exod 15:2). Across various OT literary genres, the repetitious use of this root underscores "a key biblical theme: only Yahweh, not human or military help, can bring Israel victory."[104] No one else can secure salvation, and no one can stand against him. The Lord figuratively rides in a chariot not only to defeat the wicked but also to deliver his people.

3.4.2   He Demonstrates His Rule over the Waters (3:9–10)

⁹ *You took the sheath from your bow;*
  the arrows are ready to be used with an oath. Selah
  You split the earth with rivers.
¹⁰ *The mountains see you and shudder;*
  a downpour of water sweeps by.
  The deep roars with its voice
  and lifts its waves high.

---

[101] See Deut 33:26; Pss 18:10; 68:4, 33; Isa 19:1. Canaanite mythological language and imagery depicting Baal as a "rider of the clouds" has been adapted without the theological significance to describe Yahweh.

[102] More English versions of Hab 3:8 translate *yəšûʿâ* as "salvation" (e.g., ESV, NASB, NKJV, KJV) than "victory" or "victorious" (CSB, RSV, NIV, NET). An astute reader may notice that "Yeshua" is an echo of the name "Jesus"—the Gk. form of the OT name "Joshua," which means "Yahweh saves," or "Savior." See Roy E. Hayden, "יְשׁוּעָה," *NIDOTTE* 2:553.

[103] *HALOT*, 448.

[104] Hayden, *NIDOTTE* 2:550, 553. See, for example, Pss 33:17; 37:39; 60:11; 144:10; 146:3; Isa 59:16; 63:5.

3:9 Once the Divine Warrior arrives, he engages the battle. Although the parallel section in the first panel (I:C, 1:12–17) does not mention the Babylonians' weaponry, it reports the implements with which they ruled over the sea—fishhooks and various kinds of nets. In contrast, this parallel section in the third panel (III:C′, 3:8–15) pictures the "weapons" of the Divine Warrior as bow and arrows.[105] Lamentations 2:4 declares "like an enemy" the Lord "strung his bow," with his arrows aimed at Israel. These traditional weapons of the ancient Near East were deadly in their effectiveness. The composite bow appeared sometime between the third and second millennium BC. It consisted of five pieces of wood—central grip, two arms, and two tips—bonded together and steamed into a curve.[106] Such a valuable weapon would normally be kept in a sheath to preserve it from the elements. Since arrows weighed roughly an ounce, an archer could carry up to fifty in a quiver. The size of the composite bow made it the perfect weapon for use from the platform of a chariot, a combination striking terror in the heart of many an army.[107] When the charioteer was the Divine Warrior, the arrows not only found their target; they split the earth. The distinction between this mighty warrior and the arrogant Babylonians who presumed they ruled the sea is arresting (see Hab 1:14–17). The true ruler of the waters rode his chariot over the sea and unleashed his supernatural power.

The first two lines of 3:9 are obscure in Hebrew, as demonstrated by the various English translations. The first line indicates the "bareness" of the bow made it ready for action (lit. "you have laid your bow bare"). In four of the six occurrences of this Hb. word (ʿeryâ), it appears as a synonym to the word "nakedness" (e.g., Ezek 16:7).[108] Evidently, the weapon was normally sheathed—a detail correlating to the Lord's attribute of being "slow to anger" (Exod 34:6). God's

---

[105] In Gen 9:13 the Lord explains that the rainbow is a sign of his covenant: "I have placed my bow in the clouds, and it will be a sign of the covenant between me and the earth." Not only does the rainbow resemble the shape of a weapon worthy of the Divine Warrior, but it also appears to release lightning bolts like arrows.

[106] Stringing a composite bow required great strength to bend it in the opposite direction of the relaxed curve. That force, called "weight," is measured in "pounds." Whereas a simple bow took only a few pounds to string, a composite bow required a weight of perhaps 150 pounds. The release of the string's tension would therefore propel an arrow a great distance—upwards of three hundred yards—with great accuracy.

[107] Keegan, *A History of Warfare*, 162–63, and Yadin, *The Art of Warfare in Biblical Lands*, 2–9.

[108] *HALOT*, 883.

patience does not equal passivity; at the appointed time, the Lord will remove the bow from its cover to administer justice with authority.

The Hebrew in the second line of Hab 3:9 is difficult. The word *maṭṭôt* suggests some type of shaft like a rod, spear, or staff—and by extension "tribe."[109] Here, the immediate context of the word "bow" suggests "arrows."[110] These promised (from Hb. *šābaʿ* "to promise or swear")[111] "arrows" or "staffs," God "commands" or "orders."[112] Other English versions supply various readings: "Oaths were sworn over *Your* arrows" (NKJV); "The rods of chastisement were sworn" (NASB 1995); "[You] calling for many arrows" (ESV); "[Y]ou commission your arrows" (NET); "[Y]our arrows targeted by command" (ISV). The basic understanding is that when the Divine Warrior releases his arrows, they follow his commands. They find their marks without fail. When the Lord speaks, it is as if the act is already accomplished. Elsewhere the Lord declares, "I will make my arrows drunk with blood" (Deut 32:42). No one can escape his judgment. This sobering thought calls for meditation: *Selah.*[113]

The third line suggests the strength of the Lord's arrows of judgment cleaved the earth, creating new courses for rivers. Habakkuk 3:11 links the Lord's arrows to light. Other instances of theophany compare his arrows to lightning bolts.[114] If the Divine Warrior's "arrows" in Hab 3:9 were indeed bolts of lightning, the rain that followed flowed through newly carved channels. The imagery calls to

---

[109] In the OT *maṭṭeh* is typically translated as "tribe." The LXX translates the word in Hab 3:9 as "scepter." See David M. Fouts, "מַטֶּה," *NIDOTTE* 2:917–18.

[110] *HALOT*, 573. The ASV, however, interprets the word as "tribes": "[T]he oaths to the tribes were a sure word."

[111] *HALOT*, 1399–1400. A literal rendering would be "promises of arrows/staffs he commands." A second Hb. root *šābaʿ* can denote the number "seven." In Canaanite and Ugaritic mythology, Baal typically had seven arrows, or "bolts of lightning." See John Day, "Echoes of Baal's Seven Thunders and Lightnings in Psalm XXIX and Habakkuk III 9 and the Identity of the Seraphim in Isaiah VI," *VT* 29 (1979): 143–51. Contrary to Day, Avishur, *Studies in Hebrew and Ugaritic Psalms*, 128, calls the similarity between the seven lightning bolts in the Ugaritic text and the seven staffs in Hab 3:9 "remote."

[112] *HALOT*, 67.

[113] The presence of "*Selah*" in the middle of the verse has puzzled exegetes, leading some to suggest that v. 9 should conclude with the musical notation. Avishur, *Studies in Hebrew and Ugaritic Psalms*, 176–77, mentions various solutions—deleting the third colon entirely or transposing it to the following verse or elsewhere in the psalm—before concluding that the "musical pointer" provides "no basis for separating the third colon from the previous two cola."

[114] See Ps 18:14 // 2 Sam 22:15; Ps 144:6; Zech 9:14.

mind the wadis in Israel; these sometimes dry riverbeds can suddenly flood with water following a storm.

3:10 Verse 10 expresses the results of this theophanic manifestation.[115] The mountains saw God and "shuddered" (Hb. *ḥîl*).[116] This Hb. verb frequently describes the anguish or writhing of a woman in labor (Isa 13:8; 26:17) and serves as a metaphor describing the birth of these same mountains (Ps 90:2). It describes the trembling of the earth in response to a theophany (Ps 97:4) and the "whirling" of "a storm from the LORD," sent to "whirl about the heads of the wicked" (Jer 23:19). Jeremiah also records, "The earth quakes and *trembles* / because the LORD's intentions against Babylon stand: / to make the land of Babylon a desolation, without inhabitant" (51:29; emphasis added). Similarly, in Hab 3:10 the mountains writhed in response to the Divine Warrior's appearance in judgment directed against his foe, Babylon.[117] Other OT occurrences of "downpour" (Hb. *zerem*) confirm this was a drenching, threatening, torrential storm producing hail and flooding (e.g., Job 24:8; Isa 4:6; 28:2; 30:30).[118] The subsequent flash flood swept down the hillsides on its way to the sea, where it churned up whitecap waves. Habakkuk 3:10 describes the response of the deep (Hb. *təhôm*): "The deep roars with its voice / and lifts its waves [Hb. *yādē*; lit. 'hands'] high." Perhaps the phrase figuratively implies the deep lifts its hands (i.e., waves) in surrender (Jer 50:15) or prayer (Ps 28:2) before the God who created and controls the deep.[119] This description of the sound of the water and the crests of its waves is clearly anthropomorphic.

The mythologies of the ancient Near East understood creation in terms of a struggle between various monster gods of the great deep. The Mesopotamian myth *Enuma Elish*, for example, narrates the story

---

[115] J. H. Eaton, *Obadiah, Nahum, Habakkuk, Zephaniah*, 111, argued that the torrential thunderstorm reported in vv. 10–11 was preceded by sirocco winds from the southeastern desert, presumably inferred from vv. 3–7. Based on the poem's correspondence to annual climatic changes in Israel and the description of the "death in Nature," cataloged in v. 16, Eaton conjectured that Habakkuk's psalm was composed as a liturgy for an autumnal festival (p. 117). The scaffolding for Eaton's theory seems to have little grounding.

[116] *HALOT*, 310.

[117] Terence E. Fretheim, "חִיל," *NIDOTTE* 2:126, observes that the nominative forms of *ḥîl* and its synonyms for "birth pangs" are almost always used metaphorically in the OT and often describe the trembling and anguish that accompanies God's presence or judgment.

[118] *HALOT*, 281.

[119] *HALOT*, 387.

of two such battles.[120] Several OT texts appear to be aware of these ancient myths when they personify the ocean depths in narrating God's victories.[121] Some passages refer to the Lord's defeating the "monsters" of the deep (e.g., "Leviathan" in Isa 27:1[122]; "Rahab" in Isa 51:9–10; cf. Ps 74:13–14). Other passages identify these monsters as symbols of wicked nations like Egypt and her pharaoh (Isa 30:7; Ezek 29:3; 32:2). The four "huge beasts" that emerge from the sea in Dan 7:2–3 represent successive global powers. David Tsumura observes in Habakkuk 3 there is no mention of a "dragon" even though other OT passages used "fossilized terms like Leviathan, Rahab or Taninim, a 'dragon,' for describing metaphorically the evil power."[123] He cautions against reading too much into these verses which simply reflect ancient Near Eastern battle imagery. Idol worshipers in Habakkuk's day recognized faint echoes from their own mythic cosmologies, but the prophet excised any specific pagan names or details from his account. Still, the poetic context of these OT passages "allows for . . . playful allusion to the mythological theme for polemical purposes."[124] Longman and Reid make a strong case the biblical poets intentionally drew from ancient Near Eastern myths to describe the Divine Warrior's defeat of the spiritual powers of chaos.[125] They conclude that the OT personification of the sea and the deep intentionally deconstructs the false cosmologies of other religions and poetically depicts the ultimate victory

---

[120] In the first, Ea cunningly used a sleep incantation to immobilize and slay Apsu (the Deep or Abyss). In the second, Marduk defeated the primeval mother goddess Tiamat (the Ocean) in order to become the unrivaled king of the pantheon and the national god of Babylon. The poem explains that from the two halves of Tiamat's corpse, Marduk created the heavens and the earth. See Saggs, *The Babylonians*, 330–36. Saggs, p. 330, dates the final recension of the poem somewhere between the thirteenth century and 1100 BC.

[121] See Pss 18:14–15; 24:1–2; 29:10; 77:16–20; 114:3–7; Nah 1:4. However, as C. Westermann, "תהום," *TLOT* 3:1413, notes, nowhere in the OT does *təhôm* (Eng. "deep") signify a mythical figure like Tiamat.

[122] The poetic description of the Leviathan in Job 41 corresponds to an actual crocodile as a prime example of God's creative power.

[123] Tsumura, "Ugaritic Poetry and Habakkuk 3," 45.

[124] Longman and Reid, *God Is a Warrior*, 77. According to A. H. W. Curtis, "The 'Subjugation of the Waters' Motif in the Psalms; Imagery or Polemic?" *JSS* 23/2 (1978), 245–56, this polemic was necessary because of the long-lasting tension between Baalism and Yahwism. Curtis, p. 256, traces the origin of "the motif of the subjugation of the waters by Yahweh" to this tension, arguing that "even if later such language came to be imagery, its origins lie in the battle for the affections of the people between Yahweh and Baal."

[125] Longman and Reid, *God Is a Warrior*, 78.

of the Divine Warrior over all spiritual forces of evil, a motif they see in the NT as well.[126]

In contrast to pagan mythologies, all of the OT occurrences of the "deep" (Hb. *təhôm*) demonstrate God's complete authority over the waters from the beginning.[127] The Lord created the deep and warehouses it (Job 38:8–11; Ps 33:7). He uses it both to bless and to judge humanity (Deut 8:7, 15; Ezek 31:15). He rescues people through the deep and from it (Exod 15:5, 8; Jonah 2:5). God even commands the ocean deep and the sea "monsters" it contains to praise him (Ps 148:7). The Lord threatened to judge "the great deep" along with the earth, by consuming them both with fire (Amos 7:4). In short, "[t]he LORD does whatever he pleases / in heaven and on earth, / in the seas and all the depths" (Ps 135:6). He alone is the sovereign King over the entire cosmos. Not only does the Lord's rule extend over the ocean depths but also over the heavens and the earth.

3.4.3   He Reigns over the Heavens and the Earth (3:11–12)

> [11] *Sun and moon stand still in their lofty residence,*
>   *at the flash of your flying arrows,*
>   *at the brightness of your shining spear.*
> [12] *You march across the earth with indignation;*
>   *you trample down the nations in wrath.*

3:11   The focus of v. 11 includes the heavenly lights God created. The words "sun" and "moon" frequently appear together in the OT. God made them for his purposes and fixed their order to bless all peoples.[128] Tragically, their beauty and enduring qualities captivated the hearts of even the Israelites, who began to worship them as did their neighbors (Job 31:26–28; 2 Kgs 23:5). On a future day of the Lord, both sun and moon will grow dark (Joel 2:10, 31), and these seemingly eternal lights will be replaced by the Lord, the "everlasting

---

[126] Longman and Reid, *God Is a Warrior*, 114, point to Jesus's rebuke of the storm on the Sea of Galilee (Mark 4:35–41). In Revelation 13, the seven-headed beast that arises from the sea—a composite of the four beasts in Daniel—serves as a foil but is no match for the Divine Warrior (p. 188). Finally, the introduction to a new heavens and earth in Rev 21:1 reveals that in the new creation "the sea was no more" (p. 191).

[127] *HALOT*, 1691.

[128] See Pss 104:19; 136:7–9; Jer 31:35; Deut 4:19.

light" (Isa 60:19). God, who created sun and moon, thus has complete control over them. The Divine Warrior commands them, just as he did in the day of conquest when "the sun stood still / and the moon stopped / until the nation took vengeance on its enemies" (Josh 10:13).[129] Joshua 10:14 indicates that "[t]here has been no day like it before or since, when the LORD listened to a man, because the LORD fought for Israel." Although it was not at Habakkuk's request, once again the sun and moon would stand at attention while the Lord vanquished his enemies. In Joshua's day the Lord judged the wicked Canaanites, handing their land over to the Israelites. In Habakkuk's day, he would judge the wayward Israelites, handing them over to the Babylonians. It was only a matter of time before the Divine Warrior would confront the Babylonians, as well.

The phrase "lofty residence" (Hb. zəbul, "an elevated place") personifies these inanimate bodies of light that share God's heavenly abode.[130] Solomon used the same word to describe the "exalted" house he built for the Lord (1 Kgs 8:13). Later, after the Babylonians trampled this earthly sanctuary, the Israelites would pray to the Lord in his heavenly temple: "Look down from heaven and see / from your lofty home [Hb. zəbul]" (Isa 63:15).[131] They would beseech him: "If only you would tear the heavens open / and come down, / so that mountains would quake at your presence . . . / to make your name known to your enemies" (Isa 64:1–2). Habakkuk 3 shows the Divine Warrior doing that very thing, while sun and moon look on as obedient servants of the one true God.[132]

The elements of nature quake in the Lord's presence and also serve as his instruments. Verse 11 concludes with a metaphor comparing bolts of lightning to "arrows" and a "spear." Archaeology in the Levant yielded at least two dozen inscribed bronze arrowheads dating back to the eleventh century BC. The text on the largest of these—it

---

[129] This miracle, when the sun did not go down for almost a full day, recalls a similarly miraculous sign when the shadow on the stairs reversed direction ten steps to indicate the Lord had extended Hezekiah's life by fifteen years (see 2 Kgs 20:1–11).

[130] HALOT, 263.

[131] This "lofty residence" makes a mockery of the efforts of the Babylonian who sought "to place his [own] nest on high, / to escape the grasp of disaster" (Hab 2:9).

[132] The Lord repeatedly called on heaven and earth to serve as his "witnesses" (Deut 4:26; 30:19; 31:28; Ps 50:4); he stretched out the heavens and commands "everything in them" (Isa 45:12); he created the highest heavens and all the stars worship him (Neh 9:6).

is over five inches—reads "Arrowhead of Šēmīdaʿ, son of Yiššabaʿ."[133] Evidently, the archer wanted his victim to know who shot the arrow. [134] The lightning-bolt arsenal described in Hab 3:11 needed no such inscription, since these munitions—"your . . . arrows," "your . . . spear"—belonged to the Lord alone. Although the Hebrew text does mention lightning, it refers to the "light of the arrows" that, when released, "fly." Verse 11 describes the Lord's spear with two adjectives. The first adjective, "brightness" (Hb. *nōgah*), often appears in descriptions of the Lord's theophanic presence.[135] The second adjective, "shining" (Hb. *bəraq*), denotes the reflection of light. This "shining" light, often appearing in conjunction with clouds and thunder, is typically translated as "lightning" (Ps 18:14).[136] Although a few occurrences of the word describe natural lightning bolts, even these passages stipulate that God controls and directs them (Job 38:35; Ps 135:7). Often the lightning occurs in the context of theophany. The bolts may emanate from God's presence, demonstrating his power (Exod 19:16; Ezek 1:13). They also describe weapons that gleam in the hands of the Divine Warrior: a "shining spear" (Hab 3:11), "arrows" that flash back and forth (Ps 18:14), and a sword "polished to flash like lightning" (Ezek 21:10).

The purpose of these weapons is to execute judgment and bring deliverance. These poetic images communicate both the power and authority of God and his commitment to justice—whether the wicked were found among the nations or his own people. The concept of a gleaming, polished sword of judgment surfaces in a prophecy against the sinful Israelites. The Lord instructed Ezekiel to draw a fork in a road with signposts pointing the way to the land of the Ammonites and the way to fortified Jerusalem. Although the king of Babylon

---

[133] Frank Moore Cross, "An Inscribed Arrowhead of the Eleventh Century BCE in the Bible Lands Museum in Jerusalem" *Eretz-Israel: Archaeological, Historical and Geographical Studies* (1992): 21. Cross points out that one of the clans of Manasseh was Shemida (cf. Josh 17:2).

[134] Examples of Greek and Roman cast-lead sling bullets, dating from fourth to first century BC, display winged thunderbolts on one side and a spear on the other, along with the occasional inscription of a name or place. See Jess Porter, "Roman Sling Bullet," Object #1546, Joukowsky Institute for Archaeology Old Department Collection, Archaeology at Brown. Online: https://blogs.brown.edu/archaeology/2020/08/19/roman-sling-bullet, accessed October 1, 2023. Modern soldiers have continued this ancient tradition of inscribing weapons with messages. World War II airmen, for example, often scribbled greetings to Hitler on bombs. More recently, messages on missiles have expressed sympathies for terror victims or targeted perpetrators of terror.

[135] See the discussion of *nōgah* in Hab 3:4, which notes the "brilliance" of the Lord himself.

[136] William T. Koopmans, "בָּרָק," *NIDOTTE* 1:754–55.

would practice divination—by means of arrows—to decide which road to take, the Lord had already determined to direct him to attack Jerusalem (Ezek 21:15–23). This prophecy parallels God's startling announcement to Habakkuk in Hab 1:5–6. In time, however, God's sword of judgment would turn and target the Babylonians, and he would fight to deliver his people. When he did, the Babylonian soldiers would be no match for the God over all the forces of nature. While the sun and moon remained in their lofty residence, the Lord himself came down to earth. He does not stand aloof above the fray but rather descends and engages the battle against wickedness.

3:12   Verse 12 consists of two parallel lines depicting the Divine Warrior striding across the face of the earth. The words "earth" and "nations" convey the length of his stride as he covers great swaths of land. The verb "march" (Hb. ṣāʿad, "to stride solemnly") conveys the idea of purpose.[137] Half of the eight OT occurrences of this verb appear in the context of a physical manifestation of the Lord where, accompanied by thunderstorms or earthquakes, he "marches" across the desert (Judg 5:4; Ps 68:7) or to those carrying the ark of the covenant who "advanced" six steps toward Jerusalem, as David danced "before the LORD" (2 Sam 6:13–14). Other contextual uses imply steps toward certain doom or judgment (Job 18:14; Prov 7:8, 22–23; Jer 10:5, 15). Here, the imagery of Hab 3:12 depicts the Lord striding with purpose, intent on administering justice.

The Hb. verb dûš ("trample") in v. 12b can mean "to tread on" (Job 39:15) or "to thresh" (Deut 25:4).[138] These two actions are closely related since the threshing of grain requires separating grain from stalks. In the ancient world, oxen accomplished this by walking repeatedly over piles of harvested grain stalks. The invention of the threshing sledge made the process more efficient as oxen walked and pulled wooden boards embedded with sharp stones or bits of metal (1 Chr 21:20–23). Threshing imagery readily lends itself to the figurative description of destruction, and the OT uses the verb to describe both methods of threshing in the context of judgment.[139] Micah 4:13,

---

[137] *HALOT*, 1040.

[138] *HALOT*, 218.

[139] Though the following passages do not use the word *dûš*, they too use threshing imagery to describe the judgment of both the Israelites and Babylon. Hosea 13:3 describes Ephraim "like chaff blown from a threshing floor." Jeremiah 51:33 anticipates the demise of Babylon: "Daughter Babylon is like a threshing floor / at the time it is trampled. / In just a little while her harvest time will come." The watchman of Isa 21:7–10 likewise comforts the Israelites "crushed on the

for example, describes how the Lord would use Israel to judge the nations: "Rise and thresh, Daughter Zion, / for I will make . . .your hooves bronze / so you can crush many peoples." The metaphor in Isa 41:15 describes a similar charge to Israel: "See, I will make you into a sharp threshing board, / new, with many teeth. / You will thresh mountains and pulverize them / and make hills into chaff." Even when threshing is not in view, figurative usage of *dûš* may indicate judgment: "Moab will be trampled in his place / as straw is trampled in a dung pile" (Isa 25:10 [2x]). Although some English translations render the verb in Hab 3:12 as "thresh" (e.g., NIV, ESV, KJV), the context requires the figurative usage of the term translated "trample" (CSB, NASB, NKJV, NRSV, NET). Either way, the Divine Warrior marches across the land, intent on judging the nations.

These same images appear to merge in the NT description of final harvest at the end of time when the Lord separates the wicked from the righteous:

> [The] one like the Son of Man . . . seated on the cloud, swung his sickle over the earth, and the earth was harvested. . . . Then another angel who also had a sharp sickle came out of the temple in heaven. . . . So the angel swung his sickle at the earth and gathered the grapes from the vineyard of the earth, and he threw them into the great winepress of God's wrath. Then the press was trampled outside the city, and blood flowed out of the press up to the horses' bridles for about 180 miles. (Rev 14:14, 17, 19–20)

This graphic image of eschatological judgment shows both the harvest of God's people and the trampling of his enemies. Habakkuk's concern that the Lord would allow evil to go on unchecked forever was unfounded.

Two parallel synonyms in Hab 3:12 express the Lord's emotions behind his judgment. The first Hb. word is *zaʿam* ("cursed by an indignant God").[140] Other OT translations of this word—"wrath, anger, fury"—communicate the depth of this emotion (Ps 69:24; Isa 30:27; Jer 10:10; Lam 2:6). The adjective commonly describes the Lord's

---

threshing floor" with this news: "Babylon has fallen, has fallen. / All the images of her gods / have been shattered on the ground."

[140] *HALOT*, 276.

indignation, rather than man's.[141] The second Hb. term, *'ap* (Eng. "wrath" or "anger"), also occurs in Hab 3:8, and refers primarily to divine anger rather than human anger.[142] The Lord is slow to anger, but when his fury is finally aroused, he will pour out well-deserved wrath on all who oppose him.

3.4.4 He Saves His Own and Defeats the Leader of the Wicked (3:13–15)

[13] You come out to save your people,
to save your anointed.
You crush the leader of the house of the wicked
and strip him from foot to neck. Selah
[14] You pierce his head
with his own spears;
his warriors storm out to scatter us,
gloating as if ready to secretly devour the weak.
[15] You tread the sea with your horses,
stirring up the vast water.

3:13 Verse 13 explains the dual purpose behind the imminent arrival of the Divine Warrior who comes, lit. "goes forth." He comes for the salvation of his people and for the salvation of his anointed. The Hb. nominative *yēša'* (Eng. "salvation" or "deliverance")[143] echoes Habakkuk's first cry of lament in 1:2: "How long, Lᴏʀᴅ, must I . . . cry out to you about violence / and you do not save?" The prophet mistakenly thought the Lord was unwilling or unable to step in and rescue his people. The Lord corrected his error in chap. 3 where the same root occurs four times: (1) as a description of the Lord's "chariot of salvation" (ESV) in v. 8; (2) as a statement of purpose for his coming "or salvation" in v. 13 [2x]; and (3) as a divine title, "the God of my salvation," in v. 18.

In the OT text the subject of the verb "to save" is almost always the Lord, and the object, his people.[144] Sometimes God himself inter-

[141] The one exception is Hos 7:16, but even there Ephraim stands under the Lord's judgment: "Their leaders will fall by the sword / because of their *insolent* tongue" (emphasis added).
[142] See the fuller discussion of God's anger under Hab 3:8.
[143] *HALOT*, 449.
[144] Andrew E. Hill, "יָשַׁע," *NIDOTTE* 2:548.

vened to deliver the Israelites, as he did at the Red Sea (Exod 14:13, 30). This definitive act of salvation forged disheartened slaves into a nation.[145] In other instances, God empowered an agent to rescue his people, as he did during the period of the judges and the kings (Judg 2:16, 18; 1 Sam 9:16). The Lord anointed David in particular to save, shepherd, and rule his people (2 Sam 3:18; 5:2; 7:7–8). Tragically, subsequent kings and the Israelites themselves often failed to behave as the people of God. The Lord warned he would consider them "not [his] people" and send them into exile, a threat that would come to pass in Habakkuk's day (Hos 1:9; Isa 5:13). The language of Habakkuk's psalm recalls God's monumental acts of salvation in the past. In light of the Lord's pronouncement in Hab 1:5–6, the prophet might have wondered if God would ever come to save his people again, or whether after the Babylonian rampage, would God even have a people? The wording of Hab 3:13: "You come out to save your people," provided relief. A remnant of God's people would remain, and God himself would step in to deliver them.

The Divine Warrior also comes to save his "anointed" (Hb. *māšîaḥ*, "the anointed one").[146] In the OT the "anointed" may refer to patriarchs (1 Chr 16:22 // Ps 105:15), priests (Lev 4:3, 5, 16; 6:22), a prophet (1 Kgs 19:16), or even the Persian king, Cyrus, tapped by God to deliver his people (Isa 45:1). Primarily, the word refers to the anointed kings of Israel/Judah. References to kings include a handful mentioning the increasing power or everlasting dynasty of David, a veiled allusion to a Messiah to come.[147] Three references more clearly point to the "Anointed One," as a title for the Messiah (Ps 2:2; Dan 9:25, 26).

Against this backdrop, who is the "anointed" in Hab 3:13? If the psalm follows the pattern of other ancient hymns, the verse may refer to God's parallel deliverance of his anointed king and his people (cf. Ps 28:8). Although Habakkuk could not have known that the Babylonians would carry off Zedekiah in chains—he was the last of Judah's anointed kings to sit on an earthly throne (Lam 4:20)—it was already apparent that the latest kings proved an abysmal failure. The Lord's deliverance of his "anointed" in Hab 3:13 is best understood as his

---

[145] Exodus 3:7 marks the first time the Lord called the Israelites "my people"—a phrase that reverberates throughout the book of Exodus.

[146] *HALOT*, 645.

[147] See 1 Sam 2:10, 35; 2 Sam 22:51; Pss 18:50; 132:17.

preservation of the Davidic lineage, which would eventually lead to the ideal king, the Messiah in the NT. The Latin Vulgate interprets v. 13 through a Christological lens, rendering the phrase "for salvation of your anointed" as *in salutem cum christo tuo* (Eng. "for salvation *with* your Christ"; emphasis added).[148] Jerome, who understood Christ as the fulfillment of v. 13, avoided referencing the "salvation of Christ."[149] Ironically, when the Messiah came, he did not seek to preserve his own life but willingly laid it down "as a ransom for many" (Mark 10:45). The Father then "saved" his anointed one by delivering him from the jaws of death in the resurrection. As "Moses and all the Prophets" had foretold, the Messiah had to endure suffering before being brought to glory (Luke 24:26–27).

The biblical understanding of salvation deepens across the canon. The OT concept of "salvation" implies deliverance from external dangers, like human enemies or natural disasters (e.g., famine or disease).[150] These mighty acts of God's deliverance in the OT build toward the NT understanding of "the final act of salvation" wrought by Jesus Christ, resulting in "forgiveness of sin, deliverance from its power and defeat of Satan."[151] This biblical shift from physical salvation to spiritual salvation follows a trajectory that ends in the book of Revelation with God's ultimate victory over Satan and all evil. There is a sense of eschatological finality in the victory described in Hab 3:13. The Divine Warrior accomplishes the lasting salvation of his people by destroying "the leader of the house of the wicked."

Who is this enemy described in v. 13? If the psalm is simply a reprise of an ancient hymn, the enemy is likely Pharaoh and his soldiers, who met their demise on the banks of the Red Sea. The immediate context of Habakkuk suggests alternatively the king of Babylon and his troops are in view. Although the Lord would not deliver Judah and her citizens from the impending attack by the Babylonians, the psalm provided comfort since judgment would come to these oppressors as well. The annals of history indicate the Babylonian demise was

---

[148] This translation renders the Hb. *ʾet* not as a direct object marker but as the preposition "with." See Hiebert, *God of My Victory*, 148. A few other translations follow suit: "with thy Christ" (Douay-Rheims); "with thine anointed" (KJV); "with Your Anointed" (NKJV). The titles "Christ" (Gk.) and "Messiah" (Hb.) both mean "Anointed One."

[149] Hiebert, *God of My Victory*, 148.

[150] John E. Hartley, "יָשַׁע," *TWOT* 1:415.

[151] Hartley, *TWOT* 1:414.

not the decisive battle described in the psalm.[152] That reality lends weight to the understanding the orientation of Habakkuk's psalm may be future, looking forward to a distant day when a singularly epic battle will usher in the eschaton. Unlike similar references where the Lord targets specific kings and countries,[153] the description in Hab 3:13 seems intentionally vague. The enemy's label is not "king" but "leader, or literally, "head" (Hb. rōʾš).[154] Since this word can mean "head" or "leader," both possibilities appear in various English translations. There is no mention of a specific geographic entity but rather the more generic "house of the wicked." Perhaps it is best to recognize all three orientations are in play. The psalm recalls God's deliverance of his people from wicked rulers in the past, offers reassurance that he will judge the wicked and their rulers in every age, and fortifies an enduring hope that one day the Divine Warrior will destroy Satan—the ultimate leader of the house of wickedness.

The word "house" (Hb. bāyit) has several related meanings in the OT. The noun may refer to the dwelling place of an individual or collectively, to an entire household or clan (Josh 24:15). The word also designates the temple of the Lord or the dynasty of a king (2 Sam 7:5, 11). Similarly, the phrase "house of the wicked" may refer to a proverbial individual or a collective group, just like the dwelling place of the righteous (Prov 3:33; 14:11). As Habakkuk learned from experience, residence in these "houses" was not determined by national citizenship or ethnic heritage but rather by the condition of the individual heart. The members of the household of wickedness may be geographically removed from one another; they may speak different languages; they may even attack one another. Yet they all share the same familial characteristics as the head of the household. They will also share the same fate: "The Righteous One considers the house of the wicked; / he brings the wicked to ruin" (Prov 21:12; cf. Isa 31:2). Habakkuk 3:13 contains the answer to Habakkuk's earlier pleas for justice. The Lord, in fact, distinguished between the two houses. The righteous would flourish, but the house of the wicked would one day

---

[152] See the discussion on Hab 2:12–14. Isaiah 13 describes the destruction of Babylon in similar terms of theophany and eschatological triumph.

[153] See Exod 15:4–5; Isa 14:4–23; 37:21–29; Ezek 29:2–5.

[154] In Hebrew, as in English, rōʾš or "head" can mean a person's head; the top of an object; or the leader of a family household, tribe, or group; in other cases, the term can mean "first or beginning." In construct, the word "head" could refer to the "leader" or "military commander" of the warriors. HALOT, 1166–67.

face destruction—beginning with the crushing defeat of the head of the household.

Verse 13 describes this defeat in language emphasizing its finality. The nuance of the Hb. verb *māḥaṣ* (lit. "to smash") implies the Lord "crushes" or "shatters" his foes.[155] The context of other verses containing the word suggests such a blow is irrecoverable: "I *crush* them, and they cannot get up" (Ps 18:38); "*Break* the back of his adversaries and enemies, / so that they cannot rise again" (Deut 33:11).[156] Some occurrences describe a fatal head wound, like the injury God deals his foes (Ps 68:21) or Jael's hammerblow to Sisera's head (Judg 5:26). Three occurrences appear in passages describing the work of a future Messiah. Balaam prophesied in the future a star and scepter would arise out of Israel, who would "*smash* the forehead of Moab" (Num 24:17). Psalm 110:4–6 records God's oath to a priestly king "forever according to the pattern of Melchizedek": "The Lord . . . will *crush* kings on the day of his anger. . . . / [H]e will *crush* leaders over the entire world." In this last example, the object of the verb has the same double meaning as in Hab 3:13, where the Divine Warrior would crush the leader and/or his head. These passages bring to mind the *protoevangelium* of Gen 3:15, in which one of Eve's offspring would finally deal the age-old serpent a fatal blow to the head (see NIV). According to the NT, this prophecy was fulfilled in Christ's victory over Satan (see Rom 16:20; Heb 2:14; 1 John 3:8). The parallels with messianic language and cosmic scope raise the possibility a final, eschatological victory is in view.

Habakkuk 3:13 closes with a second description of the Divine Warrior's actions against the enemy. The CSB translates this last line as "[You] strip him from foot to neck." The verb reflects the same Hb. root as in v. 9, where the Divine Warrior uncovered or removed his bow from its sheath. The image in v. 13 is of "stripping" or "laying bare" his enemy from "foundation" (Hb. *yəsôd*) "up to (the) neck" (Hb. *ṣawwāʾr*). Most English translations render this phrase to reflect the stripping of the enemy to his outer extremities: "foot to neck" (CSB, NASB); "thigh to neck" (ESV); or "head to foot" (NIV). The connotation may be stripping the enemy of his weapons and armor or even humiliating him by exposing his nakedness (cf. 2 Sam 10:1–5).

---

[155] *HALOT*, 571.
[156] Emphasis added throughout this paragraph.

The NET, however, offers a more gruesome interpretation: "laying him open from the lower body to the neck."[157] Either way, the actions of the following verse ensure the death of the head of the household of the wicked. The mixed imagery of head/body and house/foundation may serve to highlight the destruction of both the leader and the members of his household. Such welcome news deserves worshipful reflection, as indicated by the third and final *Selah*.

3:14 Verse 14 describes a third action the Divine Warrior takes against the leader of the wicked: "You pierce his head / with his own spears."[158] The verb *nāqab* (Eng. "to bore through, establish, or mark") can mean "to pierce a hole," as in the lid of chest (2 Kgs 12:9) or various body parts: for example, the nose, jaw, and hand (Job 40:24; 41:2; 2 Kgs 18:21).[159] In Hab 3:14 the pierced body part is "head" or *rōʾš*—the same word translated as "leader" in v. 13. Hebrew has several synonyms describing similar actions, which are also translated in English as "pierce."[160] For instance, four of the ten OT occurrences of the synonym *dāqar* (Eng. "to pierce through") refer either to the success of the Babylonians against Judah (Jer 37:10; Lam 4:9), or the fate of the Babylonians at the hands of the Medes and Persians (Isa 13:15; Jer 51:4).[161] The NT highlights the significance of some of these Hb. words that fall in the same semantic domain as "pierce" (e.g., *dāqar*, Zech 12:10; *ḥālal*, Isa 53:5). These synonyms play an important role in OT passages anticipating the atoning sacrifice of the Messiah in the NT.[162] Likely drawing from "a recognized *testimonium* of the early

---

[157] Roberts, *Nahum, Habakkuk, and Zephaniah*, 157, sees a parallel between this action and Marduk's ripping his opponent apart in an ancient Babylonian myth. He translates the next verse as Yahweh's scattering the sea with the dragon's supporters, using them "[a]s food for the sharks of the sea" (p. 129). Although this imagery would closely parallel the Babylonians' haul of "human fish" in 1:14–17, the reading seems a stretch for the text in 3:14–15.

[158] Because the word "head" is in construct with "warrior(s)," some English versions interpret this to mean the Divine Warrior pierces the "heads of his [that is, the leaders of his] warriors" (e.g., ESV, ISV, NET).

[159] *HALOT*, 719. This action closely resembles Jael's daring feat—driving a tent peg through Sisera's skull—with similar wording. Four verbs in Judg 5:26 communicate Jael's utter destruction of the enemy: she "hammered" and "crushed" his head; she "shattered" (Hb. *māḥaṣ*; cf. Hab 3:13) and "pierced" (Hb. *ḥālap*; "to cut through": see Job 20:24; *HALOT*, 321) his temple. Not surprisingly, Judg 5:27 records no less than three times that Sisera "collapsed and fell" dead.

[160] E.g., *dāqar*, Zech 12:10; *ḥālal*, Isa 53:5; *ḥālap*, Judg 5:26; *rāṣa*, Exod 21:6.

[161] *HALOT*, 230.

[162] See John 19:31–37; 20:19–29; Rev 1:7. First Peter 2:24 quotes from Isa 53:5d—"[W]e are healed by his wounds"—but does not mention "[H]e was pierced" (Isa 53:5a). Although the NT quotes/alludes to Ps 22:1 (Matt 27:46; Mark 15:34), v. 18 (Matt 27:35; Mark 15:24; Luke 23, and

church," Matt 24:30; John 19:37; and Rev 1:7 clearly link Christ's crucifixion to Zech 12:10: "[T]hey will look at me whom they pierced. They will mourn for him as one weeps for an only child . . . a first-born."[163] Nevertheless, the identity of the one pierced has generated much debate and speculation: suggestions include historical individuals,[164] an unknown martyr, the king (in humiliation rites), or Yahweh himself (speaking in first person; cf. Zech 12:1), who is psychologically "pierced" by the people's mockery.[165] Since piercing elsewhere never signifies mockery and the depth of mourning confirms an actual death, Douglas Moo concludes, "The pierced one must be identified as a representative of God, whose sufferings and death can be spoken of as God's"; the representative is probably the Messiah, with possible connections to Isaiah 53.[166] The NT quotations suggest the early church clearly understood Zech 12:10 was ultimately fulfilled at the crucifixion of Jesus Christ.

The instrument of piercing is the *maṭṭeh* (Eng. "spear").[167] Although the Divine Warrior has access to his own munitions (vv. 9, 11), he further humiliates the wicked leader by piercing him with his own weapons. Intriguingly, the Hb. word *maṭṭeh* originally referred to parts of a tree fashioned into a shaft-like staff or weapon.[168] Although

---

v. 22 (Heb 2:12), surprisingly v. 16 is overlooked: "[T]hey pierced my hands and feet." See Gleason L. Archer and G. C. Chirichigno, *Old Testament Quotations in the New Testament: A Complete Survey* (Chicago: Moody Press, 1983), 64–67. Douglas J. Moo, *The Old Testament in the Gospel Passion Narratives* (Sheffield: Almond Press, 1983), 283–84, labels Ps 22:16 "a well-known *crux*": in place of the LXX "they pierced my hands and feet," the MT reads "as a lion (כָּאֲרִי) my hands and feet." The *BHS* apparatus notes that some Hb. manuscripts read כארו and two Hb. manuscripts read כָּרוּ, supporting the translation "they pierced." See "בור," *HALOT*, 466; "כרה," "to be dug," 496. Moo, p. 284, concludes that the evangelists' integrity may explain their hesitancy to use a verse "whose reading was uncertain."

[163] Moo, *The Old Testament in the Gospel Passion Narratives*, 211.

[164] Mark J. Boda, *The Book of Zechariah*, NICOT (Grand Rapids: Eerdmans, 2016), 716, lists Uriah, Josiah, Gedaliah, Jeremiah, Zerubbabel, Onias III, Simon Maccabeus, and Judas Maccabeus.

[165] Moo, *The Old Testament in the Gospel Passion Narratives*, 212.

[166] Moo, *The Old Testament in the Gospel Passion Narratives*, 212. Gary Alan Long, "דָּקַר," *NIDOTTE* 1:963 points out that "[t]he Talmud understands this verse as referring to the slaying of Messiah (Sukka, 52a)." Intriguingly, the tension engendered by the improbable thought that God could die has already surfaced in Hab 1:12.

[167] In Hab 3:9, the CSB translates the same word, *maṭṭeh*, as "arrows" because of the accompanying "bow." Although no bow is present in 3:14, some versions retain the previous interpretation of "arrows" (ESV, NASB, NKJV, NRSV). The CSB, however, renders the plural word as "spears." Others choose to render the plural word as a singular "spear" (NIV, NET).

[168] David M. Fouts, "מַטֶּה," *NIDOTTE* 2:917.

Satan imagined "piercing" the Messiah would defeat him, the wooden cross became the way God wrought salvation for his people.[169] In time, the Divine Warrior will also fatally pierce the Destroyer, and the house of the wicked will fall.[170]

The leader of the house was not alone; the members of his wicked household accompanied him in droves. The origin of the rare term *pārāz*, translated here as "warriors" based on the LXX reading, may correspond to the Arabic word for "muster" or "select, distinguish" and therefore, "conscripts." Alternatively, the term may derive from the Hb. word *pərāzôn*, meaning "slaves" or "country people."[171] Some English versions translate the term as "leaders" or even "villages" (NASB, KJV, NKJV).

Those who "storm[ed] out" were submissive to or in conspiracy with their ruler. Just as in English, the Hb. verb *sāʿar* (lit. "to excite, frighten, or storm") can describe emotional rage as well as a literal tempest (2 Kgs 6:11; Jonah 1:11, 13).[172] Jonah 1:4 indicates the ferocity of this kind of squall: "[S]uch a great storm arose on the sea that the ship threatened to break apart." Some English versions translate *sāʿar* as a simile: "like a whirlwind" (ESV; KJV; NKJV) or "windstorm" (ISV). The analogy recalls the Lord's description of the Babylonian soldiers, who "gather prisoners like sand" as they "sweep by like the wind" (Hab 1:9, 11).[173] In Hab 3:14, the warriors intend "to scatter" their opponents. Scattering one's enemies was a military strategy rendering them completely ineffective. Frequently, it was the Lord who scattered his enemies, including rebellious Israel.[174] The Lord repeatedly warned his people if they pursued other gods, he himself would "scatter" them "among the nations" (Deut 4:27). Even then, he would "gather" them once more when they had repented (Deut 30:3). Two of the seven OT occurrences of *sāʿar* (Eng. "to storm") also appear in passages

---

[169] Ironically, the Lord would indeed die to make it possible for those who trust in him *not* to die. See the discussion on Hab 1:12.

[170] Those squeamish at the violent actions of the Divine Warrior do well to remember that these verses anticipate a battle to the finish on a spiritual plane. Habakkuk 3:14 amply illustrates the underhanded evil tactics of the enemy. Thankfully, justice will prevail and the leader of the house of the wicked will one day be eliminated.

[171] *HALOT*, 965.

[172] *HALOT*, 762.

[173] The wording also evokes memories of the Egyptians, who rode out to confront the Israelites hemmed in on the shore of the Red Sea (Exod 14:5–9).

[174] In Hab 3:6, even the mountains "scatter" before the arrival of the Divine Warrior.

linked to scattering—where the Lord himself sent "a windstorm" of judgment against his rebellious people in order to scatter them among the nations "like chaff blown from a threshing floor" (Hos 13:3; Zech 7:14). After judgment, the Lord promised he would extend compassion to "poor . . . storm-tossed" Jerusalem (Isa 54:11).

The enemy warriors eyed their victims hungrily. The Hb. word ʿālaṣ "to exult, triumph" (CSB: "gloating") falls in the same semantic domain as the "rejoicing" of the Babylonians who hauled in their victims as if fish on a hook or in a net (Hab 1:15).[175] The "devouring" motif is the same, but the imagery in chap. 3 resembles the hunting behavior of a pack of wolves—an animal mentioned in 1:8. A wolf pack may follow a herd for days, looking for animals that are particularly vulnerable because they are young or old, sick or injured. Working together, the pack purposefully isolates weaker animals from the herd before launching an attack. To counter this, animal herds sometimes band together in a circle in an attempt to shield weaker members from attack—a tactic recommended for humans who encounter wolves in the wild. The enemy's "scattering" strategy in Hab 3:14 appears to prey on the "poor, weak, or vulnerable" (Hb. ʿānī).[176] When the Israelites fled from Egypt, the Amalekites infamously attacked stragglers who were "tired and weary." In retribution, the Lord commanded their memory be blotted out under heaven (Deut 25:17–19). The house of the wicked was populated with warriors intent on devouring God's people. The Babylonians were guilty of the same social injustices that Habakkuk had seen carried out by his fellow Jews against the vulnerable in his own society.

The wicked thought they operated out of God's view from "a secret hiding place" (Hb. mistār).[177] This same Hb. word appears twice in Ps 10:8–9, comparing the wicked to a lion lying in wait to seize the "helpless" (Hb. ʿānî). Boasting in his cravings, the wicked person thinks, "There's no accountability, / since there's no God"; "God has forgotten; he hides his face and will never see" (Ps 10:4, 11; cf. Ps 64:4–6). Psalm 17:12 adopts this same analogy of a lion "lurking in ambush." The psalmist charges the wicked focus on "fill[ing] their bellies," while

---

[175] The NIV also translates the word as "gloating," but more English versions render it as "rejoicing" (e.g., ESV, KJV, NKJV, JPS, NET).

[176] HALOT, 856.

[177] HALOT, 608. The NIV reading suggests the "wretched" were hiding in secret to escape their oppressors.

the righteous are "satisfied with [the Lord's] presence" (Ps 17:14, 15). No hiding place is truly hidden from the one who "fill[s] the heavens and the earth" (Jer 23:24; cf. Jer 49:10). Though the wicked might think their reprehensible actions could be kept secret, the Lord already divined the motives of their hearts. Ironically, God himself is "a bear waiting in ambush, / a lion in hiding," as he waits to pierce the wicked with arrows—even when they are found among his own people (Lam 3:10–13). Because the wicked cannot hide from God, the Divine Warrior had the Babylonians in his crosshairs.

3:15   Verse 15 acts as an inclusio, closing this III:C′ (3:8–15) section in the third panel. It echoes the imagery found in 3:8b: "Or is your fury against the sea / when you ride on your horses, / your victorious chariot?"[178] Although v. 15 does not specifically refer to a chariot, the Divine Warrior "tread[s] the sea with [his] horses, / stirring up the vast water." The word "tread" (Hb. *dārak*) is one of several words in chap. 3 depicting the Divine Warrior as standing (v. 6) or walking on the earth (vv. 5, 12). In v. 15, the Lord treads on the sea rather than the earth.[179] The implication may be he causes the horses that pull his chariot to trample the sea. The effect of this trampling is literally "a heap (Hb. *ḥōmer*) of great waters," or more likely, "the great waters foamed" (Hb. participle of *ḥāmar*).[180] Either way, as swift and fierce as the Babylonians' horses were in the first panel (1:8), their spectacle fades before the Lord's steeds traversing the waves and churning up the sea.

There is a decided eschatological tone to vv. 8–15. The Lord crushed the head of the house of wickedness in order to bring salvation to those who trust in him. Elizabeth Achtemeier calls these verses "the final battle" and observes the Lord granted the prophet a glimpse of "something of an equivalent of Armageddon (Rev. 16—19)."[181] Habakkuk's vision depicts God as the triumphant Warrior King who judged all nations (v. 12) and defeated all evil (vv. 13–14). Verse 13 describes the deliverance of the Lord's "anointed," who is not King

---

[178] See the discussion of 3:8.

[179] John 6:18–19 comes to mind, where "the sea began to churn" and the disciples saw "Jesus walking on the sea." Likewise, Jesus had complete authority over the wind and waves when he calmed the sea (cf. Matt 8:26; Mark 4:39; Luke 8:24). Several psalms describe these same activities as falling under God's jurisdiction (cf. Pss 65:7; 89:9; 107:29).

[180] *HALOT*, 330. See Exod 8:14; Judg 15:16: "heaps"; and Ps 46:3: "though its water roars and foams."

[181] Achtemeier, *Nahum—Malachi*, 57–58.

Jehoiakim of Habakkuk's day. The reference is to a Davidic king like the one celebrated in Zech 9:9. Achtemeier rightly concludes that "Habakkuk's vision of the Kingdom come includes a Davidic ruler."[182] This preview of the end shifted his perspective completely. The prophet's encounter with the Lord through theophany deepened his faith and propelled him toward praise.

As the chart below illustrates, several parallels surface between this section of the third panel (III:C′, Hab 3:8–15) and the corresponding section of the first panel (I:C, Hab 1:12–17).

Parallelism in the Side Panels I:C and III:C′		
	I: C (1:12–17)	**III: C′ (3:8–15)**
Intro	Prophet questions Lord's inaction	Prophet questions target of Lord's wrath
Setting	The sea	The rivers, sea, deep, heavens, earth
Actors	Babylonian fishermen vs. nations	The Divine Warrior vs. Babylonians
Weapons	Hook, dragnet, fishing net	Bow and arrows, spears
Actions	Lord made man "fish" with no ruler	Lord slays the ruler of the wicked
	Babylonians pull them up with hook	He pierces his head with his own spears
	They gather victims in net like food	Warriors stormed out to scatter/devour
	They sacrifice to continue ruling sea	The Lord rules over earth, sky, and sea
Complaint	Lord is silent while wicked swallow the righteous: Will they continually slaughter nations without mercy?	
Shift		The Lord crushes the leader of wicked; he comes to save his people/his anointed

The previous portions (I:B and III:B′)[183] focused on the effects of warriors invading the land. In both these third sections (I:C and III:C′), the emphasis moves to the waters. In I:C (1:12–17) in the first panel, the Babylonians appeared to rule over the sea, feasting on the human bounty they harvested in their nets (1:15). Rejoicing over their haul of "food," they offered sacrifices to their nets (1:16). The prophet understandably asked, "Will they . . . continually slaughter nations without

---

[182] Achtemeier, *Nahum—Malachi*, 58.
[183] See the discussion of 3:7 for chart comparing I:B and III:B′.

mercy?" (1:17). Similarly, in III:C′ (3:8–15), the Babylonian warriors anticipated devouring the weak in secret (3:14). People are not like marine creatures with no ruler (1:14); their leader is none other than the supreme Ruler of the vast waters—rivers, sea, and deep—as well as the earth and sky (3:8–15). The answer to the prophet's plaintive question in 1:17 is a resounding "No! The Lord will not allow such evil to go unpunished." The Divine Warrior himself would come "to save [his] people, / to save [his] anointed" (3:13). He would demolish the head of the house of the wicked, along with his henchmen (3:13b–14). One day the oppressor who exulted and feasted on the weak would suffer their same fate. First, however, God's people had to endure his judgment on the wickedness within the house of Judah.

3.5   HABAKKUK'S JOYFUL SUBMISSION (3:16–19)

Habakkuk's circumstances had not changed from the opening of chap. 1. In fact, things were about to get much worse than he could have imagined. Whatever response the prophet may have contemplated while waiting on the rampart evaporated during his theophanic encounter with God. Although Hab 3:2 reveals his perspective had already begun to shift, vv. 16–19 demonstrate a remarkable transformation in Habakkuk.

3.5.1   Though Trembling, I Will Wait (3:16)

> ¹⁶ *I heard, and I trembled within;*
> *my lips quivered at the sound.*
> *Rottenness entered my bones;*
> *I trembled where I stood.*
> *Now I must quietly wait for the day of distress*
> *to come against the people invading us.*

3:16   This final section of Habakkuk opens with a recurrence of the hearing/silence motif occurring at regular intervals throughout the book.

PANEL I	PANEL III
I:A (1:2–4)	**III:A' (3:2)**
"How long, LORD, must I call for help and you do not *listen* … ?" (1:2).	"LORD, I have *heard* the report about you; LORD, I stand in awe of your deeds" (3:2).
I:D (2:1–5)	**III:D' (3:16–19)**
"I will watch [lit. "*listen*"] to see what [the Lord] will say to me" (2:1).	"I *heard*, and I trembled within; … Now I must quietly wait … "(3:16).

As the chart shows, both outer panels introduce this motif in I:A (1:2–4) and III:A' (3:2), just after superscriptions, and it recurs at the beginning of the final section in each outer panel, I:D (2:1–5) and III:D' (3:16–19).[184] The first panel opens with the prophet accusing God of failing to hear his complaint expressed in prayer: "[Y]ou do not listen" (1:2, I:A). Toward the close of the first panel, the prophet determined he would "listen to see" what answer God would give his complaint (2:1, I:D). In both instances the prophet expresses his confusion and even frustration with God. At the end of the woe section, which revealed how closely God monitors the actions of the wicked, the Lord commanded the whole earth—Silence! (2:20). The location of the hearing motif in the final panel is the same as in the first panel, but the careful parallels serve to underscore Habakkuk's transformation. The first words in chap. 3 reveal a humble, chastened prophet: "LORD, I have heard the report about you; / LORD, I stand in awe of your deeds" (3:2, III:A'). The pattern holds true toward the close of the third panel: "I heard, and I trembled within" (3:16, III:D'). The contrast between the two outer panels is instructive. Habakkuk's encounter with God profoundly changed not only his perspective but the prophet himself.

Habakkuk did not specify what he heard, but his extreme physical reaction provides a clue. Apparently, the subject matter was more than just the report he mentioned in Hab 3:2, where his response was not nearly as intense.[185] The difference was due to the intervening verses (3:3–15) describing the imminent arrival and actions of the Divine Warrior. The intensity of Habakkuk's reaction also implies his theophanic experience was rich with meaning. Habakkuk appears to have experienced the theophany described in the previous verses in

---

[184] Emphasis added.
[185] See the discussion regarding the content of the report mentioned in Hab 3:2.

a deeply personal way, perhaps through a prophetic vision—maybe even the one described in Hab 2:2–3. Whatever the exact nature of the theophany, Habakkuk's encounter with the Lord left him physically shaken.[186]

Four different clauses capture the depths of the prophet's anguish. The first clause reports that he "trembled within." The word translated as "within" (Hb. *beṭen*; "internal organs")[187] is elsewhere translated as "belly" (Judg 3:21), "stomach" (Prov 13:25), or even "womb" (Gen 25:23). Extreme emotion often produces a visceral reaction like the one described in Hab 3:16. The prophet's internal organs "trembled" (Hb. *rāgaz*).[188] The same word describes the terror the surrounding nations experienced when they heard of the Lord's mighty deeds on behalf of his people (Exod 15:14; Deut 2:25; 1 Sam 14:15). The term also designates an appropriate response to theophany, when mountains, depths, earth, peoples, and kingdoms alike all tremble before the Lord, as do the tent curtains of Midian in Hab 3:7.[189]

The second clause observes the prophet's lips "quivered" (Hb. *ṣālal*) at what he heard. In three OT instances of the verb *ṣālal*, it is the ears that "shudder" or "tingle" in response to hearing the Lord's pronouncement of disaster (1 Sam 3:11; 2 Kgs 21:12; Jer 19:3). In Hab 3:16, the prophet's lips essentially do the same "at the sound." The meaning of the Hb. word *qôl* (CSB "sound") is broad; the semantic range of the word extends from the sound of a voice to any sort of noise, and the noun often depicts the noise of cosmic upheaval accompanying the Lord's approaching presence: earthquake, thunder, great waters, galloping horses, rattling chariots, and the clamor of war.[190] Habakkuk may simply be describing a physiological response to what he heard, but the focus on his lips may point toward his prophetic role. As a spokesman for the Lord, he must relay this profound message to his fellow citizens.

---

[186] Eaton, *Obadiah, Nahum, Habakkuk, Zephaniah*, 109, suggests that Habakkuk experienced "the throes of prophetic ecstasy." Heflin, *Nahum, Habakkuk, Zephaniah, Haggai*, 108, defines "ecstasy" not as a frenzied state but rather "a higher realm of awareness and sensitivity than normal."

[187] *HALOT*, 121.

[188] A derivative of this word has already appeared in 3:2, which describes God's wrath as "shaking (in anger)." Ezekiel 16:42 similarly describes God's rage against the adulterous actions of Jerusalem.

[189] See Pss 18:7; 77:16, 18; 99:1; Isa 23:11.

[190] BDB, 877.

The third clause notes "[r]ottenness entered [his] bones." The term translated "rottenness" (Hb. *rāqāb*, lit. "decay, rottenness") metaphorically refers to the "seat of disease and pain."[191] Hosea 5:12, like Hab 3:16, links "rottenness" to the Lord's pronouncement of judgment, where he declares, "So I am . . . like decay to the house of Judah." The concept denotes the slow moral decomposition of the Lord's people. Habakkuk witnessed firsthand God's judgment executed by the Divine Warrior. As a result, dread sunk down deep into his bones—so much so that he even found standing difficult. Just as the prophet was disturbed in the first clause, in the fourth and final clause, he likewise "trembled" (Hb. *rāgaz*) where he stood.

Habakkuk's description of the physiological effects of his experience is so detailed that it surely left a deep impression long after the initial emotion subsided. Most of us have not encountered a theophanic depiction of God's judgment on the scale of Habakkuk's. Many have, however, felt the traumatic shock of a natural disaster or terror attack; the palpable grief of a sudden, unexpected loss; or even the disturbing disorientation of a panic attack. None of us can control when disaster hits or even our initial reaction to the wave of emotions that accompany it. But what is crucial is what we do next.

Immediately following this powerful theophanic experience and the sensations it evoked, Habakkuk resolved to wait on God. The Hb. verb *nûaḥ* ("settle down, rest, repose, await") denotes both "the absence of activity" and "the presence of security."[192] The OT historical narratives repeatedly mention the Lord gave his people "rest" from their enemies as they settled in the land he provided (e.g., Deut 12:10). The word can also refer to the quiet, spiritual repose one experiences in the presence of the Lord, regardless of surrounding circumstances requiring action or alarm (Ps 116:7; see also Exod 33:14; Dan 12:13). This is *not* the kind of response the reader would expect the prophet to have, knowing the disaster that awaits his people.[193] The following

---

[191] BDB, 782. Proverbs 12:4 and 14:30 link rottenness in the bones to the visceral emotions of shame and jealousy.

[192] *HALOT*, 679; Leonard J. Coppes, "נוּחַ," *TWOT* 2:562.

[193] The seeming incongruity has led some scholars to propose alternative solutions for *ʾānûaḥ*. BDB, 628, notes that Julius Wellhausen suggested an emendation derived from *nāḥam* (Eng. "to comfort") meaning "to ease oneself" (by taking revenge)" (see Isa 1:24). G. R. Driver, "Studies in the Vocabulary of the Old Testament VI," *JTS* 34.136 (1933): 377, proposed a by-form of *ʾnûaḥ* meaning "to mourn"—a term he compared to the Arabic term *nāḥu* ("cooed, moaned"): "I wailed for the day of trouble." *BHS* notes the term is probably *ʾāḥakeh* (from *ḥkh*; "to wait for";

verses reinforce this reading. Once he received assurance God would set all things right in the end, Habakkuk determined to trust in the Lord's sovereignty and to wait quietly for his perfect timing.

The prophet's resolution in 3:16 (III:D′) to "wait" quietly (Hb. *nûaḥ*; "rest") for a future day parallels 2:3 (I:D), where the Lord instructed him to "wait" expectantly (Hb. *ḥākâ*; "long for") for the vision testifying "about the end." Although the Hb. wording is not identical, English versions translate both terms as "wait." Both seasons of waiting anticipate an "appointed time" (2:3) or "day" (3:16). Both texts may well refer to the end—either the end of the wicked Babylonians and/or the eschatological end of the house of the wicked. The possibility the final end is in view increases with the understanding the vision may actually be a person—perhaps the Divine Warrior himself.[194] The prophet's instruction in I:D was to wait for a vision; the prophet's resolution in III:D′ was to wait for the fulfillment of that vision.

Habakkuk was waiting "for the day of distress." The word "distress" (Hb. *ṣārâ*) derives from a verb that means to be "narrow" or "constricted."[195] In fifteen instances, the noun is in construct with "day of" and denotes either the struggles of an individual (Ps 50:15; Prov 24:10) or the suffering of a nation during war (2 Kgs 19:3; Obad 1:14). When Israel and Judah rebelled repeatedly, God himself initiated a grueling period of uncertainty:

> In those times there was no peace for those who went about their daily activities because the residents of the lands had many conflicts. Nation was crushed by nation and city by city, for God troubled them with every possible distress (2 Chr 15:5–6)

---

see Hab 2:3). Pointing out that the LXX and Vulgate support the MT reading of *ʾānûaḥ*, Roberts, *Nahum, Habakkuk, and Zephaniah*, 146, contends that no emendation is necessary since the usage in v. 16 parallels 1 Sam 25:9, which uses *nwḥ* "in the sense of 'to cease speaking while waiting.'" As difficult as it is to comprehend, Habakkuk's decision to "quietly wait" for God's sovereign purposes to unfold as his world crumbled around him is evidence of the seismic shift that had taken place in his heart. In parallel sections in the outer panels, the prophet's waiting in stillness (*nwḥ*; 3:16; III:D′) is the perfect foil to the wicked man's inability to settle down (*nwḥ*; 2:5; I:D).

[194] See the discussion of Hab 2:3, especially regarding the conflation of Hab 2:3–4 and Isa 26:20–21 in Heb 10:37–38. The context of Isa 26 likewise pairs waiting for the Lord's wrath to pass and trusting in the Lord "in perfect peace" (Isa 26:3, 8, 20–21).

[195] *HALOT*, 1053–54.

At the same time, the Lord was the one who could rescue people out of distress, (e.g., Ps 20:1). Although Judah would endure an unprecedented "time of trouble" at the hands of the Babylonians, God promised to restore them after their captivity (Jer 33:7).

Who would have to endure "the day of distress" in Hab 3:16? Jeremiah warned Judah and Babylon alike the anguish of war would seize them like labor pangs on a woman giving birth to her first child (Jer 4:31; 6:24; 50:43). The identifier in the last line of v. 16 is ambiguous in Hebrew because the subject of the infinitive construct *ʿălôt* ("to go up"; with *lə* prefix: "to rise up suddenly")[196] is not clear. Some commentators argue the relative clause is the subject: "the ones who are invading us."[197] Habakkuk waited "[f]or the people to arise *who* will attack us" (NASB; cf. JPS 1988); in other words, distress was coming for the Judeans. Others argue "the day of distress" is the subject of the infinitive construct: The prophet waited "for the day of distress to come against the people invading [them]" (CSB; cf. NIV, ESV, NET); the Babylonians would experience distress in retribution for their attack on Judah.[198] Habakkuk demonstrated an awareness two separate days of distress were coming: the Babylonians would attack Judah and then be attacked themselves. The revelations God had given him helped the prophet realize his people were facing a conflicting scenario. The good news was that God would initiate a "day of distress" against the Babylonians. The bad news was Judah must first endure her own "day of distress" at the hands of the Babylonians. Habakkuk knew full well the horrors about to befall his people when the Babylonians came.

The pronominal suffix at the end of the phrase—"the nation invading *us*"—speaks volumes. This judgment was personal. The city and the people Habakkuk loved would face certain destruction, deprivation, and destitution on an unimaginable scale. Somehow the prophet was able to summon the courage and faith to look past the invasion to the Lord's judgment on their enemy. He humbly resolved,

---

[196] *HALOT*, 828–29, points to GKC §114k and a similar reading in Ps 62:10.

[197] Ko, *Theodicy in Habakkuk*, 95; Robertson, *The Books of Nahum, Habakkuk, and Zephaniah*, 244; Thomas, *Habakkuk*, 151.

[198] Andersen, *Habakkuk*, 345; Bailey, "Habakkuk," 373; Renz, *The Books of Nahum, Habakkuk, and Zephaniah*, 396–97; Roberts, *Nahum, Habakkuk, and Zephaniah*, 129; Shepherd, *A Commentary on the Book of the Twelve*, 341. Patterson, *Nahum, Habakkuk, Zephaniah*, 231–32, takes the unique stance that Habakkuk has both in mind: "I will rest during the day of distress (and) during the attack against the people invading us."

"Now I must quietly wait." The prophet who had once whined "how long?" now determined to wait however long it took.

When would "the day of distress" come? Judah's "day of distress" would begin in the near future and span many painful years.[199] Soon after the Battle of Carchemish in 605 BC, Nebuchadnezzar attacked Jerusalem, forcing the nation into subjugation. The Babylonians again marched on Jerusalem, besieging the city in 597 BC. The city endured yet another siege that began in 588 BC and held out for two years before Jerusalem fell to Nebuchadnezzar in 586 BC. The time of troubles lasted much longer for the survivors who were carted off into exile. Babylon's "day of distress" arrived when Cyrus the Great led Persian forces to defeat the Babylonian army at Opis in 539 BC. Soon afterward, the Persian king captured Babylon with little resistance. The city slid into a slow fade marked by occasional rebellions against the Persians. When Babylon revolted against Xerxes I in 484 and again in 482–481 BC, the Persian king responded decisively, destroying Babylon's fortifications and some of her temples. The once great city was independent no more.[200]

A final "day of distress" still awaits not only Jerusalem and "Babylon" but also all the residents of the earth. Zephaniah calls it "the day of the Lord" and describes it darkly:

> That day is a day of wrath,
> a day of trouble and distress,
> a day of destruction and desolation,
> a day of darkness and gloom,
> a day of clouds and total darkness (Zeph 1:15).

The Lord explained, "I will bring distress on mankind, / . . . because they have sinned against the LORD"; therefore, "[t]he whole earth will be consumed / by the fire of his jealousy, / for he will make a complete, / yes, a horrifying end / of all the inhabitants of the earth" (Zeph 1:17–18). Although the Divine Warrior's appearances in Habakkuk 3 and Zephaniah 1 look forward to the Babylonians' day of trouble, they also anticipate the ultimate day of distress at the end of time. His

---

[199] The date of Habakkuk is likely between King Josiah's death in 609 BC and the Battle of Carchemish in 605 BC. See "Date" in the Introduction. The exile ended after Cyrus captured Babylon in 539 BC and decreed the following year that the Israelites might return to their homeland.

[200] See the discussion of Hab 2:13.

arrival initiates judgment, but the Lord is also "a warrior who saves" and rejoices over the remnant he restores (Zeph 3:17).[201] Though the book of Habakkuk contains only the faintest of intimations of that restoration (Hab 2:4, 14; 3:3, 13, 19), the prophet was somehow able to look by faith beyond the day of distress coming soon for his own people.

3.5.2   Even if There Is No Food, I Will Rejoice in My Savior (3:17–18)

>[17] Though the fig tree does not bud
> and there is no fruit on the vines,
> though the olive crop fails
> and the fields produce no food,
> though the flocks disappear from the pen
> and there are no herds in the stalls,
>[18] yet I will celebrate in the LORD;
> I will rejoice in the God of my salvation!

3:17   Habakkuk outlined the devastating effects the Babylonian invasion would have on the people of Judah. As an agrarian society, Judah's life revolved around the annual rhythm of plowing, sowing, and harvesting. A prolonged siege would obviously suspend all these life-sustaining activities normally carried on outside the walls of a city. Besieging troops would, like locusts, consume all sources of food they could find. Invading armies would also cut down trees indiscriminately to build siege works. The Lord warned the Israelites when they entered Canaan not to cut down fruit-producing trees for such a short-sighted purpose (Deut 20:19). The only sustenance left to a city under siege was whatever food its citizens had managed to bring into the city ahead of the onslaught. Once those stores ran out within the walls, famine would begin in earnest.

Deuteronomy 8:8 lists the foods of the promised land as wheat, barley, (grape)vines, figs, pomegranates, olive oil, and honey.[202] If the Israelites kept his commands, God pledged to bless the produce

---

[201] According to Dan 12:1–2, this "time of distress" will be unprecedented in human history; however, all of God's people "written in the book will escape." They will awake to "eternal life," while others to "disgrace and eternal contempt."

[202] Most of the biblical references to "honey" are likely the product of boiled-down dates, which has over 60 percent sugar content. See Irene and Walter Jacob, "Flora," *ABD* 2:807.

of their land—"grain, new wine, and fresh oil"—along with the offspring of their herds and flocks (Deut 7:13). Habakkuk methodically
worked his way through these basic food sources—only these items
would no longer be available at any price. The list begins with the fig
tree and vine, often paired together in the OT.[203] Hosea 9:10 compares
the nation of Israel to "grapes" and "the first fruit of the fig tree." Sit-
ting under one's own vine and fig tree became symbolic of peace and
plenty (Mic 4:4; Zech 3:10). Both figs and grapes could be eaten fresh
or dried; the fruit of the vine was used primarily for wine but also for
vinegar. Fig trees and vines should normally produce annually, even
when left unattended for several years.

The wording of v. 17—"the fig tree does not bud"—suggests something more than hungry enemy soldiers eating all the figs.[204] Normally,
the flowers appear inside the fruit; the female fig wasp pollinates them,
and the figs ripen over two to three months later.[205] The failure to produce blossoms points to the reversal of the Lord's blessings. Similarly,
where there should have been grapes on the vines, "there are not"
(Hb. 'ēn). This Hb. particle emphasizes the suspension of the natural
cycle of crop development. Moses warned the Israelites if they did not
obey God faithfully, worms would consume their grapes and "buzzing
insects" would take possession of all their trees (Deut 28:39, 42; see
also Hos 2:12; Amos 4:9). The lack of peace and plenty—as well as
the absence of figs and grapes—was the result of the people's rebellion
and Israel's failure to produce spiritual fruit.

Similarly, olive trees were associated with peace and provision in
Israel (Hos 14:6–7). Their fruit was one of the most valuable com-
modities in the ancient world. Olives were not only eaten for food,
but olive oil was also used for cooking, lamps, medicine, soap, and
cosmetics. The trees grew well in rocky soil and were difficult to kill.
Bearing fruit after just seven years, a mature olive tree could live more
than a thousand years, producing olives long after its trunk became
hollow. Normally, an olive tree could be counted on to yield a half ton

---

[203] See 1 Kgs 4:25; 2 Kgs 18:31; Ps 105:33; Isa 36:16; Jer 5:17; Joel 2:22.
[204] This is the first occurrence of the Hb. word *lo'* (Eng. "no" or "not") since the chiasm in
2:13. In the thirty verses before the structural center, there are seventeen negative particles. In
the twenty-six verses following the center, there are only two, both here in 3:17. The sudden
reintroduction of the negative particle combined with two particles of nonexistence in the same
verse highlights both the chiastic turn and the prophet's resolve to rejoice in the Lord, no matter
what.
[205] Jacob, "Flora," *ABD*, 2:807.

of fruit per year.[206] The report of v. 17 indicates something was terribly amiss: "the olive crop fails"; lit. "the labor of the olive fails" (Hb. *kāḥaš*; Eng. "to deny, delude"; "to let someone down"; see Hos 9:2: CSB, "fail").[207] The curses enumerated in Deuteronomy 28 encompassed the olive crop as well: "You will have olive trees throughout your territory but not moisten your skin with oil, because your olives will drop off" (Deut 28:40). An olive tree suddenly failing to produce would be a catastrophic disappointment commanding the attention of the rebellious Israelites. The Lord reminded the people of Jeremiah's day covenant curses would result from their worship of other gods: "The LORD named you / a flourishing olive tree, / beautiful with well-formed fruit. / He has set fire to it, / and its branches are consumed / with the sound of a mighty tumult" (Jer 11:16). Not only would the olive crop fail; Judah herself would fall.

Grains likewise served as a staple food for the people of Judah.[208] Barley was a hardy grain that grew faster and in poorer soil. Passover and the Feast of Unleavened Bread marked the beginning of the barley harvest in April/May. Wheat ripened a bit later in May/June, and the Feast of Weeks commemorated its harvest at Pentecost. Since the Babylonian siege on Jerusalem began in the tenth month (January) of the year 588 BC, the fields would have been prepared and sown with seed in the late fall.[209] Just as the Lord had warned, those who rejected his commands would pay a high price: "You will sow your seed in vain because your enemies will eat it" (Lev 26:16). The Babylonian soldiers consumed the grain harvest during that first spring. Afterwards, the fields would have lain unattended and produced no food. Furthermore, God warned of the devastating results of a protracted siege: "When I cut off your supply of bread, ten women will bake your bread in a single oven and ration out your bread by weight, so that you will eat but not be satisfied" (Lev 26:26; see Deut 28:33). The Lord instructed the prophet Ezekiel, already exiled in Babylon, to enact a miniature siege of Jerusalem, including siege rations. He said, "I am going to cut off the supply of bread in Jerusalem. They will anxiously

---

[206] Jacob, "Flora," *ABD*, 2:807–8.

[207] *HALOT*, 469.

[208] Edwin Firmage, "Zoology (Animal Profiles)," *ABD* 6:1120, observes the Jewish diet was primarily vegetarian, with grains providing up to half of the caloric intake.

[209] See 2 Kgs 25:1 // Jer 52:4. The tenth month of the Hebrew calendar would be equivalent to January.

eat food they have weighed out and in dread drink rationed water for lack of bread and water" (Ezek 4:16–17). The prospect of this kind of scarcity must have filled listeners with alarm.

Ancient Israel also depended on flocks of sheep and/or goats and herds of cattle. Livestock were so valuable meat was eaten only on special occasions, often involving religious sacrifice. Sheep and goats were raised primarily for secondary products like milk, cheese, yogurt, wool, hair, and skins. Cattle, on the other hand, were valued for their ability to pull loads in the field. Habakkuk 3:17 indicates flocks were "cut off" (i.e., "destroyed) from their pens.[210] Sheepfolds, which protected a vulnerable flock from wild animals, were simple, low-walled structures made from stone or brush. Cattle would be kept in stalls since they were ten times more valuable than sheep.[211] In v. 17, however, the stalls were empty. Once again, the particle of nonexistence emphasizes the loss: "there are not." In the face of an invading army, all safety measures would be abandoned as people fled for their lives. Although some animals may have been brought into a city under siege, the amount of feed needed to sustain them made it impractical. Enemy soldiers doubtless helped themselves to any domestic animals left outside city walls, using them for meat or labor. The Deuteronomic curses warned of this eventuality as well:

> The LORD will bring a nation from far away, from the ends of the earth, to swoop down on you like an eagle, a nation whose language you won't understand, a ruthless nation, showing no respect for the old and not sparing the young. They will eat the offspring of your livestock and your land's produce until you are destroyed. They will leave you no grain, new wine, fresh oil, young of your herds, or newborn of your flocks until they cause you to perish (Deut 28:49–51; see also Jer 5:17)

The Babylonians, whom the Lord had described in Hab 1:8 as "eagles, swooping to devour," fit this profile of marauding invaders.

The repeated parallelism in 3:17 heightens the sense of escalating loss, as the prophet describes the loss of Hebrew staples. The mounting tension reaches a crescendo of alarm foreshadowing the dwindling

---

[210] The CSB's "disappear" alludes to this phenomenon. *HALOT*, 187, indicates that to be "cut off" often suggests a violent end of life (1 Kgs 3:26; Isa 53:8; Lam 3:54; Ezek 37:11).

[211] Firmage, "Zoology," *ABD* 6:1119.

food supply of a city under siege. The horrors of Nebuchadnezzar's siege of Jerusalem would last roughly a year and a half. Jeremiah 52:6 records near the end of that time, "the famine was so severe in the city that the common people had no food." Samaria faced a similar famine when the city was besieged by the Arameans two centuries previous. Thing were so bad "a donkey's head sold for thirty-four ounces of silver, and a cup of dove's dung sold for two ounces of silver"—exorbitant prices for despicable "foodstuff" (2 Kgs 6:25).[212] Far worse, the same passage relates the appalling story of two women who resorted to boiling and eating their own sons (2 Kgs 6:26–29). The curses outlined in the Pentateuch predicted such abominable actions (Lev 26:29; Deut 28:53–57). In Habakkuk's generation, Jeremiah later reminded the residents of Jerusalem they would be reduced to cannibalism during the Babylonian siege (Jer 19:9). Tragically, Lam 4:9–10 records such unspeakable things came to pass. It would have been better to die by the sword than to face the desperation of slow starvation.

3:18 Verse 18 finishes the sentence Habakkuk began in the previous verse. In this instance the Hb. conjunction *kî* conveys a sense of time with concessive force: "even when/if" or "though."[213] The six clauses that followed in v. 17 described eventualities based on the Lord's revelation to the prophet. Verse 18 completes the sentence with a clause introduced by the Hb. conjunction *waw*, translated here as "yet." Though this conjunction can join contrasting ideas, the two halves of the sentence on either side of the "yet" appear so antithetical as to be completely incongruous.[214] One might expect a lesser contrast: "[Y]et I will plod on/persist/not protest." Instead, what comes next is surprising: the "yet" is followed by praise!

Habakkuk responded to the certainty of suffering with rejoicing. He closed the sentence with a pair of cohortative clauses set in synonymous parallelism.[215] The repetition of the subject of the first clause in v. 18 is emphatic: "[Y]et I, myself, will celebrate." The phrase "in

---

[212] These amounts of silver today would equate to approximately $1,000 and $50 USD, respectively.

[213] *HALOT*, 471.

[214] This interclausal *waw* plays a disjunctive role. See *IBHS* §39.2.3.

[215] *IBHS* §34.5.1 notes that "[t]he cohortative expresses the will or strong desire of the speaker." Since the prophet theoretically has the ability to rejoice in the Lord—despite his extremely difficult circumstances—his inclination "takes on the coloring of resolve ('I will . . .'). Centuries later, Paul similarly resolved, twice over, to rejoice in the Lord even while imprisoned: "Rejoice in the Lord always. I will say it again: Rejoice!" (Phil 4:4).

Yahweh" interrupts normal Hebrew word order to underscore the object of the prophet's joy. The cohortative form of the verb "to celebrate" (Hb. *ʿālaz*) emphasizes the prophet's desire or intention to find joy in the Lord. The verb is used to describe ephemeral reasons the wicked find to celebrate: the demise of foes, evil deeds, economic profits, idolatry, revelry, plunder, and drinking.[216] The term may also refer to those who celebrate before the Lord in his sanctuary, often expressed by singing and shouting.[217] Several of these same passages also voice praise in hardship. The prophet's praise was anchored "in the LORD."

Emphasizing his resolve yet again, Habakkuk expressed his intention with a second cohortative clause: "I will rejoice in the God of my salvation!" The Hb. verb *gîl* (Eng. "rejoice") occurred once before in panel I, where the Babylonians "rejoiced" in their haul of human "food" (1:15–16). The term typically appears in cultic contexts, and 1:16 notes the Babylonians' joy led to idolatrous worship.[218] In contrast, Habakkuk chose to rejoice in the *absence* of food. Harvest normally resulted in rejoicing, so when God's judgment canceled the harvest, joy and "rejoicing" (*gîl*) normally ceased as well (Isa 16:10; Joel 1:12, 16). Ironically, Habakkuk was able to rejoice at a time when it made no sense to do so. Gowan captures the haunting incongruity in all caps: "Even though I starve to death, YET I WILL REJOICE IN THE LORD."[219] Choosing to rejoice in God in the hardest circumstances imaginable certainly illustrates what it means "to live by faith and to be faithful in our living"—even if deliverance fails to materialize in this life.[220]

Although the verb *gîl* typically describes a joyful response to God's saving activity, Habakkuk's motive for rejoicing in these bleak circumstances was God himself: "I will rejoice in the God of my salvation!" This title for God indicates Habakkuk anticipated with eyes of faith the Lord would bring the salvation he longed for in 1:2 and envisioned in 3:13.[221] It is a "confession of confidence" God will help his peo-

---

[216] See 2 Sam 1:20; Ps 94:3–4; Isa 23:12; Jer 11:15; 15:17; 50:11; 51:39.

[217] See Pss 28:7; 68:4; 96:12; 149:5.

[218] *HALOT*, 189.

[219] Gowan, *The Triumph of Faith*, 83–84.

[220] Gowan, *The Triumph of Faith*, 84.

[221] Hiebert, *God of My Victory*, 148, observes that Jerome understood v. 18 from the same Christological perspective he had in v. 13 (see above). The Latin Vulgate renders the Hb. *yišîl*

ple when called upon.[222] By adding the personal pronoun "my," the prophet staked his claim to the salvation God provides. He made a deliberate choice to worship God amid extreme hardship.[223] No matter how others might respond, no matter what the future held, Habakkuk resolved to rejoice in the Lord.

How was the prophet able to transition from the terror of v. 16 to v. 18, which expresses one of the strongest statements of faith in all of Scripture? Perhaps the intervening verse may shed some light. In v. 17 Habakkuk ironically uses poetic imagery to describe the deprivations of the coming siege. The prophet did not ignore what lay ahead, but he refused to face the future with agonized dread. Instead, with contemplation, Habakkuk meditated on all that he had seen and heard from the Lord. Through carefully recording the scarcity in poetic verse, he imagined the devastation and used that imagery to galvanize his faith before the onslaught. Whatever the outcome, Habakkuk would trust God and worship.[224] Unexpectedly, that determined choice resulted in true joy.

3.5.3 The Lord Enables Me to Walk on the Heights (3:19a)

> [19] *The* LORD *my Lord is my strength;*
> *he makes my feet like those of a deer*
> *and enables me to walk on mountain heights!*

3:19a The prophet acknowledged the source of his strength. Similar to 1:12, the final two verses of the book resound with names of God. In the previous verse, Habakkuk referred to God by his covenant name, "Yahweh," and as "the God of [his] salvation." The prophet paired two divine names together in v. 19: "Yahweh Adonai." As the covenant name by which God revealed himself, "Yahweh" evokes the memory of all God's covenant promises. It also recalls the Lord's

---

(Eng. "my salvation") as a personal name: *Iesu meo* (Eng. "my Jesus"): "I will rejoice in God my Jesus."

[222] F. Stolz, "ישׁע," *TLOT* 2:585. Other passages that describe God in this same way include Pss 18:46; 25:5; 27:9; Isa 12:2; Mic 7:7. Several of these also describe waiting on God to hear and act and exalting him in the meantime.

[223] Sawyer, *TDOT* 6:445, notes that the verb "to save" implies the Lord's "bringing help to those in trouble rather than rescuing them from it."

[224] Similarly, Job's response to incredible suffering was incredible faith. After he received news of all his losses, "[Job] fell to the ground and worshiped" (Job 1:20).

character statement in Exod 34:6–7. The Hb. term *ʾādôn* (Eng. "lord" or "master") in the OT most frequently refers to humans and is a term of polite address or deference to a superior. When used as a personal title for God as it is in Hab 3:19, *ʾădōnāy* (Eng. "my Lord) is often paired with Yahweh, though normally in reverse order: "Adonai Yahweh."[225] The name "Adonai" emphasizes God's sovereignty, which explains why some English versions translate the combined title in v. 19 as "The Sovereign LORD" (NIV, NET). The prophet would desperately need divine power to maintain his joy and perspective during the days to come. Wisely, he latched firmly to the one who is truly mighty, saying, "The LORD, my Lord is my strength."

Habakkuk's affirmation serves as a foil to the Babylonians' arrogant boasting in 1:11: "[T]heir strength (Hb. *koah*) is their god." The word *koah* usually connotes physical strength, but its frequent usage in Job describes "divine omnipotence . . . which far transcends all human power."[226] The Babylonian soldiers essentially saw their own strength as divine. In contrast, Habakkuk humbly looked to the Lord for *ḥayil* (Eng. "strength"). Although these two Hb. words for strength are in the same semantic domain, there is an interesting distinction: *ḥayil* never describes God's might. This Hb. term has a broader meaning than simply "strength." It also describes the results of that strength—capability, valor, wealth, and noble character—all gifts that come from God.[227] *Ḥayil* can also mean "army."[228] Furthermore, Deut 8:17–18 cautions the Israelites not to say to themselves, "My power and my own ability have gained this wealth (*ḥayil*) for me"; instead, they were to "remember that the LORD [their] God gives [them] the power to gain wealth (*ḥayil*), in order to confirm his covenant." Habakkuk had learned this lesson well. He knew he had no strength in himself, and so he looked to the Lord.

---

[225] "Adonai Yahweh" (CSB: "My Lord, GOD") appears more than two hundred times in the OT; "Yahweh Adonai" (CSB: "LORD, my Lord") occurs in only four other places besides Hab 3:18, all likewise in psalms: Pss 68:20; 109:21; 140:7; 141:8. The CSB, like most English versions, translates "Yahweh" as "LORD" or "GOD" with small capital letters and "Adonai" as "Lord." When the two titles occur together, translators use a variety of ways to differentiate between them.

[226] A. S. Van Der Woude, "כֹּחַ," *TLOT* 1:611.

[227] Robin Wakely, "חַיִל," *NIDOTTE* 2:116–25. See Gen 47:6; Deut 3:18; 8:18; Ruth 3:11.

[228] Roberts, *Nahum, Habakkuk, and Zephaniah*, 158, points out the irony that whereas the Babylonian soldier boasted in his military might as his god, the humble prophet declared, "Yahweh is my army."

Habakkuk closes v. 19, and the last panel, with an allusion to Ps 18:33 // 2 Sam 22:34. Like Habakkuk 3, the psalm describes a theophany, sharing similar terminology. The two differ because God answered the cry for help voiced in the Davidic psalm without the delay encountered by the prophet. The psalm may have resonated with Habakkuk for that reason. In both passages, the preceding clause speaks of drawing strength (*ḥayîl*) from the Lord. The same imagery then expresses what strength looks like in both passages:

> He makes my feet like the feet of a deer
> and sets me securely on the heights. (Ps 18:33 // 2 Sam 22:34)

> He makes my feet like those of a deer
> and enables me to walk on mountain heights! (Hab 3:19)

Habakkuk may have found the inspiration for his closing verse in his meditations on Psalm 18, reused by David in 2 Samuel. Unlike the psalmist who reported on God's deliverance from his enemies, the prophet had to believe by faith the Lord would deliver the righteous on a distant day in the future.

Other OT passages make references to deer as well. Deuteronomy 14:5–6 declared deer to be a clean animal, suitable for food, and venison was served to King Solomon on a daily basis (1 Kgs 4:23). In his theophany before Job, the Lord mentioned the roe deer's gestation and labor with reference to his omnipresence and omniscience (Job 39:1–4).[229] Like Hab 3:19, other OT occurrences compare humans to deer. Jacob's blessing compared the tribe of Naphtali to "a doe set free / that bears beautiful fawns" (Gen 49:21). The desperate thirst of a buck searching for flowing streams makes an apt analogy for the human heart's longing for God (Ps 42:1; Isa 35:6). A young bride compares her groom to the beauty and grace of a stag on the mountains (Song 2:9, 17; see also Prov 5:19). In contrast, Lam 1:6 compares Judah's leaders after the fall of Jerusalem to "stags that find no pasture; / they stumble away exhausted / before the hunter."

---

[229] Roe deer are the only deer that have the unique ability to delay implantation. This adaptation allows the animal to mate in the summer, but the embryo stays dormant for months, prolonging gestation until conditions are optimum for a spring birth.

The species referred to in Hab 3:19 is a female roe deer (Hb. ʾayyālâ), a variety once plentiful in Israel.[230] Roe deer are small: males are just over two feet tall at the shoulder and weigh about sixty pounds.[231] The sure-footedness of the deer is the focus of the analogy in Habakkuk. "Deer feet" would enable the prophet to navigate rugged terrain. Habakkuk did not have to develop this ability on his own. God himself would supply what was needed. Both verbs in the first line of v. 19 reflect this provision. The first Hb. verb, śîm (Eng. to "put, set, or place"), often appears in metaphoric language as it does here, where one object is "placed" in the domain of another.[232] The Lord thus "makes" the prophet's feet to be like deer feet. The second verb "walk" is in the causative (hiphil) stem,[233] so the Lord "causes (him) to walk/tread" on the heights. Here, as in Ps 18:33 and 2 Sam 22:34, the "heights" (Hb. bāmôtay) also has the first-person pronominal suffix: "my heights." The symbolism behind the analogy could therefore mean the Lord would enable the prophet to walk through the extremely difficult challenges laying before him. Several times the causative stem of "walk" refers to God's leading his people to walk on right paths. Psalm 25:5, for example, says, "*Guide* me in your truth and teach me, / for you are the God of my salvation; / I wait for you all day long."[234]

---

[230] Both the roe deer (Hb. ʾayyāl) and the Persian fallow deer (Hb. yahmûr; "roebuck" found only in Deut 14:5; 1 Kgs 4:23) disappeared from Palestine in the nineteenth century due to overhunting and loss of habitat. The Persian fallow deer were reintroduced to Israel in 1978 with the arrival of four female deer on the last flight out of Tehran before the Islamic Revolution. See Liat Collins, "Persian fallow deer: Roe-bucking extinction," in *The Jerusalem Post* July 23, 2020). Online: https://www.jpost.com/israel-news/persian-fallow-deer-roe-bucking-extinction-636083. There have been several unsuccessful attempts in the last few decades to reintroduce the roe deer, but lack of free water appears to be the main obstacle. See Arian D. Wallach, "Feasibility of Roe Deer (Capreolus capreolus) Reintroduction to Israel" (Master's Thesis, University of Haifa, 2005), 5–6. Online: https://www.academia.edu/ 2069057/ Feasibility_of_Roe_Deer_Reintroduction_to_Israel.

[231] Like other deer, their strong back legs enable them to run fast and jump several feet in the air; their front legs allow the animal to pivot quickly. The feet of a deer, however, make all of these moves possible. A deer foot is actually two elongated toes, capped in a hoof made of fingernail-like keratin. The outer hoof is hard and strong, absorbing shock and providing traction on soft surfaces. It can also serve as a defense weapon. The softer inner hoof provides traction and cushion on hard surfaces. Each foot has two dewclaws that give the foot a wider base in snow or mud. These features work together to ensure the deer's dexterity and stability, even on rocky terrain.

[232] Sam Meier, "שׂים," *NIDOTTE* 3:1234.

[233] GKC §53c.

[234] Emphasis added. See also Pss 25:9; 107:7; 119:35; Isa 42:16; 48:17.

Although *bāmôtay* (from the Hb. root *bmh*) can refer to mountain heights (2 Sam 1:19), the vast majority of OT occurrences refer to the "high places" situated on elevated hills. Over time, the Israelites had adopted the religious practices of their neighbors, who burned incense and offered sacrifices at cultic shrines on high places—insidious attempts to usurp the Lord's global temple as their own. Before the construction of the temple in Jerusalem, the practice appears to have been limited to worship of the Lord alone (see 1 Sam 9; 1 Kgs 3). Later, however, Solomon built high places on the hill across from Jerusalem for all his foreign wives to worship their pagan gods (1 Kgs 11:7–8), and his actions set a precedent; the remaining fifty occurrences in Kings and Chronicles refer to idolatrous worship on high places all over Israel. Occasionally, good kings like Hezekiah and Josiah destroyed the high places (2 Kgs 18:4; 23:8–20), but the stubbornly entrenched practice resisted other kings' half-hearted attempts at religious reforms (e.g., 1 Kgs 15:14; 22:43; 2 Kgs 14:4). The prophets warned idolatrous worship at high places, including prostitution and child sacrifice, would eventually lead to God's punishment of both Israel and Judah (Jer 7:31; 17:3; Amos 7:9; Mic 1:5). The Lord even declared, "Jerusalem shall become a heap of ruins, / and the mountain of the house a wooded height (*bmh*)" (Mic 3:12 ESV; see also Jer 26:18). God would severely discipline Judah in Habakkuk's generation, but Hab 3:19 symbolized the hope that genuine worship of the one true God would survive. The prophet's rejoicing, begun in 3:18, would continue, regardless of his bleak circumstances.

The symbolism of walking on the heights has yet another layer of meaning. Scripture reveals a distinct link between treading the land and possession. As the theophanic description in Habakkuk 3 illustrates, God himself treads on both land and sea (vv. 3, 5, 6, 8, 12, 15). Job 9:8 declares that God alone "treads on the waves [or "heights"; *bmh*] of the sea." Amos 4:13 likewise proclaims, "He is here: / the one who forms the mountains / . . . and strides on the heights (*bmh*) of the earth." Because God created the earth and sea and their heights, he has dominion over them and the authority to distribute them as he chooses. Deuteronomy 32:8–9 explains that the Most High graciously "gave the nations their inheritance and . . . set the boundaries of the peoples"; the people of Israel, however, he chose for his own inheritance. The Lord repeatedly promised to give the Israelites "[e] very place the sole of [their feet tread]" (Deut 11:24).[235] Just before they entered the promised land, Moses spoke his last recorded words: "Your enemies will cringe before you, / and you will tread on their backs (Hb. *bmh*)" (Deut 33:29b CSB; cf. ESV). Other English versions of this verse render this last phrase as "on their heights" (NIV), or some version of "tread/trample upon/down their high places" (NASB, KJV, NKJV).[236] God would give the Israelites victory over their enemies, and he would give them possession of their lands.

When Israel strayed from God, the Lord summoned foreign kings to capture her land. In turn they too would face God's judgment. Sennacherib of Assyria, for example, boasted he had ascended "to the heights of the mountains, / to the far recesses of Lebanon" (2 Kgs 19:23 // Isa 37:24). The Lord's counterclaim unmasked Sennacherib as a fraudulent upstart: "I will break Assyria in my land; / I will tread him down on my mountain" (Isa 14:25). The king of Babylon tried to trespass on the Lord's own territory, saying, "I will ascend above the highest (*bmt*) clouds; / I will make myself like the Most High" (Isa 14:14). The Lord countered his boast in the next verse, noting he would be brought down to the deepest levels of Sheol instead (Isa 14:15). Micah 1:3 describes how the Lord left his holy temple in order to come down "to trample the heights of the earth." Not only did he trample the earth and reclaim his land; he also trod the peoples—both his own and others—"like grapes in a winepress" of judgment (Lam 1:15; cf. Isa 63:3). The Lord had the authority to give the land back to those whom he chose. He vowed to punish the enemy who said, "Aha! The ancient heights have become our possession," and he commanded the mountains of Israel to bear fruit on behalf of his people: "I will cause . . . my people Israel, to walk on you; they will possess you, and you will be their inheritance . . . [and not] deprive them"(Ezek 36:2, 12).

Several biblical passages suggest a correlation between agricultural abundance and the heights of the land. Jeremiah, for example, paints a beautiful picture of the restored remnant in terms of the threefold agricultural fertility imagery and rejoicing on the heights:

---

[235] See also 1:36; 11:24–25; Josh 1:3; 14:9.

[236] For a discussion of the morphological and semantic variations of the various Hb. forms of *bmh/bmt,* see H. H. Hardy and B. D. Thomas, "Another Look at Biblical Hebrew *bɔmɔ* 'High Place,'" *VT* 62 (2012): 175–88.

> They will come and shout for joy on the *heights* of Zion;
> they will be radiant with joy
> because of the LORD's goodness,
> because of the *grain, the new wine, the fresh oil,*
> and because of the young of the flocks and herds.
> Their life will be like an irrigated garden,
> and they will no longer grow weak from hunger (Jer 31:12;
>   emphasis added)

The abundant fruitfulness in this passage elicits rejoicing on the heights. Other passages combine the theme of agricultural bounty with the concept of walking, riding, or "treading on the heights" (see chart below). The Lord's invitation to scale the heights is often accompanied by abundant agricultural fruitfulness as the first section of the chart shows. The Song of Moses describes God's original relationship to Israel in these terms, and Moses's final blessing promises that the Lord will enable Israel to possess the heights of their enemies (Deut 32:13–14; 33:28–29). Isaiah uses this same imagery to picture the restoration, and Ezekiel indicates this blessing refutes the previous claims of their enemies to possess their heights (Isa 58:14; Ezek 36:2, 8–12).

The second section of the chart shows there is a dark side to this motif that surfaces in the Book of the Twelve. Amos and Micah present a fearsome picture of the sovereign Lord coming to judge Israel for her rebellion and sins. The Israelites had failed to return to the Lord despite the Deuteronomic curses leveling their crops. Leaving his holy temple, the Divine Warrior would trample the heights of the earth, and the mountains would melt like wax before him. This prophetic warning was a call to repentance, to return to God before it was too late.

Positive Examples of Agricultural Fertility and the Heights[237]	
Deuteronomy 32:13–14	The Lord made Israel ride on the heights of the land and eat produce of the field, honey, oil, curds, milk, fat from herd and flock, choicest grains of wheat, and wine from finest grapes.
Deuteronomy 33:28–29	Israel dwells securely, untroubled in a land of grain and new wine, and skies dripping with dew. How happy you are, Israel, a people saved by the Lord! Your enemies will cringe before you. You will tread on their backs [or "heights"].
Isaiah 58:14	You will delight in the Lord. I will make you ride over the heights of the land. I will let you enjoy [Hb. ʾākal, "to eat"; "feast on," NIV; "I will feed you," ESV, NASB] the heritage of your Father Jacob.
Ezekiel 36:2, 8, 12, 29–30	Because the enemy said, "The ancient heights have become our possession," the mountains of Israel will bear fruit, grain, produce of the field. I will cause my people Israel to walk on and possess them.
Negative Examples of Agricultural Fertility and the Heights	
Amos 4:6, 9, 12–13	I gave you absolutely nothing to eat; I struck you with blight and mildew. Locusts devoured gardens, vineyards, fig trees, olive trees, yet you did not return to me. Therefore, Israel, prepare to meet your God— the one who forms the mountains and strides on the heights of the earth.
Micah 1:2–5	From his holy temple the Lord is coming down to trample the heights of the earth. Mountains melt beneath him like wax near a fire because of Israel's rebellion and sins.
A Unique Example of Agricultural Fertility and the Heights	
Habakkuk 3:17–19	Though fig tree, grapevine, olive crop, and grain harvest fail, though flocks and herds disappear, yet I will rejoice in the God of my salvation! He makes my feet like those of a deer and enables me to walk on mountain heights!

[237] Rather than including full quotations here, this summary chart uses abbreviated, paraphrastic statements drawn from the language of the CSB.

The above biblical texts associate "treading on the heights" with agricultural fertility—either positively or negatively. When Israel obeyed, the Lord invited his people to walk with him and share in his possession and abundance in the land. When they rebelled, he warned them by removing his blessing from the land. If they failed to heed his warning, he would come down from his heavenly temple to trample the heights of the earth in judgment. In the final chart above, Habakkuk stands out.[238] The prophet's psalm recounts a theophanic vision of the Divine Warrior who is sovereign over all the earth: "He stands and shakes the earth," "march[es] across the earth with indignation," and "tread[s] the sea with [his] horses (Hab 3:6, 12, 15). By trampling land and sea, God was reclaiming all the earth as his own. Clearly Habakkuk recognized judgment was imminent. Yet this man of faith chose to praise God through it all. Habakkuk was satisfied the Lord who owned all the earth would enable the prophet to accompany him as together they tread upon the heights. Such relationship was far better than agricultural bounty. Habakkuk had the Lord, and he was enough. Ironically, the prophet's decision to trust God in the face of unimaginable loss resulted in unimaginable gain.

Scripture often describes life in relationship to the Lord as "walking with God."[239] Enoch stands out in the genealogical record of Seth as one who "walked with God," as did Noah (Gen 5:24; 6:9). The Lord commanded Abraham to walk in his presence (Gen 17:1). Moses later included "walking in all his ways" as one of God's essential requirements, a command repeated by Joshua in his day and the prophet Micah as well (Deut 10:12; Josh 22:5; Mic 6:8). Furthermore, several OT passages connect the concept of God's walking on earth with worship at sanctuaries—both in the garden of Eden and at the tabernacle (Gen 3:8; Lev 26:12; Deut 23:14; 2 Sam 7:6–7).[240] The same theme appears in the NT as well, where Paul admonishes the Corinthians by quoting Lev 26:12:

---

[238] See 7.2 in the Introduction: "Themes Shared by Habakkuk and the Twelve" and the unique position held by Habakkuk in the corresponding chart: "Agricultural Motif in the Book of the Twelve and Deuteronomy."

[239] Although the examples mentioned in this paragraph use the Hb. verb *hālak* (Eng. "go, come, walk") instead of *dārak* (Eng. "march, tread"), the terms are in the same semantic domain as evidenced by the CSB translation of *dārak* in Hab 3:19 as "walk."

[240] See the discussion of "pathways" (Hb. *hălîkâ*) under Hab 3:6.

For we are the temple of the living God, as God said:
**I will dwell
and walk among them,
and I will be their God,
and they will be my people.** (2 Cor 6:16; emphasis in original)

God's intention all along has been that the earth would become a global sanctuary, filled with worshipers who walk with him.

In Habakkuk, not only does the Divine Warrior march across the earth to establish his dominion; he does so to reclaim the whole earth as a sanctuary. Other prophets—like Ezekiel—explain the Lord will restore Israel, filling his reclaimed possession with agricultural abundance and worshipers who walk on "the mountains and hills . . . the ravines and valleys" (Ezek 36:6, 12; cf. 1–38). Although the book of Habakkuk contains no direct mention of this restoration, it contains a few hints of life beyond the destruction of Jerusalem, tantalizing glimpses of God's mission fulfilled. Habakkuk 2:20 suggests the realm of the Lord's heavenly temple rightfully encompasses "the whole earth," and Hab 3:3 envisions the heavens filled with his splendor and earth resounding with praise. The chiastic centerpiece in Hab 2:13–14 ushers in these realities with the judgment of the wicked and the inundation of the earth with the knowledge of the most holy glory of God. The heights belong to God. They are his dwelling place, part of his cosmic temple. The high places, once sites of despicable idolatry, will be incorporated into this sanctuary of the living God in all his glory. The worship celebration begun by the prophet who rejoiced as he scaled the heights was just a prelude to the global symphony of praise yet to come.

This final section of the third panel (III:D′; 3:16–19) has several parallels with the corresponding section (I:D; 2:1–5) in the first panel.

Parallelism in the Side Panels I:D and III:D′		
	I:D (2:1–5)	**III:D′ (3:16–20)**
Setting	Prophet in prayer on lookout tower	Prophet in prayer on mountain heights
Parallel Forms	2 cohortative imperfects:[241] I will stand . . . I will station myself!	2 cohortative imperfects: I will celebrate in Lord; I will rejoice!
Actions	Petulant prophet expects reply	Chastened prophet quakes before God
	Wait for vision's appointed time!	He will wait for invaders' day of distress.
	Wicked without integrity will fall	Lord enables feet to scale mountains
Portrait	A wicked man	The prophet, righteous by faith
	His enlarged appetite is like Sheol.	Even if he loses all sources of food
	Like Death he is never satisfied.	The prophet is content to rejoice in Lord.
Complaint	The Babylonian Empire is set on gathering and devouring all nations.	
Shift		God of salvation will sustain his people and restore his dominion over the land.

Section I:D opens with the prophet confidently standing at his guard post, watching to see what God would say to him (2:1). In contrast, III:D′ opens with the prophet trembling where he stood, having heard "the sound" (3:16). Both sections contain two pairs of cohortative verbs, the only ones in the book. At the close of the first panel, the prophet intently resolved, "I will stand" and "I will station myself" (2:1). At the close of this third panel, the chastened prophet firmly resolved, "I will celebrate in the LORD" and "I will rejoice in the God of my salvation" (3:18). Both sections also involve waiting. In section I:D, the Lord instructed Habakkuk to wait "for the appointed time" for the vision, even if it seemed to delay (2:3). In III:D′ the prophet determined to wait quietly "for the day of distress" to come against the invaders (3:16). He rested in anticipation of that day, unlike the arrogant man in I:D, who "is never at rest" (2:5).

---

[241] Walker and Lund, "The Literary Structure of the Book of Habakkuk," 360, likewise point out the corresponding occurrence of double pairs of cohortative imperfect Hb. verbs in 2:1 (I:D; "I will stand"; "I will station myself") and 3:18 (III:D′); "I will celebrate"; "I will rejoice"). GKC §108a notes the added suffix (-āh) indicates an "emphatic statement of fixed determination." The cohortative verb form does not appear elsewhere in Habakkuk.

The repeated food motif recurs one last time in both parallel sections. In I:D, the focus is on the arrogant man whose insatiable appetite is never satisfied, who is as greedy as the pit of Sheol/Death (2:5). In contrast, in III:D′ the focus is on a man who is righteous by faith, who vows to rejoice in God, even in the face of death, even when deprived of all food or wine (3:16)—consumed by the gluttonous man in I:D! The first panel closes with the image of a greedy man desperately gathering up all the nations and peoples for his own possession (2:5). Because he is unstable, the wicked man will ultimately topple and perish (2:4a).

The final panel closes with the prophet treading on heights with the ease of a deer and the strength of the sovereign Lord, reclaiming the heights and possessing the land God had given his people (3:19). Because Habakkuk was a man of faith(fulness), he would ultimately live (2:4b). Robertson asks, "[Is this] an expectation of life after the last enemy has done his worst?" By the book's end he concludes that Habakkuk's faith is close to "resurrection faith": "Certainly his faith is not far from that point."[242] Shepherd concurs: although the prophet desired to see the eschaton unfold in his day, he resolved "to trust in the LORD even if he must wait until the resurrection."[243] Habakkuk was not reassured that he would merely survive the coming onslaught; rather, he was assured that his relationship with the Lord would endure into the age to come.

3.5.4   Musical Instructions (3:19b)

For the choir director:
on stringed instruments.

3:19b   Although many psalms contain musical notations as part of a superscription, Habakkuk 3 is unique in that it concludes with a musical notation in a subscription. Fifty-five psalms have superscriptions that specify "For the choir director."[244] Seven of these also indicate

---

[242] Robertson, *The Books of Nahum, Habakkuk, and Zephaniah*, 246.
[243] Shepherd, *A Commentary on the Book of the Twelve*, 343.
[244] Some scholars speculate that the notation indicates Habakkuk 3 and other psalms with this designation belonged to a "Director's Psalter," which may have been the prayer book of the synagogue during the Greek period. If so, Habakkuk's prayer was regularly sung by following generations.

that the psalm was to be accompanied "with/on stringed instruments" (Pss 4; 6; 54; 55; 61; 67; 76). Habakkuk 3 begins with a superscription (see above), but for some reason, this final musical notation was recorded after the psalm.[245] The closing instructions remind the reader of the genre of chap. 3. This passage was not for Habakkuk alone; it was intended to be sung in community. The psalm exemplifies the praise envisioned in 3:3 and commended by the prophet in 3:18. The notation serves as a call to worship for others. It encourages them, like Habakkuk, to trust God and walk by faith with him even through incredibly dark days.

Lyrics formed in the crucible of suffering tend to resonate across the ages. When Job lost all he held dear, his ancient words of praise rose from the dust where he fell in worship to find their way into today's choruses.[246] The words of Psalm 46:10 moved Katharina von Schlegel to author a German hymn in 1752. Translated into English in 1855, "Be Still My Soul" has soothed countless troubled hearts since. In 1873, a storm at sea claimed the lives of Horatio G. Spafford's four daughters. Traveling over the same spot where their ship went down, the grieving father penned the enduring lyrics to "It Is Well." His sacrifice of praise during unspeakable loss continues to comfort those who mourn. The encouraging lyrics of "He Will Hold Me Fast," composed by Ada Habershon (1861–1958), have been adopted by several contemporary artists. The myriad painful situations that forged these songs of praise have comforted those facing a myriad more.

The choice to worship by faith, even in pain, produces joy and strength in our generation as well. Not long ago I was transfixed by an online video a Canadian friend shared: in it, a few people were singing around a hospital bed, accompanied by a single guitar. In the bed lay a frail woman whose paralyzed limbs were tightly drawn. Unable to speak, she simply mouthed the words to a song that was new to me: "Raise a Hallelujah."[247] The breathtaking radiance displayed on

---

[245] Shepherd, *A Commentary on the Book of the Twelve*, 349, suggests that the Hebrew wording of the subscription has another possible translation. The word "director" can also mean "one who endures"; "on my stringed instruments" can mean "in my afflictions." Shepherd believes this to be a fitting ending to Habakkuk, as the prayer is "for the one who endures to the end in the midst of such afflictions."

[246] Job 1:21 is preserved in the title and chorus of Matt Redman's "Blessed Be Your Name" (2002). Likewise, the title of Shane and Shane's "Though You Slay Me" (2013) reflects Job's commitment to hope in God even if the Lord should kill him (Job 13:15).

[247] This song was born out of the anguish of praying for a child whose life hung in the

her face—despite her circumstances—embodied the lyrics of the song. Her worship immediately moved me to tears, and I had to know her story. As it turns out, Kim Vogel lived in my hometown in South Carolina. Diagnosed with a severe form of multiple sclerosis in her junior year of university, Kim graduated in 1997 with a cane and a broken spirit. She thought, *"This isn't what I had planned for my life!"* Kim's written testimony from 2010 explains how her perspective shifted:

> I have known for a long time that I am to count this trial as all joy. I didn't understand why or how this could be done. But now, many years later, after much stretching and growing, I can't contain the joy! I believe and embrace that my calling, from the platform of my wheelchair, is to display the unspeakable joy, the heartfelt peace, and the unshakeable security which I find in God and through the pages of Scripture. I am now able to wait expectantly on him who is faithful and who keeps his word and his covenant of love. There is no need for anyone to still feel sorry for me. I have discovered that suffering is necessary for steadfastness and maturity. The more we seek him, the more he makes himself known. I want to continue to give God the glory as he turns this earthly mess into a glorious message. Situations may not make earthly sense, but everything can be used for his glory. Knowing that we are loved by our heavenly Father gives us the joy and peace to withstand anything![248]

When she was no longer able to speak, Kim handed out cards, eloquently sharing her story with a beautiful smile to illustrate it. Kim entered the presence of her Savior on January 22, 2021. The Lord has used her message to inspire others—all the way to Canada and possibly beyond. As her life testifies, a melody can be a potent weapon, flung in the face of the enemy.

Habakkuk learned this same truth over twenty-six hundred years ago. The prophet anticipated a level of suffering most of us cannot even imagine. He could have easily rehearsed a litany of potential outcomes—and there were many: Will I die? Will I be forced into exile? Will I watch my loved ones suffer? What will we eat? When will

---

balance. It was written by Jake Stevens, Jonathan David Helser, Melissa Helser, and Molly Skaggs and released in 2019.

[248] Kim Vogel and her husband graciously granted permission to share her story.

all this take place? When will God punish those invading us? When will the Divine Warrior finally destroy the leader of the house of the wicked, Habakkuk learned to silence his anxious heart by singing in the middle of the story.

In a world that appears to be careening out of control, it is difficult to rest in the sovereignty of God. Though our own circumstances may be deeply troubling, they do not approximate the deprivations Jerusalem would experience during the Babylonian siege when every single source of food disappeared. As disturbing as it is to view the aftermath of missile strikes on a television screen, it pales in comparison to living the siege Jerusalem would endure for more than a year and a half. Her judgment for abandoning God would inevitably lead to sword, famine, and exile. We dare not think ourselves or any nation above judgment. If we faced a similar future as the prophet, would we have Habakkuk's quiet resolve to trust in the sovereignty of God?

The revelation Habakkuk experienced was a bit like one of those books where transparent plastic overlays show successive stages of a project in development. The bottom picture depicts what is right in front of you—what you can see with your own eyes. Subsequent overlays allow you to envision details of the intervening stages before the project's final completion. The book of Habakkuk contains three such overlays of pronouncements and vision. The bottom page pictured the historical Judah right in front of the prophet's eyes—the social injustice, violence, oppression, and strife that made him cry out to God in the opening verses. Why wasn't God listening? How long would he have to wait for God to do something, to step in and save?

In response to the prophet's questions, the Lord announced he *was* at work among the nations. He then held up the first transparent overlay-pronouncement—a picture of Babylonian horsemen galloping toward Jerusalem to besiege the city. Their faces etched with violence, the soldiers mocked kings and laughed at fortresses. Habakkuk recoiled at the picture. Reviewing God's names and his character, he asked how the Lord could tolerate such treachery. How could God remain silent while the wicked swallowed up those more righteous than themselves? Habakkuk's imagination added in his own details to that first overlay—blasphemous Babylonians hauling up humans like fish in a net. Would this wickedness go on unchecked forever? The prophet resolved to take his stand and wait until God turned another page. In response, the Lord announced that a vision was coming about the end. He instructed Habakkuk to record it carefully and to await its fulfillment. A preview of the vision announced in essence, "the wicked will perish, but the righteous will live by his faith(fulness)." Before the page turned, a last glance at the first overlay revealed a disgusting portrait of a wicked man gorging himself on nations and peoples, as ravenous as Sheol and Death but never satisfied.

The Lord then showed the prophet a second transparent overlay-pronouncement—a montage of five scenes illustrating the woes that would befall the wicked. The top two pictures revealed that victims would wake up, accuse, and plunder the plunderer; the house built with dishonest wealth would testify against its builder. The bottom two pictures showed that those who exploited and abused others would themselves be exposed; those who worshiped mute idols would be silenced. The image at the center of this overlay provided a snapshot of the essence and fulfillment of God's mission: the works of the wicked will go up in flames, while the knowledge of God's glory will flood the earth. Questions may have lingered in Habakkuk's mind, but they were snuffed out by the Lord's command, "Silence!"

The third and final overlay was not a pronouncement but rather a vision of God himself. Just as the Divine Warrior had come to administer justice in the past, he would do so again, both in the present and in the days to come. But life is not an endless cycle of sin and judgment set to repeat. On a future day, the Divine Warrior would step down from his heavenly temple to walk on earth. He would crush the head of the house of the wicked and deliver his people forever.

These successive overlays of revelation reordered the prophet's perspective of history, God, and even himself. The Lord's astounding work of raising the Babylonians to destroy Jerusalem was simply the next step toward fulfilling his mission. The vision was humbling, terrifying, and awe-inspiring at the same time. Seeing even the barest outlines of the overall design allowed the prophet to grasp his place in the larger divine purpose and plan. He saw his sufferings in the light of eternity. God was not ordering the world for Habakkuk's own personal health, happiness, or comfort. He did not do that for his own Son, nor will he do it for us. God's ultimate mission is to redeem a people and reclaim the entire world as a sanctuary where he will walk with them and reveal his glory.

On this side of the cross, we are able to recognize the astounding, incomprehensible work of God is to raise the dead to life—either to judgment or eternal life in his presence. Even a brief glimpse of that vision enabled the prophet to trust God and wait for the end of the story. As a result, Habakkuk experienced God himself. He settled in to walk with the Lord through the events that lay before him. Convinced of the Lord's ongoing presence and strength, the prophet was able to press on, rejoicing. From the middle of the story, in the middle of the storm, Habakkuk made the concerted choice to worship God by faith. The prophet at the end of chap. 3 was not the same man as at the beginning of chap. 1. His encounter with the Lord and his newfound eternal perspective had transformed him.

The overall structure of Habakkuk emphasizes the prophet's transformation. The intentional contrast becomes clear in chap. 3. The pronouncement mentioned in 1:1 had shifted the prophet to the prayer and praise found in 3:1. The setting for both I:A (1:2–4) and III:A′ (3:2) was the prophet's prayer closet, but Habakkuk's petitions had changed from confused complaints to humbled acquiescence. In section I:B (1:5–11) Babylonian soldiers marched across the open places of the earth to seize territories that belonged to others. In III:B′ (3:3–7) the mighty Warrior-King strode through the desert, reclaiming his land as mountains and hills bowed low before him. I:C (1:12–17) pictured the Babylonians, ruling the sea, piercing their leaderless enemies with hooks, and gathering a human feast in their nets. They offered profane worship to false gods to ensure their economic and military success. In contrast, III:C′ (3:8–15) revealed that the Lord alone is master of the sea, the rivers, and the deep. With all nature in his arsenal, he fatally pierced the leader of wickedness and the ravenous members of his household. When God appears, all heaven and earth recognize his rightful dominion.

The final sections in both panels illustrate how Habakkuk's encounter with the Lord changed him as well. In I:D (2:1–5) the prophet boldly mounted his watchtower, firmly resolved to stand his ground to see what God would say and do. In III:D′ (3:16–19), after seeing God at work and glimpsing his glory, the trembling prophet firmly resolved to rejoice as he mounted the heights in God's strength. With the Lord by his side, Habakkuk reclaimed an outpost that had been the scene of pagan practices. He courageously lifted his voice, and his praise cascaded down from the heights and wafted across a land filled with social, moral, and spiritual darkness; unspeakable suffering approached just over the horizon. Nevertheless, by faith, he completely surrendered to a God who would not be deterred from his mission to judge the wicked and save his people.

Habakkuk's determination to rejoice in such a setting is an example of faith and hope. His encounter with God had transformed and transfixed him. Even in scarcity and brokenness, his faith allowed him to experience abundant life in the present and the hope of life beyond death in the age to come. Habakkuk became a model of the faith-(-fulness) described in 2:4. He stood as a harbinger of the fulfillment of God's mission described in 2:14. Finally, the prophet also became a part of that mission as his prophetic psalm invites readers of every age to step into his story and join in the chorus so that they too might experience the same transformation. One day the anthem of the Lord's renown will encircle the earth, a global sanctuary filled with worship of the Lord whose glory and praises cover the earth "as the water covers the sea."

* * * * * * *

At the appointed time, the vision came. God the Son stepped down into human flesh and walked the dusty pathways of Judah in sandaled feet that needed washing. He sat on the hills he had made and taught about the kingdom that was to come, the kingdom that was at hand. He walked on water; he calmed the seas and stilled the waves. His disciples bowed down at his feet in recognition of his holiness. He told them where to lower their nets and haul in more fish than they had ever imagined; he promised to make them fishers of men. In an unbelievably astonishing work, the Messiah turned the weapon of the ultimate enemy—a wooden cross—into the weapon that would crush the enemy's head and bring salvation to his people. Incredibly, the palms that hide his power and the feet that tread ancient paths were forever scarred with wounds that bring many to glory.

On an appointed day in the future, the risen Lord will return a final time as the Divine Warrior, crushing Satan and destroying the ultimate house of wickedness. The Lord will reign forever, his glory will fill the earth, and every redeemed person in every place will know him. While we long for his appearing, he calls for people to believe in him and to trust in his work of salvation. He desires both our faith and faithfulness as we wait. Scaling the heights with the Lord like Habakkuk, we cannot help but be concerned about God's mission, spreading the knowledge of him and his works of salvation and judgment to every generation until his glorious return.

SELECTED BIBLIOGRAPHY

Achtemeier, Elizabeth Rice. *Nahum–Malachi*. Interpretation. Louisville: John Knox, 1986.

Ahituv, Shmuel. "The Sinai Theophany in the Psalm of Habakkuk." Pages 225–32 in *Birkat Shalom: Studies in the Bible, Ancient Near Eastern Literature, and Postbiblical Judaism Presented to Shalom M. Paul on the Occasion of His Seventieth Birthday*. Winona Lake: Eisenbrauns, 2008.

Albright, W. F. "The Psalm of Habakkuk." Pages 1–18 in *Studies in Old Testament Prophecy: Presented to Professor Theodore H. Robinson by the Society for Old Testament Study on His Sixty-Fifth Birthday*. Edited by H. H. Rowley. Edinburgh: T&T Clark, 1950.

———. *Yahweh and the Gods of Canaan: A Historical Analysis of Two Contrasting Faiths*. New York: Doubleday, 1968.

Amerding, Carl E. "Habakkuk." Pages 491–534 in *Daniel—Minor Prophets*. Expositor's Bible Commentary 7. Grand Rapids: Zondervan, 1985.

Andersen, Francis I. *Habakkuk*. Anchor Bible 25. New York: Doubleday, 2001.

Anderson, John E. "Awaiting an Answered Prayer: The Development and Reinterpretation of Habakkuk 3 in Its Contexts." *Zeitschrift für die alttestamentliche Wissenschaft* 123 (2011): 57–71.

Avishur, Yitzhak. *Studies in Hebrew and Ugaritic Psalms*. Jerusalem: Magnes Press Hebrew University, 1994.

Bailey, D. Waylon. "Habakkuk." Pages 245–378 in *Micah, Nahum, Habakkuk, Zephaniah*. The New American Commentary 20. Nashville: Broadman & Holman, 1999.

Baker, David W. *Nahum, Habakkuk, and Zephaniah: An Introduction and Commentary*. Tyndale Old Testament Commentaries 27. Downers Grove: IVP Academic, 2009.

Bakon, Shimon. "Habakkuk: From Perplexity to Faith." *Jewish Bible Quarterly* 39 (2011): 25–30.

Barré, Michael L. "Habakkuk 3:2: Translation in Context." *The Catholic Biblical Quarterly* 50 (1988): 184–97.

Barthélemy, Dominique. *Preliminary and Interim Report on the Hebrew Old Testament Text Project*. Vol. 5. New York: United Bible Societies, 1980.

———. "Yahweh Gears up for Battle: Habakkuk 3, 9a." *Biblica* 87 (2006): 75–84.

Beale, G. K. *The Temple and the Church's Mission: A Biblical Theology of the Dwelling Place of God*; New Studies in Biblical Theology 17. Edited by D. A. Carson. Downers Grove: InterVarsity, 2004.

Beaulieu, Paul-Alain. "Nebuchadnezzar's Babylon as World Capital." *Canadian Society for Mesopotamian Studies* 3 (2008): 5–12.

ben Zvi, Ehud. "Twelve Prophetic Books or 'The Twelve': A Few Preliminary Considerations." Pages 125–56 in *Forming Prophetic Literature: Essays on Isaiah and the Twelve in Honor of John D. W. Watts*. Edited by James W. Watts and Paul R. House. Journal for the Study of the Old Testament 235. Sheffield: Sheffield Academic, 1996.

Berlin, Adele. *The Dynamics of Biblical Parallelism*. The Biblical Resource Series. Grand Rapids: Eerdmans, 2008.

Berry, Donald K. "Malachi's Dual Design: The Close of the Canon and What Comes Afterward." Pages 269–302 in *Forming Prophetic Literature: Essays on Isaiah and the Twelve in Honor of John D. W. Watts*. Edited by James W. Watts and Paul House. Sheffield: Sheffield Academic Press, 1996.

Bliese, Loren F. "The Poetics of Habakkuk." *Journal of Translation and Textlinguistics* 12 (1999): 47–75.

Blomberg, Craig. "The Structure of 2 Corinthians." *Criswell Theological Review* 4.1 (1989): 3–20.

Boadt, Lawrence. *Jeremiah 26–52, Habakkuk, Zephaniah, Nahum.* Old Testament Message 10. Wilmington: Michael Glazier, 1982.

Boda, Mark J. "A Deafening Call to Silence: The Rhetorical Role of Human Address to the Deity in the Book of the Twelve." Pages 183–204 in *The Book of the Twelve and the New Form Criticism.* Ancient Near East Monographs 10. Atlanta: SBL Press, 2015.

———. *Exploring Zechariah: The Development of Zechariah and Its Role within the Twelve.* Ancient Near East Monographs 16. Atlanta: SBL Press, 2017.

Boda, Mark J., Michael H. Floyd, and Colin M. Toffelmire, eds. *The Book of the Twelve and the New Form Criticism.* Ancient Near East Monographs 10. Atlanta: SBL Press, 2015.

Booth, Susan Maxwell. *The Tabernacling Presence of God: Mission and Gospel Witness.* Eugene: Wipf & Stock, 2015.

Breck, John. *The Shape of Biblical Language: Chiasmus in the Scriptures and Beyond.* Crestwood, NY: St. Vladimir's Seminary Press, 1994.

Brettler, Marc. "Images of YHWH the Warrior in Psalms." *Semeia* 61 (1993): 135–65.

Brouwer, Wayne. "Understanding Chiasm and Assessing Macro-Chiasm as a Tool of Biblical Interpretation." *Calvin Theological Journal* 53 (2018): 99–127.

Brownlee, William Hugh, ed. *The Midrash Pesher of Habakkuk.* Society of Biblical Literature Monograph Series 24. Missoula, MT: Scholars Press, 1979.

———. "The Placarded Revelation of Habakkuk." *Journal of Biblical Literature* 82 (1963): 319–25.

———. *The Text of Habakkuk in the Ancient Commentary from Qumran.* Journal of Biblical Literature Monograph Series 11. Philadelphia: Society of Biblical Literature and Exegesis, 1959.

Bruce, F. F. "Habakkuk." Pages 831–96 in *The Minor Prophets: A Commentary on Obadiah, Jonah, Micah, Nahum, Habakkuk.* Edited by Thomas Edward McComiskey. Vol. 2. Grand Rapids: Baker Academic, 1993.

Bruckner, James K. *Jonah, Nahum, Habakkuk, Zephaniah*. NIV Application Commentary. Grand Rapids: Zondervan, 2004.

Bullock, C. Hassell. *An Introduction to the Old Testament Prophetic Books*. Chicago: Moody Publishers, 2007.

Chalmers, Aaron. *Interpreting the Prophets: Reading, Understanding and Preaching from the Worlds of the Prophets*. Downers Grove: IVP Academic, 2015.

Childs, Brevard S. *Introduction to the Old Testament as Scripture*. Philadelphia: Fortress, 1979, 2011.

Chisholm, Robert B., Jr. *Handbook on the Prophets*. Grand Rapids: Baker Academic, 2002.

———. "The Polemic against Baalism in Israel's Early History and Literature." *Bibliotheca Sacra* 150 (1994): 267–83.

Civil, M. "The Home of the Fish: A New Sumerian Literary Composition." *Iraq* 23 (1961): 154–75.

Cleaver-Bartholomew, David. "An Alternative Approach to Hab 1, 2–2, 20." *Scandinavian Journal of the Old Testament* 17 (2003): 206–25.

Clendenen, E. Ray. "Salvation by Faith or by Faithfulness in the Book of Habakkuk?" *Bulletin for Biblical Research* 24 (2014): 505–13.

Cross, Frank Moore. *Canaanite Myth and Hebrew Epic: Essays in the History of Religion in Israel*. Cambridge: Harvard University Press, 1973.

Curtis, A. H. W. "The 'Subjugation of the Waters' Motif in the Psalms: Imagery or Polemic?" *Journal of Semitic Studies* 23 (1978): 245–56.

Dangl, Oskar. "Habakkuk in Recent Research." *Currents in Research: Biblical Studies* 9 (2001): 131–68.

Davies, Andrew. "My God . . . Why? Questioning the Action and Inaction of YHWH in the Psalms." Pages 49–67 in *Why? . . . How Long?: Studies on Voice(s) of Lamentation Rooted in Biblical Hebrew Poetry*. Edited by LeAnn Snow Flesher, Carol J. Dempsey, and Mark Boda. New York: Bloomsbury, 2014.

Day, John. "Echoes of Baal's Seven Thunders and Lightnings in Psalm XXIX and Habakkuk III 9 and the Identity of the Seraphim in Isaiah VI." *Vetus Testamentum* 29 (1979): 143–51.

———. "New Light on the Mythological Background of the Allusion to Resheph in Habakkuk." *Vetus Testamentum* 29 (1979): 353–55.

Dempsey, Carol J. "Harrowing Woes and Comforting Promises in the Book of the Twelve." Pages 97–117 in *The Book of the Twelve and the New Form Criticism*. Edited by Mark J. Boda, Michael H. Floyd, and Colin M. Toffelmire. Ancient Near East Monographs 10. Atlanta: SBL Press, 2015.

Dobbs-Allsopp, F. W. *On Biblical Poetry*. New York: Oxford University Press, 2015.

Dockery, David S. "The Use of Hab. 2:4 in Rom. 1:17: Some Hermeneutical and Theological Considerations." *Wesleyan Theological Journal* 22 (1987): 24–36.

Dorsey, David A. *The Literary Structure of the Old Testament: A Commentary on Genesis-Malachi*. Grand Rapids: Baker Books, 1999.

Eaton, J. H. *Obadiah, Nahum, Habakkuk, Zephaniah*. The Torch Bible Commentaries. London: SCM Press, 1961.

———. "Origin and Meaning of Habakkuk 3." *Zeitschrift für die alttestamentliche Wissenschaft* 76 (1964): 144–71.

Emerton, J. A. "The Textual and Linguistic Problems of Habakkuk II. 4–5." *Journal of Theological Studies* 28 (1977): 1–18.

Floyd, Michael H. *Minor Prophets Part 2*. Edited by Rolf P. Knierim, Gene M. Tucker, and Marvin Sweeney. The Forms of the Old Testament Literature 22. Grand Rapids: Eerdmans, 2000.

———. "The מַשָּׂא (*maśśāʾ*) as a Type of Prophetic Book." *Journal of Biblical Literature* 121 (2002): 401–22.

Freedman, David N. "Archaic Forms in Early Hebrew Poetry." *Zeitschrift für die alttestamentliche Wissenschaft* 72 (1960): 101–7.

Fuhr, Richard Alan, and Gary E. Yates. *The Message of the Twelve: Hearing the Voice of the Minor Prophets*. Nashville: B&H Academic, 2016.

Fuller, David J. *A Discourse Analysis of Habakkuk*. Edited by K. A. D. Smelik. Studia Semitica Neerlandica 72. Boston: Brill, 2020.

Garland, D. David. "Habakkuk." Pages 245–69 in *Hosea-Malachi*. Broadman Bible Commentary 7. Nashville: Broadman Press, 1972.

Geller, Stephen A. "Were the Prophets Poets?" Pages 154–65 in *"The Place Is Too Small for Us": The Israelite Prophets in Recent Scholarship*. Edited by R. P. Gordon. Sources for Biblical and Theological Study 5. Winona Lake: Eisenbrauns, 1995.

Goldingay, John, and Pamela J. Scalise. *Minor Prophets II*. Understanding the Bible Commentary Series. Grand Rapids: Baker, 2009.

Gowan, Donald E. *Theology of the Prophetic Books: The Death and Resurrection of Israel*. Louisville: John Knox, 1998.

———. *The Triumph of Faith in Habakkuk*. Atlanta: John Knox, 1976.

Grayson, Albert Kirk. *Assyrian and Babylonian Chronicles*. Texts from Cuneiform Sources 5. Locust Valley, NY: J. J. Augustin, 1975.

Haak, Robert D. *Habakkuk*. Supplements to Vetus Testamentum 44. New York: Brill, 1991.

Hahlen, Mark Allen. "The Literary Design of Habakkuk." Ph.D. diss., The Southern Baptist Theological Seminary, 1992.

Hardy, H. H., and B. D. Thomas. "Another Look at Biblical Hebrew bɔmɔ 'High Place.'" *Vetus Testamentum* 62 (2012): 175–88.

Harper, Joshua L. *Responding to a Puzzled Scribe: The Barberini Version of Habakkuk 3 Analyzed in the Light of the Other Greek Versions*. Library of Hebrew Bible Old Testament Studies 608. London: T&T Clark, 2015.

Harris, John Glyndwr. "Laments of Habakkuk's Prophecy." *The Evangelical Quarterly* 45 (1973): 21–29.

Hays, Christopher B., and Peter Machinist. "Assyria and the Assyrians." Pages 31–106 in *The World around the Old Testament: The People and Places of the Ancient Near East*. Edited by Bill T. Arnold and Brent A. Strawn. Grand Rapids: Baker Academic, 2016.

Heflin, J. N. Boo. *Nahum, Habakkuk, Zephaniah, and Haggai*. Bible Study Commentary. Grand Rapids: Lamplighter Books, 1985.

Hiebert, Theodore. *God of My Victory: The Ancient Hymn in Habakkuk 3*. Harvard Semitic Monographs 38. Atlanta: Scholars Press, 1986.

Hiramatsu, Kei. "The Structure and Structural Relationships of the Book of Habakkuk." *The Journal of Inductive Biblical Studies* 3 (2016): 106–29.

355 Selected Bibliography

Holladay, William L. "Plausible Circumstances for the Prophecy of Habakkuk." *Journal of Biblical Literature* 120 (2001): 123–30.

Hood, Jared. "Yhwh Tsevaot before Samuel: Canonical Foundations for a Davidic Title." *Reformed Theological Review* 81 (2022): 1–32.

———. "Yhwh Tsevaot in Samuel: God of the Davidic Age." *Journal of the Evangelical Theological Society* 62 (2019): 495–513.

House, Paul R. "The Character of God in the Book of the Twelve." Pages 125–45 in *Reading and Hearing the Book of the Twelve*. Edited by James D. Nogalski and Marvin A. Sweeney. Atlanta: SBL Press, 2000.

———. "Dramatic Coherence in Nahum, Habakkuk, and Zephaniah." Pages 195–208 in *Forming Prophetic Literature: Essays on Isaiah and the Twelve in Honor of John D. W. Watts*. Edited by James W. Watts and Paul R. House. Journal for the Study of the Old Testament Supplement Series 235. Sheffield: Sheffield Academic, 1996.

———. *The Unity of the Twelve*. Sheffield: Sheffield Academic, 1990.

Hunn, Debbie. "Habakkuk 2.4b in Its Context: How Far Off Was Paul?" *Journal for the Study of the Old Testament* 34 (2009): 219–39.

Irwin, William A. "The Mythological Background of Habakkuk 3." *Journal of Near Eastern Studies* 15.1 (1956): 47–50.

Janzen, J. Gerald. "Eschatological Symbol and Existence in Habakkuk." *Catholic Biblical Quarterly* 44 (1982): 394–414.

Johnson, Marshall D. "The Paralysis of Torah in Habakkuk 1:4." *Vetus Testamentum* 35 (1985): 257–66.

Jones, Barry A. "The Seventh-Century Prophets in Twenty-First Century Research." *Currents in Biblical Research* 14 (2016): 129–75.

Kassis, Riad A. *Frustrated with God: A Syrian Theologian's Reflections of Habakkuk*. Riad A. Kassis, 2016.

Kelle, Brad E. "Judah in the Seventh Century: From the Aftermath of Sennacherib's Invasion to the Beginning of Jehoiakim's Rebellion." Pages 350–82 in *Ancient Israel's History: An Introduction to Issues and Sources*. Edited by Bill T. Arnold and Richard S. Hess. Grand Rapids: Baker Academic, 2014.

Ko, Grace. *Theodicy in Habakkuk*. Paternoster Biblical Monographs. Milton Keynes: Paternoster, 2014.

Lim, Dong-Weon. "Rhetorical Analysis of the Book of Habakkuk." *Korean Journal of Christian Studies* 29 (2003): 22–35.

———. "Structural Analysis of the Book of Habakkuk." *Korean Journal of Christian Studies* 72 (2013): 69–85.

Lim, Timothy. *The Earliest Commentary in the Prophecy of Habakkuk*. Oxford: Oxford University Press, 2020.

Lloyd-Jones, D. Martin. *From Fear to Faith: Rejoicing in the Lord in Turbulent Times*. Downers Grove: InterVarsity, 2011.

Longman, Tremper, III and Daniel G. Reid. *God Is a Warrior*. Studies in Old Testament Biblical Theology. Grand Rapids: Zondervan, 1995.

Lund, Nils Wilhelm. *Chiasmus in the New Testament: A Study in Formgeschichte*. Chapel Hill: University of North Carolina Press, 1942.

Mellville, Sarah C. "A New Look at the End of the Assyrian Empire." Pages 179–202 in *Homeland and Exile: Biblical and Ancient Near Eastern Studies in Honour of Bustenay Oded*. Edited by Markham J. Geller, et al. Supplements to Vetus Testamentum 130. Leiden: Brill, 2009.

Meynet, Roland. *Treatise on Biblical Rhetoric*. Boston: Brill, 2012.

Moo, Douglas. *The Epistle to the Romans*. New International Commentary on the New Testament. Grand Rapids: Eerdmans, 1996.

———. *Galatians*. Baker Exegetical Commentary on the New Testament. Grand Rapids: Baker Academic, 2013.

———. *The Old Testament in the Gospel Passion Narratives*. Sheffield: Almond Press, 1983.

Morris, Leon. *Galatians: Paul's Charter of Christian Freedom*. Downers Grove: InterVarsity, 1996.

Moseman, R. David. "Habakkuk's Dialogue with Faithful Yahweh: A Transforming Experience." *Perspectives in Religious Studies* 44 (2017): 261–74.

Nielsen, Eduard. "The Righteous and the Wicked in Habaqquq." *Studia Theologica* 6 (1952): 54–78.

Noble, Duncan. "Assyrian Chariotry and Cavalry." *State Archives of Assyria Bulletin* 4 (1990): 65–66.

Nogalski, James D. *The Book of the Twelve: Micah-Malachi*. Smyth & Helwys Bible Commentary. Macon: Smyth & Helwys, 2011.

Nogalski, James D. and Marvin A. Sweeney, eds. *Reading and Hearing the Book of the Twelve*. SBL Symposium Series 15. Atlanta: SBL Press, 2000.

Oates, Joan. *Babylon*. Rev. ed. London: Thames and Hudson, 1986.

O'Neal, Guy Michael. *Interpreting Habakkuk as Scripture: An Application of the Canonical Approach of Brevard S. Childs*. Studies in Biblical Literature 9. New York: Lang, 2007.

Pardee, Dennis. "YPH 'Witness' in Hebrew and Ugaritic." *Vetus Testamentum* 28 (2013): 99–108.

Patterson, Richard D. *Nahum, Habakkuk, Zephaniah*. Richardson, TX: Biblical Studies Press, 2003.

Petersen, David L. "A Book of the Twelve?" Pages 3–10 in *Reading and Hearing the Book of the Twelve*. Edited by James D. Nogalski and Marvin A. Sweeney. Atlanta: SBL Press, 2000.

Pinker, Aron. "Was Habakkuk Presumptuous?" *Jewish Bible Quarterly* 32 (2004): 27–34.

Porter, Stanley E. and Jeffrey T. Reed. "Philippians as a Macro-Chiasm and Its Exegetical Significance." *New Testament Studies* 44 (1998): 214–21.

Poythress, Vern S. *Theophany: A Biblical Theology of God's Appearing*. Wheaton: Crossway, 2018.

Prinsloo, G. T. M. "Reading Habakkuk in the Light of Ancient Unit Delimiters." *Theological Studies* 69 (2012): 1–11.

Prior, David. *The Message of Joel, Micah & Habakkuk*. The Bible Speaks Today. Downers Grove: IVP Academic, 1998.

Renz, Thomas. *The Books of Nahum, Habakkuk, and Zephaniah*. The New International Commentary on the Old Testament. Grand Rapids: Eerdmans, 2021.

Roberts, J. J. M. *Nahum, Habakkuk, and Zephaniah*. The Old Testament Library. Louisville: John Knox, 1991.

Robertson, O. Palmer. *The Books of Nahum, Habakkuk, and Zephaniah*. The New International Commentary on the Old Testament. Grand Rapids: Eerdmans, 2005.

———. "'The Justified (by Faith) Shall Live by His Steadfast Trust': Habakkuk 2:4." *Presbyterion* 9 (1983): 52–71.

Saggs, H. W. F. *The Babylonians: A Survey of the Ancient Civilisation of the Tigris-Euphrates Valley*. London: The Folio Society, 1999.

Savran, George W. *Encountering the Divine: Theophany in Biblical Narrative*. Journal for the Study of the Old Testament Supplement Series 420. New York: T&T Clark, 2005.

Schökel, Luis Alonso. *A Manual of Hebrew Poetics*. Subsidia Biblica 11. Rome: Editrice Pontificio Istituto Biblico, 1988.

Schreiner, Thomas R. *Romans*. 2nd ed. Baker Exegetical Commentary on the New Testament. Grand Rapids: Baker Academic, 2018.

Scott, James M. "A New Approach to Habakkuk II 4–5a." *Vetus Testamentum* 35 (1985): 330–40.

Shepherd, Michael B. *A Commentary on the Book of the Twelve*. Kregel Exegetical Library. Grand Rapids: Kregel Academic, 2018.

Smith, Gary V. "Prophet, Prophecy." Pages 986–1004 in *International Standard Bible Encyclopedia*. Edited by Geoffrey W. Bromiley. Rev. ed. Vol. 3. Grand Rapids: Eerdmans, 1986.

Smith, Ralph L. *Micah–Malachi*. Word Biblical Commentary 32. Waco: Word Books, 1984.

Snyman, S. D. *Nahum, Habakkuk, and Zephaniah: An Introduction and Commentary*. Tyndale Old Testament Commentaries 27. Downers Grove: IVP Academic, 2020.

Stern, Ephraim. *Archaeology of the Land of the Bible, Volume II: The Assyrian, Babylonian, and Persian Periods (732–332 B.C.E.)*. The Anchor Bible Reference Library. New York: Doubleday, 2001.

Sweeney Marvin A. "Structure, Genre, and Intent in the Book of Habakkuk." *Vetus Testamentum* 41 (1991): 63–83.

———. *The Twelve Prophets*. Edited by David W. Cotter. Berit Olam Studies in Hebrew Narrative & Poetry. Collegeville, MN: Liturgical Press, 2000.

Széles, Mária Eszenyei. *Wrath and Mercy: A Commentary on the Books of Habakkuk and Zephaniah*. International Theological Commentary. Grand Rapids: Eerdmans, 1987.

Thomas, Heath A. *Habakkuk*. The Two Horizons Old Testament Commentary. Grand Rapids: Eerdmans, 2018.

Thompson, Michael E. W. "Prayer, Oracle, and Theophany: The Book of Habakkuk." *Tyndale Bulletin* 44 (1993): 33–53.

Thomson, Ian. *Chiasmus in the Pauline Letters*. Sheffield: Sheffield Academic Press, 1995.

Tigay, Jeffrey H. *You Shall Have No Other Gods: Israelite Religion in the Light of Hebrew Inscriptions*. Harvard Semitic Studies 31. Atlanta: Scholars Press, 1986.

Timmer, Daniel C. "The Twelve." Pages 321–40 in *A Biblical-Theological Introduction to the Old Testament: The Gospel Promised*. Edited by Miles V. Van Pelt. Wheaton: Crossway, 2016.

Tsumura, David Toshio. "Janus Parallelism in Hab. III 4." *Vetus Testamentum* 54 (2004): 124–28.

———. "Polysemy and Parallelism in Hab 1, 8–9." *Zeitschrift für die alttestamentliche Wissenschaft* 120 (2008): 194–203.

———. "Ugaritic Poetry and Habakkuk 3." *Tyndale Bulletin* 40 (1989): 24–48.

Van de Mieroop, Marc. *A History of the Ancient Near East, ca. 3000–323 BC*. 3rd ed. Blackwell History of the Ancient World. Malden, MA: Blackwell, 2016.

Vanderhooft, David S. "Babylonia and the Babylonians." Pages 31–106 in *The World around the Old Testament: The People and Places of the Ancient Near East*. Edited by Bill T. Arnold and Brent A. Strawn. Grand Rapids: Baker Academic, 2016.

VanGemeren, Willem A. *Interpreting the Prophetic Word: An Introduction to the Prophetic Literature of the Old Testament*. Grand Rapids: Zondervan, 1990.

Vasholz, Robert I. "Habakkuk: Complaints or Complaint?" *Presbyterion* 18 (1992): 50–52.

Walker, H. H., and Nils Lund. "The Literary Structure of the Book of Habakkuk." *Journal of Biblical Literature* 53 (1934): 355–70.

Ward, William Hayes. "Habakkuk." Pages 1–28 in *A Critical and Exegetical Commentary on Micah, Zephaniah, Nahum, Habakkuk, Obadiah, and Joel*. The International Critical Commentary. Edinburgh: T&T Clark, 1974.

Watson, Wilfred G. E. *Classical Hebrew Poetry: A Guide to Its Techniques*. Journal for the Study of the Old Testament Supplement Series 26. Sheffield: JSOT Press, 1986.

———. *Traditional Techniques in Classical Hebrew Verse*. Journal for the Study of the Old Testament Supplement Series 170. Sheffield: Sheffield Academic, 1994.

Watts, James W. "Psalmody in Prophecy: Habakkuk 3 in Context." Pages 209–23 in *Forming Prophetic Literature: Essays on Isaiah and the Twelve in Honor of John D. W. Watts.* Edited by James W. Watts and Paul R. House. Journal for the Study of the Old Testament Supplement Series 235. Sheffield: Sheffield Academic, 1996.

Wendland, Ernst R. "'The Righteous Live by Their Faith' in a Holy God: Complementary Compositional Forces and Habakkuk's Dialogue with the Lord." *Journal of the Evangelical Theological Society* 42 (1999): 591–628.

Westermann, Claus. *Praise and Lament in the Psalms.* Atlanta: John Knox, 1981.

Whitehead, Philip. "Habakkuk and the Problem of Suffering: Theodicy Deferred." *Journal of Theological Interpretation* 10 (2016): 265–81.

Whitekettle, Richard. "How the Sheep of Judah Became Fish: Habakkuk 1, 14 and the Davidic Monarchy." *Biblica* 96.2 (2015): 273–81.

Wright, Christopher J. H. *The Mission of God: Unlocking the Bible's Grand Narrative.* Downers Grove: Intervarsity, 2006.

Yadin, Yigael. *The Art of Warfare in Biblical Lands.* Translated by M. Pearlman. Vol. 1. New York: McGraw-Hill, 1963.

Yamauchi, Edwin M. *Persia and the Bible.* Grand Rapids: Baker Books, 1996.

NAME INDEX

A

Achtemeier, E.   *11, 14, 129, 151, 315, 316*
Ahituv, S.   *276, 278*
Albright, W. F.   *39, 153, 284, 294, 295*
Allen, L. C.   *239*
Allen, R. B.   *239*
Amerding, C. E.   *50, 141, 177*
Amin, O.   *244*
Amsler, S.   *131*
Andersen, F. I.   *8, 9, 11, 13, 14, 36, 38, 39, 40, 62, 116, 123, 128, 130, 135, 145, 148, 149, 160, 170, 175, 177, 178, 184, 224, 229, 278, 295, 322*
Anderson, J. E.   *39*
Ashford, B. R.   *95*
Augustine   *195*
Austell, H. J.   *248*
Averbeck, R. E.   *135*
Avishur, Y.   *281, 284, 286, 298*

B

Bacher, W.   *181*
Bailey, D. W.   *11, 50, 140, 147, 153, 204, 224, 322*
Baker, D. W.   *7, 11, 143, 164, 177, 242, 289*
Baker, W.   *129*
Bakon, S.   *195*
Baldwin, J. G.   *220*
Bar-Efrat, S.   *76*
Barr, J.   *183*
Barthélemy, D.   *36, 142, 236, 237*
Beale, G. K.   *95, 232, 276*

Beaulieu, P.-A.   *24, 25*
ben Zvi, E.   *80, 81*
Berlin, A.   *44, 45, 46, 51, 199*
Berry, D. K.   *92*
Bliese, L. F.   *53, 58*
Blomberg, C.   *59, 62, 63, 76, 229, 235*
Boadt, L.   *113, 248*
Boda, M. J.   *80, 84, 85, 86, 125, 257, 312*
Booth, S. M.   *95*
Breck, J   *69, 70, 76, 77, 78*
Brensinger, T.   *65*
Brettler, M.   *274*
Brouwer, W.   *59, 78*
Brownlee, W. H.   *37, 125, 160, 164, 177*
Bruce, F. F.   *11, 37, 51, 123, 145, 146, 151, 152, 167, 171, 173, 177, 191, 193, 212*
Bruckner, J.   *128, 149, 157*
Bullock, C. H.   *7, 11, 51, 178, 180*

C

Caird, G. B.   *45*
Calvin, J.   *254*
Carpenter, E.   *129, 146, 147*
Chalmers, A.   *42, 46*
Childs, B. S.   *8, 49, 50*
Chisholm, R. B., Jr.   *13, 52, 147, 295*
Civil, M.   *165*
Clendenen, E. R.   *184*
Collins, L.   *333*
Collins, T.   *80*
Coppes, L. J.   *254, 320*
Cross, F. M., Jr.   *220, 262, 276, 303*
Culver, R. D.   *138*

SCRIPTURE INDEX

JUDGES

2:16   *131, 133, 307*
2:18   *118, 307*
3:8–10   *289*
3:19   *84, 257*
3:21   *319*
4:4   *113*
5   *10, 47, 49, 264, 273*
5:1–31   *47*
5:4   *294, 304*
5:4–5   *262, 276*
5:5   *286*
5:11   *294*
5:20–21   *222*
5:21   *294*
5:26   *310, 311*
5:27   *311*
6:2–3   *289*
7:1–25   *222*
13:22   *282*
14:3   *193*
14:7   *193*
14:14   *204*
15:16   *315*

RUTH

3:11   *331*

1 SAMUEL

1:1–2:11   *221*
1:3   *220*
2:2   *153*
2:10   *96, 97, 307*
2:15   *165*
2:35   *133, 307*
3:4   *133*
3:11   *319*
3:19–20   *113*
3:20   *7*
4:4   *220*
4–5   *221*
4:12–18   *173*
5:6   *180, 282*
5:6–12   *283*
5:11   *282*
6:5   *283*
8:4–6   *160*

8:7   *160*
9   *334*
9:9   *7*
9:11   *7*
9:16   *118, 307*
9:18   *7*
12:18   *268*
12:21   *247*
12:24   *268*
14:15   *319*
15:24   *268*
15:29   *153*
17:43–44   *43*
17:45   *220, 221*
17:45–47   *43*
18:6   *162*
18:20   *193*
18:26   *193*
24:17   *157*
25:9   *321*
26:23   *183*

2 SAMUEL

1:19   *334*
1:20   *329*
3:18   *118, 307*
5:2   *307*
5:6–8   *144*
5–7   *221*
6:9   *268*
6:13–14   *304*
6:19   *165*
7:5   *309*
7:6–7   *288, 338*
7:7–8   *307*
7:8–9   *221*
7:11   *309*
7:27   *265*
10:1–5   *310*
15:25   *197*
17:4   *193*
18:19–27   *173*
22   *49, 154, 273*
22:1–51   *47*
22:3   *149, 281*
22:10   *284*
22:15   *298*
22:34   *10, 332, 333*

22:47   *119, 149*
22:51   *307*
23:10   *223*
24:11   *7, 114*
24:15   *283*

1 KINGS

1:40   *162*
2:32   *157*
3   *334*
3:26   *327*
4:23   *332, 333*
4:25   *325*
4:32   *204*
5–7   *242*
8   *282*
8:5   *164*
8:10–11   *234, 279*
8:11   *232*
8:13   *302*
8:22–53   *265*
8:27   *253*
8:42   *265*
8:43   *233*
9:7   *204*
9:12   *180, 193*
10:1   *204*
11:7–8   *334*
13:30   *202*
14:14   *133*
15:14   *334*
17:20   *150*
18:22   *7*
18:27   *252*
18:28   *252*
18:29   *250, 252*
18:38   *224*
19   *262*
19:16   *307*
22:19   *220*
22:24   *146*
22:43   *334*

2 KINGS

22:18–20   *34*

ZEPHANIAH